Motorcycle Fuel Systems TechBook

by John Robinson

incorporating certain illustrations from the Haynes Motorcycle Carburettor Manual by Pete Shoemark

(3514-176)

D1421329

44089

ISBN 1 85960 514 1

British Library Cataloguing in Publication Data
A catalogue record for this book is available from the British Library

Library of Congress Catalog Card Number 98-75324

e USA

...lishing
Sparkford, Nr Yeovil, Somerset BA22 7JJ, England

Haynes North America, Inc
861 Lawrence Drive, Newbury Park, California 91320, USA

Editions Haynes S.A.
Tour Aurore - IBC, 18 Place des Reflets,
92975 Paris La Défense 2, Cedex, France

Haynes Publishing Nordiska AB
Box 1504, 751 45 Uppsala, Sverige

Contents

Introduction

This book covers fuel systems – that is, everything from the airbox intake to the exhaust tailpipe, not only carburettors and fuel injectors. It's arranged in a logical sequence. The first few chapters look at the theory: what fuels are, how they burn, the dynamics of gas flow. Later chapters deal with the construction of real carburettors and injectors, so the various components can be seen and identified.

Where jargon is used for the first time, it is explained, although there is a glossary at the back containing all the terms which have a special meaning in the world of engines.

In between there are chapters on tuning – which is broadly the same for all types of carburettor and fuel injection, after all, it is the engine that is being tuned, not the fuel system – plus sections on overhaul and fault finding.

Finally there are details on other aspects – like turbochargers, superchargers, pumps, electronics, funny fuels and methods of testing, ranging from dynamometers to race tracks.

When the book was being researched, we took the City & Guilds *Repair and Servicing of Motorcycles* (3890) syllabus and made sure each of the relevant topics was covered. As a result there is plenty of background theory on the physics and chemistry involved.

To make it easier on those who prefer not to get knee-deep in technicalities, this has been kept separate from the main text as far as possible. For 'those who want the information, for their own curiosity or for one of the automotive courses, it is all there.

John Robinson

About this manual

The text in each chapter is arranged in numbered section order and will correspond with the contents list at the beginning of the chapter. If a section in another chapter is referred to, a typical instruction 'see Chapter 4, Section 8' will be found. Certain text, relevant to, but not part of, the text section have been separated out and displayed in boxed form.

All illustrations are numbered sequentially within the chapter and referred to by their figure number (eg Fig. 6.4) in the main text.

Whilst every attempt is made to ensure that the information in this manual is correct, no liability can be accepted by the authors or publishers for loss, damage or injury caused by any errors in, or omissions from, the information given.

Acknowledgements

We all understand how to hit a billiard ball or a golf ball, or how clay is turned on a potter's wheel, but knowing about it and doing it successfully are not the same thing. They are separated by having the right aptitude plus a lot of experience and practice. You not only have to know what to do but exercise some skill and judgement in doing it.

Adjusting carburettors is much the same. It seems easy enough to correct a weak mixture by making it richer, until you find there are four or five ways of doing this and each will have a series of repercussions that could leave you worse off than when you started. I speak from experience. But I have also been lucky enough to have had the experience of watching some very skilled and talented people work with engines, some of whom were patient enough to explain what they were doing and why.

The late Leon Moss, who ran the LEDAR engine development business, was a master of carburation. He made me realise the difference – in throttle response, crispness and ease of use – between an engine that was fuelled acceptably right and one that was exactly right.

As well as developing their own jet kits and exhaust systems, LEDAR did development work for other exhaust manufacturers and for many of the major race teams between the late '70s and 1990. I did some of the test riding for Leon, in exchange for material for magazine articles, and we ran tests together on various project and race bikes. He produced full race engines that would start, idle and be as driveable as completely standard roadsters. Occasionally he would run a series of tests that were pointless for him (because he already knew), just to show me what would happen if things were changed in a particular way.

When he died in a car crash in 1990, he was working on a ram induction system, a few years before the factories' bikes appeared with it. We'd measured airbox pressure at speeds up to 170 mph and he was in the process of duplicating these pressures on bikes in his test house. To beat the manufacturers at their own game of acronyms, he wanted to call it *Fresh Air Ram Technology*. He was also the driving force behind a prototype data logger, again, at a time when only F1 car teams and people with similar budgets were using them. Already he could see the need to sample data on the track so it could be repeated in the test house and the bike be developed as a whole, not as an engine that came from dyno-testing dropped into a chassis that came from track-testing. This holistic approach was also being adopted by the manufacturers and the results appeared a couple of years later.

Above all this was Leon's immense knowledge of fuel systems, stemming from his early days at BRM race cars and Shorrock superchargers, through to manufacturing his own fuel and air jets for Japanese carburettors.

I shall never have anything like his expertise but I know better than most what it could achieve and hope I can pass some of this information on.

Over the years plenty of other experts have contributed some of their knowledge, which has been stored away and, while I was preparing the copy and illustrations, many have taken the time to answer questions, provide data and give permission for illustrations to be used. I am extremely grateful to: Phil Allen of Allen's R&D; Aprilia Moto (UK); Eddie Cheung at BMW (GB); Contact Developments (Dell'Orto importer); Paul Langley and Remco Koedam at Dynojet; John Williamson at Dynopower; Bradley O'Connor at Dynospeed Developments; John Rowland at Fuchs (Silkolene) Oils; Jon and Nick Walker at Genesis Electronics; Dave Hancock at Honda UK; Peter Yeow and Des Murray at Kawasaki Motors UK; Mortons Motorcycle Media Archive; Jeff Green at Moto Cinelli (Ducati importer); Larry Webb at PDQ Developments; Performance Bikes Magazine; Steve Burns; Roger Simmons, Peter Barber and Martyn Ogbourne at Suzuki GB; Charles Smart at Triumph; Richard Albans at TTS, who is adept at tuning carburettors and lent me some of his to strip for photographs and (more to the point) trusted me to put them back together again; Yamaha Motor (UK); Reference books published by Robert Bosch GmbH, Sudco International, Dell'Orto SPA and Fritz Hintermayr GmbH (Bing Vergaser Fabrik); Barry Johnstone of Amal not least for the story that some pre-1940 Mikuni carburettors were built under licence from Amal. During the war there was obviously no communication but production continued and Mikuni did the honourable thing and paid the royalties into a neutral bank account. At some point after the war, they presented Amal with the account, including interest…

Professional mechanics are trained in safe working procedures. However enthusiastic you may be about getting on with the job at hand, take the time to ensure that your safety is not put at risk. A moment's lack of attention can result in an accident, as can failure to observe simple precautions.

There will always be new ways of having accidents, and the following is not a comprehensive list of all dangers; it is intended rather to make you aware of the risks and to encourage a safe approach to all work you carry out on your bike.

Asbestos
● Certain friction, insulating, sealing and other products - such as brake pads, clutch linings, gaskets, etc. - contain asbestos. Extreme care must be taken to avoid inhalation of dust from such products since it is hazardous to health. If in doubt, assume that they do contain asbestos.

Fire
● Remember at all times that petrol is highly flammable. Never smoke or have any kind of naked flame around, when working on the vehicle. But the risk does not end there - a spark caused by an electrical short-circuit, by two metal surfaces contacting each other, by careless use of tools, or even by static electricity built up in your body under certain conditions, can ignite petrol vapour, which in a confined space is highly explosive. Never use petrol as a cleaning solvent. Use an approved safety solvent.

● Always disconnect the battery earth terminal before working on any part of the fuel or electrical system, and never risk spilling fuel on to a hot engine or exhaust.
● It is recommended that a fire extinguisher of a type suitable for fuel and electrical fires is kept handy in the garage or workplace at all times. Never try to extinguish a fuel or electrical fire with water.

Fumes
● Certain fumes are highly toxic and can quickly cause unconsciousness and even death if inhaled to any extent. Petrol vapour comes into this category, as do the vapours from certain solvents such as trichloro-ethylene. Any draining or pouring of such volatile fluids should be done in a well ventilated area.
● When using cleaning fluids and solvents, read the instructions carefully. Never use materials from unmarked containers - they may give off poisonous vapours.
● Never run the engine of a motor vehicle in an enclosed space such as a garage. Exhaust fumes contain carbon monoxide which is extremely poisonous; if you need to run the engine, always do so in the open air or at least have the rear of the vehicle outside the workplace.

The battery
● Never cause a spark, or allow a naked light near the vehicle's battery. It will normally be giving off a certain amount of hydrogen gas, which is highly explosive.

● Always disconnect the battery ground (earth) terminal before working on the fuel or electrical systems (except where noted).
● If possible, loosen the filler plugs or cover when charging the battery from an external source. Do not charge at an excessive rate or the battery may burst.
● Take care when topping up, cleaning or carrying the battery. The acid electrolyte, evenwhen diluted, is very corrosive and should not be allowed to contact the eyes or skin. Always wear rubber gloves and goggles or a face shield. If you ever need to prepare electrolyte yourself, always add the acid slowly to the water; never add the water to the acid.

Electricity
● When using an electric power tool, inspection light etc., always ensure that the appliance is correctly connected to its plug and that, where necessary, it is properly grounded (earthed). Do not use such appliances in damp conditions and, again, beware of creating a spark or applying excessive heat in the vicinity of fuel or fuel vapour. Also ensure that the appliances meet national safety standards.
● A severe electric shock can result from touching certain parts of the electrical system, such as the spark plug wires (HT leads), when the engine is running or being cranked, particularly if components are damp or the insulation is defective. Where an electronic ignition system is used, the secondary (HT) voltage is much higher and could prove fatal.

Remember...

✗ **Don't** start the engine without first ascertaining that the transmission is in neutral.

✗ **Don't** suddenly remove the pressure cap from a hot cooling system - cover it with a cloth and release the pressure gradually first, or you may get scalded by escaping coolant.

✗ **Don't** attempt to drain oil until you are sure it has cooled sufficiently to avoid scalding you.

✗ **Don't** grasp any part of the engine or exhaust system without first ascertaining that it is cool enough not to burn you.

✗ **Don't** allow brake fluid or antifreeze to contact the machine's paintwork or plastic components.

✗ **Don't** siphon toxic liquids such as fuel, hydraulic fluid or antifreeze by mouth, or allow them to remain on your skin.

✗ **Don't** inhale dust - it may be injurious to health (see Asbestos heading).

✗ **Don't** allow any spilled oil or grease to remain on the floor - wipe it up right away, before someone slips on it.

✗ **Don't** use ill-fitting spanners or other tools which may slip and cause injury.

✗ **Don't** lift a heavy component which may be beyond your capability - get assistance.

✗ **Don't** rush to finish a job or take unverified short cuts.

✗ **Don't** allow children or animals in or around an unattended vehicle.

✗ **Don't** inflate a tyre above the recommended pressure. Apart from overstressing the carcass, in extreme cases the tyre may blow off forcibly.

✔ **Do** ensure that the machine is supported securely at all times. This is especially important when the machine is blocked up to aid wheel or fork removal.

✔ **Do** take care when attempting to loosen a stubborn nut or bolt. It is generally better to pull on a spanner, rather than push, so that if you slip, you fall away from the machine rather than onto it.

✔ **Do** wear eye protection when using power tools such as drill, sander, bench grinder etc.

✔ **Do** use a barrier cream on your hands prior to undertaking dirty jobs - it will protect your skin from infection as well as making the dirt easier to remove afterwards; but make sure your hands aren't left slippery. Note that long-term contact with used engine oil can be a health hazard.

✔ **Do** keep loose clothing (cuffs, ties etc. and long hair) well out of the way of moving mechanical parts.

✔ **Do** remove rings, wristwatch etc., before working on the vehicle - especially the electrical system.

✔ **Do** keep your work area tidy - it is only too easy to fall over articles left lying around.

✔ **Do** exercise caution when compressing springs for removal or installation. Ensure that the tension is applied and released in a controlled manner, using suitable tools which preclude the possibility of the spring escaping violently.

✔ **Do** ensure that any lifting tackle used has a safe working load rating adequate for the job.

✔ **Do** get someone to check periodically that all is well, when working alone on the vehicle.

✔ **Do** carry out work in a logical sequence and check that everything is correctly assembled and tightened afterwards.

✔ **Do** remember that your vehicle's safety affects that of yourself and others. If in doubt on any point, get professional advice.

● **If** in spite of following these precautions, you are unfortunate enough to injure yourself, seek medical attention as soon as possible.

Chapter 1
Fuel systems: overview

Contents

1 Introduction

I believe it was Ken Tyrrell, the F1 car constructor, who said that every component of a high performance machine should do more than one job. If this is the measure of efficiency, or economy of design, then fuel systems rate very highly.

Whether they are carburettors or fuel injectors, their main job is to deliver a chemically correct mix of fuel and air to the engine. Even this is two jobs, one to get the proportions right, the other to mix them thoroughly in the few microseconds between the fuel appearing in the inlet tract and disappearing into the well of the cylinder.

'Chemically correct' means one thing on a laboratory bench; it means something else to an engine. To completely burn every molecule of fuel and have no excess oxygen left requires a mixture of about 14.7:1, air to fuel, by weight. Yet engines give maximum power on a slightly 'rich' mixture, one that has more fuel than is theoretically necessary, of around 12 to 13:1. Worse, they give best fuel economy on a 'lean' mixture, one with too much air, sometimes as severe as 18:1. So the system's next job is to be able to detect both the engine speed and load, decide whether power or economy takes precedence and adjust the mixture accordingly – starting, cold running, idling, sudden acceleration – all of which require abnormally rich mixtures.

Next, the system provides the engine's main form of control, for both load and speed. As if this weren't enough, it now performs a series of functions which enhance engine power, silence the engine, reduce pollution, improve oil consumption and protect the engine from high wear rates.

The dimensions of the intake tract and the airbox can take advantage of the fast moving, highly pulsating column of air that is being drawn into the engine. If it can be harnessed, the air's own momentum can be used to increase the amount that is trapped inside the engine's cylinder — the so-called 'ram' effect. The frequency of the pulses, one every other turn of the crankshaft on a four-stroke, can also be used because the intake is a pipe and chamber that has its own natural frequency, just like an organ pipe. When the engine frequency is in step with the system's, high-pressure waves arrive at the intake valve when it is opening and again just as it is closing.

High pressure at the valve when it first opens means gas will flow more readily through the narrow gap at the valve seat. It also means the valve may be opened slightly earlier. The opening point occurs during the final stage of the exhaust stroke and there will still be some pressure in the hot exhaust gas: the intake should not open until the pressure of the fresh gas upstream is greater than the burnt gas downstream, otherwise exhaust gas will try to exit past the intake valve, in the 'wrong' direction.

Having higher pressure in the intake tract means the valve can be opened earlier, adding more time to the intake stroke. Similarly, the valve has to close when cylinder pressure rises to the level of pressure in the intake. The arrival of a high pressure wave now means the valve can be left open a little longer, again prolonging the intake process.

This improves the cylinder filling (*volumetric* efficiency) and the *trapping* efficiency; so engine torque increases.

When the two frequencies are out of step, the opposite happens and torque is reduced (engines that have been developed to make most use of this resonance have torque curves that follow a series of peaks and troughs, at regular intervals along the rpm scale).

Vibration in the air column also makes sound. Under wide-open acceleration, engines can make as much noise in the intake as they do in the exhaust. In order to meet the stringent road vehicle noise tests, the manufacturers are forced to whittle away at every source, fitting sound-deadening materials to engine covers and inside fairings – and paying a lot of attention to intake noise. The airbox chamber and its entry are carefully designed to absorb the frequencies at which the engine is loudest. This technique is named after Hermann von Helmholtz (1821-94) who investigated the effects after noticing that the reverberant acoustics in an Austrian monastery were deliberately dulled by placing large, empty containers strategically around the room. Helmholtz chambers are widely employed to take out selected frequencies in both intake and exhaust silencers.

An offshoot of this technology is that intakes can be tuned to produce pleasant harmonics during acceleration. Some car manufacturers boast of this but, while Kawasaki have never mentioned it as far as I know, anyone who has ridden their bigger bikes will agree they've been indulging in this practice for some time.

There is another way in which intake (and exhaust) dimensions can help silencing. The drive-by noise tests are made at a certain road speed and engine rpm, under full throttle. Just as the dimensions can enhance torque curves, they can also make the torque drop and if this happens at the noise test rpm, the bike will not accelerate quite as much as it otherwise might, so the peak rpm as it passes the noise meter will be less.

The airbox does several more jobs. Its most obvious is to provide a housing for the air cleaner, filtering out airborne dirt which would otherwise cause rapid cylinder bore wear. The box is also a catch tank and separator for engine breathers, which blow a certain amount of oil vapour from the cam box, crankcase and gearbox as part of the engine's natural pumping activity. Larger oil particles

can be trapped and drained back into the sump, reducing oil consumption. Oil mist is recirculated through the engine, where it is burnt, reducing the overall hydrocarbon emissions. Some engines even have a fresh air bleed, with one-way reed valves, into the exhaust so that unburnt or partially-burnt fuel and oil is oxidised on its way through the exhaust.

Finally, airboxes are designed to make use of the bike's forward motion. Partly to make extra power from the supercharging effect (at 170 mph the available boost is about 0.6 psi, small but worth a few per cent more horsepower) and also to make sure that the pressure difference between low and high speed does not upset the fuelling.

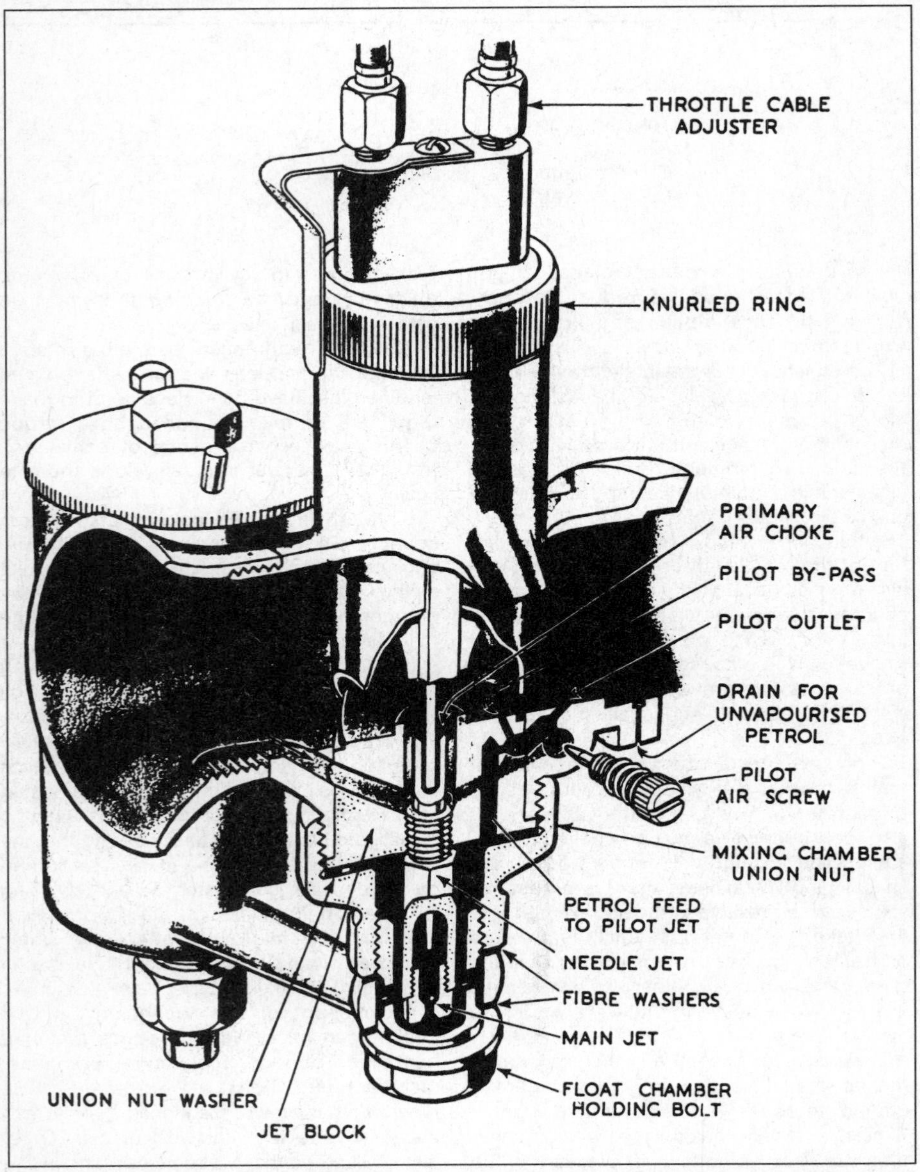

Even the throttle twistgrip gives you somewhere to rest your hand and helps steer the bike …

It is plenty for one 'simple' system to handle. The beauty of carburettors is they do most of it automatically. Their only connections to the outside world are an air intake, a gasoline feed and a throttle cable. They manage almost all the above list of feats with no other input.

If carburettors are 'smart', then fuel injection is dumb. It needs a load of sensors to tell it what's going on and then it only does what it has been told. And this is one of its attractions. Unlike carburettors, which tend to progress smoothly from one state to the next, fuel injection can make sudden, big jumps – and illogical jumps too, if the situation demands it.

This is what fuel systems do, and what the following chapters look at in more detail. It's necessary to focus on the system as a discrete part but it's a mistake to isolate it from the rest of the machine. As the above task list suggests, fuel systems are dependent on many other engine functions and even whole-bike functions. Whether you consider the exhaust to be part of the fuel system or not, it interacts with the intake to dominate the power characteristics. The fuelling also has to be closely matched to the valve timing and the engine's pumping efficiency at various speeds. The way in which it delivers the fuel has a major effect on combustion and the ignition must therefore be optimised hand in hand with the fuel mixture.

So, while this book is necessarily about fuel systems, to the exclusion of the rest of the bike, remember that the carburettor or fuel injector isn't an isolated, independent component.

In the same way, this isn't an isolated, one-off book. It doesn't give model-specific information because this is included in the Haynes range of service and repair manuals, while more information on electrical goings-on is provided in the *Motorcycle Electrical TechBook* and details of bike construction and methods of servicing and overhaul appear in *Motorcycle Basics Manual* and *Motorcycle Workshop Practice TechBook*.

2 Mixture

The first requirement of a carburettor is to mix the right amount of fuel with the air being drawn into the engine. This not only means the correct proportions, it also means the fuel has to be broken up from a cohesive liquid into a fine vapour, and evenly distributed throughout the air. When the ignition spark starts it burning, every particle of fuel needs to be very close to thirteen particles of air otherwise it will not burn completely or will not burn quickly enough and the engine's

Fig. 1.1 The air-bleeding carburettor, as pioneered and developed by a succession of Amal instruments, became the definitive motorcycle carburettor. The essential parts can still be recognised on current machines, 60-odd years later *(Amal)*

Labels in figure:
- THROTTLE CABLE ADJUSTER
- KNURLED RING
- PRIMARY AIR CHOKE
- PILOT BY-PASS
- PILOT OUTLET
- DRAIN FOR UNVAPOURISED PETROL
- PILOT AIR SCREW
- MIXING CHAMBER UNION NUT
- PETROL FEED TO PILOT JET
- NEEDLE JET
- FIBRE WASHERS
- MAIN JET
- FLOAT CHAMBER HOLDING BOLT
- UNION NUT WASHER
- JET BLOCK

efficiency will start to fall. Even at a leisurely 6,000 rpm, the two strokes that make up the intake and compression phases take a total of 0.01 seconds: not much time to give the mixture such a thorough stirring.

Some early carburettors concentrated on this aspect. Called 'hot plate' carburettors, they had a regulated drip feed of fuel on to a plate heated by the exhaust manifold, which vaporised the fairly volatile fuel and the resulting mist was drawn into the engine with the air.

Ironically, later carburettors, which use precisely-made jets and tapered needles to control the fuel flow, still rely to some extent on this hot-plate principle. A fast-moving stream of air draws the liquid fuel from a spray tube or 'atomiser' but the fuel mist it creates is not a true gas, it is made of tiny drops of liquid. Some drops are bigger than others and the heaviest ones fall out of the air flow or collide with the walls of the tract, wetting them. Liquid fuel runs down the sides of the intake port, and joins the fall-out in a pool at the bottom. This is fuel that will not reach the engine, so the mixture that does arrive at the cylinder will now be a weak one. The carburettor would have to be set to give a slightly rich mixture to compensate for this drop out.

However, the fuel is volatile and the walls of the intake port are warmed by engine heat, so the liquid pool does evaporate, joining the air/fuel stream rushing past it, albeit a few cycles later than it was intended. When an engine is in a steady state, the fuel rejoining from evaporation equals the fuel lost from drop-out, so it is not necessary to alter the mixture strength to compensate.

Unfortunately, engines do not always run in a steady state. The rate of drop-out exceeds evaporation in several conditions: when the engine is cold, when it is idling and the air velocity is not high enough to carry fuel particles efficiently, when it needs sudden acceleration and the lighter air can respond faster than the heavier fuel. In these circumstances, the fuel system needs to deliver a rich mixture to make up the difference.

During this kind of running condition, the engine does not see the same fuel as it does in steady state operation. This is because fuels are blends of different hydrocarbon compounds which have different volatilities and different boiling points. Those which are hardest to evaporate are called 'heavier fractions' and, of course these are the first to drop out of the air flow. The resulting light fractions get to the engine first, and this is what the engine runs on in critical conditions like starting, low-speed running and acceleration. As well as different vaporising characteristics, these fractions burn differently, too. Their ease of combustion, flame speed and octane rating (or resistance to knock) will all be different from the way the whole fuel behaves.

Fig. 1.2 Slide carburettors developed for Japanese roadsters: left, Mikuni two-stroke; centre, Mikuni four-stroke; right, Keihin four-stroke *(Performance Bikes)*

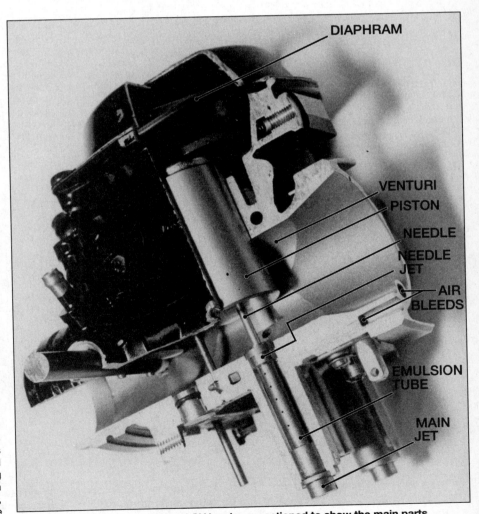

DIAPHRAM

VENTURI

PISTON

NEEDLE

NEEDLE JET

AIR BLEEDS

EMULSION TUBE

MAIN JET

Fig. 1.3 This early Mikuni CV has been sectioned to show the main parts *(Performance Bikes)*

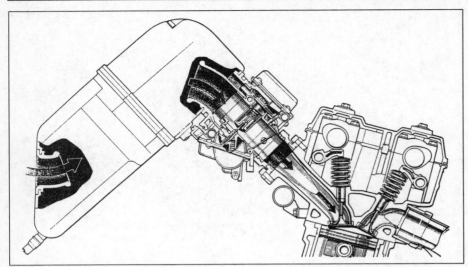

Fig. 1.4 Airbox design began as a simple housing for the air filter, then had a moulded intake (forming a tube and chamber silencer). In the mid-1980s it began to be used as a plenum chamber and its volume increased year by year. Bikes like the Kawasaki GPZ1000RX and ZX-10 (shown) were among the first to make a performance use of the airbox *(Kawasaki)*

pre-programmed 'map' to determine the necessary ignition timing for this set of circumstances. Other sensors may be added, for instance to monitor engine temperature, to detect when the starter button is being pressed, or feel the vibrations caused by detonation, etc.

All gasoline fuels are made to the same broad specifications but the specifications change, from summer to winter and from one locality to another. And although different makes of fuel meet the same specs, they do it with different blends and different additives. So if an engine feels crisper or less harsh on a particular brand of fuel or in certain weather conditions, then it probably *is* crisper or less harsh because it has run into its conditions for MBT.

4 Vaporisation

Heat supplied from the surroundings will make liquid fuel turn into vapour. The liquid will also take heat away from its surroundings in order to become a vapour. If it is forced from its liquid state into a gaseous state (by being *'atomised'* for instance), it will take the necessary heat forcibly. You can test this by dipping your finger in water and then blowing on it. The air flow will encourage the liquid water to evaporate and you'll feel the effect because it will make your finger feel cold. This is the principle of refrigeration but it also happens in carburettors. There are two side

3 Ignition advance

The engine, particularly the ignition timing, has to be optimised to allow for the fuel characteristics. The object is to achieve MBT – *minimum advance for best torque*. Old engines had fixed ignition timing or a manual lever to advance and retard it when (and if) the rider remembered. This progressed to speed-sensitive timing, where the ignition was advanced as engine speed increased. Car engines had this, plus a vacuum control that also sensed the load on the engine (or throttle position) and adjusted the timing accordingly.

Current machines have digital control. Sensors detect engine speed and sometimes throttle position, and compare this data with a

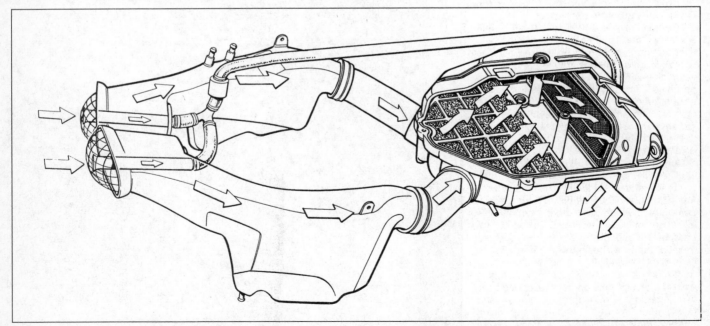

Fig. 1.5 By the time the mighty ZZ-R1100 was introduced, Kawasaki were making full use of the airbox potential, with forward facing intakes to pick up maximum air pressure from the bike's motion *(Kawasaki)*

The small tubes in the intakes are vents to the carburettor float bowls, to make sure the pressure differential between venturi and float bowl stayed in step for all road speeds

effects which are useful and one that is a nuisance.

The first good effect is that the fuel spray refrigerates the air. Cold air is more dense than warm air. That is, a given volume contains more air by weight, so the volume trapped inside the cylinder will contain more molecules of oxygen; it can burn more fuel, make more heat and the engine will produce more power. Second: in engines with very high specific outputs – usually two-strokes – the limiting factor is often combustion and piston temperature. If a rich mixture, consisting of small droplets of liquid as well as gaseous fuel, hits the piston, it cools it, reducing the distortion caused by thermal expansion, reducing piston friction and allowing the engine to make more power.

Now, a practical definition of the correct mixture is that which creates the most power. If this goes above the chemically correct proportion, even if there is unburnt or partially burnt fuel in the exhaust, yet it gives more power, then the *optimum* mixture is richer than the theoretically correct mixture. Some of the fuel is being used to compensate for drop-out, some is being used to cool the engine and in the less than ideal conditions for combustion – a few milliseconds at most – having too much fuel ensures that every last molecule of oxygen is utilised. All engines show this characteristic to some extent, highly tuned machines show it to a large extent.

The nuisance value of this 'latent heat' of vaporisation arises because air contains a certain amount of water vapour and the refrigeration effect can turn it into ice, which may build up inside the carburettor venturi – called, unsurprisingly, carburettor icing. This will be downstream of the main fuel supply nozzle but it can build up over the pilot jet outlet or its bypasses, or around the throttle valve. Blocking the jets will stop the motor idling or cause bad response when the throttle is opened. Ice on the throttle valve can make it stick, which is altogether less pleasant.

The worst conditions for icing are when there is high humidity and an air temperature of around 4 to 5°C. Warmer air can hold more moisture but then it takes more refrigeration to produce ice. Colder air does not hold as much moisture.

The oil companies put anti-icing additives in their fuels and some bike manufacturers have heated carburettors, either looping a gallery of coolant through the critical part of the carburettor or fitting small electrical heaters (which have the advantage of working when the engine is still cold).

5 Throttle

The forerunners of modern carburettors used a slide valve to control the air flow to the engine (closing it to literally throttle the

Fig. 1.6 Airbox volume continues to grow – ten times engine displacement is not uncommon, with more on some race bikes – ZX-9R shown

Fig. 1.7 As far back as 1979, the need to make carburettors compact to fit in with big engine/frame designs was becoming apparent. Kawasaki used these twin-choke Mikuni CV carburettors on their ZX1300 six-cylinder machine (*Performance Bikes*)

Fig. 1.8 This 1982 endurance racer built by Kawasaki France represents leading edge technology of the time applied to the base 1000 cc roadster engine. The carburettors are horizontal and the frame rails have to curve around them. There is no airbox but the intake stacks have tuned lengths

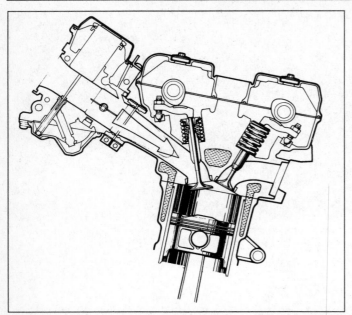

Fig. 1.9 In the search for increased, all-round performance, bike designers took a more holistic approach. In quick succession there were four-valve heads and narrower valve angles, for a more compact combustion chamber and straighter intake tracts. This was followed by steeper carburettor downdraught angles and more compact carburettors. This is the Honda CBR1000F, an engine design close to the beginning of this evolution *(Honda)*

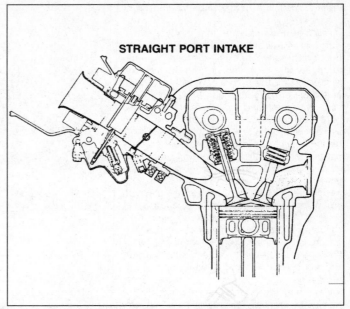

Fig. 1.10 Following on from the CBR1000F, the 1991 CBR600F takes the process a little further *(Honda)*

supply). Its up-and-down motion was also used to regulate fuel flow through an accurately made *jet* or orifice by having a tapered *needle* inside the jet, raised as the throttle was opened. When the throttle valve allowed more air to flow, the needle was lifted so a smaller diameter was in the fuel jet, permitting more fuel to flow.

A bit of experimenting with jet sizes and different needle tapers would make it possible to get the right proportions of air to fuel from small throttle openings to wide open throttle (WOT). That is, light engine load to full load. But the clever part was in making the air flow pull the fuel through the jet.

Air travelling at speed across a surface exerts less pressure on it than static air. Fuel kept at a constant level in a chamber would be at static pressure. Air travelling across the top of the jet, on its way to the engine, would not only be at lower pressure but the pressure drop would increase as the air went faster. It would lift fuel though the jet and as the engine speeded up, air velocity would increase and so would the fuel flow. By playing with the height of the fuel level and the area of the air passageway, the velocity/pressure relationship could be made to give an automatic increase in fuel flow to match the engine's needs from low speed to high speed – or nearly so. In practice, the pressure drop would get too big at high speeds. Or if you got it right at high speed, it wouldn't be big enough at low speed.

6 Air bleed

The next clever step was the air bleeding carburettor. A small orifice called an *air jet*, or sometimes an *air corrector*, supplied air into the fuel rising through the fuel jet. This flow of air had the same characteristics as the flow of fuel: low at low speed, getting exponentially higher as the main air speed rose. Thus it wouldn't have much effect at low speed (especially if the jet was small compared with the fuel jet) but it would have a significant weakening effect at high speed. Now it was possible to select a fuel jet to give the right supply at low speed and to tailor its supply at high speed by altering the size of the air jet.

And in the best tradition of using one component to do several jobs, the air bleed did two other useful things. First, it pre-mixed air and fuel, making the liquid fuel frothy. This made the fuel easier to lift through the jet when the throttle was opened and less willing to drop back down when the throttle was closed. Better throttle response.

Second, it made the fuel easier to break up – *atomise* – when the main air stream hit it. Better air-fuel mixing; faster, more complete combustion.

There were a few refinements to look after idling and cold starting but this basic carburettor now had enough adjustment to

cope with the full range of engine speed and load.

At least it would if used with some skill or if the carburettor was relatively small for the needs of the engine. Problems arose when the carburettor was big enough to let the engine develop its maximum power. Then if the rider opened it wide at low-ish revs, the light air would accelerate faster than the heavier fuel, or, if the opening was wide enough, the engine would get the air it needed without speeding the air up. Result: more air flow, same or less fuel flow, ie a weak mixture.

7 CV carburettor

This produced a division in design philosophy. One school stayed with the carburettor as described, but refined it by shaping the throttle valve, adding accelerator pumps and high speed jets. The other produced a variant which could cope with transient conditions automatically – the CV (for *constant velocity* or *constant vacuum*) carburettor.

In this design the throttle valve controlled by the rider was moved downstream of the fuel jets and needle. The relationship between velocity and pressure, so far used to draw fuel from a reservoir and through the jet block was

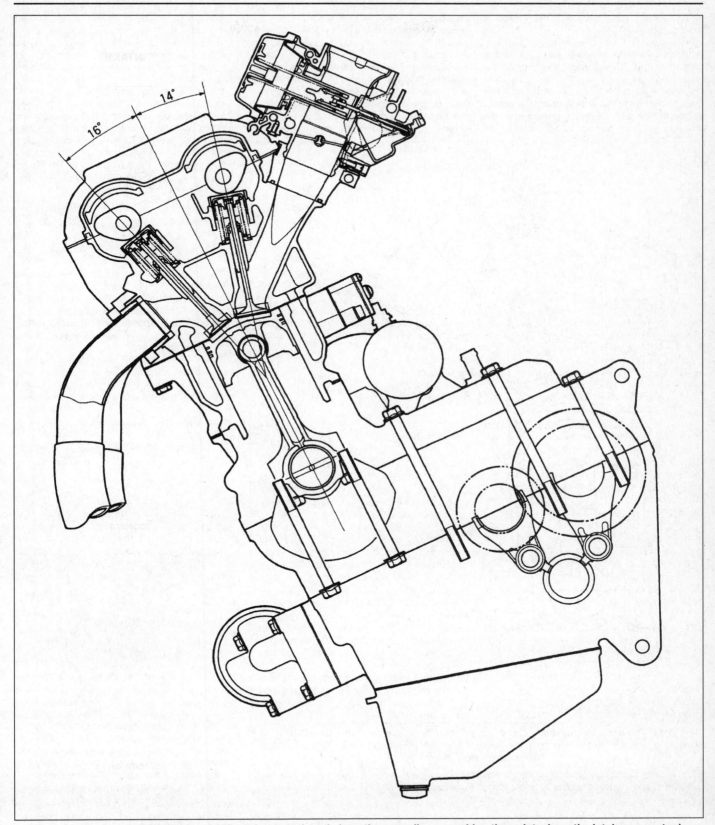

Fig. 1.11 The Suzuki GSX-R600 and 750 engines continued along the same lines, reaching the point where the intake geometry is limited by the carburettor touching the intake cam box – GSX-R600 shown *(Suzuki)*

now used to raise a slide or a piston above the jet block.

By using the air stream to create low pressure above the piston it would be lifted a certain height. This could be regulated by balancing the area in the low pressure chamber against the piston's weight plus the force of a light spring. And by using the piston to control the area of the air passage above the fuel jet, this region could be kept at constant velocity, which means constant pressure (and because it is a low pressure, called *constant vacuum* or *constant depression*).

This would greatly simplify the job of selecting jets and needles to match fuel and air flow over large ranges of engine speed and load. It would also do something else: when the rider opened the throttle wide at low engine speed, the piston would only lift according to the velocity of the air the engine was pumping. It would be like having a skilled and sensitive rider opening the throttle only as quickly as the engine could manage. No hiccups, no flat spots, just a smooth progression.

It also had all the same parts as the original slide carburettor, so it could do all the same things and it had an extra advantage, in getting a light throttle action with a small twistgrip movement. There was enough going for this design for it to dominate the street bike market and for it to continue as original equipment some 15 years after fuel injection became a practical proposition.

8 Book coverage

There are other designs of carburettor and several types of fuel injection, which are also covered in the following chapters, but the slide and CV carburettor have been used on 95% of road and competition bikes during the last 50 years, so they obviously get slightly more attention.

They have been developed to an extraordinary degree, to get ever more air flow from an ever more compact package. It is also a package that fits into a whole bike design, permitting shorter and straighter intake tracts, larger airboxes and more extreme ranges of both engine speed and power output. It is unlikely that either type of carburettor will be developed further – it's hard to see how they can be made significantly better – and with electronics becoming smaller and cheaper, plus the need to meet more stringent laws, fuel injection has more to offer and will almost certainly supersede carburettors as more new bike models are produced.

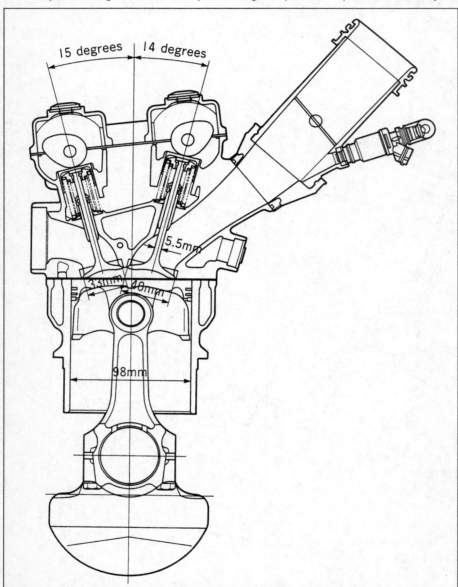

Fig. 1.12 The need for physically more compact fuelling systems, plus the difficulty of metering fuel and air to large cylinders, meant that fuel injection had useful advantages over carburettors (Suzuki)

The answer to the size problem is demonstrated by the 52 mm throttle bodies on this Suzuki TL1000S, showing ample clearance compared to carburettor bodies with a maximum 38 mm throttle

Fig. 1.13 There are other reasons for switching to fuel injection. The V4 Hondas have even more limited space and, when enclosed by tank, frame and bodywork, the carburettors can suffer heat soak problems, making the fuel boil or cause vapour locks (Honda)

Chapter 2
Basic principles: chemistry and combustion

Contents

1 Introduction

See Fig. 2.1

Internal combustion engines are heat engines. They burn fuel in air and convert the heat produced into mechanical work. The heat raises the pressure of the air and this pressure, acting on the surface area of the piston, creates the force that turns the crankshaft. For a given amount of fuel, a more efficient engine will generate more heat, more pressure and more force. Similarly, an engine that wastes heat (in raising the temperature of the engine, for example) will not have so much left to raise the gas pressure and will not be so efficient.

Although we use words like *force, pressure, work* and *energy* loosely and interchangeably in everyday language, they each have specific meanings in Physics and Engineering, as explained in the tables (see Figs. 2.2 and 2.3), and it's important not to confuse one with another. The fuel system's job has three parts:

● To regulate the amount of air fed into the engine
● Supply the precise amount of fuel that will burn with this quantity of air
● Mix the two thoroughly together

Name	Abbrev.	Meaning
yotta	Y	$\times10^{24}$
zetta	Z	$\times10^{21}$
exa	E	trillion ($\times10^{18}$)
peta	P	thousand billion ($\times10^{15}$)
tera	T	billion ($\times10^{12}$)
giga	G	milliard ($\times10^{9}$)
mega	M	million ($\times10^{6}$) *[megawatt = one million watts]*
kilo	k	thousand ($\times10^{3}$) *[kilometre = one thousand metres]*
hecto	h	hundred ($\times10^{2}$) *[hectare = one hundred ares or 10,000m^2]*
deka	da	ten ($\times10$)
deci	d	tenth ($\times10^{-1}$) *[decibel = one tenth of a bel]*
centi	c	hundredth ($\times10^{-2}$) *[one centilitre = one hundredth of a litre]*
milli	m	thousandth ($\times10^{-3}$) *[one millimetre = one thousandth of a metre]*
micro	μ	millionth ($\times10^{-6}$)
nano	n	thousand millionth ($\times10^{-9}$)
pico	p	billionth ($\times10^{-12}$)
femto	f	thousand billionth ($\times10^{-15}$)
atto	a	trillionth ($\times10^{-18}$)
zepto	z	$\times10^{-21}$
yocto	y	$\times10^{-24}$

Note: In the US, a billion is 10^9 and a trillion is 10^{12}

Fig. 2.1 Abbreviations

Quantity	Commonly used unit	Abbrev.
length	metre (kilometre, millimetre)	m (km, mm)
	foot (inch)	ft (in)
mass	gram (kilogram)	g (kg)
	pound mass	lbm
acceleration due to gravity	(is a constant, 9.81 m s^{-2} or 32.2 ft s^{-2} at sea level)	g
time	second	s (")
	minute	min (')
	hour	h
		: (eg 1h 18min 24s can be written 1:18:24.0)
velocity	metres per second	m s^{-1} (m/s)
	kilometres per hour	km/h
	feet per second	ft s^{-1} (ft/s)
	miles per hour	mph (mi/h)
rotational speed or frequency	revolutions per minute	min^{-1} (rpm)
	cycles per second (Hertz)	s^{-1} (Hz)
acceleration	metres per second per second (metres per second-squared)	m s^{-2} (m/s^2)
	feet per second per second (feet per second squared)	ft s^{-2} (ft/s^2)
volume	litres	ℓ (or L, when this sort of font isn't available, as a lower case l often looks like a figure 1)
	cubic centimetres (cc)	cm^3 (cc)
	cubic feet	ft^3 (cu ft)
	gallon (pint)	gal (pt)
force	Newtons	N
	kilograms	kg or kgf
	pounds force	lbf
pressure and stress	Pascals	Pa ($= \text{N/m}^2$)
	bar	bar ($=10^5$ Pa)
	pounds per square inch	lb/in^2 (psi)
torque	Newton-metre	Nm
	kilogram-metre	kg-m
	foot-pound (or pound-foot)	ft-lbf (or lbf-ft)
energy, heat quantity, work and torque	Joule	J
	Newton-metre	Nm
	Watt-second	W s
	Kilowatt-hour	kW h
	British Thermal Unit	BTU
power, heat flow rate	Watts (kilo-watts)	W (kW)
	Joules per second	J s^{-1} (J/s)
	kilogram-metres per second	kg m s-1 (kg m/s)
	horsepower (brake horsepower)	hp (bhp)
	Cheval Vapeur	CV
	Pferdestärke	PS
temperature	Kelvin	K
	Celsius	°C (= K – 273.15)

Fig. 2.2 Units and abbreviations

Name	Definition of SI (Système International d'Unités) unit	SI unit	Imp unit	Notes
Note: Units are either an arbitrary standard (such as mass) or are directly measured from some natural phenomenon (such as time and length), or are derived from other existing units (such as velocity: distance divided by time)				
mass	A standard: the international prototype of the kilogram is made of platinum-iridium and is kept at the International Bureau of Weight and Measures, at Sèvres, Paris. Copies are kept at similar institutions, such as the National Physical Laboratory at Teddington, Middlesex, UK.	kg	lb	kg ≡ 1000g 1kg ≡ 2.205lb
length	Once a standard, originally estimated to be 1/10,000,000th part of a quadrant of the earth's meridian, and kept in the same way as the kg (above) but since 1983 it is defined as the distance travelled by light, in a vacuum, during a time of 1/299,792,458 of a second.	m	ft	1mm ≡ 0.001m 1ft ≡ 12in 1in ≡ 25.4mm
area	length × length	m^2	ft^2	
volume	length × length × length	m^3	ft^3	
time	Originally a fraction of the mean solar day but, since 1967, the second is the duration of 9,192,631,770 periods of the radiation corresponding to the transition between the two hyperfine levels of the ground state of the caesium 133 atom.	s	s	
velocity	Distance/time (distance travelled, divided by the time taken) Note: velocity has two components - size (speed) and direction	$m\,s^{-1}$	$ft\,s^{-1}$, mph	$1m\,s^{-1} \equiv 3.28ft\,s^{-1}$, $88ft\,s^{-1} \equiv 60mph$
acceleration	Velocity/time (change in velocity, divided by the time taken) Note: the change in velocity may be in size or direction (following a curved course at constant speed produces an acceleration towards the centre of the curve)	$m\,s^{-2}$	$ft\,s^{-2}$	$1g \equiv 9.81m\,s^{-2}$ $1g \equiv 32.2ft\,s^{-2}$
force	mass × acceleration	N	lbf	$1N \equiv 1kg\,m\,s^{-2}$
pressure, stress	force/area (force divided by the area over which it is transmitted)	Pa	$lb\,in^{-2}$ (psi)	$1Pa \equiv 1N\,m^{-2}$
torque	force × distance (force times the distance of the force from its pivot point)	Nm	ft-lbf	
work	force × distance (force times the distance the force is moved along its line of action)	J, Nm, kW h	ft-lbf, hp-h	
energy, heat quantity	force × distance, heat flow rate × time (1 BTU is the heat required to raise 1lb of water through 1°F)	J, calorie	ft-lbf, BTU	1J ≡ 1N m 1J ≡ 1W s 1J ≡ 0.23885cal $1J \equiv 947.8 \times 10^{-4}$ BTU
power	energy (work or torque)/time	W	hp	1W ≡ 1 J/s 1 kW ≡ 1.34 hp also CV and PS 1CV ≡ 1PS ≡ 0.986hp
heat flow rate	energy (or heat quantity)/time	W	hp, BTU/min	1hp ≡ 0.746kW
temperature	originally scaled from the freezing and boiling points of water, (0 and 100°C), the absolute unit of temperature, the Kelvin, is 1/273.16 of the temperature of the triple point of water above absolute zero (the triple point is the combination of temperature and pressure at which water can exist in solid, liquid and vapour forms)	K, °C	°F	°F ≡ °C×9/5 + 32

Fig. 2.3 Units and definitions

Units raised to a power: mm² is the same as sq mm; a negative power means division, m s⁻² is the same as m/s², pronounced metres per second-squared or metres per second per second.

Print style: hyphens, points, space all mean the same thing (for example kilogram-metre can be abbreviated to kgm, kg m, kg-m or kg·m, the latter being the preferred SI style). Where abbreviations use two letters, then some form of punctuation is often used, eg lb-ft and kg-m (but Nm), simply to improve readability.

The / symbol means division and is read 'per', eg km/h is kilometres per hour. Thus lb-ft is a value of force times distance (torque) while lb/ft is a value of load distribution, pounds per foot as in the weight carried by the span of a bridge.

Plurals are not used, eg 20lb, not 20lbs, partly because s stands for seconds, partly because there is little point in shortening something only to lengthen it by adding an 's', and partly because in this case lb stands for libra so the plural would be librae not libras.

As the table shows, torque, work, energy and quantity of heat amount to the same thing, while power and heat flow rate are also equivalent to one another.

The throttle valve looks after the first part, and is the rider's means of controlling engine load and speed.

The quantity of fuel needed depends on the chemistry of the fuel and the air. The process reaches maximum efficiency when there is exactly the right amount of fuel to burn in the oxygen present in the cylinder. To do this, each molecule of fuel has to be close to the appropriate number of oxygen molecules, that is, the fuel and air must be mixed very thoroughly. Even if exactly the right amount of fuel was there, it wouldn't all burn if a large clump of it gathered at one end of the cylinder, while the oxygen was at the other. It also wouldn't burn if it was in large droplets, because the molecules in the centre of each drop would be shielded by those on the outside and, as they burnt, they would remove local oxygen, replacing it with burnt exhaust gas, which would also form a barrier between the unburnt fuel and the remaining oxygen.

Consequently, thorough mixing is more important than having precisely the right mixture. When maximum power is the main consideration (ie, it is important to make use of all the oxygen), then the fuel system will supply too much fuel. A few unburnt fuel particles will not make much difference to the engine's performance as they are small compared to the volume of gas. Of course this increases fuel consumption and it makes the exhaust gas dirty, because there will be unburnt and partially burnt fuel particles in it.

When maximum economy is the object, the fuel system will deliver excess air. In this way it is likely to burn every last drop of fuel and there will be oxygen left over. The engine will not give as much power as it might have – but all this means to the rider trying to hold a steady 50mph is that he has to open the throttle a touch, to, say, 30% open instead of 28%.

Excess air means the exhaust is likely to be clean in terms of unburnt fuel but weak mixtures tend to burn at higher temperatures (watch the flame of an acetylene torch as the oxygen is turned up). This in turn can persuade the normally inert nitrogen to become active and it will combine with some of the spare oxygen to form nitric oxides, which are irritants and are thought to be one of the ingredients that produce smog. Also if there is unused oxygen rushing around looking for something to combine with it will burn (oxidise) any impurities such as sulphur that are in the fuel.

Bearing in mind there are only a few milliseconds to deliver the fuel, it is important to have it broken into the finest possible spray, mixed as completely as possible with the air and kept close to the chemically correct proportions. Fuel in exactly the right proportion to air is called a stoichiometric ratio, which depends on the chemistry of the fuel.

2 Chemistry

Hydrocarbons

Most fuels are hydrocarbons, that is they are *compounds* of hydrogen and carbon and there are many ways in which these two elements can bond together. Air is a *mixture* of gases, broadly speaking, about four-fifths nitrogen and one-fifth oxygen although there are traces of other substances – mainly carbon dioxide and water vapour plus others, depending on where and when you sample it. They matter in terms of pollution but they are not usually significant to the way an engine performs.

The convention in chemistry is that single elements or compounds (substances made of two or more elements bonded at the molecular level and not simply mixed together), have a certain stability. Less stable materials will break down or combine with other materials to form a more stable material and in doing so will give off a certain amount of energy. Conversely, if you add some energy to a substance, it will become less stable and more likely to react with other substances.

Anything that is completely unstable in atmospheric conditions will no longer be around: it will have reacted with its surroundings and turned into something stable a long time ago.

So anything that stays put for more than a few seconds is fairly stable. The hydrocarbons that we use for fuels, for example. But they mustn't be too stable. We want to add a minimal amount of energy (like raising its pressure plus the electric arc in a spark plug, or, in slower motion, like the flame of a match that lights some paper that lights some wood that finally gets a coal fire burning). And once the fuel is raised to a more energetic state, it will continue to react with oxygen in the surrounding air. The fire will continue burning, and a flame will spread through the fuel mixture long after the spark has disappeared.

The reaction produces compounds that are more stable than the original fuel or the oxygen, and it liberates energy in the form of heat. Some of this heat is sufficient to keep the reaction going, the rest is given off and if you can collect it you can make use of it, to boil a kettle or to drive a piston down a cylinder bore.

Hydrogen is the simplest fuel. Its chemical symbol is H_2, meaning that two atoms are bonded together to make each molecule. A single H on its own, one atom, is not stable. Similarly, oxygen (O_2) also consists of two atoms. When hydrogen is burnt in oxygen, it makes water:

$$2H_2 + O_2 \rightarrow 2H_2O + heat$$

This means two molecules of hydrogen are needed to combine with one of oxygen, creating two molecules of water (which contain three atoms each) plus some heat. [Note there are the same number of Hs and Os on each side of the arrow, so if you started with four hydrogen atoms in two molecules, you still have four hydrogen atoms afterwards, although they're now in two water molecules. In terms of the number of hydrogen and oxygen atoms, nothing has been created or destroyed.]

Water is a stable compound: its atoms bond together in a strong way and are not easily separated. It takes more energy to separate the hydrogen and oxygen than is released when they recombine. Which is a pity because otherwise the water-hydrogen/oxygen-water cycle would be the perfect fuel. There's plenty of it, and it burns completely cleanly. Hydrogen also has a very high heat content, (more of which later) making it doubly desirable as a fuel. There is a lot of research work going on all over the world, attempting to find cheap ways of making and storing it.

Of all the other possible combinations of O and H atoms, none are as stable as water and most are unstable. It's likely that in the heat and violence of the explosion some of these exotic compounds do exist for a tiny fraction of a second. But if there are Os, Hs and OHs rushing about they will collide with others, forming more and more stable compounds, which ultimately come down to H_2O. The process is akin to trying to balance three balls on top of one another: it's theoretically possible and it's achievable for a few tenths of a second but ultimately the balls will fall to a more stable configuration on the floor.

Hydrogen is an ideal fuel but the fuels we actually use consist of bonds between hydrogen and carbon atoms, called *hydrocarbons* or HC. The simplest is methane, a flammable gas that contains one carbon atom to four of hydrogen and its formula is CH_4.

When it reacts with oxygen, this happens:

$$CH_4 + 2O_2 \rightarrow CO_2 + 2H_2O + heat$$

Each methane molecule has combined with two oxygen molecules to form a carbon dioxide molecule, two water molecules and heat. Carbon dioxide is a harmless gas (it produces the fizz in lemonade and beer) so methane is also a very clean fuel. However if you forced the combustion process at high temperature and pressure and gave it only a very short period of time you can visualise imperfections.

We're only looking at three molecules. They are, of course, surrounded by millions of others, all (in a perfect combustion chamber) behaving in the same way. But inside an *imperfect* chamber, too many methane molecules end up together. There's too much carbon and not enough oxygen in this little region. Instead of making friendly carbon dioxide, it makes poisonous carbon monoxide (CO), which may not be quite as stable, but is stable enough to exist in atmospheric conditions. This leaves an excess of hydrogen although it soon recombines with some more carbon – there are dozens of hydrocarbon compounds to choose from and some even contain oxygen, so any free oxygen floating around could also be scooped up. The exhaust gas now contains CO_2, H_2O, CO and some combination of H, C and possibly O.

Because these are not quite as stable as the ideal combustion products, there will be less heat released. If it were in an engine, there would be slightly less power compared to a cycle that gave perfect combustion. [Real engines give 0-2% CO, running up to 2-4% on full power and over 6% on a rich mixture.]

The relatively simple reaction of methane is likely to be clean running, simply because there is less chance of things going wrong. Other fuels are much more complex. Ethane is C_2H_6. Butane is C_4H_{10}. Octane is C_8H_{18}. There are families called paraffins whose formulae follow a $C_nH_{(2n+2)}$ pattern, eg C_6H_{14} and there are several similar families.

When you burn a hydrocarbon, the ideal object is to produce water, carbon dioxide and as much heat as possible. But when you burn one in less than perfect conditions there's every chance that it will burn to form another, more stable hydrocarbon. By-products may then include carbon monoxide and various nitric oxides (known as NO_x). These are the pollutants that emission laws try to restrict: hydrocarbons (HC), particulate carbon (C – soot), CO and NO_x.

Hydrogen has a molecular weight of 1, carbon 12, nitrogen 14 and oxygen 16. From this and from the structure of the chemical reactions like those shown above, it's possible to work out how many molecules of each substance are needed and the weight of each substance (assuming the reactions go to plan).

In the above example

$$CH_4 + 2O_2 \rightarrow CO_2 + 2H_2O + heat$$

We can put in the molecular weights for CH_4 (a total of 16) and $2O_2$ (64), so the reaction will require 64 weight units of oxygen to burn 16 units of methane and the ratio is 4:1 (by weight, not by volume – a gas will expand to the volume of its container but it will still weigh the same whether it is filling a 250 cc cylinder or has been compressed to 25 cc).

The oxygen is carried in air, which is mostly nitrogen, by weight 79 parts nitrogen to 21 parts oxygen. Nitrogen is a fairly inert gas that doesn't willingly react with other chemicals and it can pass through this reaction unchanged but it is nevertheless present and the equation should be

$$CH_4 + 2O_2 + (2\times79/21)N_2 \rightarrow$$
$$CO_2 + 2H_2O + (2\times79/21)N_2 + heat$$

If we now put in the molecular weights, there is 16 of methane, against 64 of oxygen and 210.67 of nitrogen, so the ratio (air:fuel, by weight) is (64 + 211)/16 or 17.2:1 for methane. This is the minimum weight of air

Pollution and global warming

Atmospheric pollution has two impacts which can be described as local and global. The local form is obvious to anyone who has found themselves behind a black-smoky diesel or suffered runny eyes and headaches after working in a test house running high performance engines. The widespread form is much more subtle. Clearly it's not a good idea to pump out irritants into the atmosphere, even if they only stay there for a short while. Less obvious is the long term damage done by things that are immediately harmless and unnoticed – carcinogens, for example. In addition to these short- and long-term health hazards, there is the problem of what our traffic and industry might be doing to the world as a whole. An ideal engine has water and carbon dioxide as its exhaust products but both of these 'harmless' substances are extremely efficient greenhouse gases that are able to contribute to the global warming phenomenon.

The greenhouse effect is an analogy to what we've all experienced in glass houses – heat radiated from the sun passes through the glass, hits the floor, plants etc and warms them up. They pass on this heat via conduction and convection to the surrounding air, but in this form the heat cannot escape through the glass walls and roof, it stays inside the greenhouse and makes the air temperature go up.

In the whole world version, the sun sends a very broad spectrum of radiation, ranging from gamma rays at the very high frequency end, through ultra-violet to the visible colours: in order, violet, indigo, blue, green, yellow, orange and red. Below this are long-wave, infra-red and radio frequencies, like those found in micro-wave ovens and radar sets. The whole lot hits the top layer of the atmosphere.

The high frequency, short-wavelength radiation is more easily deflected, either reflected back into space or absorbed by the gas, in the same way that visible light behaves when it hits a brick wall – some is reflected, some disappears forever but none emerges on the other side. Hardly any gamma radiation and very little UV gets through the atmosphere to the earth's surface.

Of the visible radiation, the blue end of the spectrum is most easily scattered, which is why the sky appears blue. Longer wave, red light has more penetrating power. When the sun is low in the sky and its light has to get through a greater layer of atmosphere to reach you, the observer, it is predominantly red light that succeeds, which is why the rising and setting sun is red. When the atmosphere is thickened with dust etc, the effect is more pronounced and the entire skyline appears red.

This accounts for the proverb 'Red sky at night, shepherd's delight; red sky at morning, shepherd's warning.' A red sky at sunset means all the dust and airborne debris of the day's activity is in the west, so the wind must be in the east, coming from mainland Europe. Crossing land, it will be dry and not bring rain. Conversely, a west wind would carry the airborne stuff to the east, where it will filter the rays of the rising sun, and a west wind comes straight off the Atlantic, bringing plenty of water with it. Obviously shepherds in different parts of the world, like the American east coast, would have different criteria for rejoicing.

The sun's radiation that does penetrate the atmosphere arrives at the earth's surface where some is reflected and some is absorbed. Of course it doesn't just disappear, its energy warms up the surface. And this surface radiates heat, just like the sun does. The difference is the sun is at a much higher temperature: it radiates over a broad spectrum with visible light at its centre (wavelengths of about 0.5 to 1.0mm). The earth's surface radiates at a much lower frequency and longer wavelength, well into the infra-red, in the region of 4 to 100mm.

Now some solids are impervious to visible radiation while others, like glass, let it through, and gases behave in a similar way. Most let visible light through but each gas absorbs certain frequencies. When water vapour is visible (ie clouds) it absorbs a fair amount of visible light, but much water vapour is invisible. In this form it still absorbs radiation in the wavelengths from 4 to 7mm. Carbon dioxide absorbs wavelengths from 13 to 19mm. Both are in the range of radiation emitted from the surface.

Water vapour and carbon dioxide in the atmosphere (which occur naturally) trap these radiations from the earth's surface, causing the troposphere (the lower part of the atmosphere) to warm up. It in turn radiates its new-found heat, in all directions. Some goes upwards and outwards, some goes downwards, where it warms up the surface again. This is the greenhouse effect and we depend upon it to maintain the climate to which we have evolved.

The risk is that it might be a finely balanced thing and adding too much greenhouse effect might start a spiral of warming which would make the climate uninhabitable.

In this context even 'zero emission' electric vehicles are no good. They may not produce local irritants but the electricity they use, apart from nuclear and hydro-electric power stations, is produced from burning hydrocarbons with the

continued overleaf

needed to burn the fuel completely and is known as the stoichiometric ratio. Any more is called excess air and if the weight is known, it can be expressed as a factor (eg 1.05) or a percentage (5%) excess air. It is calculated:

$$\text{excess air} = (r - r_{stoich})/\, r_{stoich} \times 100\%$$

Where r is the actual air/fuel ratio and r_{stoich} is the stoichiometric ratio. An excess air figure of more than 1 or 100% indicates a weak mixture. The excess air ratio is sometimes called λ (the Greek letter lambda) and sensors that measure excess air in exhaust systems are called λ-sensors.

Sometimes the same thing is expressed as mixture strength:

$$\text{mixture strength} = r_{stoich}/r \times 100\%$$

In which case a figure of less than 100 is a weak mixture (excess air), while anything above 100 is rich (excess fuel)

In these examples nitrogen is assumed to be inert, passing through the reaction with no change. In real conditions, the high temperature and pressure make the nitrogen more active. Coupled with the less than perfect mixing and the short time interval, there is a very good chance that unstable oxygen atoms will find themselves next to nitrogen, instead of the carbon or hydrogen with which they would rather react. In this case they form nitrogen oxides (NO, NO_2, NO_3, known collectively as NO_x), not as stable as CO_2 or H_2O but better than free oxygen atoms.

This implies that somewhere else in the mixture there is now a surplus of carbon or hydrogen, which may appear in the exhaust as carbon (soot), hydrogen (not very likely) or some hydrocarbon compound. Running a mixture with excess air can handle these surpluses and is more likely to oxidise the carbon and hydrocarbons before they get very far. Such a system will be economical in terms of fuel consumption. Others bleed fresh air into the exhaust, so this secondary oxidation is done outside the engine cylinder and is not productive in terms of power or economy, although it does clean the exhaust of hydrocarbons. But both systems will tend to produce NO_x emissions.

So far we've only looked at the simplest fuels. There are single hydrocarbons which contain many more atoms and gasoline is a complex blend of many hydrocarbons. They can be synthesised from virtually any hydrocarbon stock, ranging from coal to rotting vegetation (which is what coal once was) but the cheapest and most direct way is to refine crude oil. This is also known as petroleum and the English word petrol was originally a name derived from petroleum distillate.

The hydrocarbons in gasoline generally come from four families: paraffins (which have the general formula $C_nH_{(2n+2)}$), olefins (C_nH_{2n}), naphthenes (also C_nH_{2n}) and aromatics (at its simplest, a molecular ring of six carbon atoms each bonded to a hydrogen atom). As well as having different numbers of carbon and hydrogen atoms, these groups also vary in the ways the atoms bond together, which determines how stable or reactive they are. Some paraffins with four or more carbon atoms can exist in different forms, called isomers, which have different properties.

An example is a paraffin called normal octane (or n-octane) with 8 carbon and 18 hydrogen atoms bonded like this

```
    H H H H H H H H
    | | | | | | | |
H–C–C–C–C–C–C–C–C–H
    | | | | | | | |
    H H H H H H H H
```

continued from previous page

same exhaust products and inefficiencies as vehicle engines.

The question is whether vehicle emissions are enough to make a difference. 'Straws' and 'camels' backs' spring to mind. There are volcanoes that make man's emissions seem puny. There is no shortage of water to provide water vapour. Carbon dioxide comes from the world's forests, especially in (naturally-occurring) forest fires and recently another source has been noticed. The oceans, like lemonade, contain dissolved carbon dioxide. When they're shaken up enough, as in tropical storms and hurricanes, they give up the gas into the air. Wherever you see white water, you see carbon dioxide being released into the atmosphere.

Another question is whether emissions from our cities would successfully find their way to the upper troposphere (a height of 30,000 to 40,000 ft, or 9 to 12 km) where they work most effectively. Aircraft, on the other hand, with their 'clean', kerosene-burning engines, routinely fly at precisely this level. While they only consume about one-sixth of the fuel used by motor vehicles, they deliver exhaust gas exactly where it isn't needed. According to estimates by the Intergovernmental Panel on Climate Change and by Paul Wennberg at the California Institute of Technology, the effect could be between one-third and one-half of the carbon dioxide production by motor vehicles. To keep motor vehicles in perspective, electrical power stations produce almost twice as much CO_2, while industry and heating produce more than twice as much.

Catalytic converters and clean running engines don't address the problem of carbon dioxide or water vapour emissions – these already are the 'clean' components of exhaust gas. They concentrate on cleaning up the irritant, dirty emissions: hydrocarbons (HC), carbon monoxide (CO) and nitrogen oxides (NO_x).

There are problems with catalytic converters. They don't work fully if they're not in their ideal temperature range or if the air/fuel ratio deviates by more than 1 ratio from stoichiometric. On top of this, they create nitrous oxide (N_2O), which, as a greenhouse gas, is said to be 300 times more effective than carbon dioxide. By partially blocking the exhaust, catalytic converters prevent engines making full use of the exhaust system to enhance power output, so the less efficient engines have higher fuel consumption and consequently pump out more carbon dioxide and water vapour than they might. Finally, there is the global pollution caused by refining and fabricating the materials used to make the catalysts (platinum, palladium, copper or cadmium).

Ozone (O_3) is a not-very-stable form of oxygen which is produced when less stable NO_x and other oxygen-bearing compounds provide active oxygen and where three Os or an O_2 and an O are less stable than one O_3.

It varies from being a pollutant to being beneficial, depending on where it is. At ground level it is an irritant and is implicated with NO_x, other pollutants and sunlight in the formation of smog. Higher up, but still in the troposphere, it is an effective greenhouse gas. Much higher still, in the stratosphere (up to 130,000 ft or 40 km high) where the lower temperatures and pressures make it more stable, it serves a good purpose in filtering out ultraviolet light.

Finally, it must be said that our knowledge of these things is far from complete, even at the levels of the engineers and scientists who do nothing but study them. By the time politicians and marketing people have become involved, the facts, decisions based on the facts and actions based on the decisions are often removed a long way from what would be useful.

Even an honest perception of what is benign and what is harmful can change quickly. When it was decided that organic lead was too dangerous to be used as a fuel additive, there was a scramble to find replacements that would raise octane levels as effectively (which, by making engines more efficient, cuts down several other types of pollution). MTBE – methyl-tertiary-butyl-ethylene – was one of the candidates. When I researched the subject in the early '90s, it was regarded as harmless, as safe as anything semi-explosive was likely to be. The consensus was that it was a bit too tame, it didn't do any harm but it didn't do its octane-raising job particularly well either. Now, eight or nine years later, the American Environmental Protection Agency lists it as a possible carcinogen and the additive, which is very soluble in water, has leaked from filling station tanks and contaminated ground water. Its repulsive smell makes it unlikely that anyone would drink contaminated water but it's a serious problem for drinking water supplies. In California there are moves to ban the additive — but not to ban leaky underground storage tanks, it seems.

One of its isomers, iso-octane, has the same number of atoms but they're bonded like this:

```
    H  CH₃ H   H   H
    |   |  |   |   |
H – C – C – C – C – C – H
    |   |  |   |   |
    H  CH₃ H  CH₃  H
```

This particular variation is significant for us because iso-octane is resistant to knock (detonation) and has a research octane number (RON) and a motor octane number (MON) of 100 (see later in this chapter). This is not surprising because the number is obtained by comparing the test fuel with iso-octane, which, of course, behaves like 100% iso-octane. But in the same test, n-octane only gets a rating of 25, ie it behaves like a fuel containing 25% iso-octane (mixed with something that knocks very easily, like n-heptane, which has a rating of 0).

The chart (see Fig. 2.4) shows the general processes and products in a typical refinery. The final blending of gasoline has to meet certain specifications, in the UK it is BS7070 and later BS EN228 for unleaded, BS7800 for super unleaded and BS4040 for leaded, 4-star, fuel. These set out criteria to make sure the fuel is safe to handle and store, is suitable for summer or winter conditions, is compatible with other fuels made to the same specification, delivers a minimum performance in terms of knock resistance and ignitability and has limited tendencies to corrode, varnish, pollute or leave ash deposits.

These are safety and compatibility aspects. Engine designers want more: things like heat content, flame speed and knock resistance are important – and it's important they shouldn't vary between one batch of fuel and

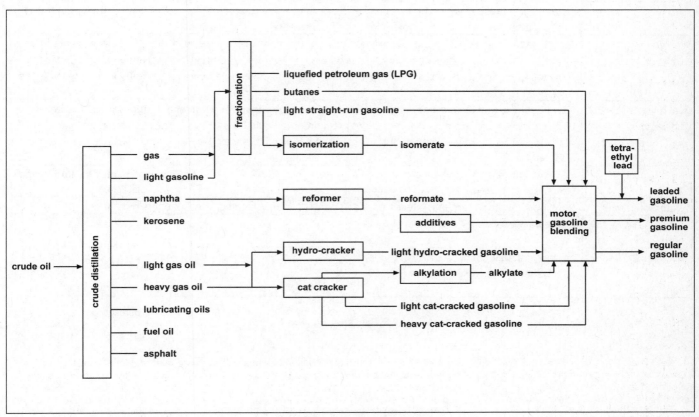

Fig. 2.4 Oil refinery process

*Crude oil consists of **fractions** which have different boiling points. A simple distillation process separates the main groups but will only give whatever the crude oil contained in the first place. In order to obtain more hydrocarbons (from which gasoline is blended), it is necessary to **refine** the process.*

*The bottom end of the distillation process is carried out at low pressure (vacuum distillation) because this lowers the boiling point. Being able to do this at lower temperature means that there is less risk of thermally **cracking** the raw material. The difference between the **light** fractions, which have a low boiling point, and the **heavier** fractions is in the size and shape of their hydrocarbon molecules. The heavier (larger) molecules can be cracked or broken down into smaller (lighter) hydrocarbons. This was first done by raising them to high temperature (**thermal cracking**), a process improved by the use of catalysts (**cat cracking**).*

*Hydrocarbons that will not crack by this method can be broken down if the process is conducted in a hydrogen atmosphere (called **hydro-cracking**). The products formed so far can be altered further by changing the shape of the HC molecules in processes called **reforming** and **isomerization**. An isomer contains the same atoms bonded in a different pattern, which alters its stability as a fuel. Alcohols – partially oxidised hydrocarbons containing oxygen in a hydroxyl (OH) group – will also form isomers called alkyls. The first point of all this is to extract the maximum amount of usable fuel from a given crude oil (and these vary enormously). The second point is that all these groups have different properties (boiling point, ignition or flash point, knock resistance and so on) from which it is possible to blend fuel to meet specifications to suit different climates etc. Finally **additives** are put into the blended fuel to reduce varnishing, icing, increase knock resistance and so on.*

Quality	Significance
octane rating	resistance to knock. Greater resistance means higher compression ratios may be used, which give more power and better thermal efficiency.
RON	relates to low-speed knock
MON	relates to high-speed knock
heat content	amount of heat liberated by unit mass of the fuel. More heat equals more power but note that the *amount* of fuel drawn into the cylinder also depends on the AF ratio. Sometimes quoted as 'high' and 'low' value: 'high' (or gross) is starting with liquid fuel and finishing with liquid water, while 'low' (or net) means liquid fuel to water vapour (which is what happens in ic engines)
heat of evaporation	the heat required to turn unit mass of liquid into gas. This is a measure of the cooling effect on the air stream. More cooling creates a denser intake charge and lowers the temperature further from the detonation point
AF ratio	ratio of air to fuel by weight, for combustion. This determines the amount of fuel present in the cylinder and, multiplied by the heat content, determines the heat release per engine cycle
ignition limits (misfire limits)	the AF ratios beyond which the fuel will not ignite. Wide limits make the engine easy to tune and able to be set for best power and best economy, although they have safety and handling implications if the fuel is too easy to ignite. The fuel's resistance to pre-ignition and autoignition (ie how much energy is required to ignite it) is also important.
volatility boiling curve vapour pressure	how easily the fuel evaporates; what proportion of it evaporates over what temperature range; the pressure of its vapour (when this equals the ambient pressure, the liquid boils). More volatility is good for cold starting, warm-up, driveability and throttle response. It also increases the likelihood of vapour lock, icing, and emissions from the fuel tank, float bowls and during refuelling
gum	deposits left when fuel evaporates (which can block jets, filters etc). Also fuel's oxidation stability for storage (oxidation creates gums)
water tolerance	the highest temperature that causes phase separation in oxygenated (alcohol-containing) fuel
copper strip corrosion	indicates presence of sulphur compounds
sulphur and phosphorus content	compounds that occur naturally in crude oil but cause pollution in exhaust fumes and therefore need to be kept below a maximum level

Fig. 2.5 Fuel specifications

another. The charts (see Figs. 2.5 and 2.6) show most of the important requirements that gasoline has to meet, and (see Fig. 2.7) compare gasoline with some alternative fuels.

Calorific content

From an engine performance point of view the fuel's heat content is important. In a way, this is a measure of its chemical instability and so has to be a compromise between potential power and ease of handling. There are substances (like nitro-glycerine) that will explode if they are shaken but a little more stability is useful in road vehicle fuels.

The heat released when a fuel is burnt is measured in a calorimeter, a heavily insulated flask containing the fuel and a compartment full of water. The definition of a heat unit is the amount of heat required to raise unit mass of water through 1° – in the metric scheme of things, one calorie is required to raise 1 gram of water through 1°C (the SI preferred unit, the Joule, is equivalent to 0.23885cal). The Imperial equivalent, the BTU (British Thermal Unit) is what's needed to raise 1lb of water through 1°F. A known weight of fuel is burnt in a calorimeter and the heat is used to raise the temperature of a known mass of water.

The heat content simply tells you what's available and gives a comparison between different fuels (see Fig. 2.7). It's not a straight comparison because an engine's cylinder fills with a mixture of air and fuel and it is the AF ratio that determines the weight of fuel used in each cycle. This amount, multiplied by its calorific value, gives the potential heat release inside the engine.

As an example, methanol has less than half the heat content of gasoline and if the same quantities were burned, would give less than

10% evaporated	50 – 70°C
50% evaporated	110 – 121°C max, 77°C min
90% evaporated	185 – 190°C
Final boiling point	225°C

Fig. 2.6 Gasoline distillation curve (ASTM D4814-94d)

Fuel	RON	MON	Lead g/L	Calorific value MJ/kg (Note 2)	Stoichiometric A/F ratio	% weight	constituents
Elf Moto 119 (made for high revving two-stroke racers, before leaded fuel was banned)	>119	>110	1.4				
Avgas 100LL	Note 1	>99.5	0.85 max	43.5		85C, 15H	
4-star BS4040 (Note 3)	97	86	0.05 to 0.15	43.5	14.7	86C, 14H	blends of various HC from C_7H_{16} through to $C_{11}H_{24}$
Premium unleaded BS EN 228:1999 (Note 4)	95	85	0.013 max	42.7	14.8	86C, 14H	
Super unleaded BS7800:1988 (Note 4)	98	87	0.013 max	41.9 - 44.2	14.7	86C, 14H	
Methanol	107	92	0	19.9	6.45	38C, 12H, 50O	CH_3OH
Ethanol	108	92	0	26.8	9.0	52C, 13H, 34.8O	C_2H_5OH
LPG (liquefied petroleum gas)	>100	-	0	46.1	15.5	82-83H, 17-18C	mainly propane and butane C_3H_8, C_4H_{10}
Hydrogen	>130	-	0	120	34.3	100H	H_2
Methane	>120	-	0	49.6	17.2	72C, 25H	CH_4
Propane	112	97	0	46.1	15.7	82C, 18H	C_3H_8
Natural gas	120-130	-	0	47.7	c17.5	76C, 24H	90% methane CH_4
Purified sewage gas	>120	-	0	37.7	c17.5	75C, 25H	95% methane CH_4
Orange oil	106	-	0	45.3	14.2		$C_{10}H_{16}$
Diesel	-	-	0	41 - 43	14.5	86C, 13H	
Kerosene			0	43	14.5	87C, 13H	

Fig. 2.7 Fuel comparison

Note 1: Aviation gasoline is octane-rated by different methods to motor gasoline. Piston-engined aircraft have a manual mixture control, going from fully lean to fully rich. The lean-mixture test is done at stoichiometric AF and approximates to MON. The rich-mixture method simulates the behaviour of fuel in a supercharged engine where a fully rich mixture is used so the cooling effect of the fuel suppresses detonation. This is the first number in an Avgas spec, eg 130 in 130/100, but doesn't have an equivalent in motor gasoline specs.

Note 2: The heat content figures are lower than the theoretical values because the exhaust products (mainly steam) take some heat with them. If the steam could be condensed into water and the heat put to some use, the figures would be higher. Liquid fuels have an advantage here because their latent heat of evaporation cools the intake charge, raising its density and moving it further from the detonation threshold. Fuels which arrive in gaseous form do not have such a good starting point.

Note 3: Leaded 4-star discontinued in the UK from January 2000. Replaced by a lead substitute fuel for use in those vehicles which cannot use unleaded fuel.

Note 4: Titles on pumps vary from country to country. UK titles are given in the table. Regular grade unleaded is defined as 90 RON and 80 MON, although may not be available in some markets.

half the heat and less than half the power. But its stoichiometric ratio is 6.4 compared to 14.7 for gasoline, so a cylinder-full of air would take in more methanol (14.7/6.4 = 2.28 times as much, to be exact).

From their calorific values, gasoline has a heat content of 43.5 mJ/kg compared to 19.7 for methanol, but 2.28 times as much methanol would liberate 19.7 × 2.28 = 43.5 - or the same amount of heat as could be extracted from the gasoline. This turns out to be true for all hydrocarbon fuels.

However, there are two final twists that give some fuels a power advantage. Running at stoichiometry, the heat release is approximately the same but when the AF ratio is optimised for maximum power, gasoline needs between 12 and 13:1, while methanol needs 4:1. We now have 3 times as much methanol going into the engine, with a heat content of 59.1 mJ compared to gasoline's 43.5. And the fuel's better resistance to knock makes it easier to get at this potential power.

3 Combustion

Thermal efficiency

The engine still has to arrange combustion in the time available, extract the heat and convert it into mechanical work. The efficiency with which it does this is called its thermal efficiency (η_{THERM} – the Greek letter *eta*) and spark ignition engines currently run at 25 to 30%, at best.

Thermal efficiency is calculated from

$$\eta_{THERM} = sfc/cv \times 100\%$$

where sfc is the specific fuel consumption and cv is the calorific value of the fuel

Specific fuel consumption is the fuel flow (in g/s) divided by the power produced (in kW), so the sfc units are g/kW-s and the heat content of the fuel will be in kilo-Joules per gram (kJ/g). As one Joule is equivalent to one Watt-second, η_{THERM} is a ratio with no dimensions: it simply compares the actual power produced to the potential power available (ie the heat content of the fuel flow rate).

The engine's compression ratio is important because it is directly linked to the thermal efficiency (see Fig. 2.8).

$$\eta_{THERM} = 1 - (1/r)^{n-1}$$

where

η_{THERM} – thermal efficiency
r – compression ratio
n – ratio of specific heats of gas at constant pressure and constant volume ($\approx$ 1.4 for dry air and about 1.3 for an air-fuel mixture, see Chapter 3)

Flame travel

While high compression ratios are desirable for thermal efficiency, the limit is imposed by detonation or knock. Fuels that resist knock, permit higher compression ratios and higher thermal efficiency.

In normal combustion the spark ignites fuel close to it and the flame spreads outwards, as a three-dimensional ripple or 'kernel', through the gas. If the flame front travels uniformly it ensures that all the fuel is burnt and the minimum time and energy is spent igniting the next layer of fuel particles. A flame that darted hither and thither in a ragged manner could leave pockets of unburnt fuel or unused air. Even if all the fuel was finally burnt, the process would take longer and the extra time would allow heat to be lost into the metal of the engine, instead of being kept to expand the gas.

Whatever time it takes from ignition to the point where the combustion heat begins to make the gas expand has to be allowed for by the ignition timing. Ideally, expansion must start as the piston moves through top dead centre (TDC), so the spark must be *advanced* some time before TDC to let this happen. If it is advanced too far, the expanding gas will work against the piston while it is still rising towards TDC, slowing the engine and raising the gas temperature. If it is not advanced enough, the expansion will start too late and part of the downward stroke will be wasted.

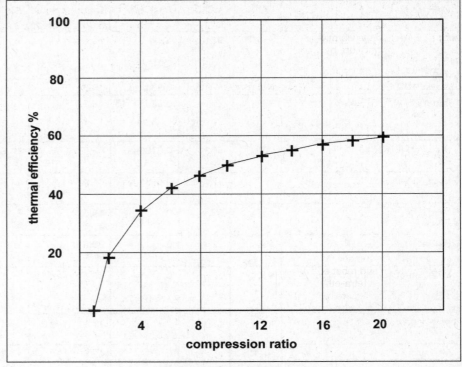

Fig. 2.8 Thermal efficiency

This graph shows the theoretical increase in thermal efficiency with compression ratio. Real engines, typically running compression ratios in the range 10 ~ 12:1 have thermal efficiencies of 30% or less, ie about half the theoretical value.

So ignition timing is critical for maximum performance, in terms of both engine torque, gas temperature and fuel consumption.

One problem is the flame travels faster through a dense mixture, such as when high throttle openings are used, compared to the thinner mixture when the engine is on light load, so the timing needs to vary with throttle position.

The ignition circuit is usually triggered by a sensor on the crankshaft, a fixed angle before TDC but as the engine speed increases, it takes less time to move through this angle, so the timing also needs to be advanced at higher engine speed.

Finally, as the engine goes through its speed range it will have regions of high and low volumetric efficiency, caused by effects of the exhaust and intake dimensions, and the cam timing. In the efficient regions (where the torque makes small peaks) the intake charge will be more densely packed and will burn faster, needing less timing advance. In the inefficient regions (dips in the torque curve) combustion will take longer and the ignition will need more advance. Ideally, whatever controls ignition timing needs to be sensitive to speed, load and the engine's characteristics.

Detonation

There is an alternative means of combustion – detonation. When the AF mixture gets enough energy from having its pressure and temperature raised, it ignites without any help from a spark or a flame front. All of the particles can ignite at once, or some particles ignite and spread combustion to the rest. This is what happens in diesel engines and is actually a very efficient process, with the minimum amount of time and heat loss. Unfortunately it's a bit too efficient for gasoline engines. The explosion is destructive and critical parts like pistons are not made as strong as they are in diesels, in order to keep the engine as light as possible.

Often there is partial knock, where ignition and flame spread begin normally but some gas ahead of the flame front is heated or compressed too far and a small pocket detonates. This happens at low engine speed and high load, when the engine's trapping efficiency is high and compression pressure goes above the fuel's limit. It's called *pinking* and can be heard as a rapid tinkling noise when the throttle is opened. It is not usually serious or likely to do any damage.

Partial knock also happens towards the end of combustion when the end gases, furthest from the spark plug, detonate. This can cause damage, usually around the edge of the piston crown and to the inside edge of the head gasket. The fuel will knock if the temperature and pressure are raised enough and these conditions can be caused if the ignition timing is too far advanced, because the increasing pressure caused by combustion is added to the compression caused by the still-rising piston. Sometimes it can be heard, and the vibrations it causes can certainly be picked up by knock sensors (Piezo-electric crystals that generate electric current when they are compressed – a signal that can be used to make the control system retard the ignition timing).

A fuel's resistance to knock is called its octane rating, because the tests compare it to the knock characteristics of iso-octane.

Additives

By refining the fuel to a high level and blending the right components it is possible to make high octane gasoline, although this is an expensive process and it tends to cream off the top few per cent of the raw material. It is better to use more of the crude oil to make a lower octane fuel and then add something to raise its knock resistance.

One of the first and most effective additives was organic lead – tetra-ethyl lead (TEL) and tetra-methyl lead. Both are highly toxic, add to exhaust pollution and coat catalytic converters. This stops the catalyst doing its job as it no longer comes into contact with exhaust gas. (TEL has one good effect: it lubricates and cushions valve seats, preventing wear and 'sinking'. Nearly all bikes produced since the '70s have had hardened valve seats and do not need leaded fuel.)

For these reasons, leaded fuel began to be phased out many years ago and where it is still used in road vehicle fuel, the amount is severely limited. Avgas (aviation gasoline for piston-engined aircraft) contains a high

CFR engine

Back in the 1920s, the Co-operative Fuels Research Council realised there had to be standards for motor fuels and that one of the most significant aspects was knock resistance. They drew up a specification for a test engine to measure this and Waukesha Engine built it during 1928. It was a single cylinder, 3.25 inch bore, 4.5 inch stroke and the whole cylinder and cylinder head could be moved up and down relative to the crankshaft. This meant the compression ratio could be varied between 4:1 and 18:1, without altering the shape or characteristics of the cylinder head.

amount, even in the so-called 100LL (low lead) grade. The effects on the fuel's octane rating can be seen in Fig. 2.7

TEL is an extremely effective octane booster and to maintain the performance we expect from bikes and cars it was necessary to replace it with something else.

There are many hydrocarbons which have higher octane ratings than gasoline, and can be added to increase the overall rating – such as iso-octane (100RON, 100MON), toluene (120RON, 109MON) and xylene (118RON, 115MON).

Alcohols (see Chapter 11) such as methanol or ethanol have high octane ratings and can be blended into gasoline (an example is the American M85, 85% methanol, 15% gasoline), usually with additional components to stabilise them and prevent separation. There are also ethers (isomers of alcohols) which are used as additives, the most

A knock meter, made by Weston, sat on top and let the operator judge the onset and the severity of detonation, so that he could match this between the test fuel and the reference fuel.

It set the standards for the RON and MON tests so successfully (and repeatably) that essentially the same engine design is used today and would give the same results as the 1928 engine. The same tests are used, despite the fact that current engines are far removed from the dimensions and speed of the long-stroke, single cylinder. Engine manufacturers and fuel producers go to a lot of trouble to correlate RON and MON numbers with real world performance.

common being MTBE (methyl tertiary butyl ether, with a blending RON of 115) and TAME (tertiary amyl methyl ether, which has a blending RON of 111).

Mixture loop

When an engine is running on load, the mixture can be altered through quite a wide range. As it is richened, the torque usually increases, reaches a maximum and then decreases. Further richening produces a misfire, which is the rich-mixture limit of the engine. Weakening the mixture beyond the optimum reduces the torque but as it also reduces the fuel flow, the *brake specific fuel consumption* (bsfc) may improve. This bsfc figure is the fuel flow rate divided by the power produced. Strictly it should be a mass flow rate, in g/min or lb/h but often, for convenient measurement, a volume flow rate is used, in cc/min or pt/h.

Octane rating – a knock-resistance test

Iso-octane is very resistant to knock and it is used as a baseline comparison for other fuels: if one behaves like a 95% mixture of iso-octane (mixed with something very prone to knock like n-heptane) then its octane rating is 95.

The test is done in a Co-operative Fuels Research (CFR) or a BASF test engine – a single, whose cylinder head and barrel can be raised or lowered to alter the compression ratio. The engine has a knock sensor and is run at a predetermined constant speed, constant temperature and fixed ignition timing with stoichiometric air-fuel mixture. The compression ratio is raised until the fuel begins to knock.

The test is repeated with the same engine settings on a mix of iso-octane and n-heptane, reducing the proportion of iso-octane until the fuel starts to knock and this percentage is the test fuels' octane rating.

To evaluate fuels whose octane rating is above 100, a reference fuel is used with increasing amounts of TEL, calibrated against iso-octane up to 100% so the effects of adding

more TEL can be extrapolated and this fuel is then used in place of iso-octane.

There are two basic test procedures.

The Research Octane Number (RON) method is ASTM D2699, and the Motor Octane Number (MON) is ASTM D2700. The MON test is more severe, running the engine at a higher speed (900 rpm as opposed to 600 rpm), pre-heating the intake charge and allowing the ignition timing to be adjusted with the change in compression ratio. In the RON test, ignition is fixed at 13° BTDC. It gives higher values.

In the UK the higher (RON) value is displayed on pumps. In the US they take an average of the two values - (RON + MON)/2, which is also known as the anti-knock index - and use this figure. The difference between RON and MON is called the fuel's *sensitivity*.

The tests for Avgas are different and yield two numbers, the higher one for a fully rich mixture and a lower one that approximates to the MON figure in motor gasoline tests.

There is a third rating, called Front Octane Number (FON or sometimes R100), which is a RON test on the fraction of the fuel that boils below 100°C. This is the fuel vapour that will

reach an engine first during cold running and sudden acceleration.

These tests are perfectly good ways to compare fuels and put them into a sort of league table of knock resistance. However, they do not simulate conditions inside a real, multi-cylinder engine running at considerably higher speed, so there is another rating, called *Road Octane Number* (RdON) which is done in WOT acceleration in a test vehicle (usually on a dynamometer).

The test is the *Modified Uniontown Procedure CRC F-28*. A series of reference fuels with increasing octane ratings are used and the ignition timing is progressively advanced until the test operator can detect 'trace knock'. From this a graph of octane number and ignition timing to give trace knock can be drawn for that engine. The procedure is repeated with the test fuel, advancing the ignition timing until trace knock is detected. The RdON for the fuel is then the octane number of the reference fuel that gave knock on the same ignition setting. Usually 10 to 15 test vehicles are used, to get results that are statistically safe from spurious effects.

In SI units, bsfc is measured in g/kW-h or cc/kW-h. In Imperial units it becomes lb/hp-h or pt/hp-h. Drawn as a graph against engine speed (rpm), the low points on the curve show where the engine is most fuel-efficient.

As four-strokes run between a best of 0.5 pt/hp-h and a worst of 0.7 pt/hp-h, it is possible to predict the fuel flow for a given power output. For example, an engine producing 80 bhp will require a fuel flow rate of 80 × 0.5–0.7 pt/h. Taking the larger number, 56 pt/h, and adding a safety margin of 20% gives us 67.2 pt/h. So the fuel tap, fuel lines, fuel filter and fuel pump must all be capable of delivering a minimum of 67.2 pt/h when the fuel tank is at its lowest level. This calculation provides a useful reference for fault-finding, simply by running the fuel flow into a measuring cylinder and timing it with a stopwatch. If the flow is at the safe level or above, then there is no problem with fuel supply.

If it is between the safe value and the minimum calculated value (80 × 0.5 or 40 pt/h in the above example) then there should be no problem but there is no safety margin. Any fuel starvation symptoms will only show up under extreme conditions, ie maximum power.

AF by weight	effect
6 to 7:1	rich mixture misfire
12 to 13:1	best power
13:1	rich limit for 3-way catalytic converter to work efficiently
14.7:1	typical stoichiometric
16:1	lean limit for 3-way catalytic converter to work efficiently
16 to 18:1	best economy (conventional engine)
20 to 22:1	lean mixture misfire (carburettor)
>28:1	lean-burn engine (fuel injection)

Fig. 2.9 Gasoline air-fuel mixtures

If the system cannot flow the calculated amount it should be improved before any further tests are made.

Note that although the fuel tap and lines may be capable of delivering the required flow, if the tank breather is blocked it will prevent air replacing the fuel drained from the tank. Low pressure inside the tank will eventually restrict the flow of fuel out of it. So any flow rate measurements must be made with the system in its normal operating condition – tank at the normal height, filler cap closed etc.

Two-strokes, tuned engines and some supercharged engines run richer mixtures because the cooling effect of the extra fuel allows them to make more power. For race-tuned two-strokes a bsfc of 1.0 pt/hp-h is not uncommon. It's obviously necessary to find the bsfc for individual engines – or to allow for the worst possible case – before deciding upon the fuel supply system.

Fig. 2.9 shows the approximate range of mixtures that an engine will tolerate – and their effects. During engine development it is usual to produce a *mixture loop* – at each

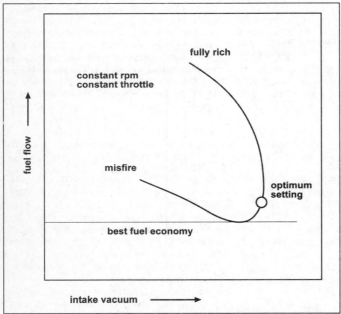

Fig. 2.10 Fuel mixture loop – small throttle opening

*Running an engine on a dyno from fully rich to fully lean produces a curve like this, which shows where the optimum settings are for both power and economy. Note: this is at one speed, and one throttle opening, with the ignition set for MBT. The exercise is repeated at other speeds, at say 500rpm intervals, and other throttle openings. The full set of curves gives a complete picture of the engine's fuelling requirements or a fuel **map**. This is a typical loop on low part throttle, using intake vacuum rather than dyno load to detect changes. The setting for best economy can be seen clearly but the optimum setting for best engine pick-up will be slightly richer. In practice, smooth idling and clean throttle response may demand an even richer setting,*

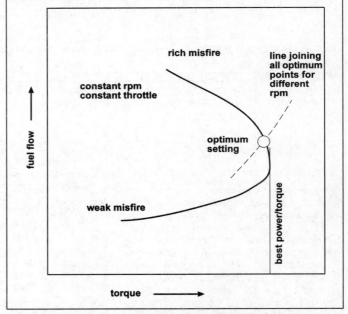

Fig. 2.11 Fuel mixture loop – large throttle opening

At high throttle openings, fuel flow is measured against dyno load or torque, keeping both engine rpm and throttle position constant. At wide throttle openings the curve will show where maximum power is produced, as in the example shown. At smaller throttle openings and lower speeds, the curve will change towards the shape shown in Fig. 2.10, giving a choice between best power and best economy. The sharpness with which the curve turns the corner and the full length of the curve indicate how sensitive the engine is to fuel mixture and how well it functions with the particular type of carburettor. A short curve with a very sharp corner means that it will be difficult to tune the carburettor and there will be no lee-way for compromise when it comes to getting the best fuel slope (see Fig. 2.12)

speed, the mixture is richened until the engine misfires, then it is progressively weakened, letting the engine stabilise and measuring the torque or power at each step. It's then possible to draw a graph of fuel flow against torque, which shows the optimum flow rates for power and economy (see Fig. 2.10 and 2.11).

Knowing the optimum flow rate for each crank speed allows you to draw a graph of fuel flow against rpm – called a *fuel slope* (Fig. 2.12). It's then necessary to select jets etc (or to map a fuel injection controller) to get as close as possible to this slope through the full engine speed range (see Chapter 3). So far these tests have been done with the engine running at steady speed. The next thing is to run transient tests, where the engine accelerates (at the same rate as it would under various road conditions) and where the throttle position is changed (again at various rates). The requirements in the transient tests have to be superimposed on the steady speed, base data. This is the basis for tuning carburettors or mapping fuel injection systems, which is covered in more detail in Chapters 4, 5 and 6.

Better burn engines

There are more ways to improve combustion – either to get better power/economy, to get cleaner running or to improve the engine's response, driveability

and its sensitivity to fluctuations in mixture strength.

Turbulence

Turbulence in the gas, either in the form of *swirl* (circular motion around the axis of the cylinder) or *tumble* (circular motion along the axis of the cylinder) will mix the fuel and air more thoroughly and will speed up the combustion process. Turbulence may be created by the shape of the intake tract, the position of the valves or by staggering the opening of a pair of intake valves by a few degrees.

It speeds up combustion, gives better fuel efficiency and lower emissions during difficult combustion, such as light loads or low rpm. But at high power, when the engine is at maximum efficiency, turbulence can spoil things because whatever causes it tends to obstruct gas flow and the swirling motion continues through combustion, so it brings more gas into contact with the metal of the engine, losing gas heat to the cooling system.

Yamaha developed a (so far) experimental variable intake port to enjoy the benefits of turbulence (mainly tumble) at part load, reverting to a conventional, straight tract on full load. It consists of a spool, fitted into the floor of the port. In one position it is flush with the port and has no effect on air flow. When rotated it creates a rounded step, which narrows the port in a venturi-like way, raising the gas speed, giving it more momentum and

making it easier to carry the fuel particles. When the flow leaves the step it imparts the circular motion that makes the gas tumble as it goes past the valves into the cylinder.

Stratified charge

It takes less energy to ignite a slightly rich mixture and this led to engines in which a ball of rich mixture is aimed at the spark plug, the surrounding gas being a weak mixture. The rich region ignites easily and burns quickly, in doing so it heats up and raises the pressure of the remaining gas, so the flame will spread through it more quickly than it normally would, carrying molecules of unburnt fuel ready to react with any excess oxygen they find. This is done with fuel injection, which gives more control over how much fuel is placed where (and when).

Lean burn

Lean burn engines are designed to run with excess air, to give maximum fuel economy and cleanest running. It's usually combined with stratified charge, in order to get reliable ignition and speed up the burn, but isn't used in bike engines.

Exhaust gas recirculation

Exhaust gas recirculation (egr) is a process of bleeding burnt gas back into the intake. It forms an inert part of the mixture, like the nitrogen in the air – it can still be heated, pressurised and used in the expansion stroke but it takes no part in the chemical reaction. This means that less air and fuel are needed; it also means that the combustion process will be slower (because the burnt gas gets in the way) and will be at a lower temperature. The net result is a small improvement in fuel economy on light loads and a bigger improvement in exhaust gas emissions, mainly due to the lower temperatures.

Used in car and truck engines, egr hasn't found its way into bikes yet but another factor might make it useful. This is the inefficiency caused by pumping losses on light load. When the throttle valve is mostly closed, the engine struggles to drag air past it. Bleeding exhaust gas downstream of the butterfly valve can alleviate this throttling loss without providing any air or fuel for the engine to burn. The pumping losses would be reduced without altering the engine load. It has also been found that egr can be used to control knock, permitting engines to be designed closer to the knock limit, where they run more efficiently, without the risk of mechanical damage caused by detonation.

Another problem on light load is that the total mixture is not so dense and can be hard to ignite evenly and quickly. It's worse on two-strokes, especially when they have large ports designed for maximum power. At low loads and low speeds, the scavenging isn't efficient and there is the opportunity for fresh charge to *short-circuit* (go from the transfer ports straight to the exhaust). The mixture trapped in the cylinder will be poorly distributed and

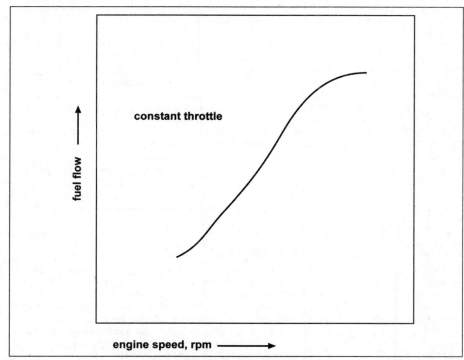

Fig. 2.12 Fuel mixture slope

For any given throttle position, the optimum fuel flow settings for all engine speeds can be joined together to produce a fuel slope. This shows how fuel flow must vary against engine speed if the machine is to give its best performance.

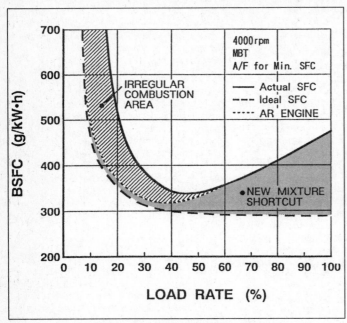

Fig. 2.13 Honda AR combustion

Two-strokes tuned for performance at high rpm have poor trapping efficiency and irregular combustion at lower revs and smaller loads. This shows the specific fuel consumption for an engine at 4000rpm, compared to its ideal performance and the performance achieved by Honda's AR combustion (Honda)

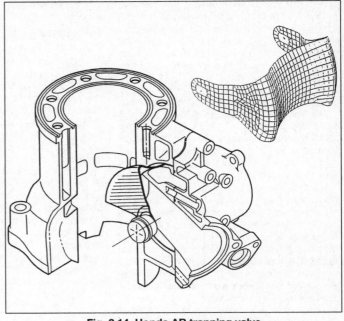

Fig. 2.14 Honda AR trapping valve

The valve is raised and lowered across the exhaust port window at the appropriate engine speeds and loads, preventing fresh mixture 'short-circuiting' through the exhaust port. Because more gas is trapped in the cylinder, compression raises it to higher temperature and pressure – enough to cause auto-ignition (Honda)

will contain exhaust gas not scavenged from the previous cycle. It is difficult to burn quickly and completely: the result is the familiar two-stroke characteristic of stuttering and misfiring at low revs and low load.

Activated radical combustion

See Figs. 2.13, 2.14 and 2.15

Honda reasoned they could stop this problem if they could encourage the mixture to detonate. If the temperature and pressure were raised enough, the fuel and air particles would burn spontaneously rather than waiting for a flame front to come along. Honda called it *activated radical* combustion because it's not really detonation in the full-blooded, piston-melting sense of the word.

Given enough energy, chemical compounds break into more active/less stable forms called radicals. As a simple example, water, H_2O might exist as H and OH radicals. In the right conditions, a similar thing happens to the fuel molecules. These temporary compounds are very unstable and will react readily with any suitable partners, without being nudged by a spark or a flame front. This is *auto-ignition*: you often see a similar effect in high-mileage engines or engines that have

got very hot, when the ignition is switched off, the motor continues to run on.

Honda found they could activate the hydrogen, carbon and oxygen components enough by using a *trapping valve* to partially close the exhaust port – how much depended on the actual speed and load conditions, monitored and controlled by the same computer that ran the bike's indirect fuel injection system.

Lowering the roof of the exhaust port traps more mixture in the cylinder and increases the length of the compression stroke. Both will raise the temperature and pressure of the gas, until it ignites. During this phase the spark ignition is switched off, being brought back in only when the engine is operated at high speeds and loads, where detonation would be dangerous.

The result is an engine that can be tuned for high speed operation, without the compromise of poor low- to mid-range running and with the benefits of clean exhaust emissions in the low-load regions where two-strokes are usually very dirty.

Honda built two EXP-2, 400 cc, two-stroke singles on this principle, producing about 43 bhp at 6300 rpm, which they raced in the Granada-Dakar rally in 1995. One bike, ridden by Jean Brucy, finished 5th out of 95 motorcycle starters in this tough 15-day event. The other rider, Richard Sainct, crashed and broke a collar-bone on the 4th day.

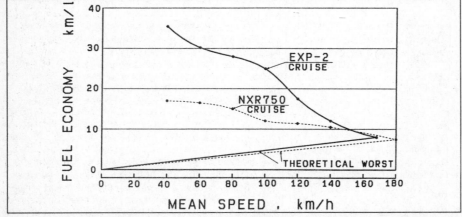

Fig. 2.15 Fuel consumption curves, for the EXP-2, 400 cc two-stroke compared with the four-stroke NXR750, Honda's conventional desert racer *(Honda)*

Chapter 3
Gas flow

Contents

1 Introduction

Engines running on gasoline are usually limited by the amount of air they can receive. Getting the right amount of fuel into the engine is not a problem, but accompanying it with 14.7 times its own weight of air, is.

Consequently, anything that can pump air efficiently is at an advantage. The most successful engines ever, in terms of power production, have been supercharged (ie air is delivered from a compressor, see Chapter 11). Two-strokes (which use their own crankcases to pump air) dominate all forms of bike competition where they're not specifically banned. Turbochargers and superchargers have been banned from most bike competitions for many years. Where there are no such restrictions and where *power density* is the main objective, engines are always supercharged: pre-war racing cars and bikes, piston-engined aircraft, F1 race cars, road cars, trucks and so on.

If it's not possible to pump air to the engine, then air flow becomes a critical design factor.

Gases have several properties, which can be used to increase engine efficiency. The relationship between pressure, volume and temperature (see Note 1), their ability to transmit pressure waves and to vibrate, their ability to mix and to transfer heat... all these things become important in various ways. But the most important, the most useful of all is called Bernoulli's theorem.

It's named after Daniel Bernoulli (1700-1782) who reasoned, quite logically, that if you neither add energy to a gas nor take it away, its total energy level will remain constant.

Note 1 *Boyle's law (after Robert Boyle, 1627-1691) states that at constant temperature, the volume of an ideal gas is inversely proportional to its pressure [$p_1V_1 = p_2V_2 = $ constant]. Real gases deviate from this.*

Charles's law (after Jacques Charles and Joseph Gay-Lussac in the 1780s) added temperature to this, saying that the volume of a given mass of gas is also proportional to its temperature [$p_1V_1/T_1 = p_2V_2/T_2 = $ constant] – an observation which followed from their enthusiasm for hot air ballooning. It implies that all gases have the same coefficient of expansion, which is only true at low pressure, when real gases approach 'ideal gas' behaviour.

An ideal gas is one in which the molecules have no size and produce no inter-molecular force.

Real gases have this equation modified according to their specific heat, (the heat required to raise one unit of mass through one degree temperature change). Gases have two specific heats, one when the pressure is kept constant (C_p) and the other when the volume is kept constant (C_v). The ratio C_p/C_v is called γ (gamma). For air at normal atmospheric conditions it is about 1.4 and the Boyle's Law equation becomes $pV^\gamma = $ constant (known as the adiabatic equation).

This total energy is made up of several components: a gas has kinetic energy (0.5mv², due to its velocity), potential energy (mgh, due to its height above a certain datum level) and pressure energy (mp/D, a combination of its pressure and density).

The sum of all these will remain constant, which implies energy can be freely transferred between them. For example, an increase in kinetic energy must be accompanied by a proportional decrease in either pressure energy or potential energy.

For a 'perfect', incompressible gas the following formula applies. Note that v is velocity, m is mass, p is pressure, D is density, h is height above a datum level, g is gravitational constant, and K is constant.

$$\frac{mv^2}{2} + \frac{mp}{D} + mgh = K$$

Note: the units must be consistent in terms of mass (M), length (L) and time (T)

mv² is	ML²T⁻²
mp/D is	ML²T⁻²
mgh is	ML²T⁻²
and energy is	ML²T⁻²

A real gas has a little more flexibility in its pressure/density relationship and the equation becomes:

$$\frac{mv^2}{2} + \int \frac{mdp}{D} + mgh = K$$

There is an analogy between this gas behaviour and a solid item, like a brick balanced on top of a wall. It's a solid so its pressure and density remain constant, it has no velocity (so no kinetic energy) but it does have potential energy, because of its height. This can be measured above any fixed datum level, as long as the same reference is used throughout. The height of the wall seems relevant here, so its energy is mgh – its mass, times the gravitational constant times its height. If it now falls off (with no energy being added, you understand, this requires a scientific, zero-energy nudge...) it accelerates downward. It is trading potential energy for kinetic energy.

When it reaches ground level, its potential energy will be all used up, so its newly acquired kinetic energy (mv²/2) must be equal to the lost potential energy (mgh): That is:

mv²/2 = mgh
so, v = √(2gh)

g is 9.81m/s² and if the height of the wall is 10 m we can expect the brick to be travelling at 14.01 m/s when it lands on our foot.

At this point the velocity (and the kinetic energy) are brought to zero, and so is the potential energy. The total brick energy cannot simply disappear. It has several possible outlets: (a) it will squash the ground

or the foot on which it lands and the strain energy will be equal to the lost kinetic and potential energy, (b) it will deflect or break itself and the strain energy will appear here or (c) it will bounce and the energy will return in the form of kinetic and potential energy as it gains both speed and height. In practice it will be some combination of all three (plus some energy being dissipated as sound and in raising the temperature of the impact zone).

A ball, instead of a brick, will bounce back up, but not quite as far as its starting point because not all the kinetic/potential energy is available, some gets frittered away in deforming the ground, the ball, making noise and air drag (in which some energy is transferred to the surrounding air).

Just as the brick's potential energy can be converted directly into kinetic energy, gases give us a three-way option to transfer energy. In practice, where things as small as carburettors are concerned, the change in potential energy is tiny and can be ignored for most practical calculations. Which leaves kinetic and pressure energy. As one goes up, the other must go down and vice versa. This has all sorts of wide-ranging implications. It is, for example, the reason aeroplanes fly – and Bernoulli established the theoretical base for this more than a century before the Wright brothers' Flyer left the ground.

The only condition attached to the energy equation is that none must be added or subtracted, so it doesn't matter if the gas is moving and you are standing still, or you are moving and the gas is standing still: it's enough to have relative velocity between you and it. The air moving over an aeroplane's fuselage exerts less pressure on it than if both were standing still, but it doesn't matter if the aeroplane is travelling through still air, or if the aircraft is parked and there is a wind blowing over it.

2 Pressure

An aircraft's wings are shaped so that air flowing over the top surface has slightly further to travel than air flowing underneath. The streamlined shape makes sure the flow doesn't break up and, to maintain this smooth flow, the air above the wing has to travel slightly faster than the air below. This means there is slightly less pressure exerted on the upper surface and slightly more on the lower surface. The difference is typically less than 0.5 psi, but if the wings have lots of square inches, they will generate lots of lb of lift.

Carburettors use this principle in many ways. The first is to lift fuel at static (high) pressure from the float bowl up into the main intake passage, where air travelling into the engine has a high velocity and therefore a low pressure (see Fig. 3.1).

This works exactly like a barometer, where atmospheric pressure, caused by the weight of a column of air many miles high, acts on the free surface of a liquid (see Fig. 3.2). Here, a vertical tube has an open end in the liquid, the other end is closed and isn't subject to atmospheric pressure. With almost a vacuum above the liquid (see Note 2) the pressure at the reservoir's surface level is due entirely to the weight of the column of liquid.

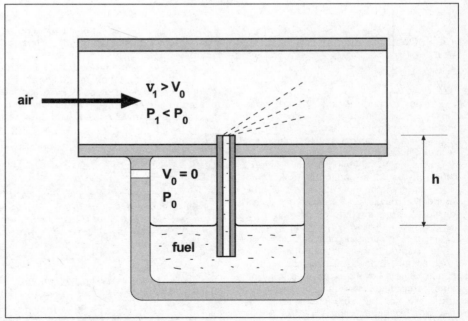

Fig. 3.1 Air being drawn into the engine reaches a certain velocity and so its pressure will be less than the static air in the float bowl. The pressure difference pushes fuel up the connecting tube

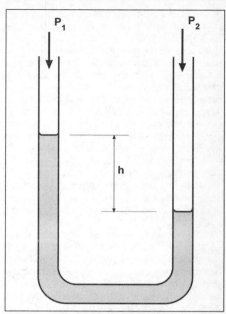

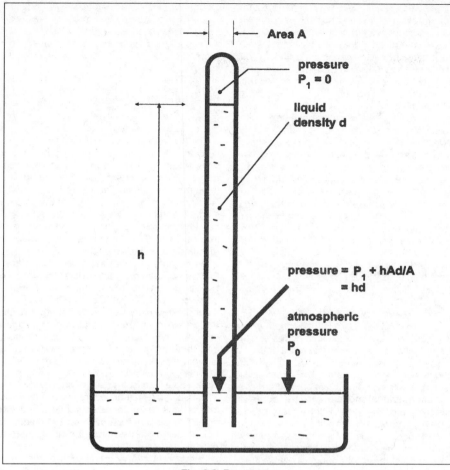

Fig. 3.2 Barometer

The pressure at the surface level of the liquid is caused by the weight of the liquid column, which is balanced by the weight of the 'column' of air above the free surface.

Fig. 3.3 Manometer

The pressure difference between the two ends, $P_1 - P_2$, is proportional to the height of the column of liquid it supports and may be measured by multiplying this height by the density of the liquid.

sources you can measure the difference by connecting one to each end. In both cases, the vertical height (see Note 3) of the column of liquid shows the pressure difference. If one end of a manometer is connected to a region of static air and the other end is placed in an air stream (so the air flows across the open end) then the difference in pressure would also be a measure of the air velocity. This is the basis of the Pitot-static tube (after Henri Pitot, 1695-1771) used to measure air speed in ducts and of aeroplanes.

> **Note 3** *Vertical height is what matters, even if the column is sloping. Some manometers for measuring small pressure drops have an inclined column, to make the liquid move further along the tube for a given change in pressure. These must always be set so the angle of the inclined scale is the same for all measurements.*

If you always use the same liquid (water and mercury are favourites, water because it's easily available and mercury because it's the heaviest liquid, 13.5 times heavier than water, so its column will only need to be 0.07 times as high as a water column) you don't need to know its density, a simple height comparison will be enough. As this is such an easy and accurate method of measuring pressure, units called 'inches of water' or 'inches water gauge' or 'in WG' are commonly used. This

> **Note 2** *When the column is tipped upright, the liquid tries to flow out, creating a vacuum at the top. Low pressure reduces a liquid's boiling point and some liquid at the top of the column will boil, supplying a vapour to fill the space between the top of the liquid and the top of the tube. This maintains a very small pressure, enough to prevent any more liquid boiling off although it's greater than the theoretical zero pressure of a perfect vacuum. It is small enough to be considered zero for practical purposes. [Boiling point: as a liquid is heated, some molecules leave its surface, forming a vapour which has its own pressure. When enough molecules are leaving the liquid to become vapour, the vapour pressure will equal the ambient pressure. This is the liquid's boiling point and is proportional to both temperature and pressure.]*

If the area of the tube is A, the height of the column is h and the density of the liquid is D, then the weight of the liquid column will be AhD and the pressure it creates at surface level will be AhD/A – that is, hD. The pressure depends only on the height of the column and the density of the liquid, not on the cross-section area of the tube.

The surface of the reservoir also supports a 'column' of air and the same principle applies: the pressure depends only on the height of the column (ie the depth of the atmosphere) and the density of the air (which would have to be an average value). The column of liquid stays put. It is in equilibrium so the pressure at the bottom caused by the weight of liquid is equal to atmospheric pressure, which can now be accurately measured simply by taking the height of the liquid column and multiplying it by the liquid density.

The next step is to make a pressure gauge which is simply a U-tube with liquid in it, called a manometer (see Fig. 3.3). You apply pressure to one end and leave the other open to atmosphere. Or if you have two pressure

refers to a column of water, if it's mercury (chemical symbol Hg) then the units are 'in Hg' or 'mm Hg'.

If you simply apply pressure to one end of a manometer, and it reads 30 mm Hg, the total pressure you're applying is 30 mm Hg plus atmospheric. The total is called the 'absolute pressure' while the direct reading is called 'gauge pressure'. Often it isn't necessary or convenient to measure absolute pressure: gauge pressure is good enough, but it is necessary to know which you're measuring.

Absolute pressure =
gauge pressure + atmospheric pressure
Gauge pressure =
absolute pressure – atmospheric pressure

Gauge pressure can be negative. If you suck on the end of the manometer, the liquid columns will reverse position and the height between them is now a negative value, written for example –30 mm Hg. It's negative because it's below atmospheric. For example if atmospheric pressure is 29 in Hg and gauge pressure is –0.7 in Hg, then when you add them to get absolute pressure, you have 29 – 0.7 = 28.3 in Hg.

This is sometimes called 'vacuum' even though a vacuum is, strictly speaking, the absence of any pressure (and it is impossible to go below zero absolute pressure because pressure is caused by molecules of fluid hitting the walls of the vessel – remove the molecules to achieve a perfect vacuum and you obtain zero pressure, but anything 'below' this is meaningless until someone discovers some matter that will 'pull' on the walls instead of 'push' on them).

3 Intake flow

The basic structure of a carburettor is similar to a barometer. The reservoir of fuel is kept at atmospheric pressure, while air drawn into the engine has a low pressure, in proportion to its velocity. A simple tube between the two will have fuel drawn through it as long as the pressure drop is greater than the height of the fuel column.

The actual velocity of the air stream depends on a number of factors. From an overall view, if the piston displaces 250 cc on each stroke, then a four-stroke at 6,000 rpm – 100 revs per second – will have 50 intake cycles, and pump a nominal 50 × 250 = 12,500 cc/second.

If the air passage through the carburettor has a section area of 11.3 sq cm (the area of a 38 mm diameter circle), then to get 12,500 cc through it in a second, the velocity would have to be (12500/11.3) cm/s or 1106.2 cm/s or 11.06 m/s.

However this figure is taken from gas flow averaged over a whole cycle. Its true value

varies: the gas velocity would start at zero, accelerate as the intake valves opened, continue accelerating until the piston reached peak speed and then it would start to decelerate, down to zero as the cylinder finally filled and the intake valves closed. This entire pulse would take 0.05 seconds or so, then there would be around 0.15 seconds of relative inactivity.

The true gas velocity is never constant, unless it's zero. The pressure conditions in the intake will also vary and, as the kinetic energy varies with the gas velocity squared, the pressure changes will be even more dramatic than the gas speed changes. The fuel supply will be a series of spurts rather than a steady flow, although there's more to come. What happens next depends on the cam timing and the dimensions of both the intake and the exhaust systems.

4 Inertia effects

When the intake valve first opens, it will be towards the end of the exhaust stroke and the piston will be travelling up towards TDC.

The precise opening point is critical because in the engine's most efficient speed region, a wave of high pressure will arrive at the intake valve and the gas pressures on either side of the valve will be more or less equal. At worst, the valve can open without the risk of burnt gas flowing from the cylinder back into the intake. At best, the intake pressure will be high enough to make fresh gas flow into the cylinder even though the intake stroke has not officially begun.

It's necessary to get the valve open before TDC so that it has a reasonable amount of lift when the intake stroke proper starts. This way the valve is of minimal hindrance to the main gas flow.

But at other engine speeds the pressure wave will not arrive at the correct time; intake gas will not start flowing past the valve, in fact, burnt gas from the cylinder might start flowing out in the 'wrong' direction. At these engine speeds the volumetric (or pumping) efficiency drops and so does the torque. This is the main reason that peak torque has a 'peak'.

The culprit is the pulsing nature of the flow and the sudden shut-off of the valves. Air has weight and it has inertia. It takes time to accelerate to speed and, once it is travelling, it takes time to stop. This is part of the reason the valves have to open early, maybe 60° of crank travel before their proper stroke starts – the inertia of the valve means it cannot be fully opened immediately and the inertia of the air means that it too needs a little time to get going.

At the end of the stroke, the engine will make use of this, letting the inertia of the incoming air continue filling the cylinder, even

though the piston has reached BDC and is no longer displacing any volume in the cylinder. This is called the 'ram effect'. When the fast-moving air gets into the cylinder it has to slow down and stop and, as predicted by Bernoulli, its pressure rises.

5 Resonance effects

Ideally, the valve will close just as the pressure on its downstream side rises above that on the upstream side, trapping the maximum amount of air inside the cylinder. But there is more air moving under its own inertia towards the valve. It hits the valve and has to stop dead, causing a sudden increase in pressure. This high pressure wave is reflected back along the inlet tract.

When pressure waves travel along pipes they are reflected if they hit a solid end, like the valve, and return with the same pressure in the opposite direction. But when they reach a sudden opening, like the bellmouth entry to the carburettor, the pressure content pops out, literally like air bursting from a balloon, and this reflects a *low* pressure wave back along the pipe. Similarly, a solid end reflects low pressure as a low pressure wave, but an open end will reflect it as high pressure.

In the intake tract, a pressure wave will reflect back and forth between the closed and open ends, changing from high to low or low to high each time it reaches the open end (see Fig. 3.4).

These reflections travel at the speed of sound in the gas and will carry on many times,

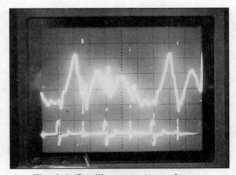

Fig. 3.4 Oscilloscope trace from a pressure sensor in the intake tract of a four-stroke

The bottom trace is connected to the ignition, so its spikes identify TDC and BDC. On the top trace, the first large peak on the left is the pressure build-up caused by the intake valve closing. Two reflections of this appear before the intake opens again, during the third peak. The steady, low pressure is where the valve is open and air is travelling into the engine, building to a sudden, high peak again as the valve closes, bringing the flow to a standstill

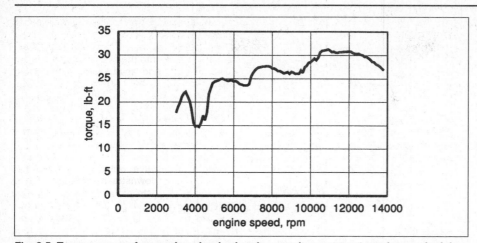

Fig. 3.5 Torque curve of an engine clearly showing regular, resonant maxima and minima
This was taken during development of a CBR400, when there was a mismatch between exhaust and intake lengths and the valve timing

slowly getting weaker, if nothing interrupts them.

They are quite useful, if you can arrange for a high-pressure wave to get the gas flow started and let you open the valve a little earlier. In the same way, another high pressure wave will let you delay the closing of the valve, effectively making the intake stroke longer than the nominal 180 crankshaft degrees (see Fig. 3.4).

The only problem is the waves travel at a substantially constant speed (at the speed of sound in the gas), so the time interval between reflecting from the bellmouth and arriving at the valve is always the same. The time interval between the valve closing and re-opening varies with engine speed.

When the two events get in step, the effect is called *resonance* and, technically, it can only happen at one speed. In practice the beneficial effects spread over a range of a few hundred rpm. And rather than pure resonance it's more likely to be a *harmonic*, that is, instead of the valve opening just as the first pressure reflection arrives, the wave might travel up and down the intake two, three or more times. Each time the pressure wave is weaker, but as long as the valve timing is in step with it, the volumetric efficiency will benefit.

However there will be other speeds where the valve movement and the pressure waves get out of step. Now, when the valve is opening the cylinder pressure will be higher than the tract pressure and some exhaust gas will push past the valve into the intake tract. During the next cycle, the engine will draw in this burnt gas, which contains no oxygen and no fuel and cannot produce any power.

Similarly, if the tract pressure drops when the intake valve is closing, some of the gas in the cylinder will escape past the valve, not as much gas will be trapped in the cylinder and engine torque will fall.

You can see the consequences clearly in some torque curves. At the in-step speeds the

torque is increased, making a little peak. At the out-of-step speeds, torque is reduced, making little dips in the curve. There is a clue that resonance is the cause: these steps occur at regular speed intervals – at, say, 3000 rpm, 6000 rpm and 9000 rpm there will be peaks, while the troughs occur at 4500 and 7500 rpm (see Fig. 3.5).

Of course the effect of these pressure waves, travelling through the moving gas, is superimposed on the fuel being drawn from the float bowl. Each time a low pressure wave passes the delivery tube, more fuel is drawn off, which tends to richen the mixture. There is a condition called *stand-off* in which a column of fuel vapour is blown out of the bellmouth, only to be drawn back in again. It appears to hang in the air upstream of the bellmouth but when this cloud of air and fuel is drawn into the engine it will collect more fuel from the delivery nozzle and the mixture that finally arrives at the cylinder will be very rich.

There are several variations on this theme. If the engine is set up to run satisfactorily like this on a dyno, then the effect of the air stream on the road might be to blow away the fuel mist, resulting in a weak-running engine. Or a second cylinder might inhale the mixture blown out of the first, so some cylinders would appear to run richer than others on the same settings.

6 Variable geometry

The resonant effect depends on the density of the air/fuel mixture as this affects the speed of sound in the gas, but in stable operating conditions it will be pretty well constant. Resonance also depends on the engine speed, the length of the intake tract and the cam timing. In conventional machines all of these factors, except engine speed, are constant, so resonance effects tend to be

restricted to a narrow band of engine speed. It's worth noting that variable valve timing or variable geometry intakes and exhausts have been fitted to many experimental engines, quite a few race engines and the occasional road machine.

Even where fixed intakes are used, it is not uncommon to find a four-cylinder engine with two longer stacks (usually the inner two cylinders) and two shorter. By making two cylinders resonate at a slightly different speed to the others, the effect can be spread over a wider range, although the maximum effect will not be as great as if all four worked at the same speed.

The exhaust system works in a similar way. By lowering the pressure downstream of the valve just before it opens and creating high pressure when it closes, the resonance effect can improve exhaust scavenging. It encourages the early flow, but discourages flow at the end of the stroke. At this point, when the exhaust valve is closing, the intake valve is also open and fresh gas is starting to flow into the cylinder. If the fresh gas is travelling at the right speed and direction it will help to push burnt gas out past the exhaust valve but there will come a point when fresh gas starts to go past the valve into the exhaust.

This not only wastes air and fuel that should be making power, it puts unburnt fuel into the exhaust, increasing hydrocarbon emissions. If the exhaust system can create pressure waves to prevent this, it will make the engine more efficient.

Highly tuned engines, like most sports bikes have, use quite a lot of valve overlap in order to be able to pump efficiently at high speeds. To achieve this, they are dependent on intake and exhaust geometry to provide the right pressure waves at the right times.

When intake and exhaust valves are open together, the engine is at the mercy of the intake and exhaust effects: it is only gas inertia and the pressure effects that keep it all travelling in the right direction.

Consequently small changes (to either the intake or the exhaust) can have serious effects on the engine's output – by changing the volumetric efficiency or the trapping efficiency, it alters the useful air flow and somehow the carburettor has to make the fuel supply follow these changes.

On a multi-cylinder engine it is possible to run the exhaust header pipes into a *collector* and then into a single *secondary* pipe and silencer can. This not only saves the weight and space of having a full pipe and silencer for each cylinder, it also means the pressure pulses can be shared between cylinders. Typically, a four-cylinder engine will run all four pipes into one secondary (a 4-1 system) or will join the pipes in pairs and then let both pairs run into the secondary pipe (a 4-2-1 system). The 4-1 type, where all four headers are the same length, gives the highest maximum torque but makes the torque curve

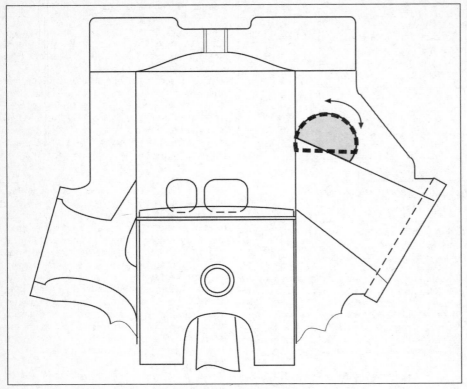

Fig. 3.6 Yamaha power valve

torque than the correct mixture, this only makes the holes deeper.

Although we've concentrated on four-stroke engines, because they're used in the vast majority of road bikes, the same theory also applies to two-strokes. In fact two-strokes depend more on their exhaust systems because there is no valve, merely a port uncovered by the piston. Its timing therefore has to be symmetrical about BDC: open it early and it has to close late.

Pressure waves in a two-stroke's intake have a similar effect to those in a four-stroke but once again it is more critical because there is no mechanical valve opened by a cam but a reed valve whose springy petals are opened by gas pressure. A suitable pressure wave superimposed on the natural gas pressure will encourage the reed valve to open or close more promptly.

Tuned pipe lengths and port timing have such a marked effect on two-stroke power delivery that they were the first engines to use *variable geometry*.

Yamaha were first put a 'power valve' in the exhaust port (see Figs. 3.6 and 3.7). This spool-shaped device formed the top surface of the exhaust port and rotated through an arc of about 30 – 40°, to raise or lower the port's top edge. This controls both the timing and the duration of the port. The valve is operated by a cable from an electric servo motor, switched by an engine speed sensor.

Since then, every two-stroke manufacturer has incorporated various types of mechanism to vary the port height and to open/close resonator cavities (see below) in the exhaust system.

Yamaha also led the way with variable geometry four-stroke exhausts, when they introduced their *Exup* system in the mid-'80s. Here a 4-1 exhaust was developed to give maximum torque at peak engine speed (see

'peaky' because it is only efficient over a narrow speed range and can create big inefficiencies (dips or *holes* in the torque curve) at other speeds.

The 4-2-1 type is not so critical. It does not give quite as much peak torque, but it creates a broader power band over a wider speed range and does not produce such severe holes at other speeds. These holes cause big

problems for fuel systems. As well as the air flow dropping off, making the engine give less torque, it is very difficult to adjust the carburettor to give the correct mixture in the efficient part of the power band and still give the correct mixture where the engine is running inefficiently. Usually the effect is to make the fuelling go weak in the inefficient regions, and as a weak mixture gives less

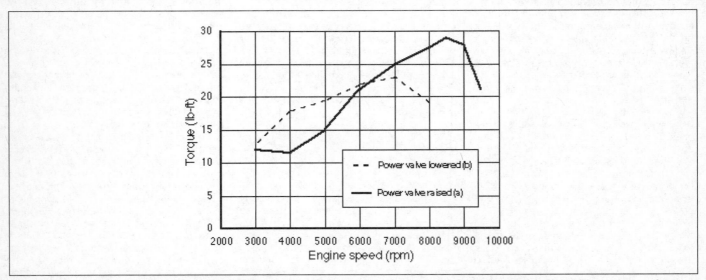

Fig. 3.7 Torque curve of a Yamaha RD350YPVS (a) with the power valve fixed open and (b) with it fixed closed. The sensor and servo motor would need to operate the valve as the engine goes through 6300 rpm

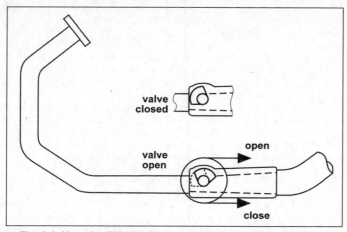

Fig. 3.8 Yamaha EXUP valve in a four-stroke exhaust system

This allows the exhaust to be developed for maximum engine output at high rpm when the valve is open, but when it closes at low engine speed, it breaks up the pressure waves that would now have bad effects on performance

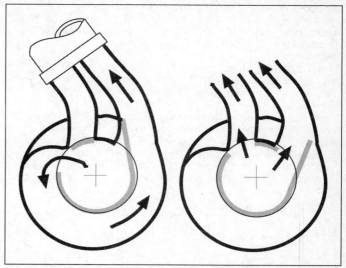

Fig. 3.9 Example of a variable geometry intake, designed by Ricardo Engineering

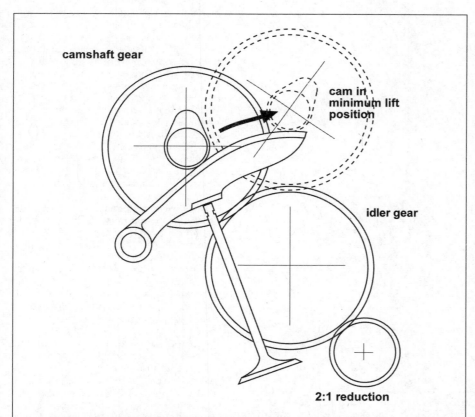

Fig. 3.10 Variable valve timing: Honda's shuttle cam is one of many approaches

There is a 2:1 reduction between the engine and the camshaft gear, the idler gear can be any size without affecting this ratio. The camshaft can be swung about the idler gear's centre, which both moves the cam along the finger rocker and alters the cam phasing, as its gear 'rolls' along the idler gear. The cam's position along the rocker alters the lever ratio between cam and valve, and therefore changes the valve lift for a given amount of cam lift. The phase change can be arranged to give optimum timing for low or high speed operation. In fact, if the lift and valve duration can be brought down to zero, the VVT mechanism can be used to control engine load, doing away with a throttle valve and the associated part-load, throttling losses.

Fig. 3.8) by making use of the tuned lengths of its component pipes. This would cause poor performance in the midrange, so Yamaha used various types of valve (butterfly and guillotine types on different models) to disrupt the pressure waves. Once again an engine speed sensor and servo motor were used to operate the valve.

There have been experimental engines, race car, road car and some bike engines that also use variable geometry intake and exhaust systems, where the lengths of the tracts can be altered to match different speed ranges (see Figs. 3.9 and 3.10).

Another way to attack the same problem is to vary the valve opening and closing, shortening the duration to suit lower engine speed and extending it at high speed. Variable valve timing (VVT) has had the attention of motor manufacturers, universities and engineering teams all over the world for many years now. Designs range from the crude but effective two-stage cam profile that depends on part of the valve train being hit very hard by the controlling device, through to very sophisticated designs that can vary valve lift as well as duration. Figs. 3.10 and 3.11 show some examples used by Honda.

7 Throttling losses

Being able to control the valves completely has some useful implications for gasoline engine efficiency. The load is controlled in spark ignition engines by regulating the air flow (unlike diesels, which flow full air all the time and regulate fuel flow to control the load). When the air intake is restricted by closing the throttle valve, the engine still tries to pump air past this restriction and these pumping losses make the engine inefficient on part load. It is this, plus the very high compression ratios, that makes diesels so fuel efficient.

If the load could be controlled by varying the valve timing, there would be no need for a throttle valve, so part of these losses could be avoided.

Balance pipes between the intakes and the small chambers tapped into some two-stroke intakes go a little way to alleviating these losses. By opening up the flow from a neighbouring cylinder (unused – the cylinders fill one at a time) or letting the relatively large

volume of a chamber ease the throttling losses, the motor runs more efficiently on part-load.

8 Airbox design

There is another chamber that contributes a surprising amount to the engine's performance: the airbox. If design efficiency is measured by the number of jobs a component does, the airbox is a winner.

It was there primarily to hold the air filter. It

became an obvious catch tank for the engine breathers – vents from the crankcases and cam boxes, which are there to reduce pressure fluctuations under the pistons because unwanted pressure here can absorb power in the same way throttling losses do, except crankcase pumping happens at all engine loads.

Crankcase gases contain oil mist and the airbox was a good place to separate the heavier droplets, letting them drain back into the engine. Lighter oil particles would go through with the air and fuel, being burnt and so minimising overall emissions.

The airbox also forms a natural trap for any stand-off – fuel mist blown out of the carburettor intakes. At least it ensures the fuel gets drawn into one or other of the cylinders and isn't blown away as soon as the bike is moving.

And this leads neatly to one of its main jobs, as a plenum or still-air reservoir – a constant, ready supply of clean, calm air regardless of how fast the bike is travelling. Airboxes have grown considerably since designers recognised their full value in the early '80s; now their volume will be a minimum of ten times the engine's capacity.

Bernoulli's theorem applies to the air travelling past a bike in the same way as it applies to air going through a carburettor. The faster it goes, the lower its pressure. The engine draws air into the carburettor because the descending piston creates low pressure on the engine side. The amount of flow depends on the difference between this and the relatively high atmospheric pressure on the outside. But if the bike's slipstream is rushing past the bellmouths, it will have less pressure than static air and less air will flow into the engine.

This is why the airbox has to be so big, so each cylinder can be filled from it in turn, with a steady flow into the airbox, yet there will be negligible air velocity inside the box, the air will be as static as possible and therefore at full atmospheric pressure. The intake can also be positioned to collect cool air that hasn't been over the engine or through a radiator (warm air is less dense, as Charles had noticed, so 250 cc of warm air would contain less oxygen than 250 cc of cold air).

As permitted sound levels were reduced in all the major bike markets, it soon became obvious that the exhaust was not the only source of noise. The pressure pulses that can increase engine performance also make sound when they pop out of the bellmouths – and quite a lot of sound. The airbox is a useful way of attenuating this noise. Initially the entry to the airbox would be a rubber or plastic piece, sometimes with webs moulded along the intake. They would reduce sound emissions, and most of them reduced air flow as well.

They weren't really necessary. The shape of the airbox could do just as well, without restricting air flow. It could even increase it

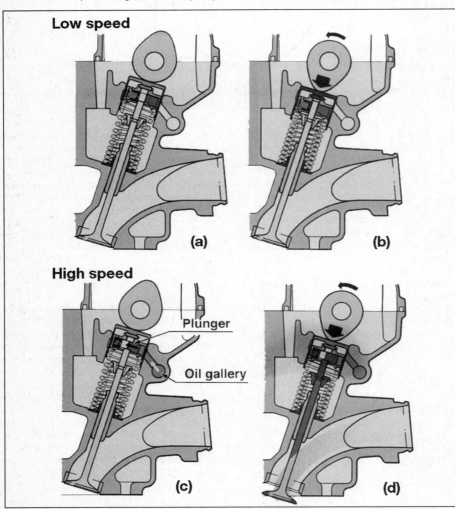

Fig. 3.11 Honda developed a more pragmatic system for production. Fitted to the Japanese-spec CB400R, it works on one of each pair of intake valves. The other functions normally

At low speed, the cam moves a bucket follower against a light spring but there is clearance so that it does not move the valve. All the gas flows past the 'normal' valve, raising its velocity, lowering its pressure and, by the asymmetric route into the cylinder, causing turbulence – see pics (a) and (b). At higher revs a spool valve is opened allowing high pressure oil to enter the gallery just below the cam follower – see pic (c). The pressure of the oil forces a plunger between the cam follower and the end of the valve stem. The cam now operates the valve normally – pic (d) – until the engine speed decreases, the spool valve closes dumping the oil pressure and a spring pushes the plunger away from the valve (Honda)

under the right conditions. The effect was first noticed in the nineteenth century by Hermann von Helmholtz, supposedly when he realised that strategically-placed earthenware jars changed the acoustics in a monastery. By absorbing sound frequencies, they cut down the reverberation time.

All pipes and containers have their own natural frequencies, which, as we can see from organ pipes and woodwind instruments, depend on their lengths and volumes. The Helmholtz resonator equation is as follows, where s is the speed of sound, A is the area of the inlet to the chamber, L is the length of the inlet to the chamber, and V is the volume of the chamber.

$$\text{frequency} = \frac{s}{2\pi} \sqrt{\frac{A}{LV}}$$

The volume of the airbox (current design is around 10 times engine displacement) also has an affect on power output characteristics (see Fig. 3.12). Typically, in-line fours with 4-1 or 4-2-1 exhausts produce a torque curve with two peaks, a smaller peak at the low end of the midrange and a larger peak at high engine speed. The peaks obviously represent regions of high efficiency (best gas flow and combustion) while the midrange dip represents low efficiency. The size of this dip is critical. When it is deep (a hole) the rate of change of airflow is high and the fuel system needs to track this change and supply fuel accordingly. There comes a point when carburettors cannot match these large changes and to get the correct mixture where the engine is running efficiently means the mixture will usually be wrong in the inefficient regions, making the hole deeper. Exhaust dimensions and the length of the intake stacks have the biggest effects on these characteristics but the chamber volume also plays a part.

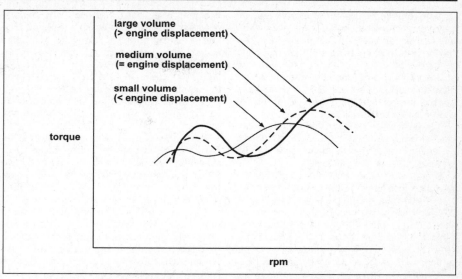

Fig. 3.12 Typical torque curve shifts produced by changing the airbox volume

If the chamber is smaller than the engine displacement, the box tends to be restrictive: it minimises the low speed peak and shifts both peaks down to lower speeds. Maximum torque is likely to be less than with larger airboxes but the midrange loss of torque is not affected. Consequently by reducing the peaks, the hole is made less deep and the result is a smoother torque curve, which is easier to carburate (and having the right mixture means the hole will be filled in some more, making the curve still smoother).

As the chamber size gets bigger, the two peaks are increased in size and are shifted to higher revs. While giving more torque and extending torque production to higher speeds, this accentuates the midrange hole.

When engines are being developed, this gives the design engineers one more tool to tailor the power characteristics. For a given set of valves and cam profiles, the torque can be manipulated by altering the exhaust dimensions, intake stacks and airbox volume. A touring bike can be given maximum flexibility, while a race engine can develop maximum high speed torque, albeit over a short rev range.

9 Pressurised airbox

See Figs. 3.13 and 3.14

So the airbox does many jobs: a still-air reservoir where the intake stacks can perform their resonant tricks; a supply of cool air; somewhere to house the air filter; somewhere

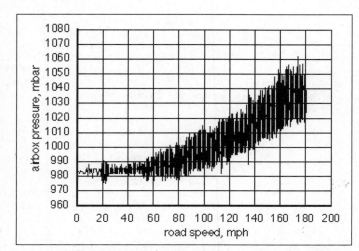

Fig. 3.13 A pressure sensor in the airbox of a Kawasaki ZX-9R picks up the violent pressure fluctuations produced by the engine on load and also registers the increasing pressure as the bike goes faster (*Performance Bikes*)

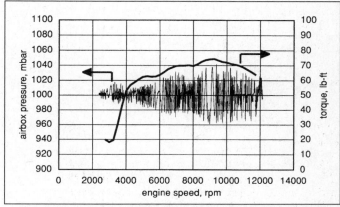

Fig. 3.14 The same set-up as Fig. 3.13 but this time the bike is standing still and driving a dynamometer

The pressure fluctuations vary clearly with engine speed and when the Kawasaki's torque curve is superimposed on it (right hand scale) it follows the same shape. When the air pressure is high, engine torque increases. Where it is low, torque falls (Performance Bikes)

to vent crankcase gases, separate out oil particles and drain them back to the sump; an intake silencer; yet there's still one more. By having the intake at the front of the bike, forward motion naturally scoops air into the airbox and will pressurise it slightly. This will have an increasing supercharge effect as road speed goes up, and the engine will give more power at higher road speeds.

It is a tantalising, something-for-nothing, offer that bike designers cannot ignore. However, the potential gains have to be viewed alongside the difficulties.

First, what are the gains? Dropping numbers into the Bernoulli equation shows that if you take a column of air travelling at 170 mph and bring it to a complete standstill, the rise in pressure is about 0.6 psi. At 80 mph, the maximum boost is about 0.15 psi. Now 0.6 psi represents about 4% of normal atmospheric pressure: simplistically, if you put in 4% more oxygen, you could expect to get 4% more power out. And 0.15 psi represents an increase of 1%, so these figures are roughly what's on offer.

This doesn't mean it's not worth bothering about. Any gains are worth having and if the air flow were working against us (eg dragging air away from the intake instead of filling it, as it would with exposed, open carburettors) then there is a potential *loss* of a few per cent. On top of that, a pressure change of 0.1 – 0.5 psi applied across the float bowl or spray tube of the carburettor could make a significant change to the fuel delivery and mixture strength.

Although the gains are not great, the potential losses are worth considering. The implication is that the difference between a very well designed intake and a very badly

designed intake could approach 10% power – at top speed. But if the badly designed bike had its carburettors adjusted to give best-power mixture at top speed, then they might not give the best mixture when the bike was flat out at low road speeds, so acceleration through the gears would also suffer.

There are two objectives: (a) to maximise air flow into the engine, (b) to maintain the optimum air/fuel mixture.

This leads us into the design difficulties. It's easy enough to open an airbox intake up at the front of the bike. If it works, you then have a machine that makes less power in first gear than it does in top (and will have a slightly different power curve in each of its gears).

This isn't necessarily a bad thing because most high performance bikes have a surplus of power in first and second gears, producing wheelies or wheelspin if the rider tries to use all of it, while every bike could employ more power in fifth and sixth gears. The problem is that this pressure difference in the airbox can easily upset the fuel mixture, so the float bowls have to be vented to the airbox, making their pressure the same as the 'still' air being supplied to the carburettor venturis. This means it is difficult to incorporate an overflow tube to the float bowl. One other solution, employed on Honda's RS250 race bike, is to place the carburettors wholly inside the airbox.

10 Physical airflow

Finally, there's the nature of the airflow itself. Air flow rigs usually compare the

pressure drop across a test piece with the pressure drop of the same air flow across a *standard orifice*. Typically this will be a circular hole with a knife-edge profile in a flat plate. You find that holes of the same diameter don't all flow as much air. Those with a sudden entry flow less than those with whose entry is generously radiussed. The bigger the radius and the further it rolls back, the better. The orifice behaves like a plain, square-edged orifice of a bigger diameter. This is why engine intakes usually have bellmouths.

The reason is that the squared-off entry creates turbulence, little whirls and vortices like you see around stones and other obstacles in a fast-flowing river. In these regions, the fluid isn't travelling at the same speed and direction as the bulk flow, so the bulk flow is effectively restricted to a narrower passage. Streamline the entrance and the flow can make use of the full width. The same applies to anything else that projects into the stream, especially sudden steps.

Turbulent flow means less gas will travel along a given tract, which is not what we want in a carburettor. It also means the local velocity at any point is unpredictable, in terms of both speed and direction. If this point is the spray tube where fuel is introduced to the flow, random turbulence is especially bad (although designed-in turbulence can be used to improve the atomisation process, see *primary choke*, Chapter 4).

As far as fuel delivery and mixing is concerned, we generally want the air flow to be as smooth and stable as possible. Further along, just before going into the engine, a certain amount of turbulence can be useful (see *Turbulence, swirl* and *tumble*).

Chapter 4
Carburettor theory

Contents

1 Introduction

Carburettors depend upon, or make use of, the chemical and physical properties mentioned in the previous two chapters. To see how they apply these features, we'll develop a full working carburettor, starting from the basic spray tube illustrated in Fig. 3.1 at the beginning of Chapter 3.

The size of the air passage needs to be big enough to supply the engine's needs at full power, yet small enough to raise the air speed to create a suitable pressure drop between the fuel reservoir and the top of the spray tube.

As the pressure above the fuel spray tube depends on the air speed, many older designs had a narrowed section in the region of the spray tube, in order to raise the air speed locally. This shape, contracting from the normal intake size and then expanding again

beyond the fuel spray, is called a *venturi* (after the Italian physicist Giovanni Battista Venturi, 1746-1822). The shape also restricts maximum air flow and hasn't been used in high-performance bike carburettors for many years, although the term is still used as a convenient description of this part of the carburettor. The narrowest section is also called the *choke* and carburettors are sized by the bore of the venturi or choke. As 'choke' is also used for the cold-start mechanism, we'll call this region venturi.

Air speed, carburettor size and power characteristics

If the piston displaces 250 cc, it will draw (roughly) 250 cc of air through the carburettor during the course of the intake stroke, which lasts for a nominal 180° of crankshaft movement. If we know the maximum engine speed (say 12,000 rpm or 200 rev/s) then each rev takes 1/200th of a second and half a rev (180°) will take 1/400th or 0.0025s.

The nominal volume flow at this engine speed will be 250/0.0025 or 100,000 cc/s. This is an average value (the real speed will start lower, reach a higher peak and finish at a lower value), but it gives us an idea of the figures involved.

To calculate the air speed through a particular section of the intake, we need to know the volume flow and the area of the cross-section at

right-angles to the gas flow. For a 38 mm carburettor, a common size on larger engines, the area is:

$$\pi(38)^2/4 = 1134.11 \text{ mm}^2 \textbf{ or } 11.34 \text{ cm}^2$$

Imagine a column of air, with this section area, and long enough to make the 100,000 cc we need for each second's-worth of flow. It would have to be 100,000/11.34 cm long. That is, 8818.3 cm or 88.183 m and so the (average) air speed at 12,000 rpm will be 88.2m/s (equivalent to 318 km/h or 197 mph).

From Bernoulli's equation (see Chapter 3, using an air density value of 1.225 kg/m^2 and assuming the flow is incompressible), this will cause a pressure drop of 4.76 kPa (0.69 psi) in the region of the fuel spray. Doing the same calculation again for an engine speed of 3000 rpm (if this is the lowest speed the rider is

likely to try to use WOT) gives an air speed of 22.05 m/s and a pressure of 0.298 kPa (0.043 psi).

These are average figures, to get an idea of the order of velocity and pressure involved. The pressure drop is quite small, particularly in low engine speed and wide throttle conditions. However if the fuel had a specific gravity of 0.7, then a head of fuel of 43.2 mm (1.7 in) would give the same pressure produced by the engine at 3000 rpm so, as long as the height between the fuel level and the top of the spray nozzle was not greater than this, the carburettor would be capable of working.

From previous experience of engines or flow bench tests, the working pressure range of carburettors would be known. Similarly, the flow capacity of each carburettor size would also be

continued overleaf

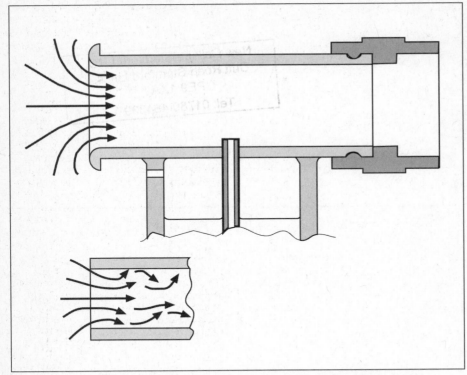

Fig. 4.1a Elementary carburettor – a fuel reservoir connected to a venturi

A radiussed 'bellmouth' entry straightens out the airflow, causing less turbulence than a sharp-edged intake, and raises the flow capacity of the unit. A rubber mounting isolates the venturi from engine vibration and heat

Fig. 4.1b The bellmouth entry supplied in Yamaha's R7 race kit

Fuel supply

The fuel is supplied by pump or gravity fed from the main tank, through a valve containing a tapered needle (see Fig. 4.2). A float in the fuel reservoir bears on the bottom of the needle and as the fuel fills the chamber it lifts the float, closing off the fuel supply at a predetermined level.

The needle usually has a sprung pin which contacts the tang of the float, to protect the valve from vibration or chattering, which would stop it sealing properly. This sort of valve is very susceptible to tiny pieces of debris, which get stuck between the face of the needle and its seat, and prevent the valve from sealing. For this reason there is usually a filter in the valve's housing and/or in the fuel line, and another at the fuel tap.

There are two forms of adjustment. First, the float height, which determines the shut-off point and the level of fuel in the float bowl. This is adjusted by carefully bending the tang that operates on the bottom of the needle. The height is measured either by directly checking the fuel level or by measuring the position of the float when the valve is fully closed. Check the workshop manual for the method and the precise measurement.

If the fuel level is to be measured, there will be a stub pipe at the bottom of the float bowl,

Our elementary carburettor is nothing more than a venturi, plus a fuel supply (see Fig. 4.1a). We can make a few practical refinements straight away. Experiments with air flow show that a simple tube is more efficient if the entry has a bell-mouth – a fairly large radius that rolls back almost a full 180° (see Fig. 4.1b). The whole of the air passage should be as straight and smooth as possible, with no interruptions and particularly no steps or sudden changes that could cause turbulence in the air stream. At the other end,

a flexible mounting, keeping the inner surface as flush as possible, protects the carburettor from both engine heat and vibration.

Raising the temperature of a gas lowers its density, so the same volume would contain less mass – fewer molecules – and couldn't burn so much fuel. Vibration causes all manner of mechanical problems. It can make fuel froth and it can prevent needle valves from sealing. A needle valve is the next refinement, to keep a constant supply of fuel at roughly the same level.

continued from previous page

known. Part of engine development is to match the carburettor, in terms of its flow capacity and suitable pressure range, to the engine designer's ambitions, in terms of power output and flexibility or power spread.

The limit is formed partly by the engine's ability to accelerate air up to such high speed in such a short space of time and partly the ability of the carburettor body to maintain this flow in a uniform, orderly manner. As the speed is raised above a critical point, the stream will tend to break up and become turbulent. In this condition the volume of air reaching the engine will not increase when engine speed is increased and the power will fall.

As the cylinder size or power requirements increase, it becomes necessary to fit a larger

carburettor to match the air flow at peak power but eventually the air speed will become too low at the lowest engine speed (and therefore venturi pressure will not be low enough).

Any carburettor size has upper and lower air flow limits. The upper limit dictates the maximum flow and hence the maximum power the engine can produce. The lower limit is where the carburettor no longer draws fuel efficiently.

It's likely that our example engine would give peak torque and peak power in the 8000 to 10,000 rpm region. Above this the air flow per cycle will drop and at its maximum safe speed of 12,000 rpm, a 250 cc cylinder would receive significantly less than 250 cc of air. We assumed a volumetric efficiency of 100% for simplicity: real engines achieve volumetric efficiencies in the order of 105% at peak torque, dropping either side of this speed. At the ends of the

useful power band, the volumetric efficiency will be 90% or less.

The engine torque and bmep curves are better than the power curve for showing air flow trends, because they depend entirely upon the amount of air received and the engine's ability to burn it and extract heat from it. Any deficiencies in air flow, mixture strength or combustion problems show up as a clear dip in the curve. The difference between torque and bhp readings is that the torque curve reflects the state of air flow/combustion per cycle, while the power curve shows what happens over a period of time so, although the torque may be less at 9000 rpm than it was at 8000 rpm, there are 1000 more revs crammed into the same minute and the power can still increase. It's not until torque falls faster than a certain rate that power also starts to fall.

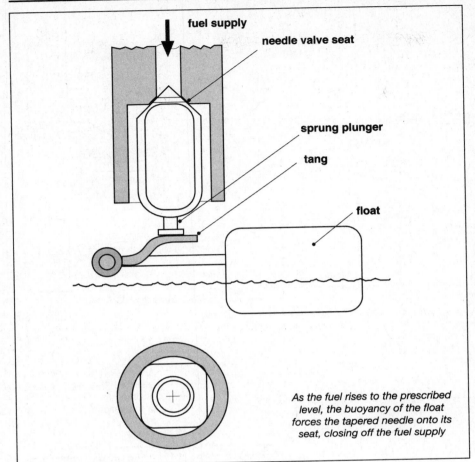

Fig. 4.2 Needle valve

As the fuel rises to the prescribed level, the buoyancy of the float forces the tapered needle onto its seat, closing off the fuel supply

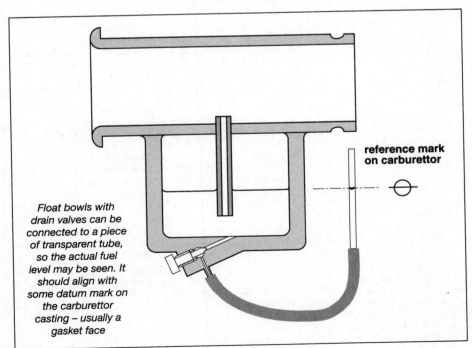

Float bowls with drain valves can be connected to a piece of transparent tube, so the actual fuel level may be seen. It should align with some datum mark on the carburettor casting – usually a gasket face

Fig. 4.3 Fuel level gauge

with a screw valve in it. Push a piece of transparent tube over the pipe (see Fig. 4.3), hold it vertically alongside the float bowl and open the valve. The level in the transparent tube will show the level of the fuel in the float chamber, usually it should align with some datum mark on the float bowl or be a prescribed distance from a datum such as the float bowl gasket face. Naturally the fuel should be switched on while this is measured and, if the machine has a vacuum-operated tap, it should be set to *prime*.

If the float height is to be checked, the carburettor has to be removed from the bike, the float bowl removed and the carburettor turned upside down. Then the height of the surface of the float is measured from the gasket surface, with the float's own weight pressing down on the needle valve (see Fig. 4.4). Usually a tool like a small T-square or squared bridge is used.

The other adjustment at the needle valve is the size of the tapered needle and valve seat. This affects the sealing pressure. The buoyancy force on the float is constant, so the sealing pressure depends on the valve area, that is the diameter of the valve seat. A smaller diameter gives a smaller area, which creates a higher pressure. This must be high enough to seal against the fuel pressure, which depends on the height of the tank or the output of the pump/regulator. If the delivery pressure is raised, it may be necessary to fit a smaller needle valve seat to prevent the carburettor from flooding.

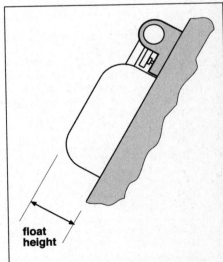

Fig. 4.4 Float height adjustment

Usually measured between the flat gasket face of the carburettor body and the surface of the float furthest from the gasket face. The weight of the float should be lightly resting against the needle valve but should not compress the anti-chatter spring in the needle. It may be necessary to hold the carburettor body at an angle, as shown, to do this

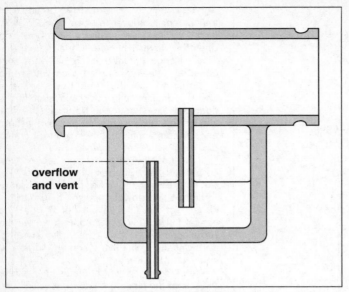

Fig. 4.5 Float vent and overflow pipe

The float bowl must be vented to static air pressure. Early types were simply open to atmosphere and the vent pipe could double as an overflow. If the carburettor flooded, excess fuel would run through the pipe instead of finding its way into the engine. Later types have the float bowls vented to airbox pressure

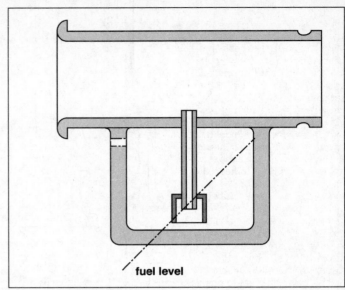

Fig. 4.6 Baffle around fuel pick-up

Sometimes a fence is fitted around the fuel entry to prevent the fuel being swilled away by the effect of heavy braking or acceleration. In car and sidecar carburettors, cornering forces have a similar effect

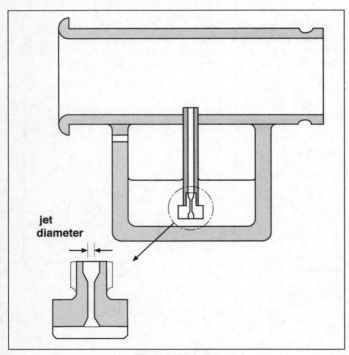

Fig. 4.7 Main jet

Usually designed as a miniature venturi to promote smooth flow over the widest possible pressure range, jets are sized either according to the smallest diameter or according to how much they flow at datum pressure on a test rig. There are different designs, different materials (usually brass or plastic) and the flow characteristics are all different.

Using the same make, same design, same material, you can be confident that a 140 jet will flow more than a 135. This may not be true if one has a different design, manufacturer or material

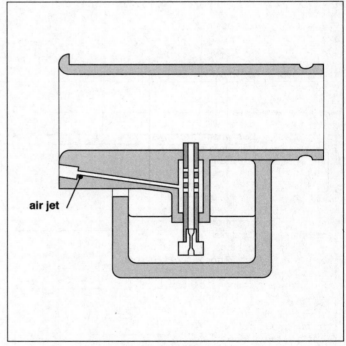

Fig. 4.8 Air jet

A narrow passageway. sometimes containing a brass jet, is used to bleed air into the fuel stream via a chamber and an emulsion tube – a needle jet with holes drilled in it

In order to let fuel into the float bowl, there must be a vent to let air out and on some carburettors this is combined with an overflow pipe, to drain excess fuel away if the carburettor floods (see Fig. 4.5). Flooding can be serious, apart from wasting fuel and making a mess. If liquid fuel runs into the engine, it can *hydraulic*, that is, fuel collects on top of the piston and when the engine is started the incompressible fuel is trapped between piston and head and can break piston rings and even connecting rods.

Bikes that use the airbox to increase engine performance have to keep the float bowls at the same pressure as the 'static' air supply in the airbox, so breather tubes are vented to the airbox and there is no drain to protect against flooding. This is a good reason to switch the fuel tap off when the engine is stopped.

We have shown the float bowl immediately below the fuel spray tube, which is where it usually is on current machines but in the past it was more often set to one side and was, in some cases, a separate part, mounted independently and connected to the carburettor via a tube. Having a remote float bowl has some advantage in mounting, where space is limited, and one bowl could feed more than one carburettor. It can also be raised or lowered to adjust the fuel height easily, although this isn't usually a critical adjustment.

The disadvantage is in fuel *swill* – the tendency of the fuel to run up the front of the chamber under braking and backwards under acceleration. If the float bowl is at the side of the carburettor, this wouldn't make too much difference and on solo motorcycles there is little or no lateral force because the whole bike leans over to balance sideways cornering force so fuel levels will stay constant. Ironically, in the days when offset float bowls were used, sidecars were also popular and these, of course, do produce lateral swill, so on left turns the fuel could be forced away from the carburettor, while right handers would force fuel into the carburettor. Sidecar racers used to fit *swill pots*, secondary chambers on the opposite side of the carburettor to the float bowl.

On modern machines, the float bowl is integral with the carburettor and the fuel spray tube is approximately in the middle of it, minimising any changes caused by swill. However, there can still be problems, caused by fuel moving away from the main spray tube. To prevent this, carburettor manufacturers have fitted baffles, like a cylindrical fence around the fuel pick-up point (see Fig. 4.6).

To keep the remaining drawings as simple as possible, we won't show any float bowl detail.

Fuel jets

We now have a plain venturi, fuel spray and constant fuel supply. The size of the venturi can be matched to the engine's demands for air and the size of the fuel spray tube can be arranged to deliver the best air/fuel mixture. Or rather, the spray tube can be designed for flow and spray characteristics and we'll fit a screw-in restrictor called a *jet* at the pick-up end. This will give us immediate control over the fuel delivery and (as there will be other jets) it is known as the main jet (Fig. 4.7).

The air speed simply depends on engine revs and the size of the venturi. The air *pressure* reduces as the square of the air speed. Provided the main jet isn't so small it reaches its flow limit (see Note 1), the force lifting fuel into the venturi will increase as the square of the engine speed. So if the engine speed doubles, the air speed will also double (ignoring influences like ram effects for the time being). This means the pressure will be reduced by a factor of 4, so although it will make more fuel flow through the jet, which is required, it will encourage too much fuel to flow. The bigger the change in air speed, the greater the discrepancy in pressure and fuel flow.

> **Note 1**
> *Fluid flowing across a surface tends to stick to it and forms a 'velocity gradient', that is, an increase in velocity with distance away from the surface, until the 'free' velocity of the fluid is reached. This depends mainly on the fluid's viscosity (shear resistance or thickness). The depth of the velocity gradient is small but even for a low-viscosity fluid like gasoline, inside the confines of a jet, the depth forms a significant part of the total size. As the fluid speed increases, the depth becomes greater until the whole jet area contains a velocity gradient. Beyond this point, it takes larger and larger increases in pressure to produce an increase in fluid flow – which eventually reaches a maximum.*

The result is that if the fuel jet gives the correct mixture at low engine speed, the AF ratio will get progressively richer as the speed rises and the air flow increases. Or if a jet is chosen for correct mixture at high speed, the mixture will get progressively weaker at lower speeds. (The change in fuel flow between high and low engine speed is called the *fuel slope*.)

The answer, in the case of motorcycle carburettors, is the *air jet*, also called *air bleed* or *air corrector*. It is fitted (see Fig. 4.8) so that air can be mixed with the fuel being drawn through the spray tube. The amount of air is controlled by the size of the jet and it, too, is dependent upon the speed-squared of the air in the venturi. Now by changing fuel and air jets, we have a means not only to control the fuel delivery at one point but to control the

slope as well. As long as the engine's demands are reasonably linear, we can match them.

The effects of the air jet are small at low speed and become significant at high speed. This means we can choose a fuel jet which gives the best AF at the bottom end of the speed range (and would become too rich at the top end). Then we can try increasing air jet sizes to lean off the top end until it's right. It might be necessary to repeat the process to get the fuelling exactly right all the way through the rev range.

The air jet has a couple of other beneficial effects. There's an infinite number of ways of introducing the air bleed to the fuel flow – the height of the air bleed, the size of the chamber, the number and pattern of holes in the fuel tube (now called an *emulsion tube*), the size of the emulsion tube and its exit into the venturi. Bleeding air into the fuel makes it frothy, so it's easier for the main air stream to break it up or *atomise* it, and we can optimise the fuel spray for the best response and combustion. The frothy liquid drops back into the float bowl less readily than neat liquid, so the response between power off and power back on again is quicker. Finally, the chamber around the emulsion tube partly fills with fuel, providing a small reservoir that has less distance to travel to the venturi when you want instant response for snap acceleration.

Apart from controlling the fuel slope, these other benefits are academic because so far we don't have a throttle to respond to. Our primitive carburettor is wide-open only, with no means of regulating air flow or engine load.

2 Basic slide carburettor

Part-load

The next step is some kind of air valve controlled by the rider, called a throttle because this is what it does to the engine's air supply (although 'full throttle' means fully open not fully closed). The obvious (and easiest to make) would be a *butterfly valve* – a circular plate which blocks the venturi but can be twisted until, edge-on, it hardly obstructs air flow at all. Positioned just downstream of the spray tube, this regulates air flow but doesn't do anything to control fuel flow, so in this type of design we find we need a succession of jets, positioned so the movement of the throttle valve opens them up progressively. In return for installing a simple throttle valve, we have a more complex jet block, with many drillings and tubes.

This type of carburettor, known as *fixed-jet* or *fixed-venturi*, was/is used extensively on car engines but there are significant differences, especially when compared to motorcycle engines of 50 to 60 years ago. On cars, one carburettor would supply four or

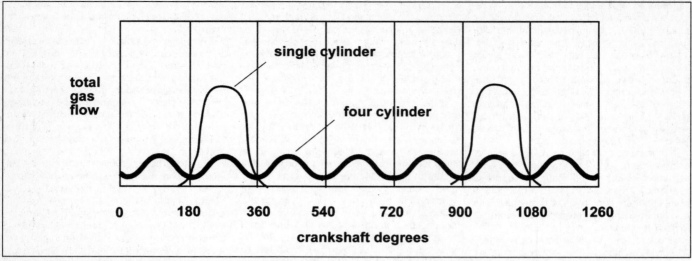

Fig. 4.9 A single cylinder creates large pulses every other revolution. Four cylinders giving the same total displacement create quarter-sized pulses every half revolution

more cylinders via a large manifold. Individual cylinder pulses would be smoothed out considerably back at the carburettor. The engine, and the carburettor, would be relatively large, in a compartment where there was plenty of space (as the cylinders go through intake strokes one at a time, the carburettor venturi can be the same size as if it fed only one cylinder – see Fig. 4.9). Fixed jet carburettors often have a lot of refinements such as spray bars and an inner venturi, in order to control the flow over individual jets and give the required progression. All this restricts air flow and so, to get the flow required for a certain power level, the whole carburettor has to be significantly bigger than a simple, uninterrupted venturi. Motorcycle engines would often be single cylinders, with the carburettor close to the engine and a limited amount of space for it; engines, and carburettors, tended to be smaller.

The manufacturing complexities become more difficult as the carburettor body size is reduced. Butterfly valve plates need a minimum thickness, for their own strength and for the need to fit a suitable spindle. In a large venturi the edge-on plate may be insignificant but many motorcycle venturis were less than 25 mm and the butterfly valve is less efficient in these circumstances.

Motorcycle development generally favoured an air slide to throttle the engine. Originally cylindrical, the same diameter as the venturi, this would be raised by a cable against a return spring (see Fig. 4.10).

Positioned immediately above the fuel spray, the valve could reduce air flow simply by reducing the size of the venturi but as it did so, it also raised the air velocity immediately above the fuel jet. This maintained, possibly even increased, the pressure drop on the fuel spray.

This is not what we want in terms of fuel quantity because reducing the air flow would tend to give the same or more fuel flow, ie to richen the AF mixture. However it does mean the fuel supply and mixing will remain efficient even when air flow in the rest of the intake tract is down to low levels, too low to make our original carburettor work efficiently.

And, as the throttle valve has a simple, linear motion directly above the fuel spray, it is easy to regulate fuel flow by fastening a

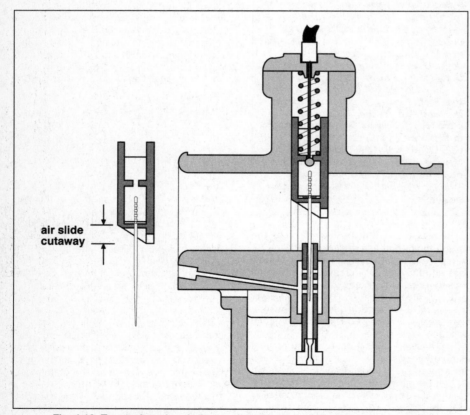

Fig. 4.10 To regulate the air flow, a throttle valve slides across the venturi

Early types were cylindrical, later types had a flat air slide, as shown. A tapered needle is carried in the slide and fits inside the needle jet to control fuel flow. The leading edge of the slide has a cutaway portion – the size of this affects air flow between idle and 1/8 throttle

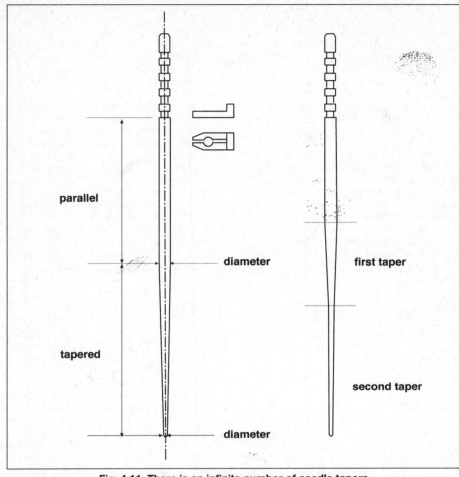

Fig. 4.11 There is an infinite number of needle tapers

The dimensions which affect fuel flow are: (i) overall length, (ii) main diameter, (iii) length of parallel portion, (iv) start and angle of taper, (v) start and angle of subsequent tapers and (vi) the groove in which the locating clip is fitted

tapered needle to the throttle valve, so it runs inside the spray tube. The spray tube now does several jobs and there are opportunities for four or five new adjustments.

The spray tube carries the main jet, it contains the emulsion tube, where air is pre-mixed with the fuel, it forms the spray nozzle into the venturi and now it houses the tapered needle (which is why it is often called *needle jet*, a name we'll use from now on).

In addition to what we had before, we can vary the size of the needle jet in relation to the thickest part of the needle, we can have different lengths and taper of needle (or two or more different tapers on one needle, see Fig. 4.11), we can raise or lower the needle into the jet and we can alter the air slide's underside shape.

On wide open throttle, the only obstruction to air flow is the small needle (some Amal carburettors like the GP model actually had the needle and jet offset in the carburettor body to the side of the venturi, so there was no obstruction to air flow at all). This is a very

efficient way to flow air, down to very small venturi sizes and it forms a compact shape (particularly in length and width, if not in height), which suited most motorcycle engine/frame layouts from the '20s through to the '60s.

The needle has a good bonus effect, because it acts as a spray bar. Liquid fuel runs up the needle, increasing the distribution of fuel over a wider segment of the air flow.

The range of part-throttle adjustment is immense, in nightmare proportions. The combinations and permutations of jet size, air slide, needle length and taper is too big to contemplate and it would probably be a life's work to start from scratch and come up with optimum settings for a given engine.

Fortunately, the development engineers progressed through simple constructions, like our model, so there was always a working version to give baseline settings from which improvements and refinements could be made. Even so, the mention of needle tapers brings a funny look to the faces of most test-house staff.

At WOT the needle must still locate inside the needle jet, otherwise it could jam and prevent the throttle closing. Consequently there are two physical parameters the carburettor must follow:
- The difference between needle jet and needle at the thinnest part of the needle must be greater than the main jet size but not so much greater that the main jet continues to govern fuel flow as the throttle is closed.
- The needle length and the depth from the spray nozzle to the main jet are governed by the venturi size. Some manufacturers list main jet extensions so that longer needles may be used and many tuners have discovered that increasing main jet size no longer affects power or mixture strength, because, beyond a certain size, the needle/needle jet is smaller than the main jet and the needle jet then controls WOT fuelling.

Jet area

As an approximate calculation to check that the main jet, needle jet and needle have compatible sizes, we can work out the area open to fuel flow.

For the main jet the formula is as follows. Note that d is the diameter of the jet.

$$\text{area mj} = \pi d^2/4$$

For the needle/needle jet it is as follows. Note that d_j is the diameter of the needle jet and d_n is the diameter of the widest part of the needle still inside the jet at WOT.

$$\text{area nj} = \pi d_j^2/4 - \pi d_n^2/4$$
$$\text{or area nj} = (d_j^2 - d_n^2)\pi/4$$

For the main jet to control fuel flow at WOT,

$$\text{area mj} < \text{area nj}$$

The area of the main jet needs to be comfortably smaller than the combined area of the needle and its jet, because the flow through a simple orifice is not the same as flow through an orifice containing a rod. If the coefficient of discharge at the main jet is higher than at the needle jet, this is effectively the same as increasing the main jet area (or decreasing the needle jet area). However, the simple area calculation will give you warning if the main jet is close to losing control over the WOT fuel flow.

The answer in this case is possibly to fit a bigger needle but as this will also affect part-throttle mixture, it will probably mean a bigger needle jet and a new needle... but this cannot be chosen until the (approximately) correct main jet has been established. As a result, all carburettor testing tends to be done in less than perfect conditions, or done over and over again, looping closer to the optimum settings with each cycle.

Operating regions

To simplify this process, it helps to split the duties of each component into regions of throttle opening and to tune them in logical steps. It's true that the main jet, for example, contributes to all fuel mixtures down to idle. But it's the only fuel control at WOT (see Note 2) and it has a dominant effect down to ¾ throttle or less, so if you want to change the mixture strength above ¾ throttle (and above ½ throttle if this is the first test on a new engine/carburettor set-up) then do it with the main jet and the main air jet. The sizes are selected for best power, at all rpm where the engine will accept WOT.

> **Note 2** Even this is not strictly true because the idle system contributes fuel all the time. Once the pilot jet has been selected (to give good progression from idle to 1/8 to 1/4 throttle and to set the tickover mixture roughly in the middle of the screw adjustment range) it is very rarely changed.

Between ¼ throttle and ¾ throttle, the needle/needle jet are dominant. The initial combination will have been chosen so they don't take over from the main jet at WOT and the next step is to find the optimum needle taper to give the best steady speed running in this region. The bottom (thinner part) of the needle covers the ⅝ to ¾ throttle range, while the top of the needle controls lower loads. At any part-throttle position, the widest part of the needle still inside the needle jet is what regulates the fuel flow.

Depending upon the combination of load and speed, the optimum setting would give best fuel consumption for light load and low speed, rising to best power production at higher load and higher speed. Detailed techniques for this sort of testing are covered in Chapter 6 – Carburettor Tuning.

Below ¼ throttle, the needle still controls fuel flow but the air slide is close to the spray nozzle and its shape affects air flow, local speed and fuel delivery. Cutting away the leading edge leans off the AF ratio in this region.

This control is too coarse for the tiny supply the engine needs at tickover and the majority of carburettors have a completely separate system to cope with idle conditions. A fuel jet

(the pilot jet) takes its supply from the float bowl and delivers fuel to a simple drilling in the base of the venturi just downstream of the air slide (see Fig. 4.12). When the throttle is fully closed, the engine displacement creates low pressure in the intake tract which is more than enough to draw fuel through the pilot system.

To help atomise it and provide air to burn the fuel, there is a pilot air jet that bleeds air into the fuel stream. Adjustment is by a tapered needle that is screwed into either the air stream or the fuel stream. Screwing the needle in restricts the flow, so depending on which system is used, it will richen the mixture if it restricts the air flow or weaken it if the needle controls the fuel flow. On some carburettors the fuel and air jets control the mixture strength and the tapered needle merely controls total flow.

The idle mixture is set either by measuring exhaust gas CO or by choosing the highest engine speed. There is an adjustable throttle stop, which is set to make the engine idle at roughly the required speed, then the mixture control screw is turned a little, waiting for the engine to stabilise, whichever way is needed to speed the engine up (or reduce the CO reading). The throttle stop is then used to bring the speed down again and the process repeated until the best setting is reached.

This needs to be done before the low-load needle and air slide adjustments are made, because the idle system supplies fuel all the time and, while it might not make a measurable different to WOT performance, it is a significant proportion of the fuel used on light load.

The difference between the idle system and low load is still too great and transferring from idle to the main spray tube is not smooth, causing hesitation and jerkiness in the way the engine picks up as the throttle is opened. To overcome this, there is usually a by-pass (or several by-passes) – drillings from the pilot feed into the venturi, under the bottom edge of the air slide or slightly further upstream.

When the throttle is closed, there is no air flow over these outlets, so no fuel flows through them. As the throttle is opened slightly, air flow starts and draws off fuel, bridging the gap between the idle system and the main system.

Transient conditions

This brings in a new dimension. So far we've concentrated on running the engine at fixed speeds and loads, now it's necessary to make the engine progress smoothly from one to the next, whether the throttle is opened slowly, or snapped open. These are known as transient conditions and obviously make a big contribution to how pleasant a bike is to ride.

In most cases, acceleration requires a richer mixture to compensate for fuel falling out of the airstream and the fact that the

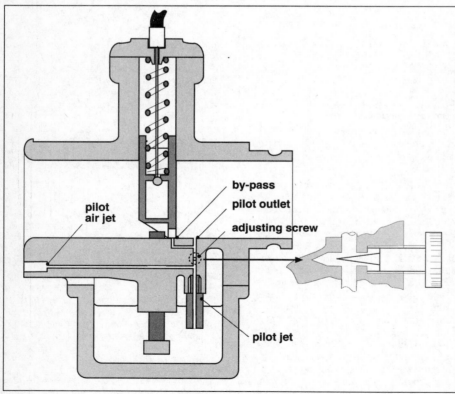

Fig. 4.12 Idle system

A separate jet, fed from the float bowl, supplies fuel to an outlet downstream of the throttle valve. Air is bled into this fuel stream from an air jet, and there is a tapered adjusting screw, which can regulate the air, or the fuel, or both (as shown). One or more by-pass outlets are positioned under the trailing edge of the throttle valve and will supply fuel when the valve is lifted slightly, to avoid a sudden step between the idle and main systems

labels: pilot air jet, by-pass, pilot outlet, adjusting screw, pilot jet engine can accelerate light air more easily than heavier fuel particles. So, to make sure the engine gets an increased dose of the *correct* mixture, the carburettor has to temporarily supply too much fuel.

The reservoir around the emulsion tube helps and many carburettors are able to follow the engine's demands closely enough with only this aid. Short, steeply inclined intake tracts help, as there is nowhere for fuel particles to fall out, apart from into the engine.

Where more fuel is needed, an accelerator pump can be incorporated. There are several varieties but usually the pump is a cylinder with a sprung plunger inside it, connected by a cam type of linkage to the throttle. This could be a part of the throttle linkage outside the carburettor or, as in some Dell'Ortos, there is a ramp on the air slide itself. The cylinder is supplied with fuel from the float bowl and when the throttle is opened, the cam mechanism pumps the fuel through a drilling to the venturi.

This is one of many add-on parts that either tailor the fuel slope or match temporary conditions:

Power jet (high speed jet)

A jet supplied from the float bowl connected to its own spray tube which is positioned in the venturi, upstream of the air slide. The nozzle of the tube is set high, around the ½ throttle position and this height is often adjustable (see Fig. 4.13). There is no air flow over the nozzle until the throttle is lifted higher, so up to this point the jet does nothing. When the throttle is lifted beyond the nozzle, air flows over it and draws off fuel. This provides a means of introducing extra fuel above a precise throttle position. Some GP two-strokes have carburettors with two or even three power jets.

Nozzle shapes

We've shown a simple plain tube as the fuel delivery nozzle. Putting a small screen upstream of it, extending 180° around the nozzle exit, creates a much larger depression at the exit and causes more fuel to be drawn through the nozzle. Changing the size and shape of the screen and also the way air is bled into the nozzle provides another way of tailoring fuel delivery and atomisation (see Fig. 4.14). This type, sometimes called *primary choke* is mainly used on two-stroke engines and the air is bled into the fuel at the nozzle, not via holes in the emulsion tube. Usually the screen is upstream of the fuel nozzle but there is an optional type on Mikuni TDMR flatslides which has a screen with a large hole that goes downstream of the nozzle.

Second air jet

This is an auxiliary air bleed, like the main air jet but whose inlet is blocked, either by the air slide or by an electronically controlled solenoid valve. This means the fuel slope can have two gradients, the second one brought in at a precise point which is either throttle-

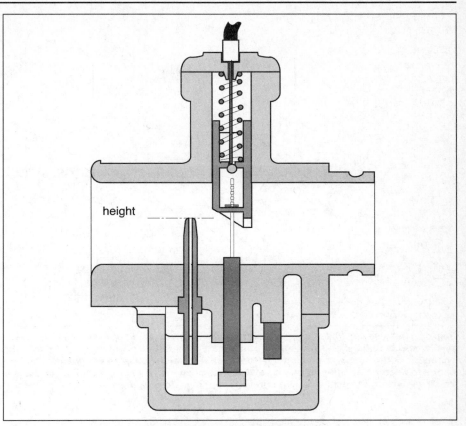

Fig. 4.13 Power jet (high speed jet)

Supplied from the float bowl, via a fuel jet (and sometimes its own air jet), the power jet is a nozzle fitted upstream of the air slide. The height of the nozzle is arranged so that air will not start to flow across it (and therefore draw off fuel) until the air slide has reached a certain position. In this way the jet will only contribute fuel flow above a certain throttle opening

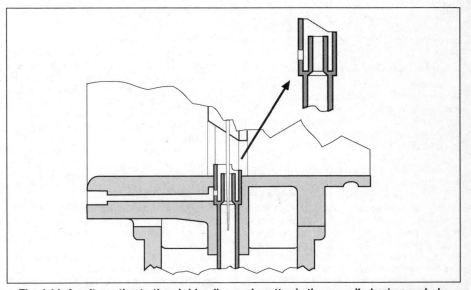

Fig. 4.14 An alternative to the air bleeding carburettor is the so-called *primary choke* type, which has a screen upstream of the fuel nozzle and only introduces the air bleed around the nozzle itself. For a given air velocity and fuel jet size, this type will produce a greater fuel flow and is used in two-stroke engines, where the air flow is less stable. The size and shape of the screen can be used to tailor the fuel delivery

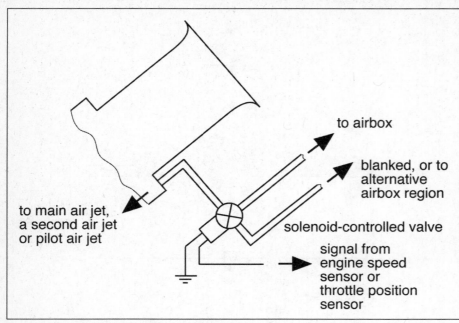

to airbox

blanked, or to
alternative
airbox region

to main air jet,
a second air jet
or pilot air jet

solenoid-controlled valve

signal from
engine speed
sensor or
throttle position
sensor

Fig. 4.15 A valve controlled by a solenoid can be triggered when the engine speed goes past a certain threshold or when the throttle reaches a certain position. It can be used to open/block the supply to an air jet, or to switch the air jet's supply from one part of the airbox to another (at different pressure). This has been applied to main air jets, additional main air jets and to pilot air jets (to prevent popping and banging in the exhaust on the overrun)

related or engine speed-related (see Fig. 4.15).

Airbox connections

Air supplied to air jets needs to be filtered and at the same pressure as normal intake air, so the feed to air jets is usually ducted to the 'still air' part of the box, downstream of the filter. If the pressure in the airbox changes with road speed, then the float bowls will also be vented to a high pressure region of the airbox.

Vacuum connections

The pressure in the venturi is lower than atmospheric and its value depends on engine speed and throttle opening. It is a useful and accurate way of measuring low throttle openings, for instance when running part-load, steady speed dyno tests to optimise AF ratios and ignition timing. It's also used to synchronise multiple carburettors, ie to make sure they all open the same amount at idle and all start to move simultaneously when the throttle is opened. It is frequently used to operate automatic fuel taps (the low pressure is connected to a diaphragm which pushes on a sprung plunger to open up the fuel passage, the spring closing it when the engine is stopped and the vacuum disappears). It has even been used as a back-bleed to lower the pressure in the float bowls (and weaken the mixture) at low loads, allowing another gradient to be built into the fuel slope. Some carburettors have small diaphragm valves operated by intake vacuum (which is very high

in overrun conditions) either to cut off fuel or to bleed fresh air to the pilot system on the overrun, to clean up exhaust gas and stop the machine popping and banging in the exhaust.

In cars it has long been used to rotate the distributor (to vary the ignition timing with engine load), to operate power-assisted brakes and even to work windscreen wipers and washers.

Additional main jets

In the late '70s Honda had several models whose Keihin carburettors had *primary* and *secondary* main jets. The secondaries were the same as the normal type already described and the primaries were constructed in the same way, with their own air jets, but had no needles and the nozzle outlet was below the trailing edge of the air slide, so they performed in much the same way as very influential idle by-passes, and gave a lot of scope to adjust the shape of the fuel slope.

Air slide shapes

The cutaway on the leading edge of the air slide influences air flow at small throttle openings but the whole slide is an aerodynamic obstruction. Even on WOT, when the slide is clear of the venturi, the machined guides in which it slides form edges and steps that can induce turbulence in the air flow. Apart from reducing the total flow the venturi could manage, these interruptions prevent the intake tract responding to resonance tuning (see Chapter 3). Amal went to a lot of trouble with their TT, GP and later

'smoothbore' Concentric to make the venturi as smooth and step-free as possible. This involved some intricate machining to let the cylindrical throttle valve pass though a 'choke adapter'. They were very efficient carburettors. Size for size they would outperform competitors on flow benches and dynamometers.

Mikuni produced a smoothbore version of their VM series before introducing the flatslide TM and RS smoothbore series. Flat air slides had first appeared in Gardner carburettors around 1970 and later in American Lektron and EI instruments. They make the carburettor more compact and in flow bench tests a 34 mm EI equalled the performance of 36 mm Amal and Dell'Orto carburettors. Their other advantage is in producing better control of the airflow, resulting in a more consistent signal pressure above the fuel spray.

Cold start devices

Originally the rich mixture for cold starting was provided by a *strangler*, simply a slide valve that blocked most of the intake upstream of the carburettor. Sometimes this took the form of a cable-operated slide housed within the air slide. Later a butterfly valve was fitted into the area between the venturi and the bellmouth (called a *choke*). Some were prone to break, while all obstructed the air flow, and it wasn't long before cold start jets replaced them. In this system, a jet feeds a drilling downstream of the air slide, exactly like the pilot system. It also has an air jet. The cold start control (still called a *choke*) operates a plunger that blocks/unblocks the air flow to the jet.

The cold start control also operates a small cam that lifts the throttle stop, raising the idle speed. This is partly because it's easier to keep a cold engine running at 2000 – 3000 rpm rather than the usual tickover of about 1200 rpm. It's also partly because the load on the nose of each cam is greatest at low engine speeds and this, combined with cold, thick oil and the fact that the cams are the furthest things from the oil pump, means that cam nose wear can be very high during cold starts. The extra engine speed both reduces the nose loading and speeds up oil delivery.

Disadvantages

The basic carburettor type we've developed was used almost exclusively on motorcycles between the 1950s and early 1970s. There were a few models with fixed jet carburettors, such as Harley-Davidson, but on the whole, the slide carburettor was boss.

However, it has quite a lot of disadvantages, especially as venturi sizes get bigger and power outputs rise:
● Despite all the tricks and dodges outlined above, if the rider snaps the throttle open suddenly from lowish rpm, the carburettor will not be able to supply a combustible mixture. The engine will stagger, misfire and possibly stall.

● Even if the rider opens the throttle too much from midrange rpm, the engine will not respond. Instead of accelerating, it will make less power and go slower. The carburettor cannot cope with such big transients: the rider must feel the effect of the throttle and only open it the maximum the carburettor can manage (that is both maximum distance and maximum rate), to get full engine response. This takes a lot of skill on the part of the rider.

● The carburettors are tall. The air slide has to be lifted the height of the venturi and the needle also has to be longer than the venturi height, so a 38 mm carburettor has to be more than 114 mm high, plus the linkage on top and the float bowl below.

● The effect of engine vacuum on the slides makes them wear and prone to stick. They need heavy return springs to overcome this. Some competition flatslide designs have the slides running on roller bearings, ironically increasing the complexity the flatslide was meant to overcome.

● It's difficult to make a neat throttle linkage, which can open several air slides 38 mm yet only use a comfortable quarter-turn of the twistgrip, especially as it has to work against the heavy return springs. The result is either very heavy throttle action, or too much travel at the twistgrip.

● As engines become more compact and use shorter, steeper, straighter intake tracts, tall carburettors run into the cam box space.

3 CV carburettor

Design and advantages

There has always been an alternative to the slide carburettor. It's called the CV carburettor and it can contain the components mentioned in Section 2 but it has one feature which answers all of the slide carburettor's disadvantages. Instead of a cable-controlled air slide, it has a slide controlled by intake pressure and a separate throttle valve (usually a butterfly valve) downstream of the air slide.

The throttle valve, operated by the rider, regulates air flow and therefore engine load. The (low) pressure of the air flow is vented into a chamber above the air slide and this is used to lift the slide (and a fuel-control needle) against its weight and a light spring (see Figs. 4.16a and 4.16b).

The idea, initially, was that the slide (now called a *piston* or *piston valve*) would lift in proportion to air pressure (ie velocity) in the main tract. As it lifted it would alter the area underneath it (above the jets) and this could be arranged to keep the local airflow constant, hence the abbreviation CV for *constant velocity* (or *constant vacuum*) or CD (*constant depression*).

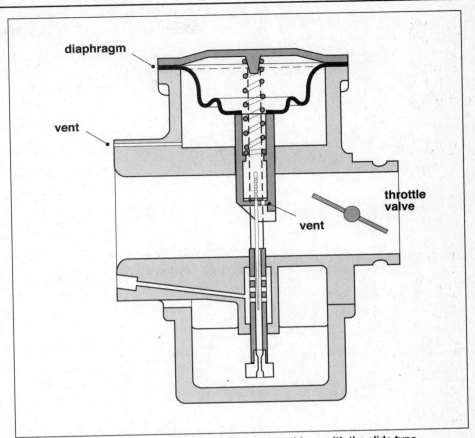

Fig. 4.16a The CV carburettor shares many things with the slide type

The float bowl, main jet, air jet, needle jet and needle are identical. The essential difference is a butterfly throttle valve just downstream of the air slide and the fact that the air slide now rises into a chamber, divided by a sealing diaphragm. An air vent provides atmospheric (or airbox) pressure to the underside of the diaphragm. Another vent in the base of the air slide ducts venturi pressure to the topside of the diaphragm. The butterfly valve regulates air flow to the engine and when this flow speeds up, its low pressure (ducted above the diaphragm) makes the air slide lift. This increases the area below the air slide, which tends to keep the local air velocity constant, providing a constant pressure drop across the fuel jet. Fuel flow is regulated by the tapered needle, which is lifted with the air slide

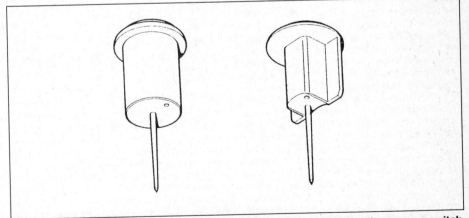

Fig. 4.16b Early CV types had cylindrical air slides. In the early 1990s, there was a switch to the semi-flatslide designs. These are Keihin slides for the 1990 and '91 CBR600. As well as making the venturi area more compact, the flatslide gives better air flow and throttle response (Honda)

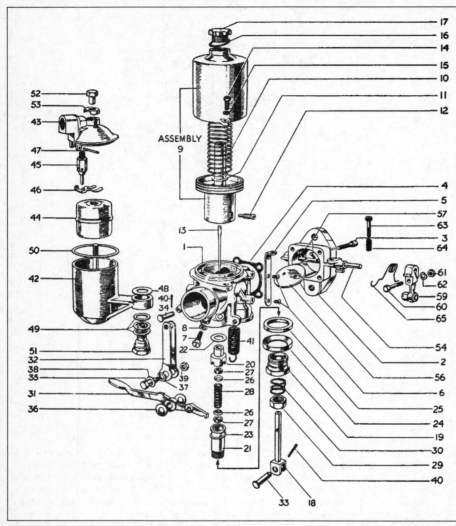

Fig. 4.17 SU carburettor. One jet size, one needle, an idle system, a float bowl and a cold start

1	Carburettor body	23	Copper washer	45	Needle and seat
2	Throttle barrel adapter	24	Sealing ring (brass)	46	Hinged lever
3	Screw – 4 off	25	Sealing ring (cork)	47	Hinge pin
4	Gasket	26	Gland washer (brass)	48	Fibre pin
5	Throttle cable stop	27	Gland washer (cork)	49	Washers
6	Screw – 2 off	28	Spring		(2 fibre, 1 brass)
7	Plug screw	29	Adjusting nut	50	Float chamber lid
8	Washer	30	Spring		washer
9	Suction chamber	31	Jet lever	51	Holding bolt
	complete	32	Jet link	52	Float chamber lid nut
10	Piston spring	33	Pivot pin (long)	53	Brass cap
11	Thrust washer	34	Pivot pin (short)	54	Throttle spindle
12	Needle screw	35	Bolt	56	Throttle butterfly
13	Jet needle	36	Fibre washer	57	Screw
14	Screw – 2 off	37	Spring washer	59	Throttle lever
15	Spring washer – 2 off	38	Washer	60	Bolt
16	Damper oil cap washer	39	Nut	61	Nut
17	Damper oil cap	40	Split pin	62	Washer
18	Jet	41	Return spring	63	Adjusting screw
19	Jet screw	42	Float chamber	64	Adjusting screw lock
20	Jet top half bearing	43	Float chamber lid		spring
21	Jet bottom half bearing	44	Float	65	Lever return spring
22	Copper washer				

This, in turn, would simplify conditions at the fuel jets. A constant pressure would result in constant fuel flow, which could then be regulated, from idle to WOT, by one needle jet and one needle. With no pressure changes, the fuel slope would, in effect, be the needle's taper.

The SU carburettor (see Fig. 4.17), used on many cars and a few motorcycles, followed this design principle faithfully. It resulted in a very simple, efficient carburettor, which was easy to assemble, with few components – but the parts list did have an awful lot of needles and, as mentioned earlier, if there's one thing that can turn a development engineer's complexion grey, it is the matter of needle tapers. However, the SU has one jet and one needle and this is the only tuning adjustment. There's a float bowl, an idle system and a cold-start system but otherwise – minimum complexity. In a car installation one carburettor would feed two, three or four, low-revving cylinders via a lengthy, large-volume intake manifold. Even the diluted pulses from this sort of set-up could make the piston flutter and it had an hydraulic damper to compensate for this. On a one-carburettor-per-cylinder bike layout, with the carburettor very close to the high-revving engine, the SU's simplicity was not such a big attraction.

The CV carburettors which began replacing slide carburettors through the 1970s were more of a mishmash of CV and slide carburettor components, in an attempt to get the best of both worlds. The fact that this isn't possible is demonstrated by racing bikes that still use slide carburettors (because they offer the best air flow and therefore power) while four-stroke roadsters almost always have CV carburettors (because they are much more rider-friendly).

Some particularly awkward designs (singles of 600 cc and upwards) have a two-barrelled combination of slide and CV – a small, responsive slide carburettor which opens when the rider turns the throttle but which, on its own, couldn't supply enough air for full power. Alongside it there is a CV carburettor that opens as and when the air flow can sustain it. In this way it's possible to have the total inlet area of, say, a single 43 mm bore carburettor but to have the low speed performance and clean throttle response of a 30 mm instrument.

Slide and CV carburettors reach a practical maximum at about 40 mm, when they are applied to bike-sized cylinders on a one-carburettor-per-cylinder basis. Bigger units will work at high gas flow rates but in high load/low engine speed conditions, the gas velocity becomes too low, even for the 'automatic' CV type.

Going away from the puritanical SU design, CV carburettors (made mainly by Mikuni and Keihin) kept the piston valve but incorporated all the other features that had been developed for slide carburettors. In this way it was possible to tune them without having to sift through millions of needle profiles.

They also kept the butterfly throttle valve, which is both the main attraction and the biggest disadvantage of this type of carburettor (see Fig. 4.18). It's a disadvantage because it is always an obstruction to air flow, even in the edge-on WOT position. If everything else is the same, then a 38 mm CV carburettor will always flow less than a 38 mm slide carburettor. But having the butterfly valve also addresses all the shortcomings of the slide carburettor:

● If the rider opens the throttle too far or too fast, there will not be enough air velocity to raise the piston valve and this temporarily becomes a throttle. As the air flow speeds up (which is now in proportion to what the engine can manage, not what the rider wants) the piston lifts until it matches the butterfly position. The butterfly valve then resumes throttle control. The piston valve has mimicked the action of a highly skilled rider, in opening the throttle at a rate at which the carburettor can maintain an AF mixture the engine finds acceptable.

● The carburettor still needs to be tall enough for the piston to lift the height of the venturi, but that's all, there's no additional linkage to go on top. It has gained a bit of width, for the piston chamber and for a throttle linkage which is now on the side of the carburettor.

● The butterfly valve pivots at its centre, so engine vacuum on the upper half, trying to open the valve, is balanced by the same vacuum on the lower half, trying to close it. A fairly light return spring is all that's needed to make the valve close whenever the twistgrip is released, under any engine conditions. The valve spindle is carried on circular bushes which have no tendency to stick.

● Regardless of the venturi size, the butterfly valve only has to turn through slightly less than 90° to go from idle to WOT. As the return spring force is not strong, the twistgrip does not need to have any mechanical advantage and it is easy to give it a light, quick action that the rider finds comfortable.

Our working model can be adapted along these lines without too much trouble. In early designs, the piston valves were round, like the early air slides. They were changed to give a flat air slide portion, for the same reasons as slide carburettors, although this doesn't affect the working principle. This requires a sealed chamber above the piston (see Fig. 4.16a). Pressure from the venturi is vented to the top of the chamber, via a hole in the bottom of the air slide. Static (or airbox) pressure is vented through a drilling in the carburettor body to the lower part of the chamber. The forces now acting on the piston valve are:

● Static pressure (upwards, on the underside of the piston portion)

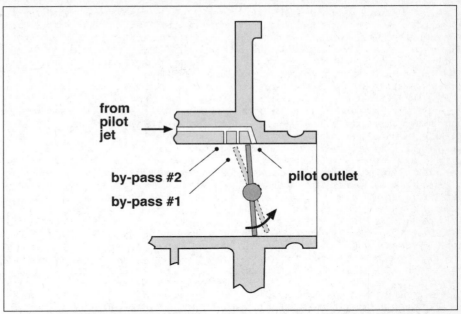

Fig. 4.18 The idle system in CV carburettors is the same as in slide types although the movement of the butterfly valve lets by-passes be brought in with more precision, achieving a smooth transition from idle to part-load

As the by-pass outlets need to follow the edge of the valve that is moving upstream, the pilot jet may supply fuel to drillings in the top of the venturi casting, as shown here. Alternatively the throttle valve can open in the opposite direction (ie clockwise) and the by-passes will be on the floor of the venturi (see photographs in Chapter 7)

● Venturi pressure (downwards on the topside of the piston portion and upwards on the underside of the air slide portion)
● Weight of the piston, needle etc (downwards)
● Spring force (downwards)

It's only a matter of arithmetic to make the piston area big enough so the upward force exceeds the downward force for the venturi pressure available. In steady engine conditions, as the piston lifts, the venturi area is increased, which reduces the air speed until a balance is reached and the piston will rise no further. For a given size of venturi, piston etc, the piston will tend to settle at a height that gives the same air speed in the venturi. So there will be constant air velocity and constant pressure for all throttle positions.

The actual values can be engineered to some extent, to keep the pressure drop between float chamber and fuel nozzle in the optimum region for fuel flow through the main jet/needle jet combination, working with the air bleed. Having this consistency means the atomised fuel spray should also be consistent for all load/speed conditions. This is an advantage over slide carburettors, where high air velocity gives the best atomisation, and the fuel spray is not so good at low speed/high load. If the spray is not broken up into a fine enough mist, then (a) the fuel will not mix so thoroughly with the air and (b) heavier fuel particles are more likely to drop out of the air flow and wet the sides of the intake tract.

The CV carburettor is also self-regulating over small changes. When the air flow lifts the piston and it settles at a height, this determines the air velocity and pressure, drawing fuel through the jets. The tapered needle controls the amount of fuel flow and its height is fixed by the piston height, so the AF ratio becomes a function of venturi size and needle taper.

If something lifts the slide slightly it will reduce the air velocity and reduce the pressure drop at the jets (weakening the mixture) but at the same time it will lift the needle (richening the mixture). The opposite happens if something lowers the slide: the effect is to speed up the air flow, lowering its pressure and pulling more fuel through the jets, while the needle is lowered and restricts the fuel flow. The two changes tend to cancel out, making the mixture self-stabilising and not prone to disruption by outside influences like vibration or road bumps.

Actual carburettors

Translating this theory into practice requires careful construction. The original SU design had a circular, alloy piston, sealed by being a close fit in its chamber. It was easy to construct and at the time I doubt if there were any suitable materials to make the diaphragms that are used to seal current carburettor chambers. The disadvantages with the SU design (I guess) are that the whole piston assembly is heavy and that it would suffer from friction. Both of these factors would slow down the response and, once moving, the inertia of the piston would tend to carry it too far. Instead of nipping smartly to the correct height it would wobble about before finally settling at the right height. Flutter, or some imprecision, was evidently a problem because SU also had an hydraulic damper – a tube on top of the piston carried engine oil and a damper rod fixed to the top of the chamber extended into the oil.

Current CV designs feature an extremely light, plastic piston attached to an elastomer diaphragm, which is trapped between the carburettor body and the chamber top. Lightness in all the moving parts is critical for throttle response. There is no mechanical damper, although flutter, as we shall see, can still be a problem.

Apart from the ability to respond quickly to throttle changes, a light piston means that less pressure difference is needed to lift it, so the topside surface area can be smaller and the carburettor more compact.

Pressure in the venturi is transmitted via a small drilling in the base of the piston and the size of this drilling has an effect on performance. For steady-state running, the size of the hole is not important but a larger diameter makes the piston respond faster, while a smaller diameter slows it down – in effect, it works like a damper. The hole size becomes a compromise between fast response and too much sensitivity.

Although CV carburettors tend to self-compensate for small fluctuations, they do not compensate exactly and the larger the fluctuation the more the mixture strength will go astray. Basically, if you physically lift the slide above its normal equilibrium point it will richen the mixture, while pushing it downwards will weaken the mixture.

When the rider opens the throttle quickly, the slide needs to follow this action as faithfully as possible. But if it moves too quickly it might get into the region where the fuel supply cannot keep up with the changing air flow and you have the slide-carburettor problem that CV carburettors are supposed to avoid. In this case the slide would need a smaller vent hole.

Also the slide is a freely suspended mass and although it is made as light as possible it still has inertia. If it starts moving too quickly it will not stop at the correct level but will overshoot and then fall back as the spring, air pressures and weight finally reach a balance. But at the critical moment when the rider opens the throttle, the slide will travel too high, creating a too-rich mixture in a slowed-down airstream. Usually, some richness is desirable for acceleration so at least the design errs in the right direction. But if it goes

too far (vent hole too big) the combination of richness and poor atomisation will spoil the engine response, possibly to the point of causing hesitation or a *flat spot*.

It works the other way, too. If the rider is using a high load and rolls the throttle off (not closed completely) then too much response will have the slide close down too far. This is not so much of a problem because when the rider backs off he wants the bike to slow, so a momentary lack of power or over-weak mixture will usually go unnoticed. But if we put the two conditions together, as in riding along a very twisty road, where the rider is continuously opening and closing the throttle, although never getting it fully open or fully closed, then the excess motion of the piston slide will make itself felt in poor throttle response and the engine generally lagging behind the rider's commands. Bouncing about between too-rich and too-weak instead of settling in between will also make the engine less fuel efficient.

Sometimes the engine itself can cause problems at the carburettor. Standard machines are well developed to give smooth power delivery and throttle response from all conditions. However, in order to get a high peak output, they are in a high state of tune – mainly in terms of valve timing, exhaust and intake dimensions, which all come together to work in harmony at high rpm (upwards of 8,000 rpm on a typical, big four-cylinder bike). This means a certain amount of disharmony at lower speeds and most torque curves show a pronounced dip in the 4000 – 5000 rpm region. It requires a lot of skill and development time to optimise the carburation and ignition timing so that the engine will pull smoothly through this inefficient region.

Further tuning (or any change that upsets the fine balance, like a change of exhaust system, airbox dimensions or even an air filter with different flow characteristics) will often turn the midrange dip into a hole.

Here the engine is running inefficiently, burnt gas is being pushed back past the intake valves because they are open for too long, the gas flow is anything but steady. If you now ask the engine to accept a wide throttle opening from this speed it will start to accelerate whenever it sees a combustible mixture but it will then decelerate when it doesn't. The effect, to the rider, varies from hesitation, a flat spot, to stuttering and finally a misfire and spitting back in the carburettors.

CV carburettors with large vent holes will respond to these surges and pulses. In the flat spot-stuttering part of the spectrum, the slides will flutter rapidly. This can obviously make the stuttering condition worse than it might have been. It also causes rapid wear

between the needle and the needle jet which, by opening the clearance between the two, causes an ever-richening mixture.

If the vent holes are too small, then throttle response will be poor. It's also possible that the slides will not lift fully at WOT and so will restrict top-end power.

4 Jet kits

Carburettor jet kits, designed to work with moderately tuned engines and less restrictive air cleaners, often contain new needles and a drill bit to enlarge the vent holes in the slides. There are two potential problems here.

First, making the vent holes too big will promote the problems described above, especially if additional tuning makes the midrange delivery worse. Second, the new needle material and finish may not be compatible with the needle jet. In normal operation this could cause wear over large mileages, which might be acceptable if the needle jet is a replaceable item. On some carburettors it isn't. Although it is pressed in and can usually be removed with some skill and care, it may not be available as a service item from the dealer.

If the two problems combine together, the jets could wear, to the extent of causing rich-mixture misfiring, in just a few hundred miles. The moral is (a) to avoid a state of tune that causes stuttering, (b) only to enlarge the vent holes when it is proven necessary, not just because there's a drill bit in the kit and (c) to check on needle jet availability. On many types of machine it's possible to run the bike on a dyno with the airbox top removed so the carburettors are visible and can be watched as the engine is accelerated through a variety of speed ranges on a variety of throttle openings.

We now have a fully working carburettor which, in practice, can perform precisely over a huge range of operating conditions. One unit can cope with up to 40 bhp, or 150 bhp per litre, yet still pull WOT cleanly from 1500 rpm up to 12,000 rpm. It can handle all part-load and speed conditions and will respond smoothly to any rate of throttle opening. It provides stable idling plus quick hot or cold starting. It's quite an achievement for something whose only connections to the outside world are an air supply, a fuel supply and a throttle cable. Yet by the mid-1990s, more and more bikes were demanding more and the only way to provide it was fuel injection.

Chapter 5
Fuel injection: theory

Refer also to Chapter 10 for details of production systems adjustment and settings

Contents

1 Introduction

See Fig. 5.1

Fuel injection has long been the alternative to carburettors. As with most mechanical things, if you delve thoroughly enough you can probably find examples dating back to the 1920s or beyond. It actually pre-dates venturi-type carburettors, as Gasmotorenfabrik Deutz were making injection plunger pumps in 1898. Certainly fuel injection was in everyday use by 1940: it gave the Messerschmitt Bf109 one of its few advantages over the Hawker Hurricane and Supermarine Spitfire, with their carburetted Rolls Royce Merlin V12 engines.

The Messerschmitt could go directly from level flight into a dive, while this manoeuvre produced a rich-mixture misfire in the Rolls Royce engines as the float bowls temporarily lost control of their contents. To avoid this, pilots had to do a half-roll and dive, keeping positive g on the engine and fuel system.

It neatly summarises the advantages of fuel injection, namely that you take a predetermined quantity of fuel and deliver it to each cylinder, independent of and

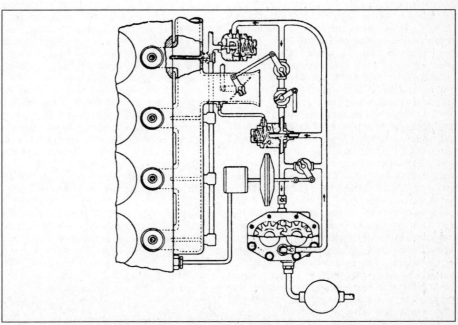

Fig. 5.1 A 1934 patent by Ed Winfield shows a mechanically controlled, continuous-flow injection system

The gear pump delivers fuel under pressure to a common rail and the pressure is regulated by throttle position, intake vacuum and engine temperature

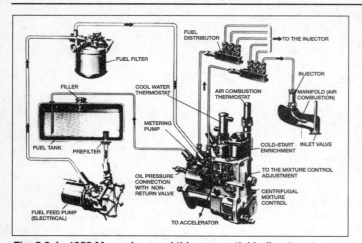

Fig. 5.2 In 1958 Mercedes used this sequential indirect system on their 220SE

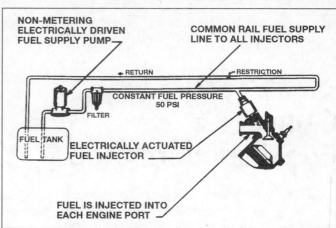

Fig. 5.3 The Bendix electrically controlled system kept the fuel rail at constant pressure and used injector-on time to regulate the fuel flow

uninfluenced by any ambient conditions. The carburettor uses its surroundings to automatically supply the correct amount of fuel.

This is also the disadvantage of fuel injection. While it can 'force' an 'unnatural' amount of fuel to the engine, permitting it to deal with difficult operating conditions or to follow sudden changes, it cannot do this automatically, it has to have a very complicated control system to tell it what to do.

During the period after World War 2 the complexity of the (mechanical) control system was the limiting factor – limiting its use to a few racing cars, as aircraft switched to jet or gas turbine engines and military vehicles switched to diesels (designed by Dr Rudolph Diesel, 1858-1913, who ran the first compression ignition engine in 1897). Diesel engines, of course, have always used fuel injection but they are helped by the characteristics of the fuel, both in combustion and as a lubricant, while gasoline only makes life more difficult in these directions.

Fuel injection consists of pumping fuel at high pressure to a nozzle, which delivers the fuel into the cylinder (direct injection – DI) or into the intake tract or a pre-mixing chamber (low-pressure or indirect injection – IDI). In the case of diesels, the air flow is not throttled, they flow full air all the time and the power is regulated by the amount of fuel injected. They run from low load (very weak) to full load (very rich – diesels deliver maximum power when they make black smoke) simply by altering the amount of fuel. This makes the control system much simpler as there is no need to regulate the air flow or to match the fuel quantity to the air flow. It also means that, as there is no throttle valve, there are no throttling losses when the engine is run on part load, which is one reason diesels are more fuel efficient in cruise conditions.

Another reason is they ignite the fuel by compression, by raising the pressure and the temperature to the point where the fuel will auto-ignite. The very high compression required for this and the very rapid combustion raise the engine's thermal efficiency. The engines run excess air, making it relatively easy to achieve combustion of all the fuel without having to mix air and fuel so completely as a spark ignition engine demands. In the region of the fuel spray, the mixture has to be of ignitable quality ($1.5 > \lambda > 0.3$) while gasoline needs to be in the range $1.25 > \lambda > 0.7$ throughout the *entire gas*. It is simply a function of nozzle design and fuel pressure to achieve this for the diesel.

The diesel engine's moving parts have to be heavy to withstand the sudden, explosive nature of the combustion. The ignition delay depends upon compression pressure (and fuel quality) and both of these factors limit diesels to a fairly narrow speed range, with speeds that are low by comparison to spark-ignition engines of a similar output (large truck engines peak around 2000 rpm).

Gasoline will not tolerate excess air or detonation. Its combustion can get so efficient it will melt pistons and valves instead of producing useful power, so the fuel system must keep to safe AF ratios, must regulate air as well as fuel, and must mix all the air and fuel very thoroughly. This takes time, an ever diminishing commodity in a high speed engine (some roadster bike engines reach 15,500 rpm). It's not enough merely to pump the fuel into the cylinder at high pressure, because it has to be broken into the finest possible particles and completely mixed with the air.

2 Early development

See Figs. 5.2, 5.3 and 5.4

In the early days, the difficulties of pumping and mechanical control were enough to ensure that fuel injection only appeared on aircraft engines (which have particular problems of negative g and of fire in their superchargers, so injection is very attractive) and in very expensive racing cars. Advances in materials and electronics gradually solved these problems and from about 1980 onwards fuel injection was a viable alternative to carburettors if the circumstances demanded it. As electronics – particularly computer memory – became cheaper, it became easier to measure air flow, monitor engine conditions such as speed and throttle position and use an electronic signal to control the injector opening.

In 1958 there were mechanical car systems made by Lucas, Bosch, Marvel-Schebler, Holley, Rochester and SU, but Bendix had an electronically controlled injection system. During the next 15 years, computer-controlled systems appeared from Volvo, Volkswagen Porsche, Bosch (fitted to Citroën and Mercedes Benz), and AE Brico (fitted to Aston Martin).

Bosch had the K-Jetronic mechanical system and the L-Jetronic electronic system available in 1973, and by 1979 had built the Motronic, with a digital processor that could also control ignition timing. The Bosch systems had the most influence for bikes because the first fuel-injected machines used versions of the German design.

Fig. 5.4 This fuel injected BMW was raced at the 1953 TT and at Hockenheim in 1954 *(Mortons Motorcycle Archive)*

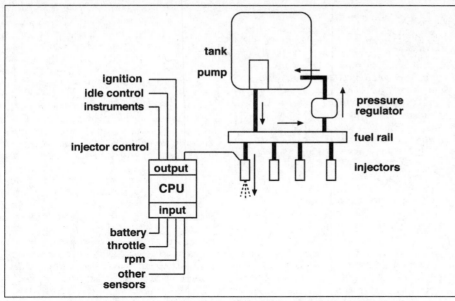

Fig. 5.5 All current systems follow the same general arrangement

A pump supplies fuel at high pressure to a fuel rail, from which the injectors are fed. The pressure is kept constant by a regulator which returns excess fuel to the tank. Fuel quantity is determined by the amount of time the injector is switched on. The CPU calculates this time from a number of sensors (mainly engine speed and throttle position) and sends a suitable electrical pulse to the injector's solenoid. The CPU has other outputs – typically it controls ignition timing and dwell, the instrument display (tacho and warning lights) and may also control idle speed (by altering an air bleed to by-pass the throttle, operating a movable throttle stop or by altering the ignition timing)

3 Typical systems

See Figs. 5.5, 5.6, 5.7 and 5.8

There are DI gasoline engines but the majority use IDI, usually with the injectors aimed at the intake valves. Positioning the injectors close to the cylinder gives better results in terms of part-load response and fuel economy. For full-load performance, placing the injectors further back along the intake tract allows more time for fuel/air mixing (in extreme applications such as F1 cars and Yamaha's OW02-R7, the injectors are placed in the airbox, just upstream of the bellmouth entry to each intake).

Multi-point injection has one (or more)

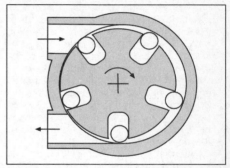

Fig. 5.6 This is the principle of the roller cell type of fuel pump

injector per cylinder – on bike designs this usually consists of a throttle body with its own throttle valve for each cylinder, although there are car designs in which there is only one throttle valve (the intake tract then branching out into individual intake 'runners' for each cylinder, sometimes with a resonator chamber feeding the runners so both it and the runner lengths can be tuned to work in harmony with the most useful engine speed range). The alternative, single point injection (in which there is one throttle body and one injector feeding all cylinders via a branched manifold) has not been used on bike engines. Given individual injectors for each cylinder, there are three broad types of injection:

● **Simultaneous** – All injectors fire at the same time. Usually the delivery is split into two short bursts rather than one long one, which means some bursts can be delivered

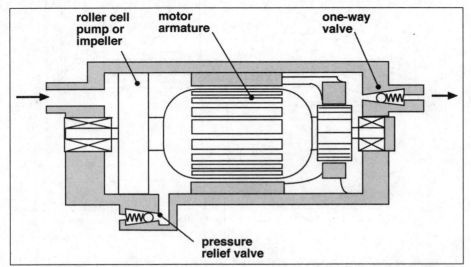

Fig. 5.7 Pumps are usually immersed in fuel, with either a roller cell rotor or impellers (or a combination of both) to move the fuel through them

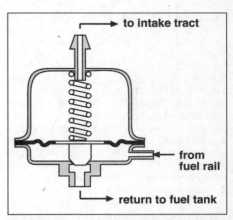

Fig. 5.8 The pressure regulator is a sealed unit in which a needle valve is held on to its seat by spring pressure, backed by intake manifold pressure

If the fuel pressure on the opposite side of the diaphragm is high enough to lift the spring, the valve opens and fuel flows back to the tank, until the pressure falls below the spring's closing load. In this way the fuel pressure is kept at a constant level above the air pressure in the port close to the injector just before the intake valves open on some cylinders (of an in-line four) but others occur when the intakes are open (not desirable as the air is expanding into the cylinder and the fuel will not have as good a chance to mix thoroughly with it).

● **Grouped** – Of a four cylinder engine, the injectors fire together on groups of two cylinders. These are single, therefore longer bursts but all can be timed to arrive just before a cylinder's intake stroke, which is the ideal arrangement.

● **Sequential** – Each injector is timed to fire just before its cylinder's intake stroke.

Of the three systems, sequential injection offers the most control over the fuelling and is better for metering precise amounts at low speeds or loads or when emissions are the prime consideration. It also requires more complex electronics. Simultaneous injection is simpler to construct and, at high speeds and loads, works just as well. Grouped injection is a half-way house between the two. As power outputs rise, the injector's 'on' time increases until, eventually, it is 'on' all the time, which is the limit for that particular system. As the 'on' time increases, the difference between sequential and simultaneous injection gets smaller.

The systems use constant pressure, so the fuel quantity depends only on the time the injector nozzle is open. Quite often there will be sequential injection at low engine speed, shifting to two injections per cycle once the engine goes above a certain speed. Alternatively, there may be two injectors per cylinder, one which works all through the rev range and one which comes in to meet high speed or high load demands.

This shows up another problem. The fuel pump and fuel injectors have moving parts that must be lubricated by the fuel, and gasoline is a poor lubricant. Typically, its viscosity (see Note 1) at 20°C is 0.66 cSt compared to diesel at 2 – 8 cSt, and an SAE30 engine oil at 1000+ cSt, or even water at 1.17 cSt (at 16°C). Until recently, diesel fuel also had a high sulphur content (sulphur is a good load-bearing lubricant), typically 0.5% by weight compared to gasoline – unleaded is restricted to 0.1% but a typical level is around 0.03%. Volatile liquids like gasoline also tend to leave deposits – gums and varnishes – which clog the precisely-dimensioned injector nozzles (which are made to tolerances of 3 to 4 microns).

One of the problems in devising gasoline fuel injection systems was in building a pump and injectors that could survive in these conditions.

But control was always the main problem and it wasn't until Eprom (erasable programmable read-only memory) chips were available that gasoline fuel injection really stood a chance. Once electronics had advanced to this stage, mixture control was no longer a problem, merely an expense. As computer memory became cheaper, fuel injection became more attractive than carburettors.

Note 1

Viscosity is the thickness of a liquid, actually defined as the force needed to shear the liquid at a certain velocity. η = *shear stress/shear rate. As moving parts, separated by a film of liquid, do just this, it's a realistic measure of the liquid's lubricating ability. Kinematic viscosity (usually measured in cSt) is absolute viscosity (usually in cP) divided by the liquid's specific gravity (1 cP = 0.001N/m² and 1 St= 1cm²/s).*

4 Applications for bikes

See Figs. 5.9, 5.10, 5.11, 5.12, 5.13 and 5.14

The first fuel-injected production bike was the Kawasaki Z1000-H1 in 1980. This used an analogue CPU (central processing unit – the engine management control) which was later changed to digital processing on the 1982 Z1100-B2 and the 1983 ZX1100-A1 (GPz1100).

Honda had their first production system on the turbocharged CX500TC (1981 and the 1983 CX650TC) and when Kawasaki and Suzuki brought out their turbocharged ZX750-E1 (1984) and XN85 (1983) they both had fuel injection. These were all turbocharged engines, in which carburettors are at a disadvantage – because you either have to pressurise the fuel system or put the carburettor upstream of the compressor and then pass an ignitable mixture through it, with serious consequences in the event of the engine spitting back. Also an electronically controlled system can monitor other dangerous conditions, such as knock, and can instantly alter the mixture strength and ignition timing to avoid mechanical damage.

As the turbocharger fad died away, so did fuel injection on bike engines – in an era when all car manufacturers were switching from carburettors to injectors. Indeed the Honda 273E, a 2992 cc V12 race car engine, had a low pressure fuel injection in 1966... so they presumably knew the pros and cons.

The exception was BMW, who put Bosch LE Jetronic and, later, Motronic systems on their K100 and K75 series (1985 onwards).

Much later, big twins like the Moto Guzzi and Ducati 851 began using injection, as did the V4 Honda RC45 and VFR800, but the first mainstream, in-line fours to get it (apart from BMW) were the 1993 Yamaha GTS and 1998 Suzuki GSX-R750.

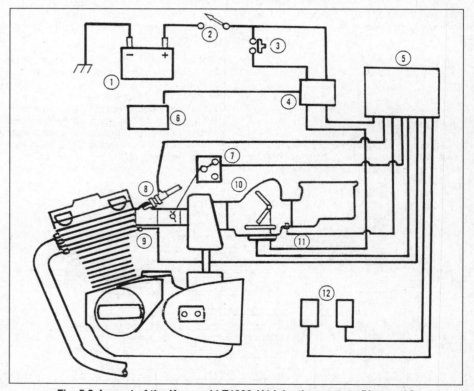

Fig. 5.9 Layout of the Kawasaki Z1000-H1 injection system *(Kawasaki)*

1 Battery	5 Analogue CPU	9 Engine temperature sensor
2 Ignition switch	6 Fuel pump	10 Air flow meter
3 Starter switch	7 Throttle switch	11 Air temperature sensor
4 Relay	8 Fuel injector	12 Ignition coils

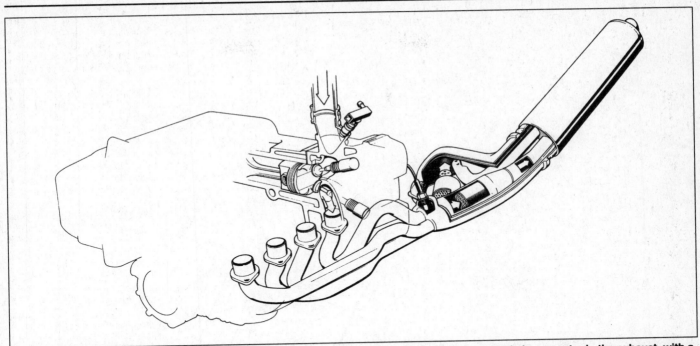

Fig. 5.10 The Bosch system used by BMW on the three- and four-cylinder models. This has a catalytic converter in the exhaust, with a λ-sensor in the exhaust collector *(BMW)*

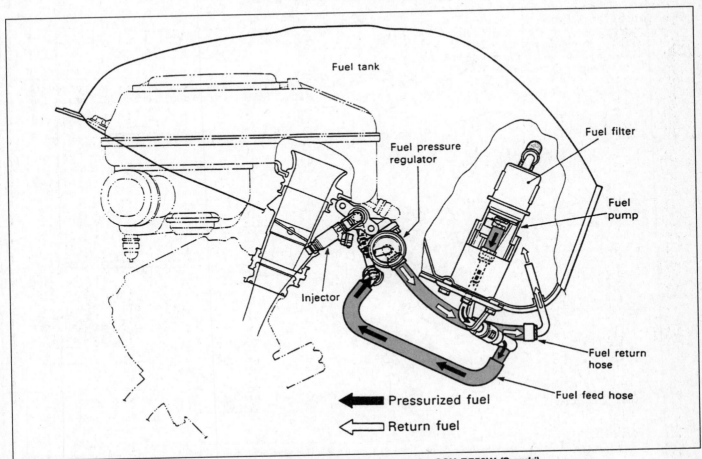

Fig. 5.11 The general layout used by Suzuki on the GSX-R750W *(Suzuki)*

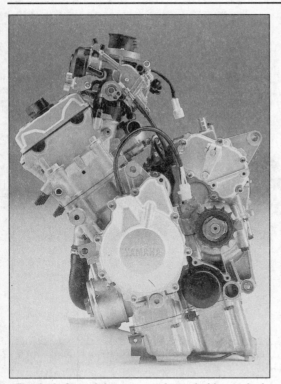

Fig. 5.12 One of the reasons for switching to fuel injection can be seen in this shot of the extremely compact Yamaha R6, where the space available and the steep downdraught angle make carburettor design increasingly difficult. With the R1/R6 family of engines Yamaha have taken carburettors as far as they can go and the later R7 had fuel injection *(Yamaha)*

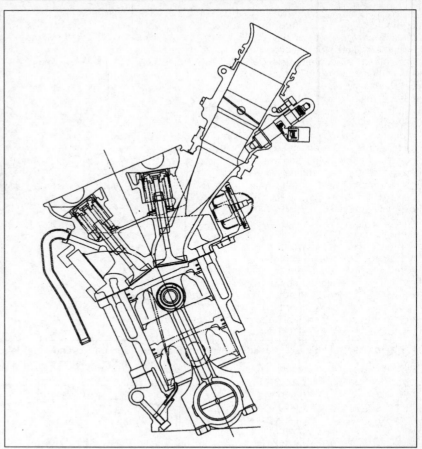

Fig. 5.13 This shows how a large-bore throttle body can be incorporated neatly in an engine with a steep intake tract and double overhead cams *(Suzuki)*

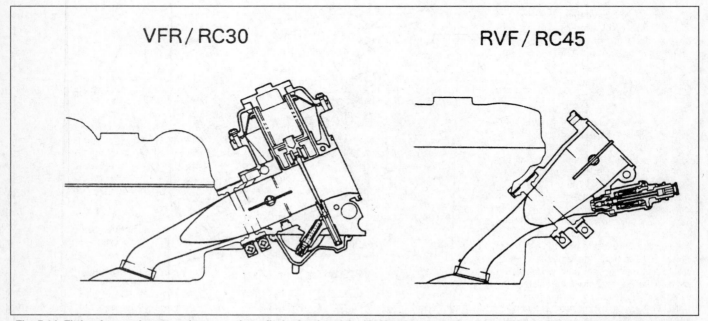

VFR / RC30

RVF / RC45

Fig. 5.14 Fitting four carburettors between the cylinder banks of the V4 Hondas was even more difficult. This drawing shows how fuel injection allowed them to use bigger throttles, with shorter and straighter intake tracts *(Honda)*

Why take so long? The bike manufacturers, particularly in Japan, are nothing if not pragmatic and tight-fisted. If they didn't swing wholeheartedly to fuel injection it means there was either a problem using it in a bike environment or it had nothing to offer over carburettors (or they had an agreement with the carburettor manufacturers).

Early on the problem was that computer memory was both bulky and expensive and processor speed was slow. To get a true picture of what the engine is doing, the CPU needs to sample the sensors many times faster than the engine is turning. At 12,000 rpm the crank goes through 200 cycles per second, so the CPU needs to look at some of the channels 1000 to 2000 times per second and this is just to make sure it has the correct information in order to make its calculation and send the appropriate signals to the injectors and ignition. Also the costs of developing entirely new systems must have outweighed any benefits in new-bike development (it's tempting to think that a programmable CPU must be easier to tune from scratch than a bank of carburettors, with myriad combinations of fuel jets, air jets and needle tapers, especially when the fuelling also has to be trimmed to cope with noise tests and exhaust emissions).

As the years went by, these possible problems must have receded dramatically, the car manufacturers were using injection on an increasing number of models (many of which had the hypercritical catalytic converters in their exhausts and so needed the unvarying precision offered by injection). Yet 20 years after Kawasaki developed the Z1000, the only models offered with fuel injection were those with special needs. The turbocharged bikes of the early '80s provide a clue: fuel injection gave them a neater method than alternatively blowing or sucking through conventional carburettors.

Similarly, big capacity, high performance twins need big intakes and it is difficult to tune large carburettors to work well at high load and low speed, because the air velocity may drop below the point at which it can both lift fuel through the jets and atomise it successfully. Fuel injection on BMW twins, Guzzis, Ducatis, the Suzuki TL1000s and the Aprilia RSV confirms this.

The V4 Hondas had the different problem of fitting four carburettors into the limited space of the V-angle, and then another problem of heat from the banks of cylinders causing vapour locks in the fuel lines or boiling fuel in the float bowls. Typically this sort of problem gets worse when the motor is asked to idle after a long, fast run, when there is a large heat soak from the engine and minimal fuel flow, so the fuel is subjected to heat for the longest possible time. Honda also used fuel injection on their experimental EXP-2 two-stroke, with activated radical combustion, which needed computer control of both fuelling and ignition to function properly.

Clearly these requirements only apply to certain engine layouts in certain operating conditions.

Equally clearly, the manufacturers see no advantage in fuel injection until these requirements arise. Years ago there used to be claims that fuel injection offered better power, better economy, smoother running – all the usual things, which, simply, were not true. If the right mixture arrives in the cylinder, the engine doesn't care whether it comes from an injector, a carburettor or Father Christmas.

Improvements

Some of the claims had a basis in truth, from very early tests on car engines where, typically one carburettor would feed four cylinders through a manifold with different branch lengths to the intake ports and with cylinders running at different temperatures. Those carburettors also had problems from high under-bonnet temperatures and from braking and cornering forces causing swill in the float bowls, so that subsequent running was a bit erratic. Working on any fuel system to address any of these problems would create improvements, as the testers usually acknowledged, so it wasn't a surprise that fuel injection gave increased performance and response.

But compared to the highly developed carburettors on late-1990s bikes, there isn't much that injectors can offer. Then, around 1998, bikes arrived at a point where carburettors could do no more. In order to develop these engines further it was necessary to use straighter intakes with larger diameters. And whole-bike development demands that the engine is shaped to permit the shortest wheelbase and positioned to give the best weight distribution. This means the venturi or throttle body region needs to be very compact, to avoid running into the intake cam box. It must also be able to work at steep downdraught angles and carry on working with acceleration and deceleration values of more than 1g. Finally, big bike engine performance was calling for intakes larger than 38 – 40 mm diameter, the practical maximum for efficient carburation. Both Mikuni and Keihin developed 41 mm flat slide carburettors for race applications but it can be seen as a tentative, last-ditch step… and a small step when big twins like the TL1000 and RSV appeared with 51 mm throttle bodies. [There are bigger carburettors that work well, but they are not slide carbs, they do not flow as much air as slide carbs and they are physically very big.]

Given these conditions, carburettors had already reached their limits as far as the highest performance bikes were concerned: witness the 1999 Suzuki GSX1300R, which makes about 150 bhp at 9800 rpm and uses fuel injection with 46 mm throttle bodies. That's 38 bhp per cylinder, while the Aprilia RSV, making closer to 60 bhp per cylinder uses 51 mm intakes. Or Yamaha's R7, which

Injector types

See Figs. 5.15, 5.16, 5.17 and 5.18

Bosch use several types of injector, varying in the way fuel is supplied and in the nozzle that delivers the fuel. In all types an electrical solenoid creates a magnetic field that lifts the central valve needle against spring pressure. The movement is typically 60 – 100 μm, which indicates the type of tolerance to which the injector is made and how it may be affected by the smallest amount of wear or varnish build-up.

Lifting the tapered needle from its seat allows the high-pressure fuel to flow through the orifice which both meters the amount of fuel and creates the spray pattern, whose job is to atomise the fuel and mix it completely with the air flow.

The ring-gap type of nozzle has a parallel bore and the needle valve has an extension (called a pintle) inside the bore. The end of the pintle is machined into a lip which makes the fuel flow break up. In other designs, the fuel is sprayed on to a plate or disc with one or more orifices to control the spray pattern, or even create two sprays (usually where the injector is feeding a four-valve cylinder head and directs a spray at each of the intake valves). In general, a wider spray pattern will introduce the fuel to more air but will also tend to wet the walls of the intake tract, losing some of the fuel for that cycle (which may either evaporate and return to the stream in later cycles or may run into the cylinder in liquid blobs).

There is another type of injector, called air-shrouded. In this design air is bled from upstream of the throttle valve and delivered to a calibrated opening on the injector disc, where it mixes with the fuel to improve the atomised spray. Its function depends on the design of the air intake in order to get the right pressure drop between the air bleed and the injector nozzle, which means this type usually works best at part-load.

Fuel is supplied to the injectors either as 'top feed' or 'bottom feed'. Top feed is a connector, sealed by an O-ring, which goes to the fuel rail. Its advantage is that the injector can be placed some way from the rail, in the best position on the throttle body.

Bottom feed is where the injector body is carried in the fuel rail and is immersed in fuel, making a compact arrangement which gives good hot-starting and response. It is also a convenient way to carry injectors that are not mounted in the throttle body, eg those that spray directly into the open bellmouth.

The response time quoted for Bosch injectors is between 1.5 and 1.8 ms, with a control frequency of 3 – 125 Hz, depending on the type and the engine's load/speed conditions.

is admittedly a race bike. But where Yamaha saw fit to use 40 mm carburettors on the 1998, 140 bhp, 1000 cc R1, they moved to injection and 46 mm throttle bodies on the 1999, 750 cc R7, which, although smaller in displacement, was intended to have the potential for more than 140 bhp.

Because injection has to be used to accommodate the performance, it will undoubtedly appear on more bikes. As it becomes commonplace (and electronics become cheaper and smaller) it will be just as easy to use it on humbler machines, which would be equally happy with carburettors. At this stage there will be little point having separate teams to develop some bikes with carburettors and others with fuel injection, so injection will spread to all except the smallest and cheapest bikes. The process will be accelerated by any other special requirements, like tougher emission laws.

5   System details and components

The systems haven't changed, in principle, since the early versions in the 1980s. There is a fuel pump, usually in the fuel tank, which delivers fuel at a constant pressure of 3 – 4 bar to a rail from which all the injectors are supplied. At the end of the rail there is a pressure regulator, which lifts off when the pressure goes above the top limit and returns excess fuel to the tank. This fuel circuit needs to have enough volume so that an injector opening does not have a noticeable effect on the fuel pressure.

There is a fuel line to each injector, which consists of a needle valve held closed by a spring. It is opened by an electrical solenoid, allowing fuel to flow through the nozzle, into the intake tract. The design of the valve and nozzle is critical: it must not wear, it must not get clogged by the varnish left when fuel evaporates and it must spray an optimum pattern of fuel. The spray has to be finely atomised and diverge at a wide enough angle

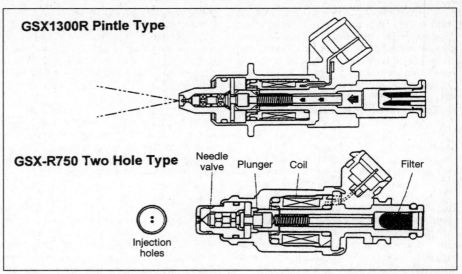

GSX1300R Pintle Type

GSX-R750 Two Hole Type

Needle valve   Plunger   Coil   Filter

Injection holes

Fig. 5.15 While all injectors work on the same solenoid/needle valve principle, there are various designs giving different spray patterns and atomisation characteristics (*Suzuki*)

to mix fuel with as much air as possible, yet not so wide that it wets the walls of the tract. Usually the spray pattern is conical, aimed at the intake valve, diverging so it is about the same diameter as the valve when it reaches it.

The amount of fuel delivered depends on the discharge characteristics of the nozzle (constant), the fuel pressure (constant) and the time the valve is opened (controlled by an electrical pulse sent from the CPU to the solenoid in each injector). The regulator keeps the fuel pressure constant, but the air pressure inside the intake tract varies with engine speed and throttle position, so the regulator's reference pressure is usually connected to one of the intakes, downstream of the throttle valves. That is, the system will supply fuel at, say, 3 bar over the manifold pressure, not above ambient. This is essential with supercharged engines.

Air flow is regulated by the rider, using butterfly throttle valves like those in CV carburettors, although any type of valve could be used – in some high performance car applications there is a flat air slide carried on

roller bearings or a barrel valve. This is a rotating valve with a hole the same size as the 'venturi' bored in it so that in the WOT position there is a completely smooth, unobstructed passage. Turning it through 90° blocks the 'venturi' completely. Although very efficient at WOT, it disrupts part-throttle flow more than the other types.

Guillotine slides and butterfly valves have exactly the same advantages and disadvantages as they do in carburettors. The slides give better air flow and are more amenable to resonance tuning, but they are prone to stick and need heavy return springs. Butterfly valves create more obstruction to airflow but they offer a short, light, throttle action and minimum throttle body height/width.

To open the solenoid for the correct amount of time to deliver the right amount of fuel, the CPU needs to know how much air is flowing this cycle and how much air is going to flow next cycle (ie whether the engine is in a steady cruise, accelerating or decelerating). It also needs to monitor dangerous conditions such as knock, running lean, running rich, approaching the safe rev limit and so on,

Fig. 5.16 Injectors simply plug into the throttle body and fuel supply, using O-rings to seal. This is a Denso 'top feed' type, in which the fuel is delivered at the opposite end to the nozzle

Fig. 5.17 This is the 'bottom feed' type of injector. The whole body is plugged into the fuel rail and is surrounded by fuel, which helps to cool the injector

Fig. 5.18 A selection of different nozzle designs

because most of these can be averted by altering the mixture strength, changing the ignition timing or cutting the ignition on one or more cylinders.

There are two basic ways the CPU can collect its information. One is to measure the air flow and this, plus a few more details is all it needs. The second seems a bit more complicated from a human point of view but works better electronically: this is to monitor more things and from this data calculate the air flow (and rate of change of air flow).

Air flow measurement

The tricky part is building a small, accurate flow meter that can survive the environment. Kawasaki's Z1000-H had an extension to its air box with a flap like a letter-box entry. The more air flow, the more the flap was lifted and this had a potentiometer to measure its position and report back to the CPU. It obviously restricted the air flow.

Ducati's 851 had a much more elegant system called a hot wire flow meter. This involves a single strand of wire, strung across the entry to one intake, carrying an electric current which heats it a certain amount above air temperature. Its resistance varies with its temperature and the air flow cools it, so when it needs more current to maintain the temperature there must be greater air flow. Once it has been calibrated, measuring the current through it gives the mass air flow.

Mapping

See Figs. 5.19 and 5.20

It turned out to be just as easy to calibrate

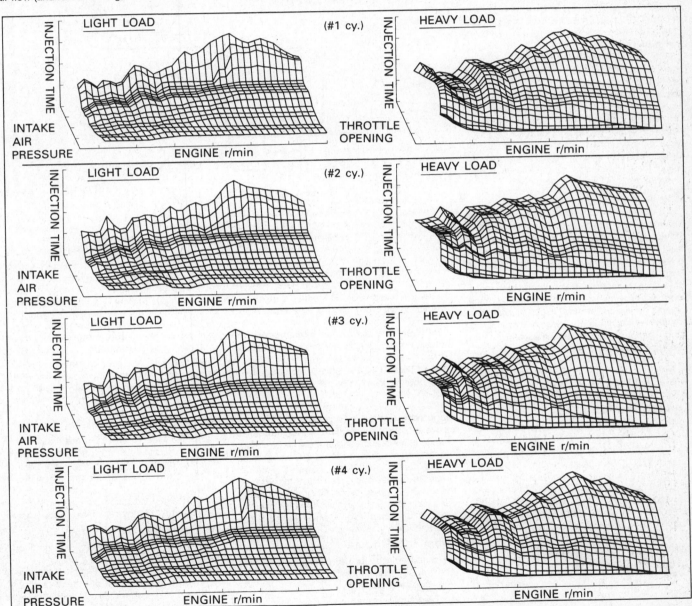

Fig. 5.19 Three-dimensional maps are a graphic way to show the data tables which the CPU uses to calculate the fuel injection quantity

The GSX-R750W has two maps for each cylinder, one for light load (which is measured by intake air pressure) and one for wider throttle positions (which is measured by throttle angle). Being able to optimise the fuelling on each cylinder allows for slight difference in temperature and the dimensions of the intake and exhaust systems (Suzuki)

the entire engine. If there were sensors to measure air box temperature and pressure, throttle position and engine rpm, it would be possible to predict air flow just as accurately. The result is a multi-dimensional map, programmed into the CPU, that is essentially a table in which you can look up the basic combination of rpm and throttle opening and see how much fuel is needed. In practice there is usually a default setting, which is good enough to keep the engine running, albeit at reduced power, if there should be a fault in the wiring or one of the sensors. This default is then trimmed and refined by the data the CPU receives from all the sensors until it results in the perfect mixture to meet the circumstances.

Both systems should be able to cope with changes such as different altitude, an air filter becoming blocked or the intake picking up more air because of the bike's speed. There are several more refinements because the CPU needs to know if there are any special conditions such as starting, cold running or if the engine has run into conditions that weren't foreseen and the mixture has started to run rich or lean. Here's a range of sensors, not all of which are used in all applications:

Engine speed

A magnetic or Hall-effect sensor, triggered by teeth or regular gaps on a wheel mounted on the crankshaft. Sends a digital signal (frequency) that represents crank speed back to the CPU. If there is one larger gap between teeth, this can identify a certain position, eg TDC. By comparing current speed to previous speeds, the software can calculate how much the engine is accelerating. It can also send a signal to a warning light (gearshift or overrev light) when a pre-set speed is reached.

Engine position

From a camshaft drive (at half engine speed) this sensor lets the CPU know which stroke a four-stroke engine is on.

Throttle position

A potentiometer connected to the throttle linkage, sends back an analogue signal (a voltage, typically 0.5V at zero throttle rising to 3.5V at WOT). This gives the throttle opening and by comparing it to previous figures the software can calculate the rate of opening. An alternative is to have a pressure sensor connected across the intake (downstream of the throttle valve) and the airbox. This is more accurate at low throttle openings and sometimes both types are used.

Airbox pressure

This is the fundamental force encouraging air to go into the engine but it will vary according to ambient pressure, resonance tuning, state of the air filter and forward motion of the bike. Pressure sensors are usually made of a thick diaphragm with piezo-electric resistors or strain gauges on it, wired in a bridge circuit. Deformation of the

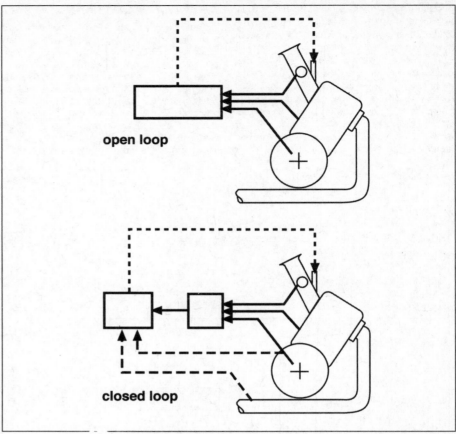

Fig. 5.20 The two methods of control

In open loop operation, sensors measure engine speed and throttle opening (and other parameters). From this, the CPU calculates the air flow, the necessary fuel flow and sends a signal to the injector

In closed loop control, the same process happens but now the results are also monitored by sensors – typically to check the exhaust gas and the engine speed. Depending on this feedback, the injector signal for the next cycle is modified, to bring the mixture back to the required AF ratio. Closed loop control is used to keep AF ratios close to stoichiometric (because catalysts only work in a very narrow range of mixtures) and sometimes to control idle speed

diaphragm caused by a pressure difference between one side and the other causes a change in resistance and in the voltage output of the bridge circuit, which can be calibrated in pressure units. Some sensors connect pressure to just one side of the diaphragm, the other being open to ambient pressure; some connect two pressure sources to either side of the diaphragm, and measure the difference between them.

Airbox temperature

Combined with the airbox pressure, this lets the CPU calculate the air density on its way into the engine.

Ambient pressure

With temperature, lets the CPU calculate base air density.

Ambient temperature

With pressure, lets the CPU calculate base air density.

Intake pressure

Lets the CPU know when the engine is on the overrun, so it can cut off the fuel supply. Also may be used to measure throttle position at light loads and to derive the difference in pressure between the airbox and the intake tract. This sensor is essential on supercharged engines to measure the boost.

Engine temperature

Warns the CPU of cold running conditions, when the engine will need a richer mixture. The *cold start* control on injected engines is merely a device to open the throttles slightly to raise the idle speed. Mixture changes are handled automatically. The CPU can also send a signal to a warning light if the engine temperature exceeds a preset value.

Fuel pressure

Part of the built-in diagnostic/safety features – if the fuel pressure goes outside the system's limits, the injectors will supply a mixture that is too rich or lean because they depend upon a constant pressure while their open time determines the amount of fuel flow.

Starter motor

If the starter is engaged, the CPU knows the motor is being cranked and not idling, and so will need a richer mixture.

Knock sensor

Usually a piezo-electric crystal, which gives an electrical signal when strained (the same phenomenon is used to make the spark in some cigarette lighters), screwed into the cylinder block. The vibration caused by detonation generates a signal to the CPU, which can then retard the ignition or richen the mixture, sometimes on individual cylinders.

λ-sensor (excess air) – see Note 2

See Figs. 5.21, 5.22, 5.23 and 5.24

Fitted into the exhaust header pipe, it gives a signal when the mixture strays from stoichiometric and the CPU immediately corrects the mixture back until the signal disappears. This is called closed-loop control, while the systems described previously are known as open-loop control.

Fuel level

Either a float arm connected to a potentiometer, or a heated element which is cooled by the fuel. Gives a warning when the fuel reaches a critical level.

Wheel speed

Usually a Hall effect trigger picking up a signal from the teeth of a sprocket, mounting bolts on a sprocket or brake rotor, or from the teeth on a transmission gear. Lets the CPU know the road speed and, by dividing it into the rpm, which gear is engaged.

Battery voltage

The CPU monitors this as part of its diagnostic operation. It and its sensors usually work from a 5V supply, although other parts, like the fuel pump and ignition, need full battery voltage. Also the injector solenoid's opening and closing rates are affected by battery voltage, so the CPU can compensate for voltage fluctuations by altering the duration. The same applies to the ignition system, which needs a longer dwell when the voltage is low.

Virtual channels

In addition to reading the channels supplied by the sensors before it makes a calculation, the CPU can also derive data from what it has been given. Examples are: the ability to calculate rate of change of engine speed and throttle position; to integrate wheel speed over time to determine the distance travelled; to use this to calculate fuel consumption; to compare engine speed with wheel speed to determine what gear the bike is in or if it is standing still.

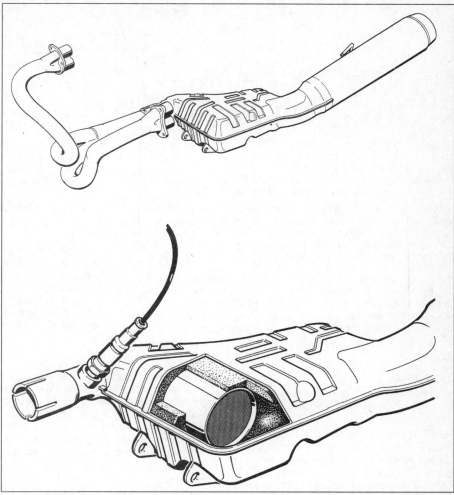

Fig. 5.21 Exhaust catalyst and λ-sensor used by BMW on their twin-cylinder engines *(BMW)*

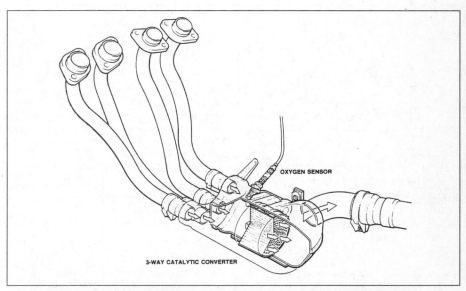

Fig. 5.22 Catalytic converter and λ-sensor used on the GTS1000 *(Yamaha)*

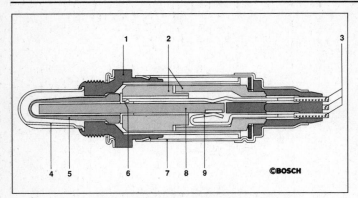

Fig. 5.23 Construction of a heated λ-sensor

The sensors, as well as the catalysts, have a critical operating range and must be positioned so they are not too close to the engine in case they get too hot and not too far away in case they cool below their working temperature. During cold running, the sensor is heated electrically (Bosch)

1 Sensor housing
2 Protective ceramic tube
3 Electrical cable
4 Protective slotted tube
5 Active sensor ceramic
6 Contact section
7 Protective sleeve
8 Heating element
9 Clamp terminals for heating element

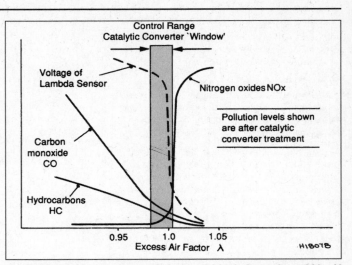

Fig. 5.24 The λ-sensor voltage drops suddenly from about 800 mV to about 100 mV when the mixture goes from about 5% rich to 5% lean. Exhaust catalysts need to operate in this narrow window because when the mixture goes outside it they cannot control emissions. If the mixture is more than a few per cent rich, hydrocarbon and carbon monoxide levels rise dramatically (as shown) while a lean mixture produces increasing amounts of NO$_x$

Tilt switch

Detects extreme angle of bank, ie when the bike has fallen over, and switches off the fuel pump and ignition.

Ignition key

An anti-theft feature. As the ignition key is pushed into the lock it operates a switch that sends a predetermined low voltage to the CPU. If the correct voltage isn't received before switching on (and sending full battery voltage to the CPU) then the unit will not switch on. An alternative method is to have a chip embedded in the key, which sends a coded signal to the CPU. Both methods prevent hot-wiring because the system cannot be armed if the correct key is not present. These methods are not confined to fuel-injected machines, as they are also used on carburetted bikes with digitally-controlled ignition.

Idle control

See Figs. 5.25 and 5.26

Sensors such as speed and throttle position are needed to detect idle conditions and then there are various ways to provide the no-load mixture, usually with an air supply that by-passes the throttle. This can be adjusted like a carburettor idle system or it can have a valve that varies the air flow automatically. Using closed-loop feedback from the engine speed sensor, air flow is increased or decreased to bring the speed back to the required tick-over. Another way to do this is to have a movable throttle stop, connected to a servo motor and use closed-loop control to maintain the idle speed. In conjunction with an engine temperature sensor, this can automatically provide a fast idle during cold-running. It's also possible to have a closed-loop control which senses crank speed and advances the ignition timing when the speed begins to drop. This produces more torque, which speeds the engine up.

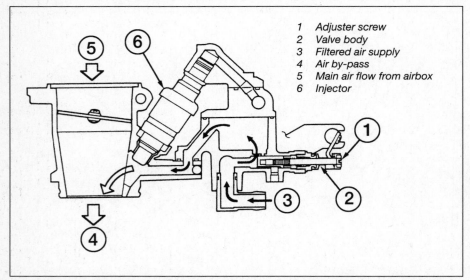

1 Adjuster screw
2 Valve body
3 Filtered air supply
4 Air by-pass
5 Main air flow from airbox
6 Injector

Fig. 5.25 The air by-pass used to control idling on the Honda RC45. When the throttle is closed, air flow is regulated by an (adjustable) valve (Honda)

Fig. 5.26 This solenoid valve can be operated electrically to control idle by-pass air flow

The obvious way to control idle, by varying the fuel flow, is not used because of emissions control regulations.

Controlling idle on bike engines is relatively easy because there are few extra loads that come in: the most that's likely to happen is the extra electrical load of a headlamp, stop lamp, etc, plus the considerable change in friction/oil drag as an engine warms up. On cars and other vehicles there are greater loads from things like air conditioning and power steering and it is necessary to detect these extra loads before they make the engine stumble.

> **Note 2** *Three-way catalytic converters have a very narrow operating window and if the mixture strength strays beyond this region the catalyst will not work properly. If it richens to λ < 0.98 then hydrocarbon and carbon monoxide emissions are not cleaned effectively. If it leans beyond λ > 1.01 then NO_x emissions are barely affected. Closed-loop control can keep the engine within this narrow working range. One type of λ-sensor consists of a ceramic, zirconium dioxide, body with a gas-permeable layer of platinum over it. The sensor is mounted so that part of it is in the exhaust stream and the rest is open to atmospheric air. When the ceramic is up to 300°C it conducts oxygen ions, producing a voltage across the platinum electrodes if there's an imbalance between the oxygen available at either end. There's a sudden jump in this voltage as the exhaust λ passes through the value 1.0 (from no-oxygen to some-oxygen) and this sudden change is used as the signal to the CPU.*

General arrangement

In a typical system there will be a default map based on throttle opening and rpm (often called an α-n system). This will have a correction factor applied to it for battery voltage and another based on information gleaned from whatever sensors are fitted.

If a fault in the wiring or an individual sensor means the correction factor would be incorrect, then the system defaults to the basic map, to provide limited, get-you-home, running.

Advantages

Apart from its ability to control mixtures accurately for emission control purposes, fuel injection has a few other advantages over carburettors. There are no float bowls, so no swill problems and no vapour lock problems. The fuel system can operate at any angle the vehicle can. The throttle bodies are more compact than carburettors and are easier to install in short, straight intake tracts, regardless of the cylinder configuration. This in turn leaves more space for cam boxes and airboxes, so by giving the designer a freer hand it permits further engine development.

Where large cylinders are used, a large diameter throttle body can be designed to permit the necessary air flow for maximum power yet still provide good driveability and response at low load and low speed because the air velocity is not needed to draw fuel into the venturi or to atomise it; the air only has to carry the fuel spray with it into the engine.

Air flow which pulses back and forth along the inlet tract tends to pull fuel from a carburettor's jets with each pass, so the mixture becomes richer each time. This does not happen with fuel injection.

Finally, the injection system already monitors engine conditions and it can prevent the engine going into potentially dangerous regions of speed, knock, temperature or mixture strength. The same electronics usually have a self-diagnostic mode to warn of faults. The instrument display can have various screens through which the rider or driver can scroll, showing things like trip mileage, average speed, fuel consumption, ambient temperature, time of day, tank range left, peak speed, peak rpm etc. With the addition of non-volatile memory, it can store data on engine running time, fuel consumption etc to provide an operational history and give the user a warning of impending services, which some car systems already do.

6 Further development

In the same way that the CPU can send out signals to an instrument display, warning lights or a rev limiter, it can be made to send a signal whenever a particular set of circumstances arise, eg when the engine reaches certain combinations of load and speed. The signal can then activate other equipment. Examples exist on carburetted models, too: Yamaha used a speed sensor to switch on the servo motor that operated the variable exhaust geometry in their RD350YPVS and later in the four-stroke EXUP systems. Suzuki had a solenoid-operated valve that brought in a second air jet on their RGV.

The kind of ancillary equipment includes:

Variable geometry exhaust

As already pioneered by Yamaha on two- and four-stroke engines, altering the height of a two-stroke's exhaust port or the effective length of an exhaust system means that it will work in harmony with the engine at more than one speed range (unlike fixed geometry, which can only 'work' at one speed). The CPU's sensors allow the operating conditions to be monitored more closely, making more efficient use of the equipment than a simple on/off switch triggered at a fixed speed threshold.

Exhaust gas recirculation (EGR)

A system to bleed a carefully controlled amount of exhaust gas back into the intake. Initially used to improve exhaust emissions, particularly on diesels, although later tests showed there are potential uses in spark ignition engines, to lower combustion temperature, control knock and to reduce throttling losses on part load.

Variable geometry intake

As with exhaust systems, the intake lengths can be tuned to increase torque at a certain speed but this doesn't work at other speeds and can reduce an engine's torque outside the working range. There are several designs which change the intake proportions, letting it work effectively over a wide range of speeds.

Traction control

By sensing the speed of a driven wheel against that of a non-driven wheel (or ground-tracking radar in the case of some car systems), wheelspin can be detected and controlled by reducing engine power (or in the case of cars, by operating a control on the differential gear to transmit more torque to the non-spinning wheel). Some cars also have yaw control: by comparing the speeds of pairs of wheels, steer angle and yaw (rate of turn),

How the fuel quantity is calculated and then 'trimmed'

Fuel quantity	injector open duration and fuel pressure
	rpm and throttle position x voltage correction x correction factor
Correction factor	air density [intake air temperature and pressure]
	intake vacuum [detects overrun, idle conditions and small throttle opening]
	coolant temperature [detects cold running or overheating]
	excess air [detects rich/weak AF ratio from exhaust gas]

the system can detect when the car is starting to spin and correct it by applying brake pressure to the appropriate wheel.

Variable valve timing

Data acquired by the sensors can provide electronic control to alter the valve lift, duration and timing in certain VVT designs. In other experimental types, the valve lift and timing have been used to control engine speed and load (in place of the throttle valve). In this case, the throttle twistgrip would be connected to the CPU, which would sense the operator's wishes, alter the valve lift/timing to the required setting and simultaneously provide the correct fuel flow.

Turbocharger boost control

Electronic input is added to the pressure-sensing wastegate control, using closed-loop feedback to maintain constant boost pressure or to avoid conditions such as knock, high exhaust gas temperature, compressor surge etc. This fine control gives better fuel efficiency and faster throttle response.

Knock control

Using sensors that pick up the vibration caused by detonation, or simply to avoid running conditions like high combustion temperature or high boost pressure, the CPU retards ignition timing, richens the mixture or could operate some other function such as variable geometry, wastegate control, EGR etc.

Speed control

Works in the same way as a rev limiter but senses wheel speed rather than crank speed. Race cars already use it to limit their speed in the pit lane. Some Japanese-specification bikes have an ignition cut-out set to operate at just above the national speed limit. There is a lot of experimental work going into 'smart' highways, which can communicate with the vehicles on them. Part of this is to enforce speed limits and to slow down vehicles in bad weather or where there is traffic congestion.

By 1999, most of these were only possibilities for production bike engines, although they have all been used experimentally or in car and truck engines.

7 Tuning

Most production systems only allow a limited amount of adjustment, typically to synchronise the throttle valves and adjust the idle settings. For some systems there is software that can be used to re-map the Eprom chip, so that the fuelling can be optimised for new conditions – such as a new exhaust system or other engine modifications. Even where the CPU is re-programmable, the software may be difficult or very expensive to obtain and is often restricted to franchised dealers.

One step down from fully programmable systems, there are units that can reprogram the CPU to something like ±10% of the fuel flow, the equivalent of 2 or 3 main jet sizes in each direction. Yoshimura supply equipment like this for some of the fuel injected Suzukis.

The next option is an aftermarket, plug-in electronic circuit which intercepts the input/output signals from the CPU and allows you to modify them to alter the AF ratio at various speed/load stations.

Finally there is the option to replace the chip with another that has been mapped either by the manufacturer or by a third party supplier.

If none of these options are available it is still possible to fool the CPU into doing something it didn't intend. One method is to use an adjustable pressure regulator to raise or lower the pressure in the fuel rail. This is not a good way to alter the fuelling because a higher pressure will increase fuel delivery everywhere, at all speeds and all loads, which is not usually what you want to achieve. Similarly a lower pressure will weaken the fuel mixture everywhere. Raising the fuel pressure also makes the pump run hotter and most pumps that run in the 3 – 4 bar region have a pressure relief valve which lifts when the pressure reaches 5 bar, to avoid the risks of overheating the pump.

If the engine temperature sensor's output range is measured, it can be replaced by a variable resistor covering a similar range and this can be used to fool the CPU into thinking the temperature is low and therefore richening the mixture. This and altering the fuel pressure are only last resorts when there is no other possibility of altering the mixture.

Chapter 6
Carburettor tuning

Refer also to Chapters 7 and 8 Construction and adjustment

Contents

1 Introduction

The carburettor's job is to regulate the total air flow to control engine power and deliver the optimum AF ratio to suit the occasion. Tuning the carburettor is a matter of finding this optimum mixture, first for each speed station and then making sure the carburettor can progress smoothly from one station to the next. As both load and speed are variable, fuel flow makes this a three-dimensional array with a vast number of possible combinations.

The only way to make sense of it is to break it down into manageable steps – coarse steps at first, because we can go over it again in finer steps later – and to rule out any other dimensions, like temperature changes, by keeping all the ambient conditions constant.

The next requirement is to run the tests in a logical sequence and only to change one thing at a time. The final rule is to remember that, where engine safety is concerned, richer is better than weaker. Weak mixtures are good at burning all the fuel but in doing so they can (a) raise the gas pressure too quickly, causing the remaining fuel to detonate, or (b) liberate the fuel's heat too quickly, causing engine temperatures to rise, which can damage parts like pistons, valves and spark plugs, while hot components can cause pre-ignition in the next cycle, raising temperatures further.

Setting up an unknown carburettor from scratch is a formidable task but fortunately the worst that most of us are likely to face is to re-tune a carburettor to suit a modified engine. Whether it is the carburettor from that engine or from a (presumably) more powerful machine, it will already have settings that are known to work. Carburettor manufacturers, importers, and jet kit manufacturers are usually helpful in making recommendations, given criteria like the proposed engine size, speed and power delivery. Tuning procedures are the same for slide and CV carburettors, with only minor changes caused by the different methods of operation.

Safety procedures

⚠️ **When working on machines in test houses you should follow all safety procedures carefully, particularly those with respect to fire, moving behind the dyno while it is running and leaving tools or other loose equipment on the bike or the test bed, where they could fall off and hit a moving part.**

Gasoline vapour is heavier than air and tends to settle at ground level, so all electrical connections, sockets, switches etc should be kept above waist height, and ventilation/ extraction fans should be used whenever burnt or unburnt fumes are likely to gather. Small concentrations of carbon monoxide are fatal (once absorbed by the bloodstream it prevents the blood from carrying oxygen) and other fuel by-products attack the nervous system and liver. Some are carcinogenic.

As if that weren't enough, sound levels above about 90 dB can cause permanent hearing damage and as even silenced bikes inside a test house can produce well over 110 dB on load, you should always use ear defenders.

2 Basic settings

The first step is to get the carburettor in a safe, workable state, which means the engine can run and that anything to do with high loads is set too rich. Then go though the following steps:

1 Idle settings – not so much to get the best tickover but to let the engine pick up without hesitation from a closed throttle. In the beginning this is most important simply to get under way but as the other settings come together there are conditions at higher revs, where you've closed the throttle and then need to open it gradually, as if at the apex of a corner, when the engine needs to pick up smoothly. The pilot jet controls this region and it supplies fuel throughout the rest of the rev/throttle range so it's important to get this right early on, and with any luck it won't need to be changed again.

2 At the other end of the scale, the main jet and air jet control WOT and this should be tested next, as long as the part-throttle settings let the engine run tolerably well. Start with WOT runs at the lowest revs the engine will accept and change the main jet to get this right or slightly rich. Then progress to higher speeds and use the air jet to control the mixture. If this isn't possible, or if you need very small air jets, repeat using a bigger main jet. Sometimes it just isn't possible – in one of their race kit manuals, Honda recommend a size zero air jet (ie the passage is blocked off completely).

3 Go through the part-load settings, at different (but steady) speeds and different throttle openings. Make a chart of where the engine goes rich or weak (along the same lines as Fig. 6.1), which will suggest the best components to change for maximum effect. Correct any obvious deficiencies but don't try to get too precise.

4 From the data gathered so far, make a decision about the state of the intake and exhaust geometry. Does the engine need longer intake stacks or a bigger airbox? Is the exhaust responsible for any flat spots or holes in the torque curve? Is it worth altering the ignition or cam timing? Run some experiments to find out. Carburation can be used to compensate for poor exhaust and intake design, but only up to a point. If you have the ability to change intake or exhaust dimensions, now's the time to do it.

These tests beg the questions: 'What is rich? What is lean? How is it measured?'

Chemically, a rich mixture will produce hydrocarbons and carbon monoxide in the exhaust. A weak mixture will leave oxygen in the exhaust. Sensors can detect these things. From an engineering point of view, the optimum mixture is the one that gives the greatest torque or the best fuel economy, depending on whether the engine is running on high load or light load. To determine this it's necessary to run the engine on a range of mixtures, measuring its torque and the fuel flow.

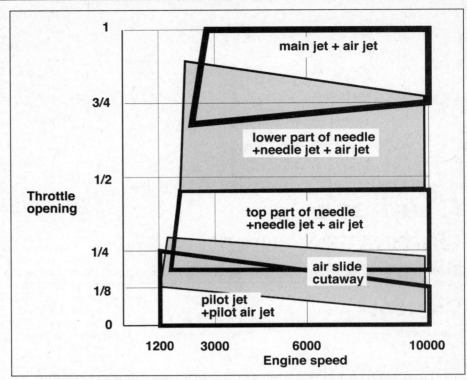

Fig. 6.1 Carburettor parts and the regions of load and speed they dominate

This is a general principle, it's not fixed and will vary from machine to machine. Some parts have an effect through the entire range, for example the pilot jet contributes at all speeds and throttle openings, but you wouldn't use it to alter the mixture at full power

Some very high output engines use fuel for cooling: most of the fuel is burnt, the rest is merely evaporated, taking its latent heat with it and keeping critical parts like pistons at a safe working temperature. Chemically speaking, this is a rich mixture but it permits the engine to produce more power than the chemically **correct** mixture. For this reason you should keep increasing main jet or decreasing air jet size until the motor is obviously over-rich at peak speed.

5 Repeat steps 1 to 3.

6 By now the engine should be running acceptably, in an overall sense. Go though the part-throttle settings, working from where the engine is best, towards the regions where it is worst. It helps to keep a clear record of the settings and the results, so that you can keep returning to the best settings. Where previous tests concentrated on maximum output, you are now looking for best pick-up, smoothest running and best fuel efficiency, which aren't so easy to measure.

7 Fine tune the whole sequence. Synchronise the carburettors (see Chapter 11). Find the optimum idle settings.

These steps are covered in more detail further on, depending on the methods and equipment available to you. The methods are, broadly:

a) *Track or road test (last resort, this is very difficult and impossible without highly developed skills and aptitude).*

b) *Track with specialised equipment (still difficult, because it's impossible to control the ambient conditions and you may have to do whole laps, whether the engine is running well or not).*

c) *Dynamometer with fuel flow meters and/or exhaust gas analysis. Best option by far.*

Carburettor size

The venturi size must be big enough to supply the quantity of air the engine needs to develop full power. However, the bigger it is, the less well it will perform at low speed, narrowing the useful power band and not giving such precise throttle response or good engine pick-up. The size tends to be a compromise between good acceleration, clean running and full power. As a rule of thumb:

bhp of cylinders supplied by	min slide carb size 1 carb	min CV carb size
5	14 mm	
10	22 mm	
15	26 mm	
20	30 mm	34 mm
25	32 mm	36 mm
30	34 mm	38 mm
35	36 mm	40 mm
40	38 mm	
45	40 mm	

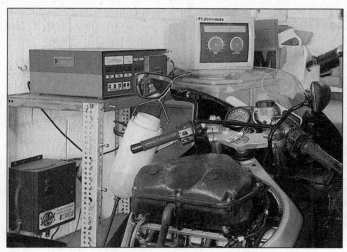

Fig. 6.2 Typical test house set-up

The bike's tank has been removed and it is being supplied by a remote tank hooked over the mirror/fairing bracket so the fuel level is roughly the same as in the proper tank. The instrument immediately behind the remote tank is an exhaust gas analyser which gives readings for hydrocarbons, carbon monoxide and carbon dioxide

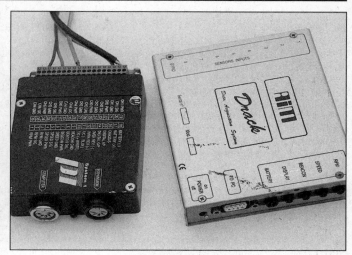

Fig. 6.3 Data recorders

These are fairly basic types: System 1 made by Pi Research (left) and Drack, by the Italian AIM srl. Both record engine rpm, wheel speed and lap times, and the Drack logger can accept eight analogue sensors plus a gyroscope, while the Pi version has six analogue channels

---

3 Dynamometer testing

See Figs. 6.2 and 6.3

If we cover dyno testing first, you'll see what can be achieved and the limitations of track testing will be pretty obvious. There are several types of dyno although the most commonly available, bike-dedicated type is the Dynojet. This is an inertia roller type and models made by Bosch, Factory, Dynopower and Fuchs all work on the same principle, which is that the back wheel drives a roller with typically ½ tonne or 1-tonne mass. As the engine accelerates against this load, a speed sensor on the roller feeds data to a computer. Software then calculates the acceleration and the horsepower needed to

> **Note 1** *John Dalton (1766-1844), derived the law of partial pressures, which states that in a mixture of (ideal) gases, each gas exerts a pressure that it would exert if it alone filled the container, at the same temperature. The pressure of the mixture is the sum of all the partial pressures.*

Correction factors

Engine output depends upon air density and this varies continuously. Higher ambient pressure or lower temperature increase air density, which means an engine will make a little more power. Lower pressure or higher temperature reduce the air density. Humidity (the amount of water vapour in the air) also makes a difference. It exerts its own pressure (called partial pressure (see Note 1) and thus makes the air pressure appear higher) and water molecules displace oxygen molecules, effectively reducing oxygen density if not air density.

The changes are large enough to compare with the type of change you see in carburation tests so, unless all the tests can be completed in the same conditions, it is important to correct for the differences.

Correction factors try to allow for these changes and bring the engine power back to what it would be under standard conditions: typically normal or standard temperature, pressure and humidity at sea level. These values vary with the organisation that has produced the correction factor (examples are SAE J1349, DIN 70020, EC80/1269 and ISO 1585, all of which are available in Dynopower

software). Dynojet software gives a choice of SAE or DIN correction factors. From running different bikes that always gave consistent power, it seems the SAE factor is the most realistic in correcting the output back to the same base level from a variety of weather conditions. This is the SAE correction where cf is the correction factor, p is the dry absolute ambient pressure (inches Hg), and t is the intake air temperature (°F).

$$cf = 1.18 \times \frac{29.92}{p} \times \sqrt{\frac{t + 460}{537}} - 0.18$$

The SAE is an American organisation, which is why the temperature is in Fahrenheit, but as you can see, it is correcting to 29.92 inches of mercury and 537°FABS, or 77°F (25°C).

Altitude makes a considerable difference, and in a country like North America there are significant changes, hence the 'absolute pressure', which is calculated as follows, where p_0 is the absolute pressure (in Hg), p_1 is the relative (ie measured) pressure (in Hg), and h is the altitude in feet above sea level.

$$p_0 = p_1 - \frac{h}{1000}$$

Humidity is measured by a wet and dry bulb thermometer. The wet bulb is whirled around in

the air, which prompts the water to evaporate and thus cool the bulb. The drier the air, the more water will evaporate and the cooler the bulb becomes. The difference between the wet and dry temperatures indicates the relative humidity, which can be converted to the partial pressure of the vapour and incorporated in the correction factor calculation. Humidity changes are significant in the tropics but are generally ignored in Europe. In the UK climate, weather variations account for differences of up to ±3%, rarely more, and most correction factors are not meant to be accurate beyond ±5%.

All of the torque and bhp figures are multiplied by the correction factor to obtain corrected figures (usually written corrected bhp or corr bhp, etc to distinguish them from the raw data). **Note:** *If torque is derived from corrected bhp (or vice versa) then there is no need to apply the correction again.*

If you run tests over several days, you should run the machine on day 2 in a configuration that gave stable results on day 1. This will show whether the correction factor is good, or, if the results are not repeatable, that something else has changed.

overcome the roller's inertia, and can plot this as a graph against wheel speed.

Instruments monitoring air temperature, humidity and barometric pressure can be used to produce a correction factor for air density, based on SAE or DIN standards. Finally, another sensor connected to the ignition system can monitor engine speed (optional but recommended for carburation tests). From this and the horsepower, the software calculates torque, plotting graphs of bhp and torque (corrected or uncorrected) over rpm. Torque is calculated using the following formula, where T is torque in lb-ft, P is power in bhp and N is crank speed in rpm.

$$T = \frac{33000P}{2\pi N}$$

The problem with inertia dynos is they cannot hold the engine at steady revs, which is what you need to do in the initial stages. There are dynos that will do this, either eddy current or water brakes made by Froude, Schenck, Superflow, Factory, Sun etc but those that have to be driven by chain or by shaft from an adapter on the gearbox sprocket, do not match the convenience and speed of simply sitting a complete bike on the dyno and running it.

A few types combine an inertia roller with a controllable load – usually an eddy current generator – and can hold the engine at steady speeds. Some makes of inertia dyno list eddy current generators as optional extras, offering the best of both worlds. One problem here is that when an engine is held at constant speed, its full power output is eventually converted into heat and this heat has to be removed from the test house. Some eddy current machines are liquid cooled, which is the most convenient method. Air-cooled types can create major problems with extra fans and ducts.

Later on in the programme, inertia dynos are excellent tools for running transient tests because the fuel system can be tuned to give the smoothest pick-up and fastest response to changing throttle.

One final distinction between inertia dynos and those that apply a load to the engine becomes important if the engine suffers a mechanical failure like a melted piston, dropped valve or broken connecting rod. Dynos applying a load will simply stop – and the higher the load, the faster they'll stop. Inertia dynos will carry on, driving the engine with their full inertia – the higher the speed, the higher this will be. Until the operator pulls in the clutch and shuts down the engine, this will maximise any damage.

The most useful figures are torque corrected to SAE J1349, over rpm. This correction factor gives a realistic comparison between tests done on different days, as long as the ambient conditions don't vary too much. Be deeply suspicious of anything producing correction factors of more than 5%.

Torque, rather than horsepower, shows fluctuations in air flow more clearly. Where the torque falls, the engine clearly isn't getting enough air or isn't able to burn the right amount of fuel in it. This could either be because it isn't receiving the right amount of fuel or because something else is inhibiting the flow/combustion/heat extraction process. The object of these tests is to identify the region and then identify the cause.

If it is possible to measure fuel flow then this can be used as a straight indication of what's happening (strictly, it should be in weight per unit time, eg g/h, but in practice it is often easier to measure volume flow, eg cc/min or pt/h).

From this more data can be calculated: specific fuel consumption (sfc) or brake specific fuel consumption (bsfc – to show it was obtained from dynamometer tests, although I'm not sure where else you'd get it). This is the fuel flow divided by the power produced, so the units are g/kW-h or, more commonly in the UK, pt/hp-h and is a measure of efficiency: what you have to pay for divided by what you get in return, so the lower the number, the better for you.

Ideally, lower fuel flow is the ultimate target

and, if you were developing a totally new type of engine, this is what you would look for. But conventional engines have well-established limits, so the target is usually to match what is already known to work. Four-stroke engines run with an sfc of about 0.5 pt/hp-h around peak torque, higher at other speeds. Two-strokes run richer, about 0.6 – 0.7 pt/hp-h for roadster models, going up to 0.9 – 1.0 pt/hp-h for race engines although, as explained earlier, this extra fuel is used for cooling rather than combustion.

Knowing these typical values means it is possible to calculate approximate maximum fuel flow, eg a 100 bhp engine at 0.5 pt/hp-h would require 50 pt/h so the capacity of the tap, fuel lines, filter, pump and needle valves must exceed this by a comfortable safety margin – say 20%, giving a figure of 60 pt/h.

During the development stages it would need to be higher still because the engine may be running at 0.6 or 0.7 pt/hp-h (although it's fair to say it wouldn't be making its full 100 bhp in this state) and there's no point in risking fuel starvation, which would make a complete nonsense of any jet changes. In the case of race engines you need the capacity to go fully over-rich to the point where the engine misfires, which could mean an sfc of 1.0 pt/hp-h or more.

Other measuring equipment usually involves exhaust gas analysis – a probe which needs to be pushed deep into the tailpipe/silencer and fastened in place, because the gas flow will blow it out, or a λ-sensor screwed into the exhaust header pipes. The probe gives the percentage of carbon monoxide (CO) and sometimes an indication of hydrocarbon (HC) content, while the λ-sensor indicates excess oxygen (see Chapter 2). The only problem with probes (and with most types of fuel flow meter) is they take a little time to stabilise and give a reading. If the engine is accelerating, it's anyone's guess at which rpm the reading occurred. However, fast-reacting gas analysis sensors are becoming fast enough (and cheap enough) to be used. One type is available to monitor exhaust gas during

Torque and power

Power is torque multiplied by engine speed (and by a constant to keep the units in line). So where P is power in hp, N is engine speed in rpm, T is engine torque in lbf-ft, and K is a constant (= 2π/33000):

$$P = \frac{2\pi NT}{33000}$$

or P = KNT

As speed (N) increases then constant or increasing torque (T) will make the power increase. Even when torque falls, if speed is increasing fast enough, power can still increase or at least remain constant. Only when torque falls faster than speed increases will the power

also fall. This is why most engines have peak torque at one engine speed, yet power carries on increasing and peaks at a higher speed.

Torque is the force that appears on the output shaft (multiplied by the radius of the shaft). If, for example, the shaft were a convenient 1 foot in radius and had a rope wrapped around it to work as a winch, then an engine developing 20 lb-ft of torque would be able to lift a weight of 20 lb attached to this rope.

Power is the rate at which this is developed. An engine producing 20 lb-ft at 2000 rpm would be able to lift the weight at (2000 × 2π) ft/min, while another engine producing the same torque at 4000 rpm would be able to lift the same weight but do it twice as quickly, at (4000 × 2π) ft/min. While having the same torque output, the second engine would have twice the power output.

These values, as measured, are averages over many (sometimes many thousand) engine cycles. Another way to look at them is that torque represents an average value of the force produced during a single cycle and this force depends upon the air and fuel drawn into the cylinder and the effectiveness of the combustion process. If something restricts the intake process, or alters the AF ratio, or affects combustion, or impedes the exhaust scavenging, then the torque will not be as high as it might have been. Changes in carburation, whether they are in gas flow, AF ratio or mixture distribution, will therefore have a clear effect on the torque reading.

If torque represents an average performance per cycle, power represents the same average but over time. Now we are not looking at the

the test and overlays its results on the engine output curves displayed on screen, giving an instant impression of fuelling variations through the rev range.

Being able to run the engine at a steady speed removes this problem although, with a lot of practice, inertia dynos can be used: by using the highest gear to slow the rate of acceleration, by choosing the start rpm carefully and using the probe's readings as a rough indication of richness rather than a precise value.

Fast-reacting sensors are getting faster and cheaper all the time and it is already possible to run dyno tests in conjunction with a data recorder which can store λ-sensor output along with other useful things like spark plug temperature, exhaust temperature, knock sensor output, airbox pressure and temperature. It's possible to use spark plug voltage as an indication of mixture strength, because a moderately rich mixture is easy to burn and will ignite at a low voltage, while weaker mixtures take longer and the plug builds up a higher voltage.

Power losses

There is one other dyno test – called a Morse test – which is designed to measure pumping and frictional losses but can be adapted to this sort of programme, to show if one cylinder or one carburettor is behaving differently from the others.

It involves running the engine on load at a steady speed and then shorting out individual spark plugs in turn. One problem here is finding an effective way to short out the plug without making a powerful ignition system damage its insulation or, where plugs are fired in pairs, without affecting its partner.

In the full test, the dyno load is reduced to bring the engine back up to its original speed and the new load measured. A four cylinder motor running on three cylinders has the same frictional and pumping losses as before but only three cylinders'-worth of power, so the loss of power equates to that cylinder's

full power, before the losses are deducted. This is called the indicated power or ihp, and bhp = ihp – losses

It is not strictly accurate because the non-firing cylinder runs at a lower temperature, does not have the piston thrust on the cylinder wall of a fired cylinder and its gas flow does not benefit from the sudden expansion of hot gas into the exhaust and subsequent pulse effects in the exhaust system.

However it can be a good method to check that all cylinders are behaving in the same way, either to locate a mechanical fault or to show that one intake is performing differently to the others (eg if its intake stack is a different length it will contribute more or less to the total, depending on the engine speed). If some cylinders are running too rich or too lean, they will contribute less to the total than cylinders whose mixture is at an optimum.

To show up these kinds of differences, the test can be abbreviated to simply measuring the rpm drop when a plug is shorted out. Naturally it should be the same on all cylinders if they're all working equally.

The engine doesn't have to be run on full load. It can be fixed on part throttle and the test can even be done at idle (that is, no load) as long as the engine will keep running.

4 Engine check

Before doing any carburation tests it's essential to check the rest of the engine is working perfectly. If it is a standard machine this is simple enough:

- Valve clearances.
- Spark plug grade and condition.
- Coil and ht lead condition.
- Ignition timing, checked with a stroboscope through the full rev range.
- Exhaust system, physical condition and function of any variable-geometry valves.
- Fresh air bleed into exhaust, working

properly or disabled for purposes of test.
- Air cleaner, physical condition.
- Correct oil quantity and viscosity.
- Cylinder compression pressures, at normal working temperature, must be within manufacturer's limits and not vary by more than a few per cent from one cylinder to the next. Race engines are often run-in on dynos, with cycles of increasing load/speed followed by an engine-off heat soak and cooling, until the cylinder pressures come up to the specified figure.
- Leakdown test to confirm condition of piston rings, valve seats and head gasket.

If the machine is modified then the same conditions apply, except you may not know, for example, the optimum ignition timings or even plug grades. In this case start at the safe end of the scale, using minimum ignition advance and the hardest, coolest running spark plugs. It's then a matter of configuring the engine so it will run safely, making it possible to reach some working carburettor settings – again safe, rather than optimum. At this point other unknown quantities, like ignition timing, exhaust system dimensions etc should be optimised before attempting any fine tuning in the fuel system.

The rest of the machine needs to be in perfect condition before you can make any sense out of carburettor changes, and you also need to check the carburettors. Typical faults include:
- Blocked or kinked breathers (tank vents and float bowl overflows).
- Dirt in the fuel filter or float bowl can partly block the supply or cause carburettor flooding. This is a particular problem with new fuel tanks, which need to be thoroughly swilled out (and still manage to hold enough debris to jam needle valves open).
- Loose or unscrewed jets.
- Wrong type (or different types) of main jet fitted.
- Loose spray nozzles or nozzles fitted wrong way round.
- Needles not clamped properly.

effect on each working cycle but on as many cycles as can be fitted into a second or a minute. This has subtly different implications. For example, closing the throttle by 25% will reduce the air flow and will reduce torque by a proportionate amount because each cycle will have less air to work with. If you then increase the number of cycles, ie raise the engine speed, by the same proportion, there will still be less torque but the power will remain the same.

The torque has indicated the throttle change quite precisely. The power reading, incorporating engine speed, can be more confusing to interpret when the engine is not running at constant speed but is moving through a range of speeds.

Both torque and power are average values. If we could watch a slow-motion replay of an

engine cycle we would see the crankshaft accelerate soon after combustion, when torque would also increase dramatically. At the end of the power stroke, the engine would start to slow down and the torque at the crankpin would not only drop it would become negative – the engine is now relying on the inertia of its flywheels to keep it moving, while it goes through the processes of pushing out exhaust gas, pumping in more fresh gas and compressing it. This inertia also damps down the speed fluctuations until they are perceived merely as engine roughness, similar to vibration.

The nett torque is the positive amount from the power stroke, minus the negative amounts when the engine is doing work on the gas and not getting work from it. As long as the engine is turning at a high enough speed, this appears as

an almost steady load rather than a series of off-on switches.

In addition to these fluctuations, the engine may not perform quite the same from one cycle to the next, possibly because the mixture formation is not the same or there's something different about the turbulence, or because one of several other factors has changed slightly. These are called cyclic variations. As engines are already non-steady in their operation, it doesn't help to have any more fluctuation superimposed, especially as carburettors are speed-sensitive and these fluctuations could cause cycle-to-cycle changes which alter the mixture strength, which in turn increases the cycle-to-cycle variation. In this case the engine would appear to run less smoothly, or would even be unstable at certain speeds.

● CV carburettor diaphragms torn or not clamped well enough to seal.
● Carburettor mountings damaged or leaking.
● Incorrect float heights.

The engine (and the test house) need to be thoroughly up to temperature. This can take a surprising amount of time but until the conditions are stable it will not be possible to get repeatable results. The dyno should be equipped with a thermometer for ambient intake temperature, a wet and dry bulb thermometer to check humidity (not usually necessary in temperate climates like the UK) and a barometer to measure atmospheric pressure. The thermometer for intake air temperature should be mounted as close as possible to the carburettor or airbox intake, so it measures the air that goes into the engine.

Ideally the cooling fan should be arranged to supply cold air to the intakes as well as to the radiator because during the course of a series of tests, the engine will warm up the test house and the air density will fall. Cooling should be arranged so the engine runs at the same temperature it normally reaches on the road or track, usually at a coolant temperature of 65 – 80°C. If the fan cannot keep on top of a very powerful engine it may be necessary to loop in an additional radiator.

It is essential to run the tests with the engine's bulk oil temperature at a constant level. When the oil is cold, viscous drag absorbs a significant amount of power. When the engine gets hotter than its normal working range, power fades quite dramatically because engine clearances close up and friction increases.

These changes (hot or cold) can amount to more than the difference seen in carburation tests. If there is any doubt, the test should be repeated two or three times, monitoring all temperatures. If the results are not repeatable although the temperatures stay constant, then there is some other fault which must be eliminated before testing can continue.

The set-up for any dyno test is with the bike as close as possible to its road or track condition. If it's necessary to run a remote fuel tank, make sure the fuel height (or the pressure at the carburettor feed) is the same as it would be with the normal tank fitted.

Although it is easier to work on bikes with the bodywork removed, this sometimes disguises problems. For example, the fuel tank on the Honda RC30 restricted air flow to the carburettors. While running an engine on load, with the tank in place but not bolted down, a LEDAR dyno operator happened to lift the front of the tank to check something or other and the load immediately increased. The resulting jack-up mountings for the tank were one of the cheapest go-faster goodies ever. And such is the power of race paddock gossip that for years afterwards all sorts of bikes appeared with their tanks raised, whether they needed it or not.

The essential part of all the tests is to see how the output varies with fuel flow and then to choose the optimum setting, whether this is for maximum power or best economy.

The chart in Fig. 6.1 shows where each component has a dominant effect, although there is a much greater degree of overlap than this suggests. It's clear that if you wanted to change the mixture at 3/8 throttle and 6000 rpm, the upper section of the needle taper would have the greatest effect. Changes of, say main jet or idle jet, would also make small differences here, but they would make greater differences elsewhere, which might not be what you wanted to achieve.

Alternatively if you wanted to make changes between 1/8 and 1/4 throttle, in the 2500 – 3000 rpm speed range, you would have a choice:
● The pilot jet and its screw control will have a significant effect here, although the changes would also be felt at idle and would make some difference all through the speed range.
● The needle is lifting so the parallel portion may no longer be in the needle jet and the first part of the taper is beginning to come into play. Raising or lowering the entire needle would shift this point and make a considerable difference to the progression as the throttle was opened. So would changing to a needle whose taper started at a different point. The needle has an effect over a wide region of part loads, and unless the mixture was uniformly adrift, any changes here would require compensation at other speeds/loads.
● 1/8 – 1/4 throttle at low speed is on the edges of the pilot jet and needle ranges, but it is in the middle of the air slide cutaway zone, so this would be the best part to change, as it would cause less disturbance everywhere else. If the engine needed a huge change, this might suggest it would be better to share the burden, making, say, a moderate change at the air slide, followed by another small change at the pilot jet and possibly a shift in needle position.
● There is one other component, not shown on the chart, which could make a difference in this area and this is the idle by-pass(es). As they are merely drillings into the pilot feed, the three ways to alter them are to blank them off, increase the size of existing drillings or make new ones, none of which is an easy task, especially as there is no way of predicting where and how big to make any new drilling. Ironically, if the problem is a flat spot just above idle, the by-pass is probably responsible, but because of the physical difficulty, modifying it is not recommended.

The only definite boundaries are where the needle taper changes. These are clearly defined when the needle is lifted out of the needle jet. Some others can be described fairly closely – idle speed, the lowest speed at which the engine will accept WOT and the lowest speeds at which it will take other throttle openings against a load.

The rest can only be guessed at but the chart still gives a good idea of which parts to concentrate on for a particular load/speed region.

The chart also shows there are some places the engine cannot go. For example, half throttle at idle speed – for the simple reason that by the time you'd got the throttle half open, the engine would either have speeded up or would have stopped.

Starting point

If you have a working carburettor from the engine or from a similar machine, then its stock settings will make a starting point from which the engine can at least be run. Removing restrictions upstream of the carburettor (air filter, airbox, intake silencer) will make the whole thing run weaker, so you'll know that you'll probably have to go richer on the main jets, needles and pilot system.

Other modifications can't be guessed so easily but carburettors are to a large extent self-correcting. Flow more air through them and they will supply more fuel and – as long as the increases are fairly small – it will stay in roughly the right proportions. The biggest problem with tuned engines is in having to fit a larger-than-standard carburettor, which will have low air velocity when the engine is running at low to mid-speeds and the throttle is wide open. Ultimately, if the carburettor size is necessary for top end power, you have to accept some shortening of the WOT rev range because it will not pick up properly from as low rpm as a smaller carburettor.

If you are using a different type of carburettor altogether and have no basic settings, you could check what jets etc are used on similar engines to which this type of carburettor is fitted. The manufacturers and importers are usually very helpful and will also recommend the best type of carburettor for your application, along with starting-point settings. They need to know:
● The engine type – model, displacement, year.
● The carburettor type and size – or if not yet known, the type and size of mounting on the engine.
● What modifications have been made to the engine – in some detail, where it affects gas flow.
● Details of the airbox and filter.
● The proposed output – peak power and rpm, peak torque and its rpm.
● The type of fuel.
● The type of use.
● Details of the operating conditions, climate and particularly altitude.

They probably won't be able to give exact settings but they will be able to provide a safe starting point for you to begin testing, and they'll point out any areas where you might have problems, be expecting too much of the carburettor or where a different carburettor would have an advantage.

5 Road loads

Before trying to optimise steady-speed, part-load settings, it helps to know what combination of throttle and revs the engine needs to hold a steady speed on a level road. The combination is called a 'road load' and it is measured by fitting a vacuum gauge to the intake stubs, riding at a steady speed and taking the vacuum reading. This is done from the lowest rpm at which the engine is happy, at regular intervals until at high speed the vacuum is too low to get a reliable reading.

Later, with the bike on a dyno, these conditions of load and rpm can be reproduced by running the engine at the required speed and then increasing the dyno load and throttle opening to get the road load vacuum reading while keeping the speed steady.

A much cruder way of doing this is to mark a scale on the twistgrip. This is OK for tests where the exact throttle opening isn't important, eg for road loads above half throttle.

Having got a full set of road loads, the engine can be tested in realistic part-throttle conditions, to find a matching set of optimum adjustments.

6 Idle settings

Although the pilot jet only supplies a small amount of fuel, it does so under all conditions. Consequently it is necessary to find the best jet size at the beginning. Its output will be added to that of the needle jet and the main jet, so we need to get this established before we start changing the other parts.

Usually it's not necessary to change the pilot jet or its air jet in an existing set-up, because there will be enough adjustment at the tapered screw. If this runs out of adjustment then a new jet might be needed.

This may be the case for a radically tuned engine although race engines usually have the idle speed turned up to 2000 – 3000 rpm, partly to avoid this very problem, partly to avoid high loadings on the cam noses in four-strokes and to make sure two-stroke engines are not starved of lubricant on the overrun, but mostly to prevent the rear wheel chattering during braking.

In the race engine's case it means the pilot system only has to do one of its two jobs. These are to supply the off-load mixture for a smooth tickover and to give a smooth throttle response just above idle. The latter is most critical at low engine speeds, when pulling gently away from a standstill or riding along as slowly as possible in traffic, but it also applies

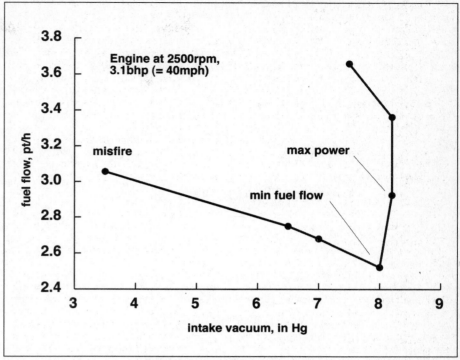

Fig. 6.4 Part-throttle mixture loop

The bike is run at a steady speed on the road to obtain rpm and intake vacuum readings. This 'road load' is then transferred to a dyno, which is adjusted to hold the engine at the same speed, while the mixture is changed from fully rich to fully weak. At each setting the fuel flow is measured and plotted against intake vacuum. The best economy and power points are shown on the loop. The test is repeated at other road loads to obtain the optimum settings. This procedure also shows how much each component contributes at any given stage

at high engine speed, whenever you close the throttle to slow down and then slowly open it again. As this usually happens in the middle of a corner, you want the engine to respond precisely, with no hesitation.

Fig. 6.4 shows the results of an engine test, turning the idle mixture screw half a turn at a time from the fully rich position. With such small flow rates the fuel consumption is usually measured by running the engine in a steady state and timing the interval for a given quantity of fuel to flow from a measuring cylinder, connected like a remote tank at roughly the height of the fuel level in the normal tank.

The characteristic, hook-shaped graph is called a mixture loop, which clearly shows the points at which the engine achieves best power and fuel consumption. At low part-throttle conditions, economic cruising is the target, so the lowest fuel reading would be chosen. This would be the case with the idle setting, although it's important to have adjustment to richen it up later, in order either to get a smooth tickover or to improve the progression when the throttle is opened slowly. If the optimum point had not left much adjustment in this direction, it would have been worth trying a larger pilot jet.

7 WOT settings

Having got the idle system running happily, the next step is to optimise WOT, which is the main jet and air jet combination. These two affect fuelling in almost all areas (the needle etc merely trim the main jet's supply to match the bike's needs for steady cruise conditions), which is why they're next on the list.

Mixture loops on WOT require no road load data, you simply hold the bike wide open and use the dyno to bring it down to the required speed, let it stabilise, measure the power and repeat going one step weaker at the main jet. By now the fuel flow is high enough to read with a flowmeter and the results follow the type of curve shown in Fig. 6.5, clearly indicating the jet that gives maximum power, although to avoid damaging the engine you would normally choose one size larger.

This test is repeated at 500 rpm steps from the lowest speed the engine can manage up to its maximum safe speed. Joining all the optimum points together produces the

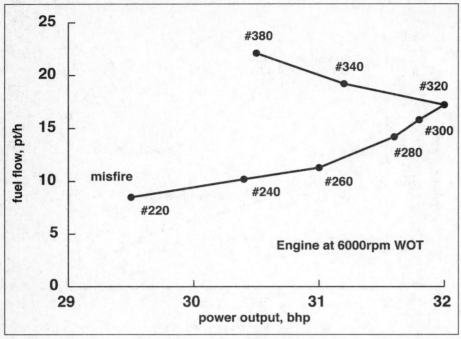

Fig. 6.5 WOT mixture loop

In this test the engine is held at a steady speed on a dyno and the power and fuel flow is recorded with different main jets, going from fully rich (size #380) to fully weak (#220). The result is a characteristic loop which shows the optimum main jet size (#320 in this case, although for the sake of the odd half-horsepower, the #340 would be a safer alternative)

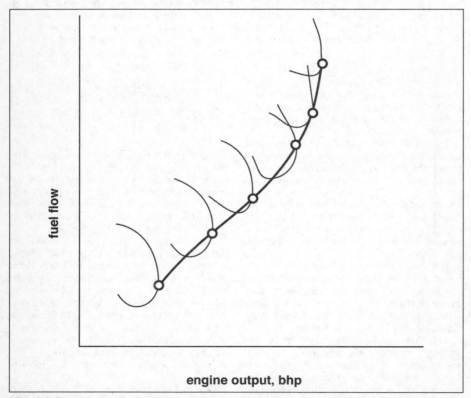

Fig. 6.6 The mixture loop test is repeated at 500 rpm intervals through the full rev range to obtain the fuel slope, ie a line drawn through all the optimum jet sizes. This is what the engine requires to give maximum power at all speeds

engine's fuel slope (see Fig. 6.6) but at this stage you usually find that the best jet for low speed is different to the best jet at high speed.

This is corrected by changing the air jet. If the best low speed jet is too rich for high speed, then a bigger air jet is needed. If the best low speed jet proves too weak at high speed, then a smaller air jet is needed. Fig. 6.7 shows the trends available by changing main jet and air jet size.

Sometimes you reach a point where the air jet size tends to zero. Quite often the air passage is simply blocked – which is acceptable but not desirable. It means you cannot adjust further in this direction – you cannot make the fuel slope any steeper. Should the bike run into conditions that make the top end lean off, it will go too weak, which could damage the engine. All you can do to tune it out is to increase the main jet size, which will then become too rich at the bottom end, effectively narrowing the useful power band. It also means you lose the other benefits of bleeding air into the fuel stream – better atomisation etc. One other method, often used on two-strokes, is to use a screened nozzle, or primary choke, to increase fuel delivery. Different heights and shapes of screen (see Fig. 6.9 opposite) have varying effects but they will apply through all on-load running conditions.

If it is impossible to get the best fuel slope, there is another option: to run a main jet/air jet that gives the right mixture at low speeds but goes too weak at high speed and then to bring in an additional jet – called a power jet or high speed jet – to richen up the top end. This jet is independent of the main jet system and has its own spray nozzle which is fitted into the venturi upstream of the air slide. Fig. 6.8 shows a common arrangement, while Fig. 4.13 in Chapter 4 shows the working principle. There are two adjustments, first a jet to regulate the fuel flow and second the height of the fuel nozzle. Fuel will not flow until the air slide is higher than the nozzle, so it need not disrupt part-throttle carburation and it can be positioned to come in at a precise throttle opening.

This system, like the main system, will follow the speed-squared principle, delivering increasing amounts of fuel as the air speed goes up. Consequently it will add very little at low speed, contributing most at high speed, and the overall delivery will be increased progressively, not in a sudden step. Some types have their own mixing chamber with an adjustable air bleed, so the additional supply from the power jet can be tailored over a wide rev range in exactly the same way as the main fuel and air jets.

8 Part load settings

Road load tests, similar to those described for idle settings, are run all the way through

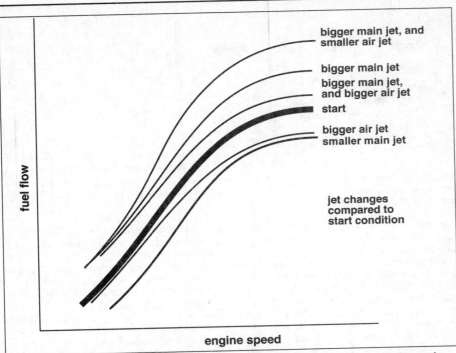

Fig. 6.7 The actual fuel slope plotted against engine speed may not match the engine requirements over the full rev range

It can be tailored: start – slope with original main jet and air jet. Fitting a larger air jet will weaken the high speed fuel delivery without making much difference at low speed. Fitting a bigger main jet will simply lift the curve, increasing flow at all speeds. Fitting a bigger main jet and a smaller air jet will lift the whole curve but increase the top end delivery more than the bottom end. The curve can be shifted up or down by changing the size of the main jet and the steepness of the slope is altered by changing the size of the air jet

Fig. 6.8 The nozzle set in the venturi in the 5 o'clock position is from an accelerator pump

A similar arrangement is used for power jets, with a fuel jet in the float bowl and the nozzle fixed at a certain height – air will not flow over it until the throttle slide is opened above this height

the part-throttle range, changing the appropriate part – air slide, needle taper or needle height – to get mixture loops at constant speed. These tests show how much effect each component has and how much this is echoed across other regions. Fortunately most of us will only have to experiment with needle positions, for there is a bewildering array of needle tapers and heights and someone else will already have done the groundwork, narrowing down the

choice to one or two needles, each with perhaps five positioning grooves.

In fact most powerful bikes are only just off idle at 80 mph, so the bulk of the work concentrates around the low part-throttle region. The rest of the settings are not so critical, partly because 120+ mph steady-speed cruising is not something that happens for long periods and even when it does, things like fuel economy are not the main criteria. It's a different story for low-powered bikes, which

do need to cruise on high part-throttle and therefore need rather more testing than high performance machines.

It's possible to run part-throttle tests in the same way as WOT tests, by fixing the throttle position. In the steady-speed cruising range the choice is likely to be for the most fuel-efficient setting, while best power is the object for wider throttle openings. So the higher part-throttle conditions are more likely to be tuned for transient conditions – throttle response, best power and smooth running where, like WOT conditions, the mixture will stray into the slightly rich area, rather than be stoichiometric or run weak.

Of course, the development engineer's job is made worse because emissions tests have to be added to all this, with cycles of varying loads and speed over which the engine must keep its exhaust products below maximum levels.

9 Transient tests

So far all the tests have involved running the engine at steady speed, which helps to let the engine and instruments stabilise and gives ample time to see what's happening. It's the easiest way to get basic settings but apart

Fig. 6.9 The main nozzle may be just a plain tube or may have a screen (sometimes called a primary choke)

The effect of this is to create localised low pressure over the fuel jet and turbulence which helps break up and distribute the fuel stream. For a given needle, fuel jet and air jet, a screened nozzle will deliver more fuel than a plain nozzle

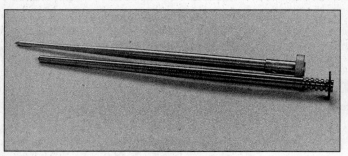

Fig. 6.10a Needle options

The type with grooves and a locating circlip can be raised or lowered in the air slide (and in the needle jet) to provide fine tuning. The plain type can sometimes be adjusted by fitting shims under its head

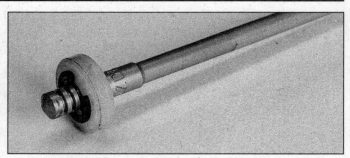

Fig. 6.10b This detail shows the needle grooves and circlip

The top groove (closest to the end of the needle) is numbered #1 and it will hold the needle in the lowest (weakest) position

from road loads, it is mostly an artificial region, which the engine will never see in real operating conditions. There's a lot to be said for testing the engine in real-world conditions, and certainly the final fine-tuning has to be done this way.

It's possible to modify some of the above tests to fit the way an inertia dyno works. For example, when running tests for mixture loops, no-one runs the engine at 5,000 rpm, changes the jets five or six times and then goes to 5,500 rpm and repeats the process. With each jet, you run the engine at all the speed stations, then change to the next jet and run the engine again. So it's possible to do this on an inertia dyno, doing one complete run with each jet size, and compare the resulting torque curves.

Where low part-throttle road loads are concerned, the dyno won't accelerate very much anyway. It may not give time for flow meters to stabilise, and requires more skill and experience on the part of the operator to interpret results, particularly where exhaust gas analysis is concerned. But as long as the speed range and throttle position are kept the same, you can get valid comparisons. Dynojet

data files include the time interval between each speed, so pick-up and acceleration are directly measured.

Data recorders are becoming more widely used and this is one way of keying real-time measurements to exact engine speeds, so the data can be overlaid on the torque curve.

At this point, inertia dynos come into their own. As fuel flow becomes a secondary consideration, you are looking for best acceleration between two speed/load stations, smooth running and clean throttle response,

all of which can be checked quickly and easily on this type of dyno. You can test the engine in different rates of acceleration by using higher or lower gears, you can test different rates of throttle movement, through to the sudden off-on snap in upward gearshifts, by running the bike through all the gears.

Adjustment is easy in principle, you identify the part that has the most effect, usually one part of the needle taper, and raise or lower the needle to richen or weaken the mixture respectively (see Figs. 6.10a, 6.10b and 6.11).

Fig. 6.11 If the part-throttle mixture needs to be changed, it helps to know exactly where the throttle slide is, because this allows you to measure the point on the needle where it emerges from the needle jet. The length of needle to this point and its diameter at this point are dimensions you'll need to compare with other needles to establish which is leaner or richer in this region

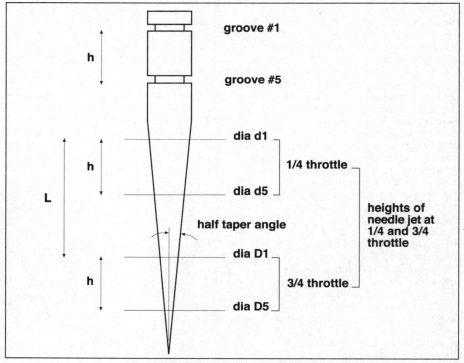

Fig. 6.12 Estimating a new needle taper

The needle positions in the needle jet are shown for ¹/₄-throttle (needle diameters shown by d) and for ³/₄-throttle (needle diameters D), for the needle in groove #1 (suffix 1) and groove #5 (suffix 5). The distance L is the needle movement from ¹/₄- to ³/₄-throttle and the existing needle taper is $(d_1 - D_1)/L$

Some manufacturers list the needle taper as an angle 2θ, where $\tan\theta = (d_1 - D_1)/2L$

If groove #1 is best at ¹/₄-throttle and groove #5 is best at ³/₄-throttle then the required taper is $(d_1 - D_5)/2L$ (which is also the tangent of half the taper angle)

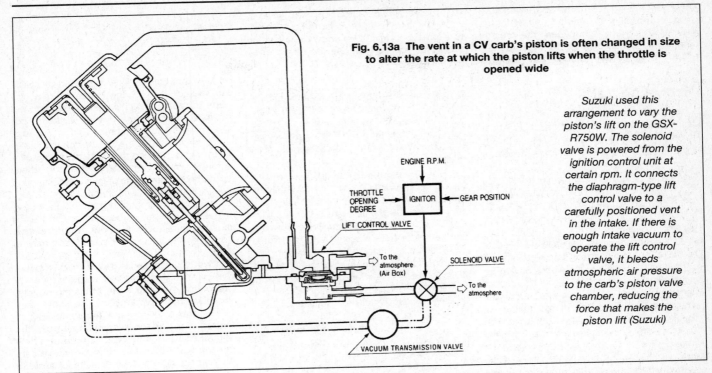

Fig. 6.13a The vent in a CV carb's piston is often changed in size to alter the rate at which the piston lifts when the throttle is opened wide

Suzuki used this arrangement to vary the piston's lift on the GSX-R750W. The solenoid valve is powered from the ignition control unit at certain rpm. It connects the diaphragm-type lift control valve to a carefully positioned vent in the intake. If there is enough intake vacuum to operate the lift control valve, it bleeds atmospheric air pressure to the carb's piston valve chamber, reducing the force that makes the piston lift (Suzuki)

Where an engine has been extensively modified, you may find that the best needle position for low load is not the same at high load, that is the taper is wrong (or where there is a double taper, the point at which it changes is no longer in the right place). However, having a needle that works tolerably well means you can run tests at different throttle openings and can pinpoint the working position on the needle corresponding to the throttle position. This is the point where the needle emerges from the needle jet. Measure its diameter at this point with a micrometer or go/no-go gauge, and measure it again at the second throttle position. These figures give the taper over that length of the needle, which is, say, the best setting for low-load operation, as shown in Fig. 6.12.

Now measure the taper again with the needle in the optimum groove for high-load operation, so the two points will be shifted by the distance between the two grooves. You can now define the optimum taper because you know the two optimum diameters and what the distance should be between them and can look this up in the manufacturer's needle codes (see under individual manufacturers, Chapters 7 and 8, for the way they code needle tapers).

10 CV carburettor: part load

This is about the only place where CV carburettor tuning varies from slide carburettors, partly because it is difficult to tell

where the piston slide is at any given throttle position and partly because there is the option to make it rise a different amount and at a different rate. The vent hole in the base of the piston and the strength of the spring (and the weight of the piston slide) control this (see Figs. 6.13a and 6.13b). A smaller hole means the piston will not rise as far or as fast and a stronger spring will have the same effect. The ideal balance is to have a hole size that lets the piston lift fully at the lowest suitable

engine speed, yet isn't so big the piston flutters. Its part-load travel is controlled by the spring.

On some machines it is possible to run the engine with the airbox top removed and to watch the piston slides move, although this is only valid at lower power levels – at higher levels the airbox pressure is significant and will change the piston slide's behaviour. However if you know that raising the needle a distance x is better at high load, then you

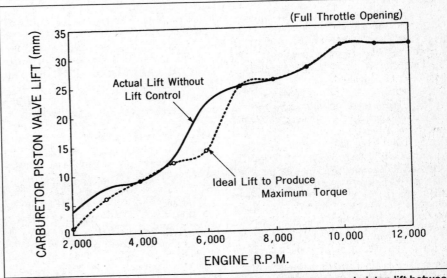

Fig. 6.13b The reason for the lift control valve is shown here: normal piston lift between 5000 and 7000 rpm would be too great. Reducing it by about 10 mm at 6000 rpm allows the engine to make more torque (Suzuki)

know the taper needs to be shortened by x over an approximate length L (which is the estimated distance between the needle heights on low throttle and high throttle – assume the piston follows the twistgrip action, as a slide carburettor would). Now you know whether the taper needs to be greater or less (greater in this case) and by roughly how much, so you can choose the next closest needle in the list and test with it.

Exporting data

If you use a computer-controlled dyno for testing it is possible to export the data it stores to an ASCII text file which can be read by any text editor, word processor, spreadsheet or graphing program. It will copy this file to a floppy disc which can then be transferred to any other PC or an Apple Mac with a PC translation utility. The data may then be used for further analysis, edited and compared to data from other types of dyno or data loggers.

It's also possible to use the 'channels' of data to create 'virtual channels' (also called 'derived' or 'maths' channels). As simple examples: multiplying power or torque data by a correction factor will give output corrected from the ambient to standard conditions: multiplying horsepower by 0.746 will give the output in kW. As more complex examples: if you have the time interval between figures, you can calculate the rate of change of torque (ie pick-up) by subtracting one torque value from the next and dividing this by the time taken (you only have to do this once, spreadsheets and graphing applications will then do it for the remaining data); if the roller speed is available, you can divide engine speed by roller speed (rpm/mph) to get the effective gear ratio and if this changes through the speed range it will highlight problems such as wheelspin, clutch slip or tyre growth.

Dynojet: (*MS-DOS software*) from the menu bar run TOOLS | OTHER TOOLS | SETUP and choose PRINTER PARAMETERS. Press the *Enter* key until *Text Device Destination* is highlighted and use the arrow keys to select FILE. Press *Enter*, select EXIT SETUP and press Y when it asks if you want to save the changes. This diverts text files from the printer to the PC's hard drive and should be changed back to its original setting (COM or LPT1) afterwards.

Select up to three runs to display on the screen. You must display engine output against rpm, not mph. Use the F2, arrow and *Enter* keys to crop tightly around the data you want. Use the F3 key and select *Numbers*. Then select the rpm interval you want: 500, 250, 100, 50, 25 or 10. The bigger steps give smaller data files but jerkier traces. The smaller steps give better resolution but create very long files (from 3000rpm to 10000rpm in 10rpm steps requires 700 lines of data). Press *Enter* and the file will be saved as *nmbrfile.nnn* in the working directory (usually *c:\djpep\nmbrfile.001*). The .nnn extension is a number, the latest addition will have the highest number. You can copy this file to a floppy disc, or another directory, renaming it

to make it recognisable, and delete the original nmbrfile. The file consists of test details, and columns of rpm, raw bhp and torque, SAE corrected bhp and torque, DIN corrected bhp and torque and the time interval between each reading.

(*Later software for 32-bit Windows*) select a run (or multiple runs) and display in graph form. From the *Print* menu (or right mouse click anywhere on the graph), choose *Print Numbers* and *Export* or *Export delimited*. Select *Delimiter* and the step size (see above) and click on the *Export* button. A standard *Save As* dialogue box is opened so you can choose the name and place for the .txt file. (Delimited means the way in which the file separates the columns of data – typically by a tab, spaces or a comma. It is then called eg tab delimited, and when you import it into another application you should specify the same type so that the new application keeps the data in its correct format.)

Under a separate *Export Dialogue* function you can also create a bitmap (.bmp) file of the graphs displayed.

Dynopower: Choose *Graph Parameters* from the first menu and set *Ascii Resolution* to the rpm interval you want (eg 250). Display the graph, place a disc in drive a: then press the *Options* button and choose *Output Ascii Data* from the menu. The file will be copied to the disc, with the same name as the test name. The file contains test details, including which correction factor was selected and columns of rpm, roller speed in mph and km/h, corrected bhp and corrected torque.

Fuchs: the software can display numerical data using *Notepad* (a text editor built into 16- and 32-bit Windows). First display the test in which you're interested or make sure it is in Box 1. From the menu bar choose LIFTS | TESTS and then you are offered a choice of sampling frequency (see Dynojet, above). The GROSS option lists all the data. The software then loads *Notepad* and displays the data file. You can SAVE the file as text, choosing a suitable name and location, or can edit it (using COPY and PASTE to move relevant parts) and SAVE the result.

These text files can be IMPORTed directly into spreadsheets, graphics applications etc, or relevant parts of them can be COPYed and PASTEd between different applications. It's not a bad idea to keep the original data file untouched and always do any editing work on a copy. If you edit a file, save the result as text only because this will not include any word processor formatting characters.

11 Final adjustments

Even though the tests are run in the most logical sequence, changing the fundamental parts first and adding the refinements later, it is often necessary to repeat whole sections, if not the entire test programme. This is because there is a wide range of overlap and later adjustments may add to or subtract from earlier settings, which then need a small correction, sparking off a new cycle of tests. Also, although you optimise ignition timing, valve timing, exhaust dimensions etc before doing anything to the carburettors, it's common to find that as the fuelling improves, the power characteristics alter, meaning these other components may no longer be at their optimum.

A typical example is when a main jet/air jet combination gives more top-end torque. By preventing the load from falling too rapidly, this gives more peak power and shifts peak torque and peak power a few hundred rpm higher up the speed scale. At this point the engine could well take advantage of a new ignition advance curve, retarded intake cam timing or a slighter shorter exhaust system. Any of these could improve the top-end delivery further and, once the engine is flowing more air at higher rpm, the carburation may need altering again.

12 Road tests

It's possible to run at least some of these tests on a road or track. In fact it was traditional to do the fine tuning this way, to make sure the pick-up and throttle response were good under real conditions. The problems are obvious – mainly in getting consistent ambient conditions and finding a rider who can be completely consistent and detect small changes, while doing all the other things necessary to ride the bike. Testing high power outputs is more difficult because of the amount if room it needs and because the greater acceleration demands more rider skill.

Setting-up a bike to race at a specific track is another matter. Assuming the carburation is already optimised for best power and smoothest response, it's necessary to look for other problems. For example, heavy braking may cause carburettors to flood or starve, making the pick-up erratic when the rider needs to get back on the throttle. In one example, when this couldn't be cured at the carburettors (without upsetting their behaviour somewhere else), a stop-light switch from a road bike was fitted and used to switch off the fuel pump whenever the brakes were used.

Particular corners may produce load/speed combinations that haven't been encountered before, where throttle response can be improved (or needs to be damped down... GP bikes have different ignition advance curves in the lower gears to make them less prone to wheelie when the throttle is opened).

Before the advent of data loggers which can keep track of such things, it was also necessary to know how safe the plug temperature was because this, on a race engine (particularly a two-stroke with few other protuberances to run hotter than the rest of the engine) is directly related to pre-ignition, detonation and piston failure. This is how the 'plug reading' saga began.

The condition of the electrodes and the insulator on the engine side of the spark plug can tell you useful things about its history. One of them is how hot the plug has been, assuming it was clean at the start of the test. To make sense of this, you need to understand how plugs work (see sidebar) but the information is limited and is only useful in fairly narrow circumstances.

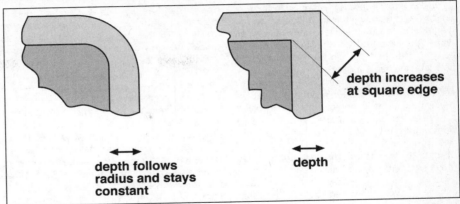

depth increases at square edge

depth follows radius and stays constant

depth

Fig. 6.14 Charge density

Whenever a layer of something is built up on an object, the depth increases over sharp edges. It doesn't matter whether it is plaster on a wall, icing on a cake or electrical charge on an electrode, which is what we're concerned with. The point (literally) where the charge is deepest is where the spark will occur. It is known as point discharge and the more acute the point, the greater the effect, which explains the shape of lightning conductors, among other things

Spark plugs

The electric arc produced at the plug's electrodes is what triggers combustion. It has to have enough energy to start local fuel burning and it has to happen at precisely the right time. This is all the engine needs but the plug itself needs more [see Haynes *Motorcycle Electrical TechBook* for full details]. First it must conduct heat away so the centre electrode stays in a temperature range where it is self cleaning. This is between 400 and 800°C. At lower temperatures combustion deposits build up and the plug gradually fouls. At higher temperatures the metal oxidises and the electrodes wear away quickly. The sharp edges become rounded (see

Fig. 6.14 for the reason square edges are important), the gap increases and the voltage requirement increases. Ultimately the electrodes get so hot they can start pre-ignition, a condition in which the mixture is ignited before the spark occurs. This is potentially dangerous because it is equivalent to advancing the ignition timing and will raise operating temperatures further, possibly melting either the plug's electrodes or the piston alloy (see Fig. 6.15).

The state of the plug will show whether it has been operating in the right temperature range and, within this range, a darker colour on the central insulator shows the plug to have been running cooler, a lighter colour, eventually looking bleached, then blistered, shows it to have been running hotter.

A rich mixture makes the plug run cooler and a

weak mixture makes it run hotter. This is the rationale of the 'plug chop', where the rider cuts the engine at the fastest part of the circuit, pulls in the clutch and coasts to a halt.

If the engine has already been optimised and has no running faults, this type of plug reading will show whether the operating conditions are safe or not. This is all racers are looking for and some two-stroke tuners prefer to remove the cylinder heads and even the pistons to look for signs of combustion overheating, rather than rely simply on the spark plugs.

For other testing purposes, consider this. The plug's temperature depends upon:

● The plug's own heat range (the heat path is varied so more or less heat is conducted away and in the same engine, an NGK CR9 will run cooler than a CR8 and hotter than a CR10) (Fig. 6.16).

● Ignition timing. Increasing the advance will raise the plug's temperature.

● Power output. More power means more heat flow and higher temperatures.

● Tightening torque. Too little torque or a damaged washer will not bring the plug into perfect contact with the rest of the cylinder head and it will run hotter.

● Electrode gap. Changing the voltage requirements at the plug by this or any other means will alter its running temperature.

● Exhaust restriction (or anything else that raises combustion temperature) will also increase the spark plug temperature.

● Mixture strength.

If all the other factors have been optimised, then the plug's condition will vary with AF mixture but it's not a very reliable indicator when the engine is being developed.

Fig. 6.15 Reading spark plugs is not always straightforward

The NGK B10 in the centre would run cooler in the same engine as the B8 (left). In this case it has black, probably oil, deposits on both electrodes, yet the centre insulator is white, suggesting too much heat. High performance plugs, such as the surface discharge type on the right, leave even less room for interpretation

Fig. 6.16 This two-stroke piston crown has overheated and been eaten away in the area below the central spark plug. The metal has expanded and eventually seized (see marks on piston skirt) yet the carbon deposits on the crown are the usual dull black of a normally-running engine

Road or track testing, other than for fine tuning, is extremely difficult. This is not to say it's impossible, but there are many factors, all working against you, on top of which it is not easy to maintain the high level of skill and consistency that is essential.

Many years ago we tried an experiment to see how effective fine tuning at a track could be, using very basic equipment. This involved a friend's 250 cc two-stroke twin, which had been lightly modified for production racing and would be set up at a track, with a series of tests devised to get the carburation at its most efficient. We had access to a proving ground, which is similar to a race track except, having travelled down the main straight, it was possible to turn off and loop back to the pit area. It meant we didn't have to do full laps – a major saving in time, fuel and engine wear, the first of the things that conspire against you (especially if the weather changes during the course of the test, or the engine is running close to a dangerous condition like detonation).

We spent a day preparing the bike in the workshop, making access easier to parts we knew we'd have to adjust, putting marks on the ignition rotor and the twistgrip (so we need not measure things on the day, we could simply use the pre-measured reference marks), and getting a selection of spark plugs and jets ready.

The tests would involve timing the bike between markers, using a stop watch and the bike's tacho. The rider would have to be very consistent in his line, approach speed, throttle position and riding position, otherwise the tests would not make valid comparisons. The initial runs gave us some baseline figures for acceleration times and terminal speeds, starting at various combinations of throttle

opening and engine speed. We then tried to optimise the ignition timing and spark plug grade. With the pre-marked rotor this was quick and easy to do. It also gave us some valuable practice in the test procedures.

We found we could measure small changes. More reassuringly, we found we could go back to a particular set-up and repeat the results. This is important during a long series of tests because if something else changes (typically a shift in wind direction or strength) you must go back to a known reference point so you can assess the effect of the new conditions. It's also important that the rider isn't asked to do anything difficult, such as acceleration runs through corners, because as he gets practice, he will get better.

Continuing the tests, we moved on to main jets and needle positions and, having gone too far, were able to go back to the best settings and at the end there was a consistent improvement in the bike's performance. This had taken two days' work, one at the track and one in the workshop, plus travelling and plus the work needed to put back the various bits and pieces we'd removed to make trackside adjustment easier. We could have done all this in one day in a test house. And someone with more experience would have run a final set of track tests: with one step richer mixtures, retarded timing and cooler plug grades.

The result, in the bike's next race, was more or less as the tests had suggested. There was a small but consistent improvement in its lap times. It qualified a few places higher than it usually did and halfway through the race, the rider felt the ominous vibration and momentary lack of power caused by detonation, before he could pull in the clutch

lever. In that fraction of a second, the engine had holed both pistons – an unusual feat in itself as one piston usually suffers before the other(s).

The conclusion is that given a suitable amount of space and time and not-too-variable weather, plus a consistent rider, it is possible to work out a set of tests to optimise the machine's transient performance, but better ways are available.

13 Aftermarket jet kits

See Figs. 6.17, 6.18, 6.19, 6.20, 6.21, 6.22 and 6.23

There are various aftermarket kits available for most popular models, often in stages to suit different states of tune (eg high-flow air filter, filter plus 4-1 exhaust, etc). Marketed by firms like Dynojet, Dial-a-Jet, K&N, Cobra (both developed by Dynojet) and Factory, they are often offered with a particular type of air filter or exhaust system (see Fig. 6.17).

Most contain main jets, air jets, needles and sometimes a drill bit to open (or some epoxy resin to close) the vent hole in the piston slide. A different type is made by Dial-a-Jet, whose kit contains a separate power jet for each carburettor (see Fig. 6.18). It takes its supply from the float drain plug, through a fuel jet to a mixing block with 5 air bleeds on a rotating chamber. Turning the chamber lines up each air bleed in turn. From here the mixture goes to a delivery nozzle clipped into the bellmouth or airbox hose. This can make the existing fuel

Fig. 6.18 Aftermarket kit supplied by Dial-a-Jet, consists of a power jet which takes its fuel supply from an adaptor in the float bowl drain screw, which also contains the fuel jet

The fuel is supplied to the black mixing chamber shown, which has a 5-way adjustable air bleed, and from there to the fuel nozzle. The nozzle is positioned in the airstream by boring a hole in the intake trumpet, pushing the nozzle through and cable-tieing the unit to the bellmouth

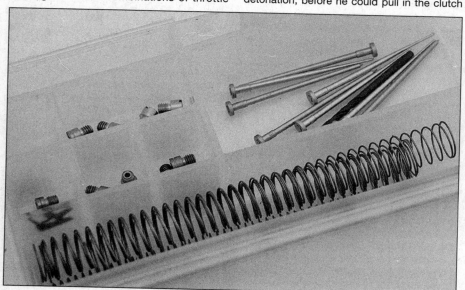

Fig. 6.17 Parts of an aftermarket jet kit, supplied by Dynojet. They include a selection of main jets, air jets, new needles, new piston valve springs and a drill bit to enlarge the piston vent hole

Fig. 6.19 Main jets vary in their internal dimensions but the type is usually identified by the thread size and the shape of the head. However different makes may not flow the same amount of fuel even though they are meant to be of the same type, so choose the correct *type* and stick to one *make*

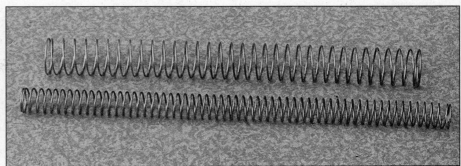

Fig. 6.20 The rate at which the piston valves lift determines engine torque and throttle response. It can be fine tuned by altering the diameter of the vent holes and by using stronger or weaker springs

slope richer by progressive amounts at high loads and speeds but cannot make it weaker (although you can, of course, use a weaker combination of main jet and air jet, and then use the kit to bring in the extra fuel).

The main problem with any of these kits is that you, the customer, don't know how difficult it was to tune a particular engine for a particular set of filters or pipes.

It could be that the kit gets the mixture slope exactly right. It could be that it's right at the top end but drifts off in the midrange. It could be marginal with one type of filter and/or exhaust – with another type or when the filter has been used for a few hundred miles, it might get rather worse than marginal.

Without doing all the work yourself, you won't know and, of course, the point of the kits is to save you the trouble and cost of doing all the work. For anything more than the simplest filter kits, they should be regarded as convenient starting points.

There are a few aspects which you should bear in mind, and which give clues to how well the kit works.

● **Jets** – Don't mix different makes, even if they appear to be the same type. Choose one and stick with that range. The reason is that a #140 made by XYZ may not flow the

same as a #140 made by ABC, even though the jets look the same (see Fig. 6.19). If they look different (different length, different taper to jet bore, plastic instead of brass) then they certainly will not flow the same.

● **Air jets** – If the instructions tell you to blank off the main air jet, then you know you're going outside this carburettor's range of adjustment. You'll be able to get the fuelling right at high revs but the odds are you won't be able to keep it right in the midrange. It is probably something you'll have to live with if you want the improved top end and ultimately, if there are further tuning steps like camshafts and valve timing, a midrange hole will probably appear.

● **Air slide vent holes** – If these need changing, leave it until last. Test the other modifications first and approach any changes in progressive steps, rather than simply opening the hole out to the suggested size. Also, using a power drill in plastic is likely to make a hole considerably larger than the bit, so do any drilling by hand.

● **Needles** – Steel needles may not be fully compatible with the original needle jets, especially if the stock needles are the anodised type. They may cause wear in the needle jets after a high mileage – or after a low mileage if some other deficiency makes the piston slides flutter.

14 Two-stroke lubrication

See also Chapter 9, Ancillary parts.

Two-stroke oil is either injected into the intake tract from a pump whose output is controlled by the throttle, or it is mixed with the fuel. While running tests it is important to maintain proper lubrication as the power output of a two-stroke is closely related to its piston clearance, which in turn is related to cylinder temperature, which is dependent upon lubrication.

While there has to be sufficient quantity and quality of oil, more is not better. More quantity simply increases carbon fouling at the rings, spark plug, exhaust port, 'power valve' and in the absorption material in the silencer. Too high a quality is, at best, a waste of money. At worst, a high load-bearing competition oil will be too viscous for the oil pump on a small commuter, possibly damaging the pump or not arriving in the engine in sufficient quantity to do its job.

It is necessary to select the right type of oil

Fig. 6.21 The central hole in the piston locates the needle, the offset hole is the vent into the piston chamber

Fig. 6.22 Aftermarket high performance air filters are free-er flowing than the standard items. As they offer less resistance to the air, they create a smaller pressure drop, which in turn means the original carburettor settings tend to be too weak

Fig. 6.23 Earlier machines had restrictive air boxes, which were often removed altogether or could not be adapted to fit new frames and bodywork, as on this Bimota. The individual filters were better than open bellmouths but would still be in a low-pressure region when the bike was travelling at speed and were prone to partial blockage during wet conditions

for the engine and, initially, to follow the oil manufacturer's recommendations for oil/fuel mixtures, which is covered in Chapter 9. Follow the recommendations of the oil company rather than the bike manufacturer because oils change, while the bike maker's recommendations will apply to the oil that was available when the bike was made.

Testing pumps. Make sure the oil is suitable for injector pumps, which are usually designed for a viscosity of about SAE30. Check the cable adjustment: that it returns to the minimum position when the throttle is closed, opens smoothly with the throttle and either reaches the maximum position on WOT or reaches the calibration marks at the correct throttle position.

Disconnect the line from the pump to the engine intake and run it into a measuring cylinder. Run the engine temporarily on an oil/ fuel mixture, typically 2 – 3% oil by volume – but use whatever the manufacturer recommends.

The engine now needs to be run at a steady speed for a given length of time but with the pump linkage fixed in the fully open position, and the pump's output measured.

This will vary from model to model and must obviously be checked in the workshop manual. As an example, the Suzuki RGV250 should flow 3.5 – 4.6 ml when the engine is run at 2000 rpm for 2 minutes.

Power fade test. If an engine is being developed, it will reach a stage when you need to determine the best oil, whether the pump (if fitted) is still adequate or what will be the best oil/fuel ratio. The engine should be run on a dyno, preferably at a steady speed, around the rpm for peak torque. Fit a thermocouple with a washer under the spark plug as its hot junction. Get a succession of torque readings with increasing amounts of the radiator blanked from the cooling fan, monitoring the load and the plug temperature very carefully. As the temperature goes up, the dyno load (torque) will fall. This is called power fade. Avoid large increases in temperature or large drops in load as this could indicate detonation or piston overheating which will quickly cause mechanical damage.

Having established the power fade characteristics, repeat the tests using different oil or different ratios. It will be necessary to run the engine on light load, with full cooling, in between tests, partly to let it stabilise and partly to make sure all traces of the previous oil have disappeared. The object of the tests is to find the oil and the mixture ratio that give the most stable resistance to fade. It's possible that one set-up will actually give more torque or let the engine make the same torque at a higher speed.

You may also notice differences in combustion quality, which will not show up in terms of engine load or temperature but as perceptible changes in engine roughness (or smoothness). Because the oil is burnt with the fuel it obviously affects the rate of burn, knock-resistance etc.

Once the best lubrication has been established for the toughest engine conditions, it should then be used for a range of part- and full-load tests to make sure that it works in all conditions.

Chapter 7
Carburettor construction and adjustment –

Keihin and Mikuni

Contents

1 Introduction

This chapter and the following one deal with the carburettors that are fitted to the majority of post-war bikes. In essence, all slide and CV carburettors are built along similar lines. Their components will be in roughly the same positions and can be identified from the data given in Chapter 4. Tuning, fault finding and overhaul procedures are also broadly the same and are covered in Chapters 6, 12 and 13. Where carburettors differ is in their detail: things like jets have different shapes and the way the manufacturers size or code parts is also different. These chapters take a look at the actual construction of the carburettors and explain manufacturers' codes.

To define a needle you must have: root diameter, length, taper angle and a point at which the taper starts (twice for needles with

two tapers). Keihin and Mikuni use alphanumeric codes for these baseline dimensions, including letter codes for the needle taper angle, starting at A (0° 15' in Mikuni and 0° in Keihin) and increasing in 15' steps through the alphabet.

When replacing jets and needles in any carburettor, it is preferable to use original equipment or parts calibrated to the same scale as the originals. There are two reasons. One is that components from a different manufacturer may have different calibration, that is, two jets marked with the same size code may not flow the same amounts of fuel. In this case, if you switch makes, stick to the new one for all subsequent tuning. The second is that there can be incompatibility between materials, resulting in premature wear between the needle and needle jet.

In the following data, the # mark is either used to denote size (as in #130 meaning a size 130 jet) or a place holder (as in ###, where the actual size is included in the part number).

2 Keihin carburettors

The picture sequence (Figs. 7.1 to 7.25b) shows a bank of four CVK carburettors of the type fitted to the Kawasaki ZX-9R. These are typical of the original equipment Keihin carburettors, which most people are likely to deal with on a service basis, while the smoothbore CR and later FCR flatslide (Figs. 7.26 to 7.31) are aftermarket/competition carburettors which are more likely to be confronted on a tuning basis.

Keihin use several types of main jets, for different carburettor models and, as the main jet is carried by the emulsion tube it is essential to use the correct matching pair for the carburettor that is, the correct type as well as the correct size. Similarly the needle length must match the lift of the slide, that is the venturi size, and the

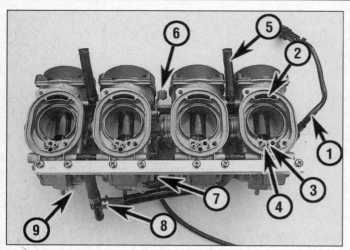

Fig. 7.1 Bank of Keihin semi-flatslide CV carburettors, from the air filter side

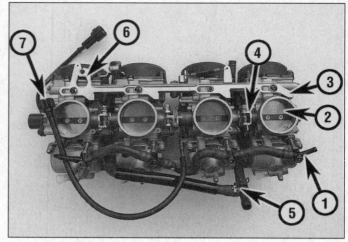

Fig. 7.2 Bank of Keihin semi-flatslide CV carburettors, from the engine side

1   *Electrical connection to throttle position sensor*
2   *Vent (atmospheric or airbox pressure) to underside of diaphragm*
3   *Main air jet*
4   *Pilot air jet*
5   *Float bowl vent (all four bowls are connected together to one hose which leads to the airbox)*
6   *Throttle cable clamp*
7   *Throttle stop adjuster cable*
8   *Fuel supply*
9   *Float bowl drain plug with plastic funnel to guide screwdriver*

1   *Coolant hose from engine, to heat carburettors*
2   *Throttle valve*
3   *Sliding rail to operate cold start plungers*
4   *Throttle adjuster between #1 and #2 carburettors*
5   *Fuel supply*
6   *Cable mount for cold start mechanism*
7   *Throttle stop adjuster cable*

needles are coded for different lengths as well as their diameters and angles of taper.

Main jets

Jets are identified by their overall length, thread size and type of head (flat screwdriver slot or hexagon). Jets are sized by diameter (mm × 100) and go up in increments of 0.025 mm in the lower ranges (up to #200) and 0.05 mm above this. The final digit is dropped, so the sizes go 120, 122, 125, 128, 130). Types are:

99101-393-###

Note: Also called SRS (small, round, slotted).
● Overall length 8 mm
● Round head, flat screwdriver slot
● Thread 5 × 0.8 mm
● Sizes from #90 to #200 (OEM – the Factory range, claimed to be calibrated to the same scale, goes from #50 to #250)

This is the most common Keihin road bike type, used in VB, VD, VE and some PD and PE series (Honda) and in CV and CVK (Honda and Kawasaki), also as the main air jet in FCR flat slide carburettors.

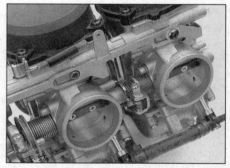

Fig 7.3 There is a throttle adjusting screw between each pair of carburettors so each throttle valve can be synchronised to its partner

Fig. 7.4 Immediately downstream of the throttle valve there is an outlet for the pilot system, which supplies fuel for tickover (to the left of the venturi) and another, on the right, a vacuum take-off for the 'coast richening' circuit

Fig. 7.5 The float bowls are secured by four cross-head screws, one of which also clamps the carburettor heater hose in position. The plain screw (recessed in the curve of the heater hose) is the pilot mixture adjusting screw

Fig. 7.6 On the upstream side of the venturi there are several holes: two contain brass jets (the pilot and main air jets), the three around them are blanked off, the larger, threaded hole to the right is where the plastic intake stack (or bellmouth) is secured

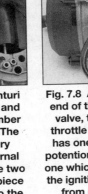

Fig. 7.7 Looking directly into the venturi shows the black plastic piston slide and the 'coast richener' diaphragm chamber on the left of the carburettor body. The float bowls are not open to ordinary atmospheric pressure. Instead, internal vents lead to the bosses between the two carburettor bodies, joined by the T-piece with the hose that ultimately leads to the airbox, so float chamber pressure is the same as airbox pressure (or, in some applications, leads to a valve so that the source of pressure may be switched to suit different engine conditions)

Fig. 7.8 At the right end of the bank, on the end of the spindle that carries the throttle valve, there is a potentiometer to sense throttle position. The three-pin connector has one terminal to supply voltage to the potentiometer, one as a ground (return) and one which carries the signal voltage back to the ignition control unit. The signal will vary from (say) 0.5V at idle, to 3.5V at WOT

Fig. 7.9a Idle by-pass. As the throttle valve is opened slightly from idle, it uncovers a pattern of small drillings, which progressively supply more fuel (from the pilot system) until there is sufficient air-fuel flow from the main system to let the engine pick up smoothly

Fig. 7.9b The full pattern of by-pass drillings. The size and rate at which they are uncovered is determined by experiment during engine development and is responsible for clean initial pick-up, with no flat spot just above idle

Fig. 7.10a The outlet in the top of the venturi, downstream of the throttle valve is for the cold start system. It is connected, via internal drillings and a fuel jet, to fuel in the float chamber

Fig. 7.10b The choke cable pulls the flat rail across the bank of carburettors, pulling the brass plunger (to the top right of the venturi) with it. This opens an air passageway from the underside of the diaphragm (at ambient or airbox pressure) across the top of the fuel feed, working like a miniature carburettor to deliver extra, atomised fuel-air mixture to richen the normal fuel supply during cold running

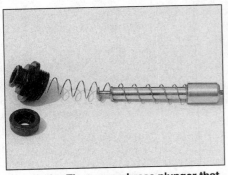

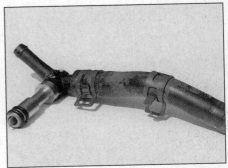

Fig. 7.10c The sprung brass plunger that controls the cold-start circuit

Fig. 7.11 Small diaphragm chamber on the side of the carburettor body is a 'coast richener', which supplies a rich mixture during overrun conditions to prevent popping and banging in the exhaust system. When the vacuum downstream of the throttle is high enough it lifts the diaphragm inside the housing against spring pressure, releasing another sprung valve in the body of the carburettor, to increase flow in the pilot system

Fig. 7.12a The carburettor heater consists of a brass tube with a central baffle, filled with engine coolant

Fig. 7.12b The tube is a push fit, sealed by two O-rings in a boss below the venturi, close to the pilot gallery, which is where icing is most likely to occur

Fig. 7.13 Most carburettors have an ID number somewhere on the body casting. This identifies the model to which the carburettor was fitted, allowing original jet sizes etc to be found

Fig. 7.14a Removing the four screws that hold the float bowl reveals the white plastic float that pivots on the steel pin (bottom left of the pic). Undoing the brass screw unclamps the pin so it and the float can be lifted out

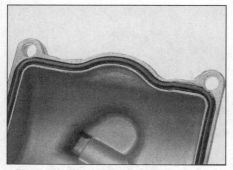

Fig. 7.14b The chamber is sealed with a captive O-ring – do not disturb it unless it has already been damaged

Fig. 7.15 The needle valve sits on the tang of the float pivot and is hooked on to it with a wire clip, so the whole assembly may be removed and replaced easily. The needle valve fits into the brass seat, which is a push fit in the float chamber casting, is sealed by an O-ring and clamped by a screw

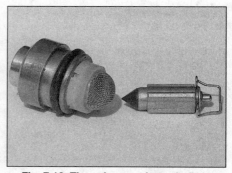

Fig. 7.16 The valve seat has a built-in gauze strainer, which should be cleaned by washing/blowing in the reverse direction to fuel flow. The rubberised tip of the needle and its mating surface inside the brass seat must be scrupulously clean and have no marks on the sealing area

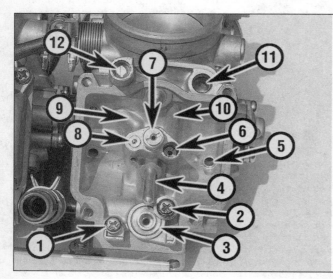

1   Clamp for float pivot
2   Clamp for needle valve seat
3   Needle valve seat
4   Sheath covering needle (steeply angled carburettors have the main jet and emulsion tube located more or less vertically, while the needle and piston slide have to be at right angles to the venturi)
5   Float bowl vent (to external T-piece and tube)
6   Pilot jet
7   Main jet
8   Cold start jet
9   Cold start fuel gallery (leading up side of venturi to air bleed and outlet at top of venturi)
10 Pilot fuel gallery (leading across venturi, below by-pass outlets, to pilot mixture screw and pilot outlet in venturi)
11 Carburettor heater gallery
12 Pilot mixture adjusting screw

Fig. 7.17 View into the float chamber

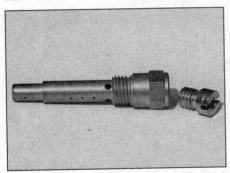

Fig. 7.18 The main jet (smaller) is screwed into a carrier, which is the base of the emulsion tube and itself screws into the alloy casting of the carburettor

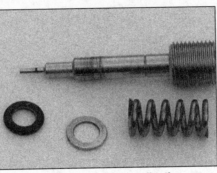

Fig. 7.19 The pilot mixture adjusting screw has a fine taper, to regulate fuel flow, an O-ring seal, a spring to hold the screw in the adjusted position and a washer to prevent the spring damaging the O-ring

Fig. 7.20 Removing the four cross-head screws from the cover on top of the carburettor reveals the diaphragm that seals the piston valve chamber and the light return spring

Fig. 7.21a The diaphragm's beaded edge fits in a groove in the alloy casting, with a locating tab to prevent it being twisted during assembly. The tab contains a small brass jet

Fig. 7.21b Inside the chamber (below the diaphragm) there is filtered air at airbox pressure, which is used to supply the cold start system (1) (brass plunger shown half-way across vent) and the coast richener chamber (2)

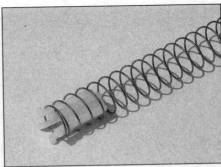

Fig. 7.22 Inside the piston, the spring seats on a plastic clip whose feet locate in recesses so the clip (and the spring force) hold the needle against the bottom of the piston

Fig. 7.23 The piston. The curved cutaway at the bottom of the cylindrical part controls air flow at very small throttle openings. The central hole locates the tapered needle and the smaller hole vents venturi pressure (low) into the chamber above the diaphragm, encouraging the piston to lift

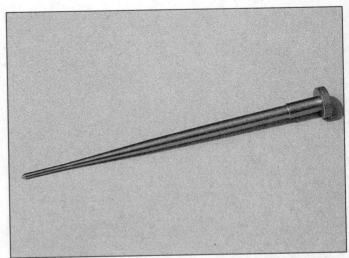

Fig. 7.24 The tapered needle (controls part-throttle fuel flow), sits inside the piston with the spring on top of it. There is no adjustment provided on this type (although it is possible to raise it by fitting shims underneath its head

Fig. 7.25a The small cover on the side of the carburettor contains a spring-loaded plunger, sealed by a diaphragm, which is a 'coast richener'. Intake vacuum is vented to the far side of the diaphragm via the small hole in the alloy casting

Fig. 7.25b Behind the brass insert is a spring loaded plunger. The vent in the 11 o'clock position connects to the underside of the main diaphragm chamber (ie to filtered, ambient air)

Fig. 7.26 Keihin FCR flatslide (aftermarket) carburettors are available with custom-made mountings and intake stacks for various applications. This is a screw-in spigot type mount (left) and a bolt-on bellmouth

Fig. 7.27 Keihin FCR, intake side. With the intake stacks removed, the main and pilot air jets can be clearly seen. The upper, plastic T-piece vents the float bowls to the airbox, while the lower T-piece is the fuel feed. The bottom, flexible hose is the delivery from the accelerator pump

Fig. 7.28 Keihin FCR, engine side. The throttle control spindle with its heavy return spring runs across the top of the bank of carburettors. The casting for the accelerator pump and its plunger can be seen on the lower left of the end carburettor. The operating linkage is attached to the end of the throttle spindle

Fig. 7.29 The accelerator pump and its linkage. One pump is used to supply four carburettors

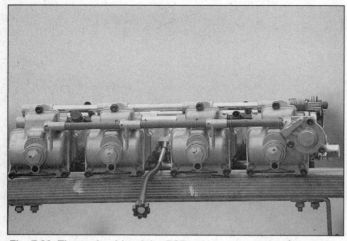

Fig. 7.30 The underside of the FCRs shows the accelerator pump layout. The large hexagons under each float bowl are drain plugs, big enough to allow dirt and water to be removed, and provide access to the main jet, without removing the float bowl itself

Fig. 7.31 Lifting the flat throttle slide shows the almost-smooth bore construction, the screen around the main fuel nozzle and, further upstream, the nozzle for the accelerator pump

99101-357-###

Note: Also called long hex.
● Overall length 16.5 mm
● Hexagonal head 6 mm AF
● Sizes from #80 to #230
  Used in CR, FCR, PD, PE, PWM, PJ and Harley Davidson OE.

1001-806-###

● Overall length 9 mm
● Round head, flat screwdriver slot (head is smaller diameter than thread)
● Thread size 6 × 1.0 mm
● Sizes #90 to #185
  Used on Harley Davidson OE fixed jet carburettors.

N427-27

Note: Visually similar to 393 series but does not have a groove around the outside edge of the head.
● Overall length 8 mm
● Round head, flat screwdriver slot
● Sizes #150 to #220
  Used on Harley Davidson OE CV carburettors.

Pilot jets

Vary in the position of the thread and the overall length. Types are:

N424-21-###

● Overall length 28 mm, thread on wider section
● Sizes #35 to #85
  Used on PJ, PWK, PWM and some smoothbore carburettors.

N424-22-###

● Overall length 28 mm, thread on narrower section
● Sizes #35 to #80
  Used on some PE carburettors.

N424-24-###

● Overall length 32 mm, thread on narrower section
● Sizes #35 to #82
  Used on CR carburettors.

N424-25-###

● Overall length 15 mm, thread on wider section
● Sizes #35 to #100
  Used on some PE carburettors.

N424-26-###

● Overall length 23.5 mm, thread on wider section
● Sizes #35 to #80
  Used on some PE carburettors.

Needles

The most popular aftermarket Keihin is the FCR, which is available in 28 to 33 mm (series 90###) and 35 to 41 mm (series OC###). The needles are coded with the series number followed by three letters (eg 90FST).
● The first letter (F) denotes a taper angle of 1° 15'.
● The second letter (S) denotes a length from the top (#1) adjustment groove to a point on the needle where the diameter is 2.515 mm. It is measured from the bottom edge of the groove (ie the edge closest to the needle taper) and in this case is 63.45 mm.
● The third letter (T) denotes the diameter of the parallel section of the needle (immediately below the adjustment grooves, before the taper starts. T denotes a diameter of 2.775 mm.

The taper code starts at A, which represent 0° and increases in 15' steps (eg G is the 6th step, so will be 6 × 15' = 90' or 1° 30').

The length to 2.515 mm diameter goes up in increments of 0.45 mm, starting at A = 56.25 mm for the 90-series and A = 72.2 mm for the OC series (eg G is the sixth step, so represents 6 × 0.45 = 2.7 mm plus the base length or 58.95 mm for the 90-series and 74.9 mm for the OC series).

The parallel diameter code starts at A = 2.605 mm and goes up in steps of 0.01 mm (eg G is the sixth step and represents 6 × 0.01 = 0.06 plus the base diameter, or 2.665 mm).

Usually for fine tuning, there is enough adjustment available at the needle grooves (the FCR needles have seven, the topmost being #1 which gives the leanest mixture, because the needle is lowered further into the needle jet in this position).

Raising the needle (using a higher groove number) richens the part-throttle mixture everywhere, but because the needle has most effect in the ¼ to ½ throttle range, any change will be most noticeable here.

A needle with the same base diameter but a shallower taper (letter closer towards the beginning of the alphabet) will not make much difference at small throttle openings, but will make the mixture increasingly weaker at wider openings. A steeper taper (letter further towards end of alphabet) will make wider throttle openings richer.

To make small throttle openings richer or weaker, raise or lower the needle as a first step. If this isn't enough, go to a needle with a smaller or larger diameter, respectively. However, the same taper angle will then give the same change in mixture all the way through the needle's range. To prevent such a change at wider throttle openings, the taper angle must be changed. If a smaller base diameter is used, to richen the mixture, a shallower taper will prevent too much richness at high load. If a larger diameter is used (weaker mixture) then a steeper taper will prevent the mixture leaning out at high load.

The value of the second code letter (the length to the point where the diameter is 2.515 mm) is that you can roughly calculate any compensatory changes, as outlined in the last paragraph. If the needle is already on groove #1 (or groove #7) and it's necessary to go still leaner (or richer) then you can use this dimension to find a needle that is longer to this point, which is similar to lowering the original needle further, to weaken the mixture (or one that is shorter, which is roughly equivalent to raising the needle). In this way you can find a needle that gives the best mixture on one of the middle grooves, leaving room for fine tuning in both directions.

Needle jets

Not usually a tuning item, but jet nozzles with a variety of screens are available. In general, the screen creates a local depression over the jet, so the larger the screen, the more fuel will be delivered.

Float height

Measured from the bottom of the float surface to the carburettor flat-bowl gasket face, with the float resting on but not compressing the sprung pin in the needle valve.

FCR	9 mm
CR	14 mm
PWK 28 mm	19 mm
PWK 35 – 39 mm	16 mm
PJ	16 mm
PWM38	6.5 mm
PE 24 – 28 mm	14 mm
PE 30 – 34 mm	20 mm

Idle mixture screw

On the FCR carburettors the mixture screw controls the volume flow. Turning it out tends to richen the mixture at idle and just above. On other types (CR, PWK, PJ and PE) the screw regulates the air flow to the pilot system (identified by the adjusting screw being upstream of the throttle slide) and turning it out will weaken the idle mixture.

Accelerator pump (FCR)

There is a certain amount of free play built into the linkage, before throttle travel starts to move the pump. This can be adjusted – more free play will reduce the amount of fuel pumped and bring it in slightly later, and will be needed if there is evidence of rich mixture during acceleration.

Reducing the free play will bring in the pump earlier, and should be used if the mixture is too lean during acceleration.

3 Mikuni carburettors

Mikuni also have a wide range of original equipment and aftermarket carburettors, including the VM and BS roundslide, TM flatslide, TMX, TMS and the later RS flatslide, plus the HSR42/45 (flatslide carburettors for Harley Davidson). Refer to the picture sequence in Figs. 7.32 to 7.54.

Fig. 7.32 Mikuni semi-flatslide CV carburettors, used as original equipment on many four-strokes, showing the main throttle stop (with remote, cable adjuster to control idle speed), the fuel feed T-pieces and the air jet entries in the carburettor bellmouths. The central one is the main air jet, the offset one is the pilot air jet. What looks like a hole in the top of the bellmouth is just a blind drilling

Fig. 7.33 The bank of four carburettors shows the adjustable linkages on the throttle spindle and the throttle stop adjuster. The float bowls have tapered drain valves

Fig. 7.34 The pipe running up the side of each carburettor is a fuel feed from the cold start jet in the float bowl to the chamber above the venturi. Here a plunger (manually operated by the 'choke' control) opens or blocks the air-fuel supply, which is delivered through the aperture shown at roughly 10 o'clock in the venturi

Fig. 7.35 The vertical pipe running through the top cover flange should have a blanking cap over it. It is a vacuum take-off point which utilises the cold start orifice

Fig. 7.36 When the throttle plates are opened slightly, the pattern of small pilot by-pass holes is visible. Note the dark ring around the venturi left by fuel deposits that accumulate and evaporate when the throttle is closed

Fig. 7.37 Viewed from inside the float chamber, the same pilot by-pass drillings can be seen. Usually there is a blanking plug over the top of them. It's possible to alter the by-passes – by blanking them, enlarging them or drilling new holes – which may be necessary to cure hesitation or flat spots immediately off idle, but the only way to find the best pattern is by an extremely tedious trial and error method

Fig. 7.38 Two cross-head screws hold the float chamber, which has a tapered drain valve in the base. Check that the O-ring gasket fits its groove and has not been damaged

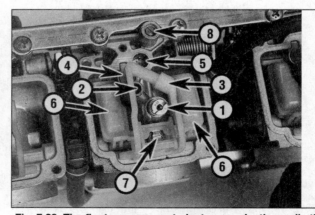

1 Main jet
2 Pilot jet
3 Cold start pick-up
4 Cold start jet
5 Pilot by-pass
6 Floats
7 Tang which closes needle valve
8 Pilot adjusting screw

Fig. 7.39 The float arrangement pivots on a plastic cradle that also provides the pick-up for the cold-start jet

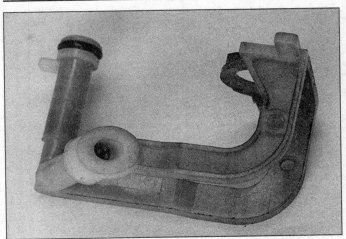

Fig. 7.40 The plastic cradle plugs in around the cold start jet, sealed by the O-ring, and clips into the other side of the float bowl

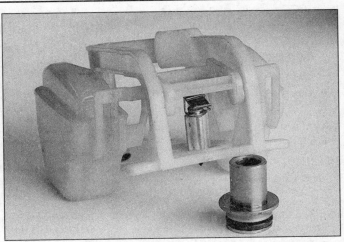

Fig. 7.41 Floats and needle valve in position on the (inverted) cradle, with the brass, needle valve seat in the foreground

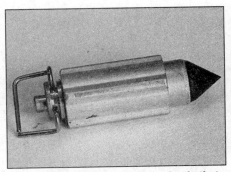

Fig.7.42 Needle valves have a plastic tip to give a more reliable seal. At the other end there is a wire clip that goes over the operating arm, helping assembly and making sure the valve follows the float motion without sticking. The central pin is spring-loaded

Fig. 7.43 Main jet

Fig. 7.44 ID number etched on carburettor body identifies the model to which the carburettors were originally fitted

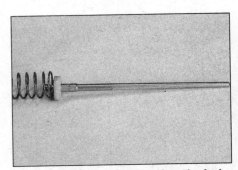

Fig. 7.45 Tapered needle. Note the fuel varnish stains on the parallel portion and wear marks where the taper starts. This implies that when the engine is running on the parallel portion (up to quarter throttle) liquid fuel climbs up the needle and then evaporates, leaving varnish deposits behind. At larger throttle openings fuel is either atomised before it can run along the needle or the needle's movement in the jet keeps it clean

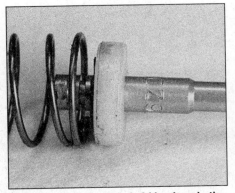

Fig. 7.46 The needle is held in place in the air slide by the slide's return spring, which butts up to the plastic washer. The needle's identity code can be seen just below the washer

Fig. 7.47 Mikuni's semi-flatslide design. The central hole in the base is where the needle fits, the other hole is the vent between the venturi and the top chamber. Check the diaphragm is not damaged, particularly where it is joined to the plastic slide

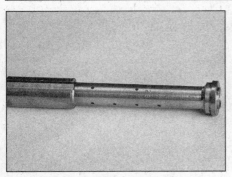

Fig. 7.48 The emulsion tube. There is a keyway in the thicker, lower portion, which engages with a projection in the carburettor body to make sure the tube is fitted the right way round. The main jet screws into the bottom of the tube

Fig. 7.49 Mikuni RS flatslide (aftermarket) carburettors have a plunger-type accelerator pump. Each carburettor has a casting for the chamber of the pump, but only one in a bank of four has the pump fitted. The operating rod is moved by the stop on the throttle spindle, which can be adjusted to control the point at which it makes contact with the rod

Fig. 7.50 Delivery from the accelerator pump is through the small nozzle just upstream of the needle. The two air jets can also be seen here – the main air jet is central, the pilot air jet to the right of it

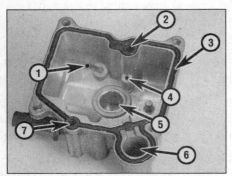

Fig. 7.51 The RS float bowl

1   Overflow pipe
2   Cold start jet
3   O-ring
4   Cold start feed
5   Drain plug
6   Accelerator pump chamber
7   Accelerator pump delivery

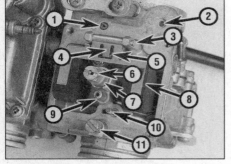

Fig. 7.52 RS float and jet arrangement

1   Accelerator pump delivery jet
2   Hole for accelerator pump plunger
3   Pivot
4   Tang
5   Needle valve
6   Main jet
7   Emulsion tube/needle jet
8   Float
9   Pilot jet
10 Cold start jet
11 Pilot adjusting screw

Carburettor series

These numbers refer to the type of carburettor and are used to prefix part numbers.

Series	Carburettor type
159	30 – 36 mm spigot
166	38 mm spigot
169	28, 30 mm small body
171	30 mm flange
172	28 mm flange
175	28 mm spigot
176	30 – 36 mm spigot
182	26 mm spigot
188	Kawasaki, 32 mm flange
192	26 mm flange
193	24 mm flange
205	34 mm flange
211	Kawasaki KR250/350/750
224	40 – 44 mm spigot
235	30 mm flange
247	Yamaha YZ250/400, IT400
258	Yamaha TT, SR, XT500, Suzuki DR, SP, GS550, GS750/850 Kawasaki Z650/1000
261	VM29 and VM33
389	TM32, 34, 36, 38, 41
499	TM33
568	RS34, 36
568	RS38, 40

Main jets

The threaded portion is similar in appearance on all Mikuni main jets, so they are most easily identified by the size and shape of the head, either hexagonal or flat screw slot.

4/042 large hex

Identified by very deep hexagon.
Sizes #50 – #200 in steps of 5, #200 – #720 in steps of 10.

M10/14 small hex

Hexagon has usual proportions for a set screw.

Sizes #50 – #200 in steps of 5.

N100/604 large round

Flat screwdriver slot, round head.
Sizes #50 – #210, in steps of 2.5

N102/221 small round

Same size thread as N100/604 but smaller head.
Sizes #50 – #200 in steps of 2.5

N208/099 press-in

No thread. Used on some Ducati and Yamaha models.
Sizes #110 – #140 in steps of 2.5

Pilot jets

Vary in the position of the thread and the dimensions of the emulsion tube

VM22/210

Used on most Mikuni carburettors. Short thread, up close to flat screwdriver slot.
Sizes #10 – #30 in steps of 2.5, #35 – #95 in steps of 5.

VM28/213

Fitted to 1972 Kawasaki Z1.
Sizes #15 – #40 in steps of 5.

Fig. 7.53 The throttle spindle has rocker arms clamped to it to lift the air slide when the spindle is turned

VM28/486

Threaded portion in centre, flat screwdriver slot, emulsion tube much narrower than thread.
Fitted to VM28, RS36 and RS38.
Sizes #12.5 – #65 in steps of 2.5

M28/1001

Longer thread, takes up half of jet.
Sizes #15 – #65 in steps of 2.5

BS30/96

OEM for CV carburettors, similar appearance to VM22/210 but only one pair of holes in emulsion tube.
Sizes #30 – #60 in steps of 2.5

N151/067

OEM for CV carburettors, similar appearance to BS30/96.
Sizes #30 – #60 in steps of 2.5

N224/103

OEM for TMX36 on Yamaha YZ
Sizes #35 – #65 in steps of 5

Air jets

BS30/97

Fitted to 26 – 44 mm spigot mount carburettors.
Sizes #0.5 – #2.0 in steps of 0.1

BS42/55

Same external size as BS30/97 but with completely different range of jet sizes. Used for pilot air and main air jets on OEM Suzuki carburettors.
Sizes #70 – #300 in steps of 10

Needle jets

Mikuni have two basic needle jets, the 'bleed' type (which is an emulsion tube with air bleed holes in its stem and a plain nozzle) and the 'primary choke' type, which has a screen on the upstream side of the nozzle and a single air bleed hole at the base of the screen. Some later RS flatslide carburettors have a screen with an aperture, which is located downstream of the nozzle.

The jet must also match the carburettor series for both length and the type of main jet that it carries, so the part number (eg 389/P-4/P) has three figures denoting the carburettor series (389 is the TM series), then a letter-number combination (P-4) denoting the size, and a final letter describing the type (P for primary choke or B for bleed).

The size code starts at N which is 2.550 mm and each letter represents an increase of 0.5 mm (so P would be 2.650 mm) and the numbers represent increments of 0.005 mm (so P-4 is 2.650 + (4 × 0.005) or 2.670 mm). Usually the size codes run from N to R, but one exception is for the 224 series (40 to 44

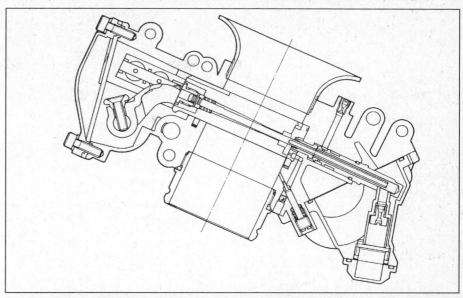

Fig. 7.54 Mikuni TDMR40, supplied with the Suzuki GSX-R750W race kit. Note the angled float bowl and offset main jet, designed to keep the carburettor compact and let it operate at a steep downdraught angle. To prevent sticking, the air slide runs on roller bearings *(Suzuki)*

mm spigot mounted), where the letter sizes run from Z continuing through AA, BB to CC (increments of 0.05 mm as before) and the numbers are 0 or 5 (increment of 0.025 mm).

Needles

There is a needle code that reveals the dimensions of the needle, for example 6DH2. The first digit (6) is the carburettor series number and will affect the overall length of the needle. The next digit (D) refers to the needle taper and the third (if a letter) refers to the second taper, furthest from the mounting grooves. The final number is a factory reference and later, flatslide, types have an extension, eg -60, added to the end. This signifies the diameter of the needle before the taper and is hundredths of a mm above 2.00, so -60 represents a diameter of 2.60. Where other needles are listed for a specific model a similar extension in the range -1 to -5 indicates the groove in which the needle clip is fitted for that model.

Series (first digit)
4 all 18 mm carburettors
    22 and 24 mm flange
5 26-32 mm spigot
    28-34 mm flange
6 30-38 mm spigot
7 40 and 44 mm spigot
8 42 mm HSR
9 RS and HS carburettors

The taper codes begin at A (= 15') and increase in 15' steps (so D is 1° and H is 2°).

Broadly speaking, a shallower taper (letter closer to the beginning of the alphabet) will give leaner mixtures, giving the greatest change as the throttle is opened further. A steeper taper will give a progressively richer mixture. To alter the mixture at small throttle openings it is necessary to raise or lower the needle (which alters the point at which the parallel portion changes to taper), to fit a needle with a different parallel diameter or to use a different needle jet size.

Mikuni manuals have many tables that list the actual needle diameter at 10 mm intervals along its length, for all needle profiles.

Air slides

The cutaway number refers to the height of the leading edge above the base of the slide, so a #3 will be greater than a #2 and will give a leaner mixture in the 0 to 1/8 throttle position.

The slides are also available in different materials: chrome plated zinc alloy, chrome plated brass, anodised aluminium alloy, and plastic.

Some older slide carburettors have windows in the body casting, plugged either with Perspex or a removable set screw, to give a view of the slide. The slides have marks (usually the indentation of a drill bit), which, when aligned with the holes allow two carburettors to be synchronised or set a throttle position at which a two-stroke's oil pump is adjusted. This type was mainly used on two-stroke singles and twins.

Notes

Chapter 8
Carburettor construction and adjustment

Amal, Dell'Orto, SU, Gardner, EI, Lectron. Fixed jet carburettors: Bendix, Tillotson, Keihin and Mikuni

Contents

1 Introduction

Despite the enormous range of motorcycle engine size and types since 1950, carburettor design can be condensed down into something like four basic formats. Different makes of carburettor obviously have their own features and style, but if you are familiar with the basic family type, you can quickly find your way around any carburettor.

There are a few particular makes that have either been used on a wide variety of machines or, if not used themselves, have influenced other designs that were. It is worth looking at them in some detail, partly to see how their influence has permeated through to current design (in fact some of them are still current). The other part of the reason is that many of these carburettors will be fitted to older, now classic machines and will need to be restored and overhauled, so some detail explanation may be useful.

There are plenty of other carburettors used on bikes but not mentioned specifically in this Chapter (eg Bing, BVF, Hitachi, Jikov, TK (TeiKei) and Weber) but their construction and operating principles are very similar to the types that are described.

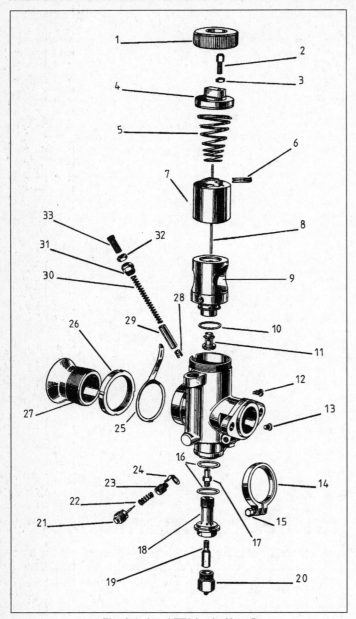

Fig. 8.1 Amal TT9 body *(Amal)*

1 Mixing chamber cap	18 Jet holder
2 Throttle cable adjuster	19 Main jet
3 Locknut	20 Plug screw
4 Mixing chamber top	21 Pilot needle
5 Return spring	22 Friction spring
6 Needle clip	23 Pilot needle insert
7 Throttle valve	24 Spring catch
8 Jet needle	25 Lock spring
9 Choke adaptor	26 Lock ring
10 Seal	27 Air Intake tube
11 Jet choke tube	28 Nipple holder
12 Adaptor locating screw	29 Air valve
13 Plug screw	30 Spring
14 Outlet clip	31 Air barrel top
15 Screw	32 Locknut
16 Seals	33 Adjuster
17 Needle jet	

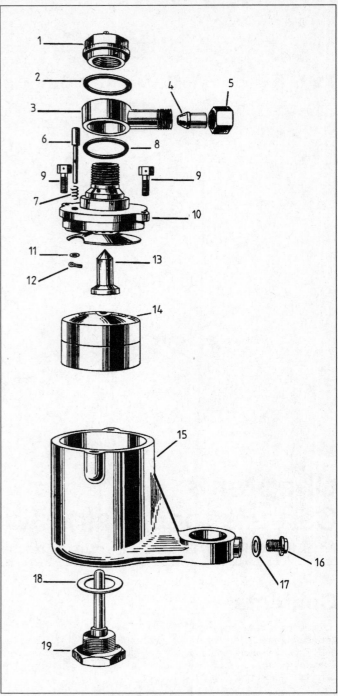

Fig. 8.2 Amal TT9 float bowl *(Amal)*

1 Banjo nut	11 Washer
2 Sealing washer	12 Spilt pin
3 Banjo union	13 Float needle
4 Ferrule	14 Float
6 Gland nut	16 Float chamber
6 Tickler	16 Plug screw
7 Spring	17 Sealing washer
8 Sealing washer	18 Sealing washer
9 Screw	19 Plug and guide pin
10 Float chamber top	

2 Amal carburettors

See Figs. 8.1, 8.2, 8.3, 8.4, 8.5, 8.6, 8.7, 8.8 and 8.9

Amal emerged after WW2 as the main motorcycle carburettor, being fitted to virtually all British bikes (which in those days meant a majority of world bikes) and setting the standard for this type of carburettor. There were other air-bleeding, slide type carburettors, such as Dell'Orto, Bing and Mikuni, but it's not clear whether they arrived at their designs independently or how much they were influenced by Amal and its Amac predecessors. Certainly, during the 1970s, Mikuni referred to this kind of carburettor as Amal-type.

In fact there is a long list of Amal types. In 1969 they had five distinct types (19, 32, GP2, 379 and the 600/900 series Concentric, descended from the 375/376/389 Monobloc).

The GP2, a development of earlier TT and RN carburettors was designed for race bikes. It used a separate float bowl, whose height could be adjusted to align the fuel level with the base of a circle scribed on the carburettor, permitting the carburettor itself to be installed at any angle. It had a round air slide but the needle was attached to the side of it, moving in its own chamber and not obstructing the venturi (RN stood for Remote Needle).

The needle ran in a conventional needle jet, with the main jet at the bottom and an air jet bleeding air into a primary choke arrangement at the top. The spray nozzle was angled from the top of the needle jet into the venturi and, on WOT, this was the only disturbance to air flow. The thin-walled air slide ran in a 'choke adapter', leaving a narrow slot in an otherwise completely smooth-bore venturi.

Outside air supply to the air jet came through a small chamber, with a cable-operated plunger in it. The rider could control this from a lever on the handlebar – lowering the plunger restricted the feed to the air jet

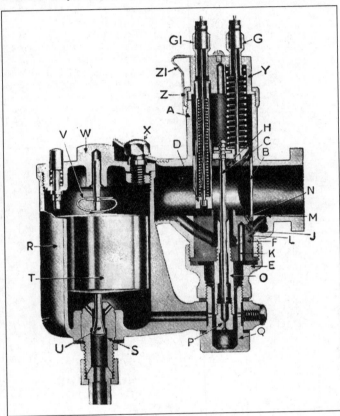

Fig. 8.3 Amal 289 *(Amal)*

This Amal Instrument proved popular for many years, and was standard equipment on the majority of machines of that era. Note the similarities between it and the TT9 racing carburettor.

A	Mixing chamber	O	Needle jet
B	Throttle valve	P	Main jet
C	Jet needle and clip	Q	Float chamber union bolt
D	Air valve ('choke')	R	Float chamber
E	Mixing chamber union	S	Float needle seat
F	Jet block	T	Float
G	Cable adjusters	U	Float needle valve
H	Jet block barrel	V	Clip
J	Pilot jet	W	Float chamber cover
K	Pilot passage	X	Lock screw
L	Pilot air passage	Y	Mixing chamber top
M	Pilot outlet	Z	Mixing chamber lock ring
N	Pilot bypass	Z1	Lock spring

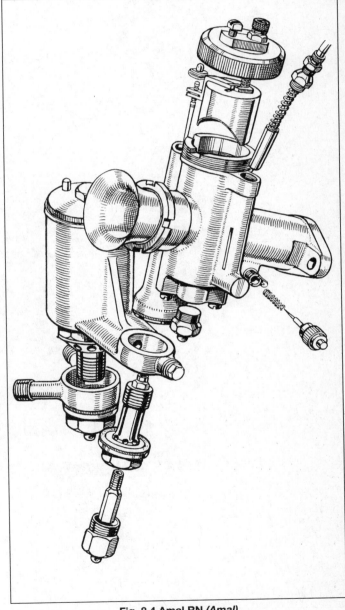

Fig. 8.4 Amal RN *(Amal)*

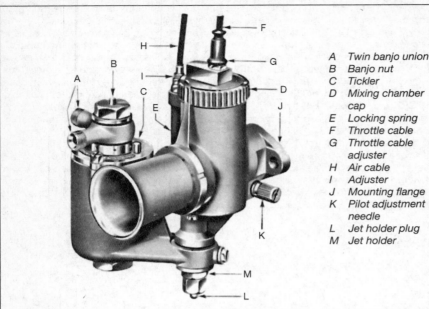

A	Twin banjo union
B	Banjo nut
C	Tickler
D	Mixing chamber cap
E	Locking spring
F	Throttle cable
G	Throttle cable adjuster
H	Air cable
I	Adjuster
J	Mounting flange
K	Pilot adjustment needle
L	Jet holder plug
M	Jet holder

Fig. 8.5 Amal GP (Amal)

and would richen the mixture, primarily for cold running (although riders often used it to increase the narrow powerband of some race engines as it allowed them to alter the fuel slope as the engine revs changed).

Amal's Monobloc had a completely different shape and is immediately recognisable as the forerunner of current carburettors. The needle was central in the round air slide, the main jet, air bleed and pilot system are in the same places as they are on carburettors like the Keihin FCR and Mikuni FSR. The float chamber was cast into the main body, although it was offset to the side, right or left, depending upon the installation.

This was the main change in the next model. The Concentric carburettor had the float bowl below the jet block, concentric with it.

The Concentric was developed into a smooth-bore version, taking over from the GP race carburettor. The final development was a power jet kit, which replaced the detachable bellmouth with another containing a nozzle fed from a jet in the float bowl.

The important thing about this family of carburettors is they were so efficient, both in

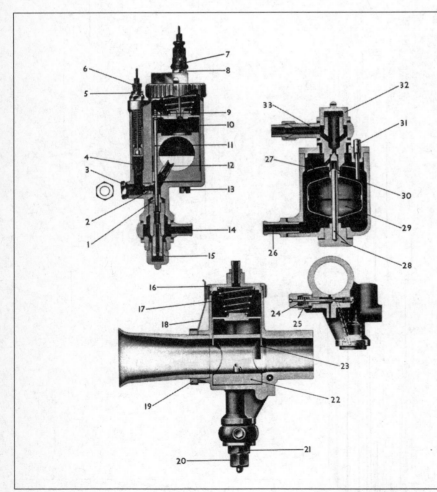

1	Needle jet
2	Air jet
3	Air jet plug
4	Primary air slot
5	Locknut
6	Air valve cable adjuster
7	Throttle cable adjuster
8	Locknut
9	Needle clip
10	Needle clip screw
11	Jet needle
12	Spring tube
13	Screws
14	Banjo union
15	Main jet
16	Mixing chamber cap
17	Return spring
18	Lock spring
19	Air tube lock ring
20	Jet plug
21	Jet holder
22	Choke adaptor
23	Throttle valve
24	Pilot jet adjusting needle
25	Pilot adjuster lock spring
26	Petrol outlet connector
27	Baffle plate
28	Base plug and guide rod
29	Float
30	Float needle
31	Tickler
32	Banjo nut
33	Banjo union

Fig. 8.6 Amal GP section (Amal)

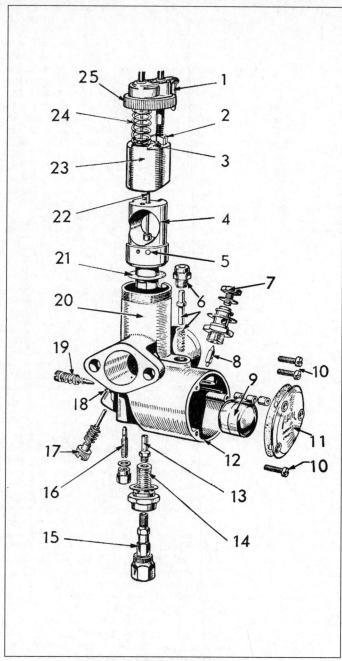

Fig. 8.7 Amal Monobloc (Amal)

1 Mixing chamber top lock spring
2 Air valve
3 Needle clip
4 Jet block
5 Pilot bypass
6 Tickler assembly
7 Banjo bolt
8 Float needle
9 Float
10 Screws
11 Float chamber cover
12 Float chamber
13 Needle jet
14 Jet holder
15 Main jet
16 Pilot jet
17 Throttle stop screw
18 Locating screw
19 Pilot air screw
20 Carburettor body
21 Fibre washer
22 Jet needle
23 Throttle valve
24 Return spring
25 Lock ring

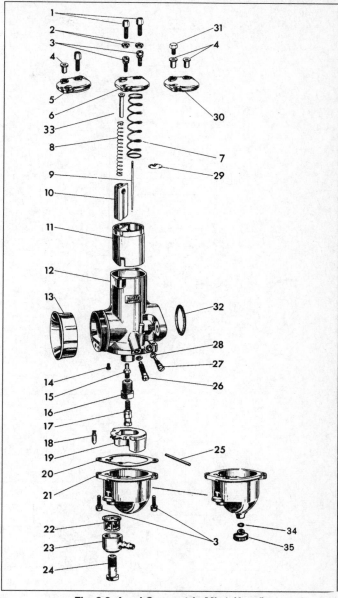

Fig. 8.8 Amal Concentric Mk 1 (Amal)

1 Cable adjuster
2 Cable adjuster locknut
3 Screw
4 Ferrule
5 Mixing chamber top (optional)
6 Mixing chamber top (standard)
7 Throttle return spring
8 Choke return spring
9 Jet needle
10 Choke valve
11 Throttle valve
12 Carburettor body
13 Velocity stack
14 Pilot jet (2-stroke applications)
16 Needle jet
16 Jet holder
17 Main jet
18 Float valve
19 Float assembly
20 Float bowl gasket
21 Float bowl (standard)
22 Filter
23 Banjo union
24 Banjo bolt
26 Float pivot pin
26 Throttle stop screw
27 Pilot air screw
28 O-ring
29 Needle clip
30 Mixing chamber top (optional)
31 Blanking plug
32 O-ring
33 Choke valve guide
34 Fibre washer (optional)
35 Drain plug (optional)

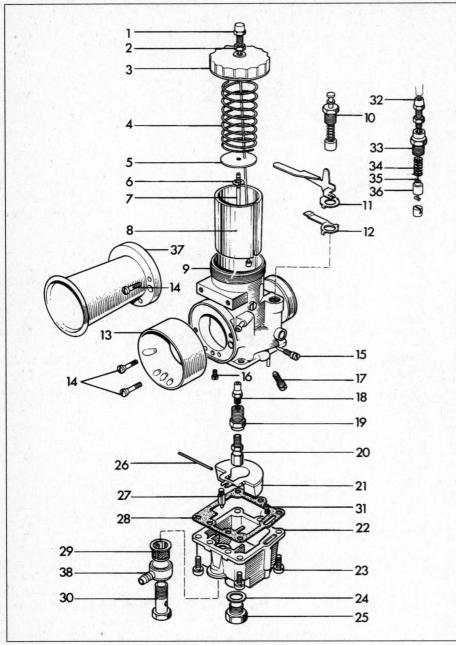

Fig. 8.9 Amal Concentric Mk 2 (Amal)

1 Cable adjuster
2 Locknut
3 Mixing chamber top
4 Throttle valve spring
6 Needle retaining disc
6 Needle clip
7 Jet needle
8 Throttle valve
9 Carburettor body
10 Cold start plunger
   assembly
11 Cold start lever and
   bracket
12 Cold start click spring

13 Air Intake adaptor
14 Screw – 2 off
16 Pilot air adjusting screw
16 Pilot jet
17 Throttle stop adjusting
   screw
18 Needle jet
19 Jet holder
20 Main jet
21 Float
22 Float chamber
23 Screw – 4 off
24 Drain plug gasket
25 Drain plug

26 Float pivot pin
27 Float needle
28 Float chamber gasket
29 Filter
30 Banjo bolt
31 Blanking screw
32 Cable adjuster
33 Body
34 Return spring
36 Cable
36 Plunger
37 Velocity stack
38 Banjo union

air flow and in fuel atomisation. It meant, to an owner or engine builder, that they gave good power and were easy to tune. So easy in fact, that Amal only listed a few needles, a couple of air jets (and none on the Monobloc or mark 1 Concentric – the air bleed was simply a passage in the casting) and a few throttle cutaways, plus a wide range of main jets. The jets are calibrated in cc/min flow under fixed conditions on a test rig. The range of sizes (roughly 100 to 400) overlaps with the mm diameter codes used by most other manufacturers.

Needle jets are coded 105, 106, 107 etc, where this is the diameter of the jet in thousandths of an inch (eg 105 means 0.105 in).

Throttle valve cutaways are coded in tenths of an inch, from 2 to 5, in increments of 0.5.

Air jets, where fitted, are sized by the diameter of the jet, in inches (eg 0.125).

Evidence of the ease of tuning comes from the wide misfire limits shown by the carburettors. Most of the data for mixture loops shown elsewhere in this book comes from Amal smoothbore carburettors. In one example, a 40 mm Amal was fitted to a Honda XBR500 (not a powerful or high revving engine, so gas flow through the carburettor would not be high) and at 6000 rpm WOT, it went through seven main jet sizes between a lean misfire and unstable running caused by a rich mixture. You would expect that an engine pulling more air through its intake would create better conditions for atomisation and fuel mixing, giving even wider misfire limits.

The problem with Amal carburettors came in two parts. The disintegration of the British bike industry took away opportunities for original equipment contracts and the joint development processes that this brings. Second, the carburettors had been developed for singles and twins in layouts where carburettor height was not important. British industry hadn't got beyond in-line three cylinder engines and most were 360° twins. When it came to adapting these carburettors to suit the next generation of in-line fours from Honda, Kawasaki and Suzuki, there was no provision to join the units in a bank and, worse still, no throttle linkage to connect all four together.

Initial installations used separate cables running from a junction box with one or two cables going to the twistgrip. Routing the cables cleanly was a problem. Amal tried one or two prototype linkages, like the spindle and rocker arm type used later by Mikuni and Keihin. But where these were built into the carburettor body, Amal used an external linkage, with short cables connecting the rockers to the air slides. It only made the installation bigger and taller. It still didn't address the slide carburettor's difficulties with sticking throttles or heavy return springs and meanwhile Japanese manufacturers were coming along with neater linkages for slide carburettors and banks of CV carburettors that side-stepped the problems of height and sticking air slides.

3 Dell'Orto carburettors

See Figs. 8.10. 8.11, 8.12, 8.13 and 8.14

Dell'Orto carburettors, used as original equipment on many European bikes and scooters as well as competition machines and aftermarket conversions, are air slide, air bleed types. The earlier type (PH-series) had round slides while the square-slide VHB and later flat-slide, smoothbore VHSA and VHSB were added to the range.

They cover a range of sizes from 14 to 41 mm. The PHF and PHM series goes from 30 to 41 mm bore, while the flat-slide VHSA series covers 28 – 32 mm and SB covers 34–39 mm (although 42 and 44 mm throttles have been made especially for the Aprilia grand prix race bikes). The flat-slide versions have oval bores. In this case the nominal size is an average of the longer and shorter diameters.

Float bowl

There are two types of float (a) connected to a pivot and (b) separate, able to slide on guides. Both are available in two weights, heavy to provide a higher fuel level (for four-stroke engines) and light to provide a lower fuel level (for two-strokes). The weight, in grams, is marked on the float.

The needle valve seat has a size stamped on it in hundredths of a mm (eg 200 = 2.0 mm) and, for gravity feed, should be 30% larger than the main jet. For pump feed, a smaller seat size is necessary. A too-large seat will

1 Screw
2 Fibre washer
3 Fuel filter
5 Dust seal
6 Cable adjuster
7 Locknut
8 Screw
9 Carburettor top
10 Gasket
11 Throttle return spring
12 Throttle slide (valve)
13 Cold start plunger
14 O-ring
15 Needle jet
16 Special nut
17 Clamp
18 Clamp screw
19 Insulation sleeve
20 Throttle stop screw
21 Mixture screw
22 Friction spring
23 Main jet
24 Float needle
25 Float
26 Float pivot pin
27 Emulsion tube
28 O-ring
29 Float bowl
30 Screw

Fig. 8.10 Dell'Orto SHB *(Dell'Orto)*

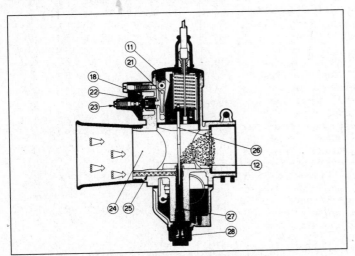

Fig. 8.11 Dell'Orto PHM *(Dell'Orto)*

At 3/4 to full throttle openings the idle circuit and needle/needle jet (26) combination will have little noticeable effect. Where an accelerator pump (22) is fitted, as in this example, it will have operated to cover the transition to main jet operation. Air velocity through the main bore (24) is high, a proportion of which is drawn through the primary air passage (26) to aid vaporisation. Fuel is drawn through and metered by the main jet (28), flows through the needle jet (27) and is discharged into the main bore (12)

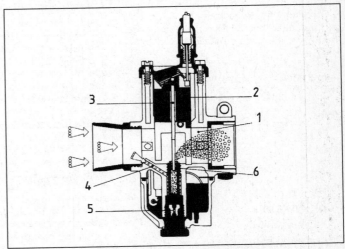

Fig. 8.12 Dell'Orto VHB *(Dell'Orto)*

Note that on some VHB types an air bleed arrangement Is employed, and is still operating at full throttle settings

1 Main bore
2 Throttle valve
3 Jet needle
4 Air passage
5 Main Jet
6 Needle jet holder

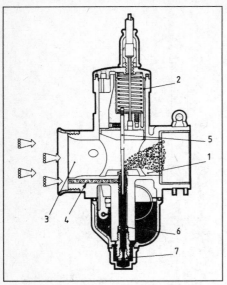

Fig. 8.13 Dell'Orto PHB (Dell'Orto)

1 Main bore
2 Throttle valve
3 Air entering bore
4 Air passage
5 Jet needle
6 Needle jet
7 Main jet

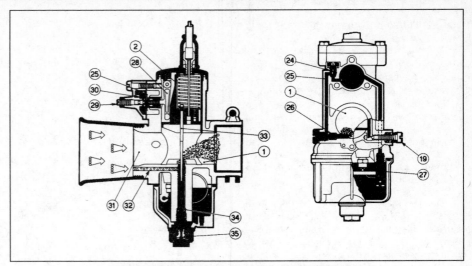

Fig. 8.14 Dell'Orto accelerator pump (Dell'Orto)

As the throttle valve (2) rises, the pump lever (28) is displaced, pushing the pump diaphragm (25) outwards. Fuel in the diaphragm chamber (30) is forced past the non-return valve (24) and is sprayed into the main bore via a discharge jet (26).
When the throttle is closed, the diaphragm returns under spring pressure. The non-return valve (24) closes, and the inlet valve (27) opens, allowing a fresh charge of fuel to enter the diaphragm chamber. The pump can be set by moving the adjuster (29) to give the required amount of fuel

cause flooding problems if its sealing pressure is not greater than the pressure in the fuel.

Float height adjustment

For pivoting floats, hold the carburettor body with the float bowl gasket face vertical and measure from the 'bottom' surface of the float to the gasket face.

For sliding floats, remove the floats, hold the carburettor body upside down and check that the float arms are parallel to the gasket face.

Carburettor	Float height
PHBG	16 ±0.5 mm
PHBL	24 ±0.5 mm
PHBH	24 ±0.5 mm
PHBE	18 ±0.5 mm
PHF	18 ±0.5 mm
PHM	18 ±0.5 mm
VHB	24 ±0.5 mm
VHSA	11 ±0.5 mm
VHSB	11 ±0.5 mm

Pilot system

There are two types of idle circuit:

Mixture adjusting screw

Located downstream of the throttle valve, controls the volume of pre-mixed air and fuel that is drawn into the venturi. Turning the screw out allows more air-fuel to flow. As the AF ratio is fixed and some air also flows past the throttle valve, turning the screw out tends to richen the mixture. Example: if the pilot jet and pilot air jet deliver a 6:1 AF ratio and the flow past the throttle is 6 units of air, the total

mixture is 12:1. If the pilot system is now doubled (a flow of 12:2) the total will be 18 of air to 2 of fuel, or 9:1.

Air adjusting screw

Located upstream of the throttle valve, adjusts the air flow in the pilot system. Turning the screw out weakens the pilot mixture.

Adjustment – mixture and air screw

Make sure there is about 1 mm free play in the throttle cable, when the throttle is closed. With the engine fully warmed, turn in the throttle stop screw slightly, to raise the idle speed to about 1200 rpm for four strokes and about 1400 rpm for two-strokes. This is a tapered screw at the base of the throttle slide, so turning it in lifts the slide.

Now turn the mixture or air adjusting screw a small amount (less than 1/8 turn) in whichever direction is necessary to make the engine speed up or to run more smoothly. Wait several seconds to give it a chance to stabilise. If the speed rises, bring it back to the initial speed using the throttle stop. Repeat the process until the best idle is obtained, then use the throttle stop to get the normal idle speed.

Check there is still clearance in the throttle cable. If the engine staggers when the throttle is blipped or when pulling away, it may be necessary to richen the idle mixture or increase the pilot fuel flow.

Needle jet/nozzle

Four-stroke engines usually use a plain nozzle, while two heights of screened nozzle are available on some carburettors for two-

strokes. The shorter type (7 mm screen height) produces richer mixtures all through the range, while the longer type (9 mm) makes the mixture go weak at low speeds and rich at high speeds. Where there isn't a choice, the screen height is 8 mm.

There are also plain nozzle emulsion tubes with various patterns of holes. Those high up (above the fuel level) let the air jet work at maximum efficiency and give weaker high speed mixtures for a given needle jet or main jet. Those with holes below the fuel level restrict the action of the air jet at low speed or during initial acceleration and give a richer mixture in these conditions.

Needles

Dell'Orto needles are defined by the diameter of the parallel portion, the diameter of the tip and the length of the tapered section (plus the length of a second taper and the diameter where it starts, if the needle has a second taper). For each carburettor type there is a code number stamped just below the clip grooves, in the range 1 to 40. Dell'Orto manuals list the relevant diameters and lengths for each code number.

In most carburettors there is a spring that pushes the needle against the surface of the nozzle, to discourage flutter and wear.

Jets

All jets are stamped with their size, in hundredths of a mm (eg 320 = 3.20 mm).

Throttle slides

Usually four or five cutaway sizes are available, marked in tenths of a mm, ranging from 30 to 60 or 70 (ie 3.0 to 6.0 or 7.0 mm) in steps of 10. The larger numbers give weaker mixtures in the 0 to 1/4 throttle region.

PHF and PHM slides (with ramps for accelerator pumps) have a size marking on the lower part of the throttle valve casting. The number (eg 40/2) has two parts, the first (40) is the height of the cutaway in tenths of a mm (ie 4.0 mm) and the second (2) is a code which gives dimensions of the ramp:

Code	Start of ramp from top of slide	End of ramp
1	10	20
2	13	23
3	2	30
4	13	26
5	2	20

Accelerator pumps

Dell'Orto use piston type pumps and cam-operated pumps (see *throttle slides*, above) in some carburettors.

In the piston type, the tip of the jet needle bears on top of the piston, in a wider than usual needle jet. There is a spring underneath the piston, between it and the main jet, so it follows the motion of the needle as the throttle is opened and closed. There are ports through the piston to allow fuel flow and a ball check valve to prevent fuel falling back into the float bowl. When the throttle is opened quickly, the spring pushes the piston up, forcing the contents of the needle jet through the nozzle.

The more common type of pump is operated by a ramp on the leading edge of the throttle slide. A rocker arm follows the ramp and bears against a spring-loaded diaphragm. Behind the diaphragm there is a chamber, which draws fuel up from the float bowl past a ball check valve and, when the cam pushes the diaphragm against its spring, forces fuel out past another check valve through a nozzle on the floor of the venturi just upstream of the throttle valve.

The start and duration of the pump stroke is determined by the slope of the ramp (see *throttle slides*, above), while the quantity of fuel pumped can be adjusted by a screw on the front of the carburettor body, above the venturi intake, which regulates the travel of the diaphragm. Turning the screw out increases the amount of fuel injected into the venturi. The check valves prevent fuel draining or being pumped back into the float bowl and also stop the system working as a power jet when the throttle is in a constant position.

4 SU carburettors

See Fig. 8.15

There are two main types of CV carburettor, often called SU-type (in which the piston slide is constructed like a piston and sealed in the same way) and Stromberg-type (in which a diaphragm is used to seal the chamber, allowing a lot more freedom in piston design). Some early motorcycle CV carburettors were SU-type (some were even SUs) but the vast majority are Stromberg-type, if not actually made by Stromberg (most are Keihin, Mikuni, Hitachi and Bing).

The SU's main claim is one of simplicity. Virtually all tuning is done by changing the tapered needle and there is a very large number of needles. The apparent simplicity of

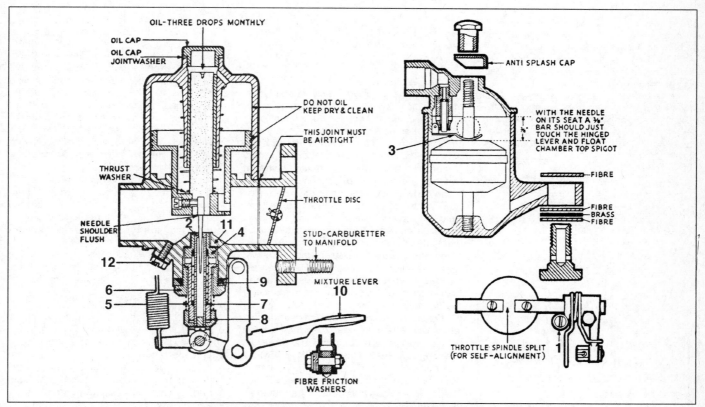

Fig. 8.15 SU MC2 carburettor, used on Triumph Thunderbird (early 1950s)

1 Throttle stop screw
2 Jet
3 Float lever
4 Jet bush (upper)
5 Jet bush (lower)
6 Locking screw

7 Gland washer (lower)
8 Jet adjusting nut (idle mixture control)
9 Gland washer (upper)
10 Mixture lever (lowers jet block to richen mixture for cold running)

11 Bridge (supports piston when engine is not running)
12 Blanking plug (removal allows the piston to be lifted using a thin rod to temporarily weaken the mixture for test purposes)

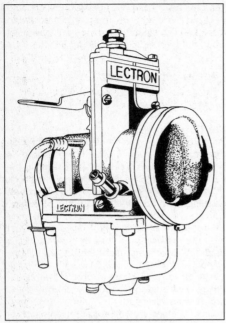

Fig. 8.16 Lectron body

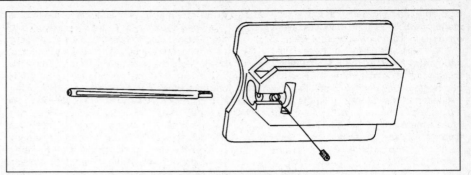

Fig. 8.17 Lectron air slide and needle

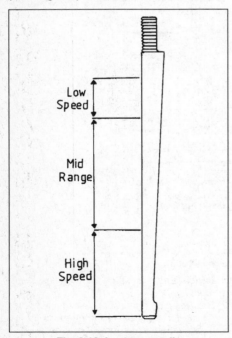

Fig. 8.18 Lectron needle

having only one thing to change is offset by the huge range of conditions it has to meet and the complexity of having several needles that are best in different conditions and finding one needle that blends all of these dimensions into one taper.

The carburettor uses one fuel jet and no air jets. The fuel jet size can be altered and it is held in a bearing which can be raised or lowered to provide tuning for idle mixture (lowering the jet richens the mixture and on some carburettors the cold-start mechanism is a lever which lowers the jet further). A throttle stop screw is used in conjunction with the jet height to control idle speed.

Given the correct jet and idle settings, the needle taper then controls everything else. To prevent the air slide fluttering and to slow down its reaction to sudden throttle opening (and therefore create a slightly rich mixture for acceleration) there is an oil-filled damper built into the slide.

5 Gardner, El, Lectron carburettors

See Figs. 8.16, 8.17 and 8.18

There is one other type of slide carburettor, made initially by Ron Gardner in Kent, in about 1970, and later by El and Lectron in the US, which combines complete simplicity with several features found on much later, high-performance carburettors – flat slide throttle, smooth-bore venturi and compact sizing. In bench and dyno tests performed by Weslake in the early 1970s, a Gardner gave better air flow than same-sized OE carburettors, including the Amal Concentric, and was on a par with the Amal GP (a much bulkier and more expensive instrument). Gardner carburettors are still popular among Classic racers, where they are a natural replacement for GPs on bikes like Matchless G50 and Manx Norton (or their current descendants).

The flat slide gives the carburettor a very short venturi and there is no main jet or pilot jet. Fuel metering is done solely by a parallel needle, with a flat taper formed on one side. The original Gardner had no float bowl, a separate unit being used (which was common practice on competition engines at that time). The later American carburettors had integral, concentric float bowls.

Tuning is by changing needles and the only other adjustment is to raise or lower the needle (carried in the air slide on a thread, locked by a grub screw) to provide idle mixture.

The El carburettor came in sizes from 30 mm up to 40 mm and three needles were claimed to cover the normal range of adjustment (two-strokes and four-strokes had different needles). There was also an air jet, available in four sizes from 0.5 up to 2.0.

6 Fixed jet – Bendix, Keihin, Tillotson, Mikuni carburettors

Over recent decades there have been very few motorcycles with fixed jet (or fixed venturi) carburettors. Harley Davidson, Suzuki's Wankel-engined RE5 and the LE Velocette spring to mind, along with various modified machines, usually with turbochargers. Some car carburettors, notably the twin-choke Weber, have also been adapted to motorcycle applications.

As the name implies, fixed jet carburettors are rugged devices with the minimum of moving parts: a float and needle valve, and a throttle valve are the essential components, but there is likely to be an accelerator pump and a choke valve as well.

At its simplest, the carburettor is a venturi with a butterfly-type throttle valve to control air flow. A fuel jet with a series of by-passes (not unlike the pilot system delivery in slide carburettors) are brought into play as more throttle is used.

Each fuel delivery orifice is only effective over a fairly small load/speed region, so there may be more delivery nozzles or spray bars to bring in more fuel as the engine load increases.

The position of the nozzles/orifices relative to the throttle valve should make it obvious where they are meant to be most effective. To extend the range of the carburettor, more venturis are added, sometimes with a small venturi tunnel mounted inside the main venturi, to ensure a region of smooth, fast-flowing air which can pick up its own fuel (to be added to the total arriving at the engine).

There needs to be a smooth progression as each additional feed is brought into play, whether the throttle is opened slowly or quickly and this is either achieved by having a greater number of fuel nozzles and by-pass outlets, or by using a plunger type accelerator pump whose output depends on the speed and distance of the throttle movement.

The more fuel feeds there are, the smoother the progression and the more precise the fuelling can be. This obviously makes the construction much more complicated and is not very adjustable (as in re-tuning for a modified engine) unless each fuel outlet is controlled by a jet or has a nozzle whose position can be changed. As most of these outlets will be simple drillings, they are fixed and not adjustable.

Adjustment/tuning is usually by a tapered mixture screw and by changing jet size(s), plus whatever might be provided at the accelerator pump. The throttle stop and float height arrangement is generally the same as for slide and CV carburettors, although the Tillotson carburettor uses a diaphragm instead of a float to maintain a constant head of fuel. The tuning procedures are also the same as for other types of carburettor (see Chapter 6) but it is essential to distinguish which part of the carburettor is responsible for which set of load and speed conditions.

The same precautions as for other carburettor types apply, especially cleanliness. As these carburettors depend on more jets and drillings and have few internal moving parts (that tend to be self-cleaning) they are more prone to blockage caused by dirt in the fuel, corrosion and varnishes or gums left by evaporating fuel. Anything that has been stored for a long period should be thoroughly cleaned using a carburettor solvent, while machines that are running (particularly those that are laid up for the winter period) should be treated with a fuel additive of the type designed to clean fuel injectors, through a couple of tanksful of fuel.

Bendix, Keihin and Tillotson carburettors

See Figs. 8.19, 8.20, 8.21, 8.22, 8.23, 8.24 and 8.25

Float level

Bendix. With the carburettor inverted and the weight of the float holding the needle valve closed, there should be a 3/16 inch gap

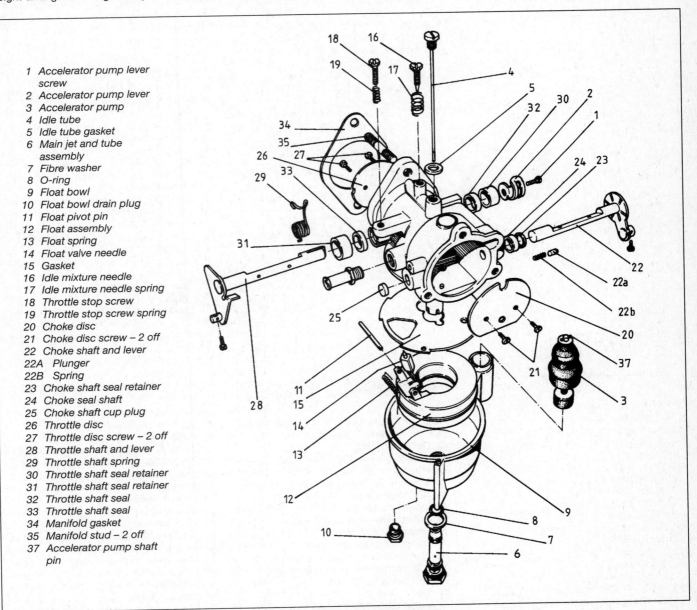

1   Accelerator pump lever
    screw
2   Accelerator pump lever
3   Accelerator pump
4   Idle tube
5   Idle tube gasket
6   Main jet and tube
    assembly
7   Fibre washer
8   O-ring
9   Float bowl
10 Float bowl drain plug
11 Float pivot pin
12 Float assembly
13 Float spring
14 Float valve needle
15 Gasket
16 Idle mixture needle
17 Idle mixture needle spring
18 Throttle stop screw
19 Throttle stop screw spring
20 Choke disc
21 Choke disc screw – 2 off
22 Choke shaft and lever
22A Plunger
22B Spring
23 Choke shaft seal retainer
24 Choke seal shaft
25 Choke shaft cup plug
26 Throttle disc
27 Throttle disc screw – 2 off
28 Throttle shaft and lever
29 Throttle shaft spring
30 Throttle shaft seal retainer
31 Throttle shaft seal retainer
32 Throttle shaft seal
33 Throttle shaft seal
34 Manifold gasket
35 Manifold stud – 2 off
37 Accelerator pump shaft
    pin

Fig. 8.19 Bendix 16P12 fixed jet carburettor

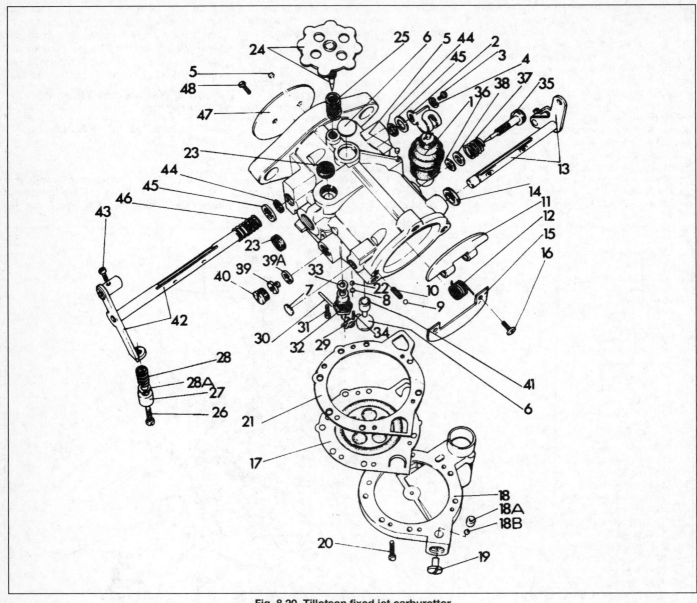

Fig. 8.20 Tillotson fixed jet carburettor

1 Accelerator pump
2 Accelerator pump lever
3 Accelerator pump screw
4 Accelerator pump lever screw lockwasher
5 Channel plug – 2 off
6 Welch plug
7 Welch plug
8 Welch plug
9 Choke shaft friction ball
10 Choke shaft friction spring
11 Choke shutter (top)
12 Choke shutter spring
13 Choke shaft assembly
14 Choke shaft dust seal
15 Choke shutter (bottom)
16 Choke shutter screws
17 Diaphragm

18 Cover
18A Accelerator pump check ball retainer
18B Accelerator pump check ball
19 Diaphragm cover plug screw
20 Diaphragm cover screws – 6 off
21 Diaphragm cover gasket
22 Economiser check ball
23 Fuel filter screen – 2 off
24 Idle adjustment screw
25 Idle adjustment screw spring
26 Throttle stop screw
27 Throttle stop screw cup
28 Throttle stop screw spring
28A Throttle stop screw spring washer
29 Inlet control lever
30 Inlet control lever pin
31 Inlet control lever screw
32 Inlet needle and seat

33 Inlet needle seat gasket
34 Inlet control lever tension spring
35 Intermediate adjusting screw
36 Intermediate adjusting screw packing
37 Intermediate adjusting screw spring
38 Intermediate adjusting screw washer
39 Main jet
39A Main jet gasket
40 Main jet plug screw
41 Main nozzle check valve
42 Throttle shaft assembly
43 Throttle lever wire block screw
44 Dust seal – 2 off
45 Washer- 2 off
46 Throttle shaft spring
47 Throttle shutter
48 Throttle shutter screws

1   Nut
2   Plain washer
3   Pulley
4   Return spring
5   Throttle cable abutment
6   Screw/washer
7   Throttle stop screw
8   Spring
9   Idle mixture screw
10 Spring
11 Screw/washer
12 Choke cable bracket
13 Throttle pump stroke
    adjuster screw
14 Screw
15 Spacer clip
16 Float pivot
17 Grub screw
18 Float
19 Low speed jet
20 Main nozzle
21 Main jet
22 O-ring
23 O-ring
24 Needle clip
25 Float needle
26 Float bowl
27 Screw/washer – 4 off
28 Throttle pump rod
29 Boot
30 O-ring – 2 off
31 Diaphragm
32 Spring
33 Accelerator pump cover
34 Screw
35 Overflow tube
36 Clip – 2 off
37 Union
38 O-ring

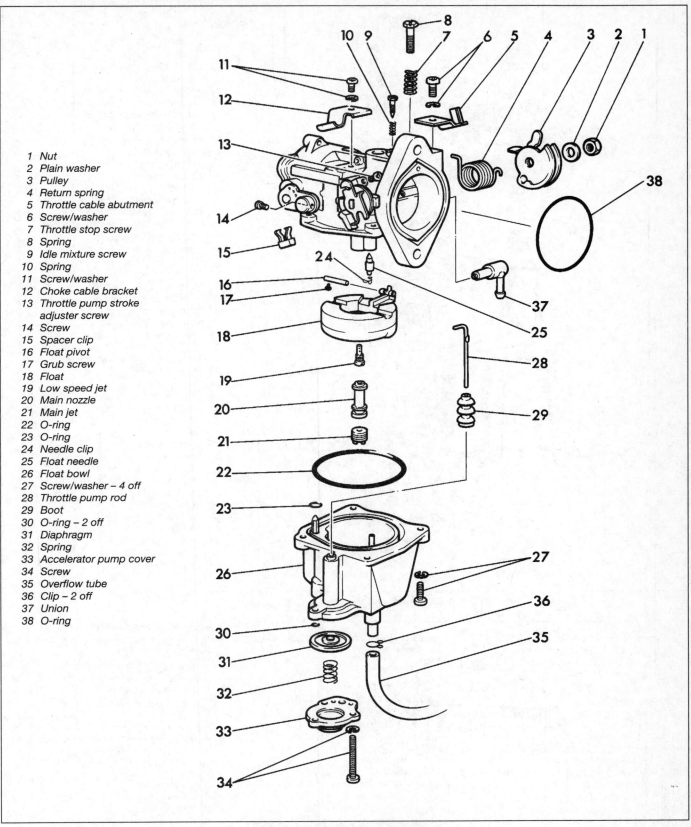

Fig. 8.21 Keihin fixed jet carburettor

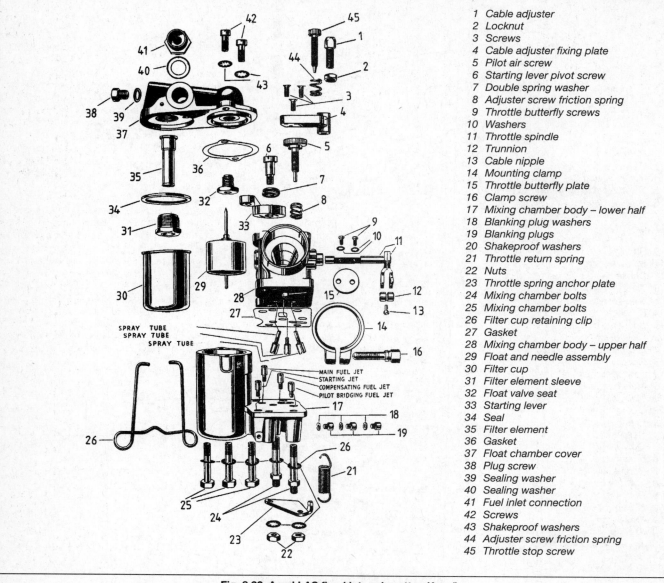

1 Cable adjuster
2 Locknut
3 Screws
4 Cable adjuster fixing plate
5 Pilot air screw
6 Starting lever pivot screw
7 Double spring washer
8 Adjuster screw friction spring
9 Throttle butterfly screws
10 Washers
11 Throttle spindle
12 Trunnion
13 Cable nipple
14 Mounting clamp
15 Throttle butterfly plate
16 Clamp screw
17 Mixing chamber body – lower half
18 Blanking plug washers
19 Blanking plugs
20 Shakeproof washers
21 Throttle return spring
22 Nuts
23 Throttle spring anchor plate
24 Mixing chamber bolts
25 Mixing chamber bolts
26 Filter cup retaining clip
27 Gasket
28 Mixing chamber body – upper half
29 Float and needle assembly
30 Filter cup
31 Filter element sleeve
32 Float valve seat
33 Starting lever
34 Seal
35 Filter element
36 Gasket
37 Float chamber cover
38 Plug screw
39 Sealing washer
40 Sealing washer
41 Fuel inlet connection
42 Screws
43 Shakeproof washers
44 Adjuster screw friction spring
45 Throttle stop screw

Fig. 8.22 Amal LAS fixed jet carburettor *(Amal)*

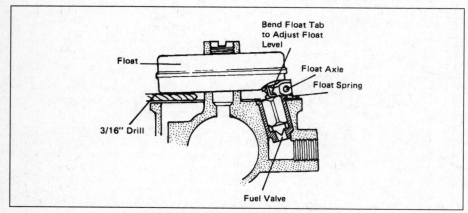

Fig. 8.23 Bendix float height adjustment

between the float bowl gasket face and the float (see Fig. 8.23); check by inserting a 3/16 drill bit shank.

Keihin. Have two measurements. With the carburettor inverted the gap between the float bowl gasket face and the float should be 14 – 16 mm and with the carburettor right-way-up, the float hangs against a stopper with a separate tang that can be bent so the distance of the bottom face of the float is 28 – 30 mm from the gasket face (see Fig. 8.24).

Tillotson. Non-adjustable but in the event of flooding, check the diaphragm's condition and seal.

Main jet

Controls full load fuelling, as on other types of carburettor, and tests should be run at high

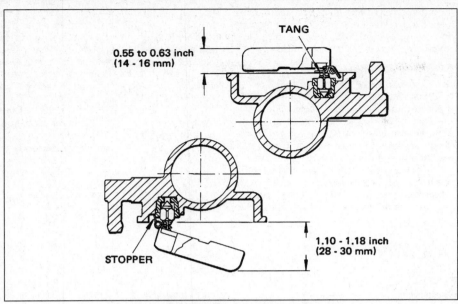

Fig. 8.24 Keihin float height adjustment

Part-load

Bendix and Keihin have a pilot mixture screw which is screwed in until it is lightly seated, then backed out 1 1/2 turns. With the throttle stop set to give an idle speed of 700 – 900 rpm, the mixture screw should be turned small amounts, up to 1/8 turn, allowing the engine to stabilise, to get the best tickover combined with smooth throttle response. Once the best setting has been found, use the throttle stop to bring the idle speed back to the 700 – 900 rpm range.

Tillotson have two mixture control screws, the low-speed control (large knurled head, on top of the carburettor body) and intermediate control (smaller head, located in the side of the carburettor). Both should initially be screwed in until they seat lightly, then backed out 7/8 turn. With the engine warmed up and running, turn the low speed screw in small amounts (waiting for the engine to stabilise) to get the highest idle speed. If the effect isn't clear, turn the screw out until the engine falters, then screw it in, counting the turns (in 1/8 turn steps) until the engine falters again. Now back the screw out to the midpoint between the two positions.

Use the throttle stop to raise the idle speed to 2000 rpm and repeat the mixture

load to WOT. The combination of main jet plus all the other fuel systems supply fuel at full load. Changing the proportions, but keeping the same overall total, will alter the WOT fuel slope from low speed to high speed, but will also change the part-load settings.

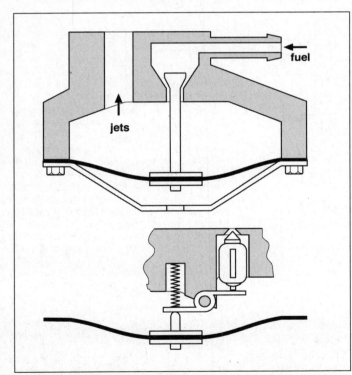

Fig. 8.25 Working principle of a diaphragm fuel chamber

When fuel enters the chamber its weight stretches the diaphragm and finally closes the needle valve. As fuel is consumed the elasticity in the diaphragm plus ambient pressure beneath it raise the fuel, keeping the head constant, and opening the valve to allow more fuel in. The bottom arrangement shows how a conventional needle valve can be incorporated, as in Mikuni's Super BN, fixed jet carburettor

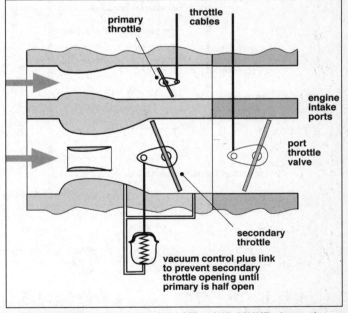

Fig. 8.26 This schematic of the Mikuni 18-32HHD shows the primary and secondary chokes and the position of the throttle valves that control air flow

The primary and port valves are opened by cables from the twistgrip. Greater opening creates more vacuum in the secondary choke and this low pressure is connected to a chamber sealed by a spring-loaded diaphragm. As the low pressure overcomes spring tension, the diaphragm moves a linkage to open the secondary throttle plate. There is another linkage (not shown) which connects the primary and secondary throttle spindles and prevents the secondary opening until the primary has reached at least half way open adjustment, using the intermediate screw. When the optimum position is found, back the screw out 1/8 turn further. Adjust the throttle stop to get an idle speed of 1000 rpm or less, and check the throttle response, going over the slow or intermediate adjustments if there is any hesitation in the bike's pick-up.

As there is such a limited range of adjustment, there is little to go wrong. Apart from blockages of the fuel ways, the main areas for faults are wear in the throttle spindle bushings, allowing air leaks, and wear in the accelerator pump mechanism. The first will cause an unstable idle and reduce the effectiveness of the adjustments, the second will cause poor throttle response when accelerating under load.

Having drillings which need to turn corners means that two intersecting drillings are made and the unwanted exits blocked by plugs, which may work loose or develop leaks.

Mikuni carburettors

See Figs. 8.26 and 8.27

A brief description of the Mikuni18-32HHD (fitted to the 1974 Suzuki RE5) is useful, for the sake of completeness and as a comparison with the above instruments, which are kept to minimum complexity and are fitted to engines with short rev ranges.

The Mikuni, a two-choke, two-stage device has all the refinement needed to cover a wide range of operating conditions. It has more jets and there is an air bleed to each fuel jet, so

the carburettor not only gives more progression/overlap between systems, it is possible to alter the individual fuel slopes as well as the overall fuel quantity. The engine depends upon two-stroke oil to lubricate the rotor and the float bowl has dual inlets, for fuel and oil, so a metered amount of oil is mixed with the fuel in the float bowl.

A list of the settings gives an idea of the overall layout, while Figs. 8.26 and 8.27 show the arrangement for air and fuel flow:

Part	Primary	Secondary
Choke size	15 mm	27 mm and 8 mm
Main jet	87.5	180
Main air jet	80-A	80-A
Pilot jet	45	70
Pilot air jet	145	140
Throttle valve tilt angle	#80 (8°)	#120 (12°)
Port valve tilt angle	#150 (15°)	
Bypass diameter	#1: 0.8 mm	
	#2: 0.6 mm	1.0 mm
Main nozzle dia	1.8 mm	3.5 mm
Pilot outlet	1.8 mm	
Valve seat dia	3.0 mm	
Acc pump nozzle	0.4 mm	
Acc pump capacity	0.5– 1.0 cc/stroke	
Acc pump start of stroke	35 ± 5°	
Fast idle opening angle	25.5 ± 0.75°	
Port valve lever contact	36 ± 1°	
Choke unloader opening	37.5 ± 0.75°	
Float level	43.3 mm	

Operation – air flow

The twistgrip has two cables (see Fig. 8.26), one opens the throttle valve in the primary choke, connected to the smaller of two intake ports on the engine and the other opens a throttle valve downstream in the secondary choke, fitted close to the intake port (called the port valve). The actual secondary throttle is operated by a vacuum device controlled by the pressure drop in the secondary venturi – that is, the secondary throttle opens on engine demand rather than rider demand, in the same way that the piston slides lift in CV carburettors.

There is also a cold start valve, which blocks the primary choke completely for starting. It opens the primary throttle slightly to give a fast idle and there is a vacuum-operated plunger (or 'unloader') that opens the cold start valve slightly once the engine has fired.

Within the secondary choke, there is a smaller venturi that carries the secondary main nozzle. This guarantees smooth, fast air flow over the nozzle in all throttle positions, so fuel delivery will be properly atomised.

Operation – fuel flow

At small throttle openings, the primary throttle controls the air flow. When the throttle

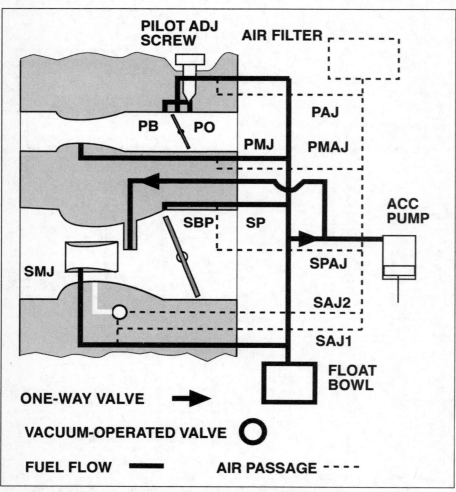

Fig. 8.27 This shows the fuel flow arrangements used in the Mikuni 18-32HHD

Note that (with the exception of fuel delivered by the pump) fuel will only flow along a particular line when there is air flowing over its nozzle or outlet, making the pressure here less than the ambient pressure in the float bowl. Key to abbreviations:

PB	pilot by-pass		SP	secondary pilot jet
PO	pilot outlet		SPAJ	secondary pilot air jet
PAJ	pilot air jet		SMJ	secondary main jet
PMJ	primary main jet		SAJ1	first secondary main air jet
PMAJ	primary main air jet		SAJ2	second secondary main air jet
SBP	secondary by-pass			

is closed, air-fuel mixture is delivered through the pilot outlet, adjusted by a tapered screw. As the throttle starts to open, the pilot by-passes are brought into play and air flow over the primary main nozzle increases, drawing fuel through the primary main jet. All fuel jets have air bleeds, so the fuel delivery is emulsified.

The secondary throttle plate is closed until the primary throttle is about half open. At this point the secondary is opened by intake vacuum and as it starts to move it brings in the secondary pilot system.

Air flow in the secondary choke now draws fuel through the secondary main system. This has a normal air jet and there is also a vacuum-controlled valve, which lifts against a spring when the secondary vacuum is high enough. This opens up another air bleed to the secondary fuel system, altering the fuel slope in proportion to intake vacuum.

Finally there is a nozzle upstream of the throttle plate in the secondary choke. This is connected via one-way check valves to the float bowl, with the accelerator pump plunger supplying the same line. When the throttle is opened, the contents of the pump are forced through the nozzle. This also behaves like a power jet, whenever there is air flow over the nozzle, the low pressure will draw fuel along the line, so this provides another way to increase fuel flow at high load.

This is the logical development of the fixed-jet design and is similar to the types of carburettor used on many cars. For the same total choke area it does not flow as much air as slide or CV carburettors. The number of small fuel and air ways, plus the necessary external linkages make this type prone to blockage by dirt or water in the fuel and by a build-up of road dirt on the exterior.

Notes

Chapter 9
Ancillary parts

Refer also to Chapter 12, Fault finding and Chapter 13, Overhaul

Contents

1 Introduction

Parts that join the fuel system together are mainly passive components like fuel lines and filters, which only suffer from ageing, dirt or careless assembly. There are some active parts, like fuel pumps, which have a service life although mostly they are non-serviceable items which must be renewed when they fail.

2 Tanks

The essential parts are a tap to let fuel out and a vent to let air in, although many tanks have more connections such as vents to the airbox to prevent evaporative emissions, fuel pumps fitted inside the tank and fuel level sensors, both with sealing gaskets and electrical connections, while inside the tank there will be baffles to prevent fuel swill and a filter at the entry to the fuel line.

Most models have the tank fastened at the front, either bolted to the frame or held with a tongue and groove sort of arrangement, and bolted to the frame at the rear, usually under the front of the seat squab. Sometimes one of these mountings is a hinge, allowing the tank to be tilted up for service access, without disconnecting the fuel and electrical lines (see Fig. 9.1). In this case there is usually a prop, either clipped under the tank or kept separately in the tool compartment under the seat.

In other cases, or to remove the tank, it must be lifted slightly so that hoses and electrical connectors may be undone.

Supporting it on a block of wood leaves both hands free and reduces the risk of scratching the bodywork.

Usually the electrical connector blocks have a unique shape, which means they can only be reconnected the right way round and it is not possible to confuse two nearby connectors (eg for fuel pump and fuel level sensor). If this is not the case, make a note of which wires go where.

Similarly check overflow pipes, breather pipes and any other connections to the tank, so they can be replaced in the correct position and routed correctly down past the engine.

Fig. 9.1 The early Honda CBR600 was one of the first bikes to have a fuel tank prop so that service work could be carried out without having to disconnect the fuel lines and remove the tank

On some designs it is easier to leave the pipes connected to the tank and pull them out of their clips on the frame or engine; in other cases it is quicker to disconnect them at the tank, leaving them attached to the bike.

On bikes with remote fuel taps (or no fuel tap) there may be a service tap fitted under the base of the tank, simply to stop the flow so that the hose may be disconnected. Remember to switch it on when the tank is refitted.

Other types have self-sealing connectors in the fuel line: the joint is snapped apart by pulling sharply at either end or it has a sprung lever which must be held compressed before the joint can be broken.

Note that on some models, where the fuel tap is positioned below a frame rail, it is necessary to remove the fuel tap (or the operating 'dial', held by a central, recessed screw) before the tank can be lifted clear of the frame.

If a new tank is fitted it must be thoroughly cleaned out, ideally hosing it with plenty of water if it is possible to drain it thoroughly and dry it afterwards. It's amazing how much debris an apparently clean, new tank can harbour and if it is not removed it will block filters, cause carburettor flooding or block jets.

3 Hoses

Low pressure fuel lines and vent pipes are usually a push fit over stub tubes, and held in place with wire circlips. High pressure hoses are reinforced, with threaded fasteners or hose clamps at either end. Problems are caused by ageing, which makes the material crack, damage (caused by cutting or melting on hot engine parts), and incorrect fitting (stretching or kinking, effectively closing the pipe). Check routes carefully, especially when the tank is lowered into place.

4 Taps

Bikes used to have a fuel tap bolted to the base of the tank, with simple ON-OFF-RESERVE positions. While taps often have these positions marked, the convention with fluid flow valves is that when the operating handle is in line with the direction of flow, the valve is open; when the handle is at right angles to the flow, the valve is closed (see Fig. 9.2).

The part of the tap located inside the tank had a gauze filter (which would need cleaning after long intervals or if the fuel had been contaminated) and entry tubes of different heights to provide the main and reserve fuel quantities.

Later types used a vacuum-operated tap, in which intake vacuum from one cylinder was connected to a chamber, sealed by a diaphragm, in the back of the tap (see Fig. 9.3). Here a spring would hold a plunger closed, blocking fuel flow. Engine vacuum would lift the plunger against the spring, opening the fuel way. The tap would have ON and RESERVE positions, connecting to the high and the low tubes inside the tank respectively and the third position would be PRIME. There is no need for an OFF position because fuel is shut off whenever the engine stops (and fuel lines downstream of the tap may then be disconnected without spilling fuel).

The PRIME position opens a by-pass around the vacuum plunger, connecting the fuel line to the RESERVE position in the tank. This is so that fuel can flow when the engine is not running (eg if the bike has been standing for a long time or if the carburettors have been

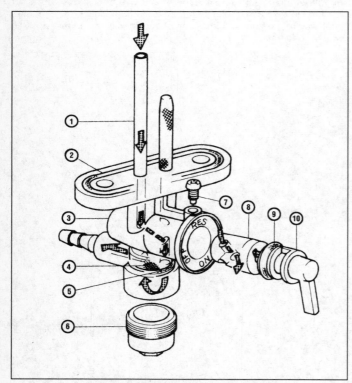

Fig. 9.2 Gravity-operated fuel tap

1 Fuel tap inlet	6 Filter bowl
2 O-ring seal between tap and tank	7 Screw
3 Tap body	8 Rotor (valve)
4 Filter gauze	9 Seal
5 Sealing washer	10 Operating lever

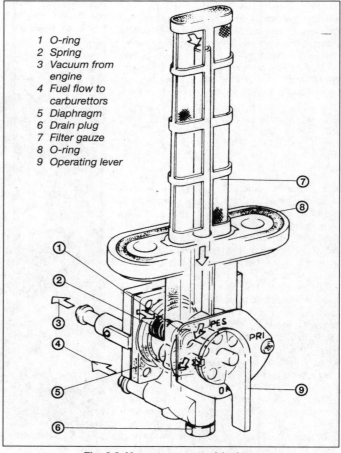

1 O-ring
2 Spring
3 Vacuum from engine
4 Fuel flow to carburettors
5 Diaphragm
6 Drain plug
7 Filter gauze
8 O-ring
9 Operating lever

Fig. 9.3 Vacuum-operated fuel tap

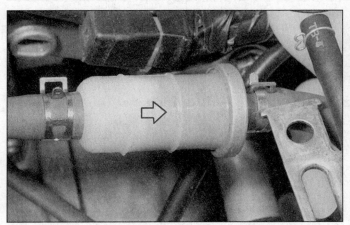

Fig. 9.4 In-line type fuel filter. An arrow usually indicates direction of fuel flow

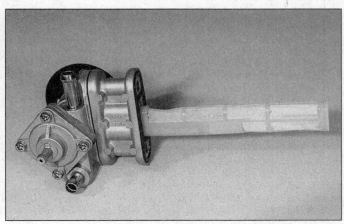

Fig. 9.5 Gauze filter fitted on tap stack

overhauled and the float bowls are empty – in these cases there is no fuel to run the engine and create the vacuum needed to open the tap). The PRIME position is also needed when the intake vacuum take-off is being used by a vacuum gauge (eg when synchronising the carburettors, see Chapter 13).

The PRIME position must not be used for normal running as its flow capacity is limited and it may not be able to supply enough fuel for full power. If the vacuum tap fails for any reason, the engine can be run temporarily in the PRIME position, avoiding high revs or high loads.

One other problem with vacuum taps is that they are set up so engine vacuum will overcome the spring force in all riding conditions, with the engine in standard form. If it is modified, typically using a less restrictive air filter and airbox intake, then the vacuum in the intake tract will be reduced (which is the reason for re-jetting when such modifications are made). There may not be enough vacuum, especially on WOT, to keep the fuel tap open, in which case the tap should be swapped for a manual version.

Some taps are serviceable, the moving element being removable so that seals can be renewed and passageways cleaned, although it is often the case nowadays that the only

parts available are those which attach the tap to the tank.

5 Line filters

Fitted in the fuel line between the tap and the rail feeding the carburettors (although where a pump is used, the filter will usually be immediately upstream of it), filters should be checked at regular service intervals and renewed when there is an obvious restriction to fuel flow (see Fig. 9.4). Note also that there is usually a gauze filter inside the tank and another at the entry to each carburettor or injector (see Figs. 9.5 and 9.6). These also need to be checked at each service and cleaned by flushing gasoline or blowing air in the reverse direction to normal fuel flow.

6 Fuel pumps

For carburettor systems, low pressure pumps are used (typically around 0.1 to 0.2

bar) while fuel injection typically runs at 2 to 4 bar, with a pressure relief return to the tank.

Electric pumps are used. The low pressure, reciprocating plunger type, works like a solenoid switch. Power in a coil winding moves the plunger against spring force. At one end it has a diaphragm seal and the movement increases the volume in the diaphragm chamber, drawing fuel in past a non-return valve. At the other end of the plunger there is an electrical contact, which is broken when the plunger reaches full stroke, switching off the current in the coil and removing the magnetic force. The spring then returns the plunger to its start position, forcing fuel out of the diaphragm chamber, past another one-way valve. This motion restores electrical contact, energises the coil and the cycle starts again.

High pressure pumps, designed to run with minimal lubrication are either fully immersed in fuel (see Fig. 9.7) or have fuel running through them over the electric motor to cool it. Types used (see Figs. 5.6 and 5.7 in Chapter 5) include roller cell (capable of pressures above 6 bar), internal gear (<4 bar), peripheral channel (<3 bar) and side channel (<1 bar).

Electrical power is supplied via the ignition switch to a relay (solenoid switch), often with

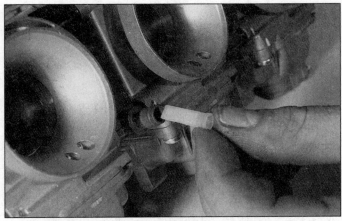

Fig. 9.6 Gauze filter at fuel inlet union on carburettors

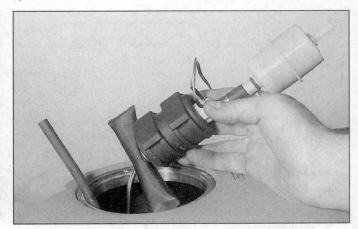

Fig. 9.7 Pump is immersed in fuel on Ducati 900SS

an additional relay (a transistor controlled switch) connected to the ignition unit, so the pump will only be powered when the ignition is switched on and the crankshaft is turning. There may be an additional relay connected to a tilt switch (or lean angle sensor), which will turn power off if the machine falls over.

Pumps are usually tested by connecting to a 12V source and measuring the pump's output over a timed period. The service limits are shown in the workshop manual, using kerosene (paraffin) as it is harder to ignite and thus safer. Make sure the electrical connections are sound and use a switch rather than holding a cable on to a battery terminal, which will make a spark when the circuit is broken.

For a low-pressure system feeding carburettors, the minimum flow rate can be calculated if the manufacturer's figures are not available, as shown in Chapter 6. For high-pressure pumps in fuel injection systems the output can be three times as high and it is not possible to predict the service limit figures.

The pump's output pressure is measured in the same way as its flow rate, except that a pressure gauge is connected to the output and, once the pump is operating, the outlet is blocked, by holding the tube firmly kinked. If the system pressure is raised by changing the pressure regulator, the pump will run hotter, which may cause wear in the pump and may produce vapour bubbles in the fuel.

Using jump cables to by-pass the solenoids will show that the pump is serviceable (or not)

and by bringing in the relays one at a time, will isolate any fault in each relay or its circuit. This process can locate a fault without any specific knowledge of the relay and its connections. See Haynes *Motorcycle Electrical Manual* for more information on pumps and relays.

Pumps are generally not serviceable and if the flow rate is out of spec the unit will have to be renewed.

7 Pressure regulators

To keep fuel rails at a constant pressure, the pump is given more capacity than the engine needs and excess fuel is returned to the tank via a pressure regulator. This takes the form of a pressure vessel in which a piston is sealed by a diaphragm and held under spring tension. When fuel pressure on the opposite side is greater than the spring force it lifts the piston, opening a valve which returns fuel to the tank. As the pressure drops, the spring pushes the piston back to close the valve. Usually the non-fuel side of the piston is vented to one of the intakes downstream of the throttle valve, so the fuel pressure is always a constant amount above intake air pressure. This is essential in supercharged applications.

Some regulators have an adjusting screw that alters the preload on the spring, so the lift-off pressure can be regulated. Raising the pressure in a fuel injection system has the

effect of richening the mixture all the way through the range.

Regulators are tested by applying pressure, either from a pump with a pressure gauge or a deadweight pressure cylinder, to see if the valve opens and closes within the specified range. Kerosene, as a less volatile and ignitable liquid, is used for this kind of test.

8 Electrical connections

Full battery power (12V) is applied to working parts such as pumps and solenoid-controlled valves, although sensors (such as airbox pressure or throttle position) may have a 5V supply, provided via the CPU, or may have their own internal resistance so their output is in the range 0 to 5V.

Check that wires have not been trapped, corroded or damaged, especially where they join a terminal block or connector. To test continuity in the circuit, identify the supply (live) connection and the ground (earth) connection. When power is switched on, there should be battery voltage (or 5V for certain sensors) between the supply and ground. There should be continuity (ie an ohm-meter reads zero) between the ground connector and the bike chassis or battery negative terminal (assuming negative earth: some very early machines may have positive earth).

Analogue sensors have three-wire connectors, supply, ground and signal. The signal voltage will vary typically from a minimum of 0.5V through to a maximum of 3.5V (above ground) as the sensor goes through its full range (eg as the throttle is moved from idle to wide open).

Fuel gauges with a float on a pivoting arm can be tested by moving the arm through its full travel. Other types use a heated element which is cooled when immersed in liquid and the change in current/resistance as its temperature increases is used as a signal for a low fuel-level warning. Check the precise output figures and test method in the workshop manual. See Haynes *Motorcycle Electrical Manual* for more information.

9 Solenoids

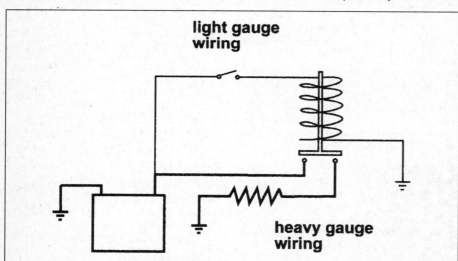

Fig. 9.8 Principle of a solenoid

A coil carrying electric current produces a magnetic field, which can be used to move an iron core, usually against a spring. The movement is used to close a switch (as shown here) permitting a control circuit in light gauge wiring, while heavy gauge is used for the full electrical load (to cope with, eg a starter motor). Alternatively the movement caused by the solenoid can be used to operate a valve, to open a fuel injector, to displace fuel in a pump, etc. When the exciting current is switched off, the spring returns the core to its start position. In the case of pumps, moving the core to its full extent operates a switch to break the circuit and when the core is returned the switch is closed, so the motion continues until enough fuel pressure builds up to prevent the initial movement

These are electrically-operated switches. When power is applied to them it is connected to a coil whose magnetic field forces a steel rod to move against the force of a spring. This movement closes the contacts of the main switch (see Fig. 9.8).

Solenoids are used for one of two reasons:
● Where the component needs a large current and heavy cables but it is desirable to use light wiring to the operating switch. An example is the fuel pump, with fairly

heavy cables between the battery, solenoid and pump, but light gauge cable from the solenoid to the ignition switch, to minimise the bulk and stiffness of the wiring loom that has to turn with the steering.
● Where an electrical signal is used to operate the switch. An example is solenoid-operated valves to open/close carburettor air bleeds, triggered by an engine speed sensor.

A solenoid has two sets of terminals:
● An input consisting of a supply (live), which will be connected to the operating switch or the CPU, and a ground (earth) connection. We'll call this the signal voltage.
● An output consisting of one terminal connected to the battery supply (+12V) and one terminal connected to the load (eg the fuel pump) which then has its own ground (earth) connection to complete its circuit.

To test, check there is ground continuity and that the input has battery voltage when the operating switch is on. When battery voltage is applied to the input terminals there is usually an audible click as the output contact is made. With the load disconnected there should be continuity across the output terminals and both terminals should then be at battery voltage above ground.

To eliminate faults in the signal voltage supply, make a separate ground (earth) connection and a separate supply directly from the battery positive terminal. If the solenoid then works, the fault is either in the operating switch circuit (or whatever supplies the signal voltage) or in the ground connection. See Haynes *Motorcycle Electrical Manual* for more information.

10 Control cables

Throttle cables

The throttle is controlled by cable from the twistgrip. Usually there are two cables, one to open the throttle and one to close it – a system known as 'push-pull' even though both cables pull, on opposite sides of the operating pulley. Two-strokes usually have a single throttle cable with a junction box from which one cable operates the throttle linkage and another goes to the oil pump. Possible faults:
● Outer cable damaged or kinked. Makes throttle action stiff.
● Inner cable frayed. Jams cable movement in one direction.
● Cable broken or nipple pulled off.
● Dirt or corrosion. Makes action stiff.
● Incorrect routing or adjustment. May open throttle when steering is turned or interfere with steering movement.

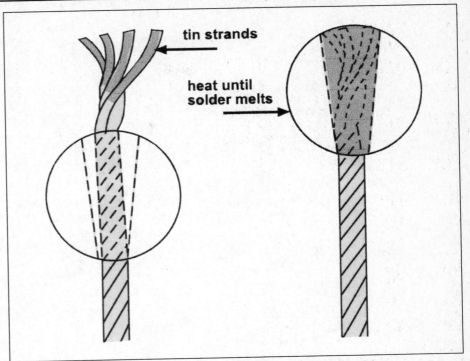

Fig. 9.9 Nipples on cable inner wires are soldered in place
The cable strands are separated slightly and tinned with solder. The nipple is pulled over them and heated until the solder melts into its tapered hole, forming a wedge that is firmly bonded to the steel strands of the cable

Set-up and adjustment

The cables must run freely over the full length of travel and must be routed in the smoothest possible way, particularly around the steering head. When the steering is moved from lock to lock, the cables must not be stretched, trapped or kinked and they must not restrict steering movement in any way.

The cables have screw adjusters which effectively alter the length of the outer. Loosen the locknut, turn the adjuster until the free play on the inner cable is correct, then hold the adjuster with a spanner while the locknut is tightened.

Free play: when the throttle is closed, the opening cable should be adjusted so there is 2 – 3 mm of play at the twistgrip, measured in terms of twistgrip rotation. Check that the throttle valve is fully open on full twistgrip travel. The closing cable should be adjusted so that it has some free play on WOT and doesn't prevent the throttle valve closing on to the throttle stop when the twistgrip is closed.

With the engine idling, check that the throttle stop adjuster controls the idle speed and that the speed doesn't change when the steering is moved. Blip the throttle quite hard, releasing the twistgrip so the return spring closes the throttle: the engine should settle immediately to its idle speed.

Soldering cable nipples

If a nipple has pulled off or the cable has broken where it joins the nipple, a new one can be soldered on (assuming there is still enough adjustment to give full travel). The end of the inner cable should be thoroughly cleaned and degreased. The nipple has a tapered hole through it. Push the cable through the narrowest end of the hole and splay out the ends of the last 3 or 4 mm of the cable. Tin (see **Note**) the individual strands with solder (see Fig. 9.9). Pull the cable back into the nipple and heat it until the solder melts, allowing the cable to be pulled gently until the ends are flush with the nipple surface. Trim off any surplus solder/cable ends.

Cold start cable

Cold start controls have similar cables, which are adjusted in the same way, usually with rather more free play when the control lever is in the off position. There is usually a clamp or friction device to prevent the control closing automatically.

> **Note** *Tinning – heat one side of the wire strand while holding the solder against the other. When the wire is hot enough to melt the solder, it will run over the surface of the wire.*

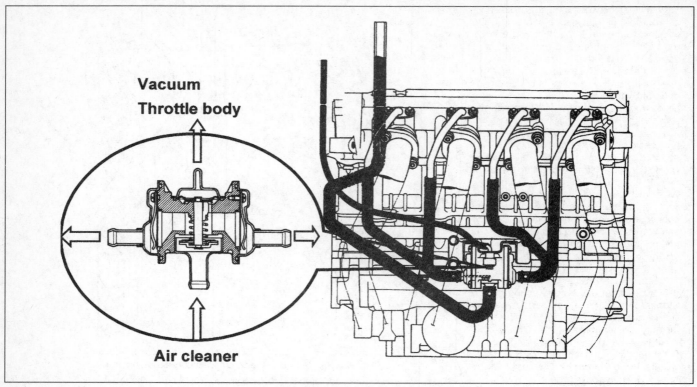

Fig. 9.10 Intake vacuum is used for many purposes

On the Suzuki Hayabusa, intake pulses operate this plunger which bleeds fresh air into the exhaust ports, to oxidise unburnt hydrocarbons and carbon monoxide. A similar diaphragm-plunger arrangement is used for fuel taps, and to operate valves or flaps in variable geometry intakes etc (Suzuki)

11 Vacuum-operated devices

As well as fuel taps, there can be intake vacuum connections to other parts (see Figs. 9.10, 9.11a, 9.11b and 9.12). Suzuki use a flap inside the airbox on some models to regulate the air speed/pressure conditions between low and high speed, which is moved by a vacuum-operated plunger. Vacuum connections are also made to pressure sensors, either as a means of measuring engine load/throttle position or to detect the pressure difference between the airbox and the intake tract.

Check that the connecting tube isn't blocked, by blowing through it, and that it isn't leaking, by blocking the end and trying to blow through it. If a sensor has an analogue (voltage) output, test the supply voltage to it (12 or 5V), test its ground (earth) connection and test the signal voltage (probably in the range 0.5 to 3.5V but check with the workshop manual). To test the signal, apply normal voltage to the sensor with a voltmeter connected across its output terminals, push a tube over the vacuum pipe and suck on the end of the tube.

Other devices, such as pumps (see Fig 9.13) usually have a diaphragm and one-way valves. Check that the diaphragm and its housing are not leaking or damaged and that any check valves give free flow in one direction and resist pressure in the other.

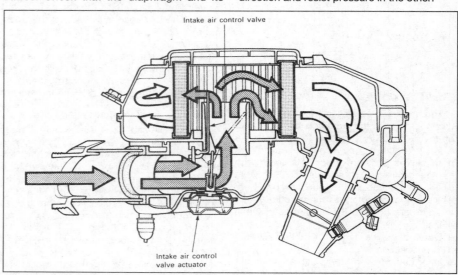

Fig. 9.11a Some machines use variable intake geometry to get the best power at both high and mid-range engine speeds. This is the system used by Suzuki on several models (GSX-R750W shown)

The central valve, in the entrance to the air cleaner is fully opened at high speed but is closed by a vacuum-operated linkage when the speed drops into the lower half of the rev range (Suzuki)

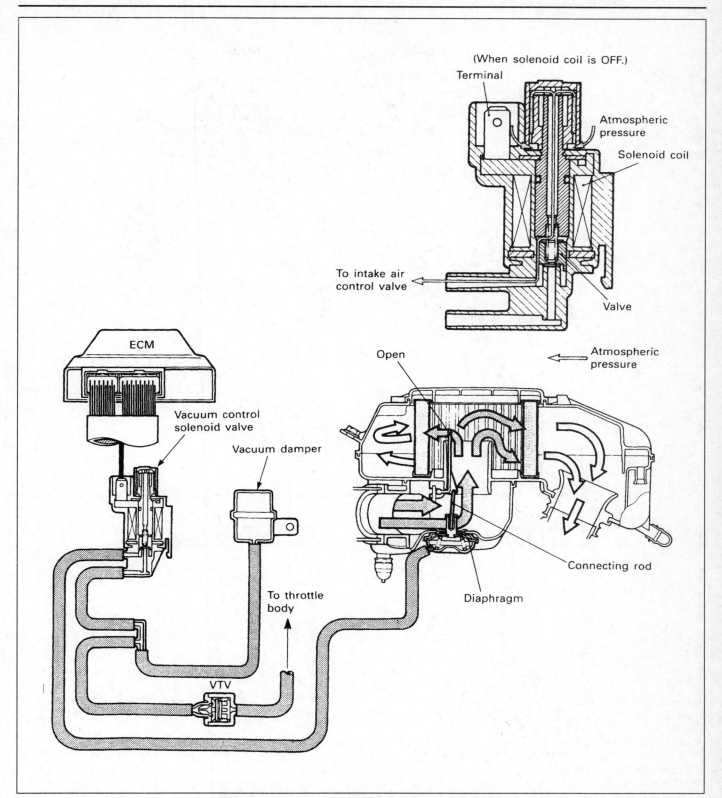

Fig. 9.11b Suzuki's operating mechanism is shown here

At the rpm threshold the ECU sends a signal to a solenoid valve which opens intake vacuum to a diaphragm chamber that has a link to the airbox valve. The part labelled VTV is a vacuum transmission valve; the vacuum damper is a small chamber, designed to take out pulsations which could make the linkage flutter (Suzuki)

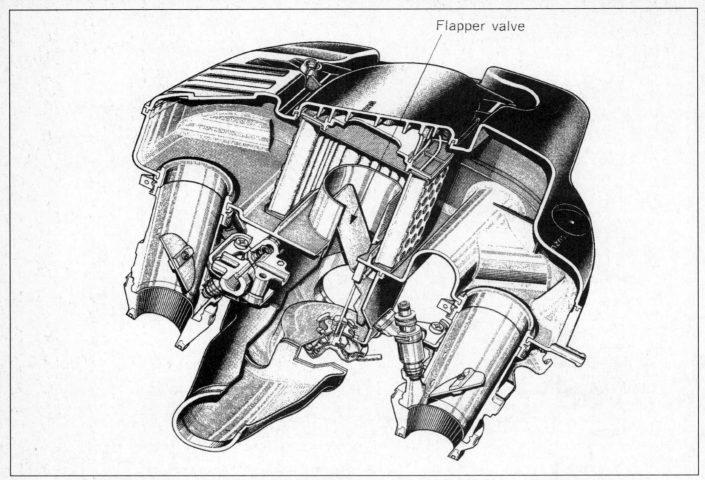

Flapper valve

Fig. 9.12 This version, fitted to the Suzuki TL1000S, shows the valve in the closed (low speed) position *(Suzuki)*

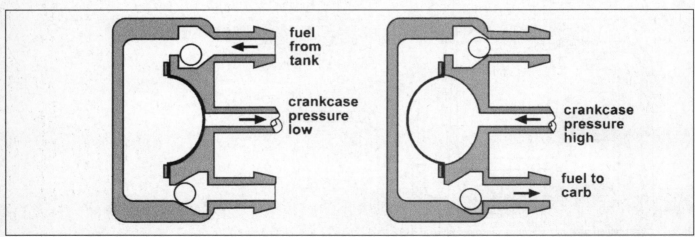

fuel
from
tank

crankcase
pressure
low

crankcase
pressure
high

fuel to
carb

Fig. 9.13 Diaphragm fuel pump, operated by crankcase pressure, which is connected to the centre tube

As the pressure changes from high to low it moves the diaphragm in the pump chamber, displacing this volume of fuel past one-way valves in the inlet and outlet tubes. The operation makes this design suitable mainly for singles, parallel twins and two-strokes but it can supply a constant head of fuel regardless of the attitude of the bike or the position of the fuel tank and without the complexity of an electric pump. It has been used on trials machines

On very basic engines the fuel tank can be placed lower than the carburettor and with this kind of pump the carburettor can have a simple weir type reservoir – a chamber with an overflow back to the fuel tank, the height of the overflow determining the fuel level, without the complexity of floats and needle valves

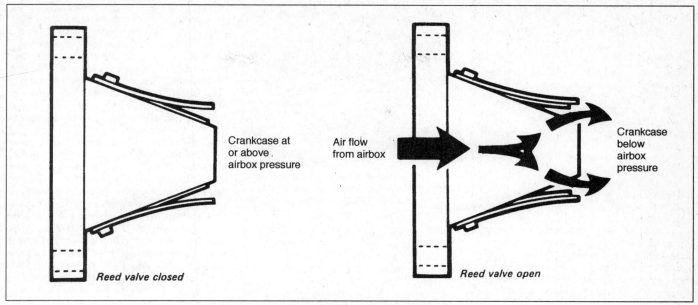

Fig. 9.14 Reed valve operation

Crankcase at or above airbox pressure

Reed valve closed

Air flow from airbox

Crankcase below airbox pressure

Reed valve open

Reed Valves

Reed valves are one-way valves used to control gas flow (see Figs. 9.14, 9.15, 9.16 and 9.17). Their main uses are in two-stroke intakes, four-stroke engine breathers and systems to bleed fresh air into the exhaust (to oxidise unburnt combustion products).

Typically the valve consists of a triangular frame, through which the gas flows, with the tip of its V at the downstream end. Thin, flat petals, made of metal or flexible fibrous material are fastened to the frame at the outer, upstream edges. In the static position, the petals lie flat against the V-frame, blocking the passage completely. Gas flowing in the 'right' direction can lift the petals away from the frame, pushing them out against carefully shaped stops. These are curved to match the natural bending of the petals, to prevent the petals flexing too far and to stop them fluttering in non-steady gas flow, both of which could make the petals fatigue and break.

When the gas flow drops, the springy petals return to the static position and if the gas tried to flow the 'wrong' way, it would simply push them harder against the frame, blocking the passage and preventing flow.

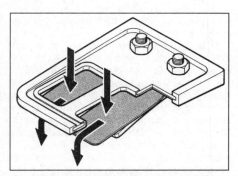

Fig. 9.15 Reed valves are one-way valves which control gas flow in several areas. This is used by Suzuki on the TL1000S as part of the crankcase breather

Usually the crankcase is vented to a separator in the airbox, which returns oil droplets to the crankcase sump but this would need to have a narrow passageway because of the big pressure fluctuations caused by two large-displacement pistons. Instead, Suzuki use a large port, with this reed valve in the floor of the separator. When crankcase pressure is low, the valve opens and returns oil quickly (Suzuki)

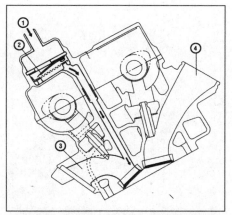

Fig. 9.16 Reed valves are also used in emission control air bleeds. This, used by Honda on the CBR1100XX, acts as a one-way valve in an air bleed to the exhaust port (Honda)

1   Incoming fresh air
2   Reed valve
3   Exhaust port
4   Intake port

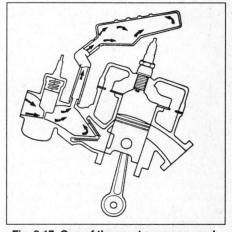

Fig. 9.17 One of the most common reed-valve applications is in two-stroke intakes, where they form infinitely variable valves that open purely on engine demand. To reduce the throttling losses on light load, Yamaha connected large chambers to the intakes on many of their two-strokes (Yamaha)

12 Emissions control and engine breather connections

There can be a variety of hoses connected to the airbox. Their jobs may be:
● To connect airbox pressure to the carburettor float bowls.
● To provide an exit for crankcase/cambox breathers into the catch-tank compartment of the airbox.
● To provide a drain for liquid oil back into the sump.
● To provide a manual drain for oil or water accumulated in the airbox (used during routine service, blocked in normal operation).
● To provide a fresh air bleed into the exhaust (via some control which is vacuum controlled and contains a one-way valve such as a reed valve).
● To provide a route for a fuel tank breather and overflow, which prevent evaporative emissions.

It's obviously necessary to distinguish which is which and to ensure the hoses are connected to the right components. Otherwise inspections and checks are the same for all. They must not have any cracks or splits, and should be clean on the inside, with no blockage. Sealed drain tubes and overflow pipes should be resealed after use and all hoses must be correctly routed, to avoid being trapped, kinked or burnt on the hot engine parts.

Some emissions control systems have connections to intake vacuum and use one-way valves, which should be checked for correct operation and kept clean. As these parts work at very small pressure differences they can usually be tested by connecting to a length of tube and blowing or sucking through them.

13 Sensors

See also Electrical connections in Section 8.
Digital ignition control and fuel injection systems rely on an increasing number of sensors around the bike. Sometimes there is a diagnostic socket, sometimes a diagnostic display is available on the machine's tacho/speedo instrument, or sometimes there is simply a warning light to let you know something (but not what) is amiss.

Without the right instruments and data from the workshop manual it is not possible to check these precisely. Sensors with analogue output, like potentiometers used to measure throttle position, can be checked with a voltmeter.

Fig. 9.18 Airboxes have increased in size and the number of jobs they do. This is a Kawasaki ZX-9R airbox

In the absence of the correct workshop equipment, the circuits can still be tested sufficiently to isolate a fault by checking continuity from the sensor to the CPU, checking ground (earth) connections and voltage supply. If the circuit is good, test by substituting a sensor that is known to work, or by breaking the circuit to the sensor. If this produces the same symptoms as the original fault then it's likely to be caused by the sensor itself. If not then the fault is likely to be in the CPU or its output connections. See Haynes *Motorcycle Electrical Manual* for more information.

14 Air filter

See also Chapter 13, Overhaul
Some air filter elements can be cleaned,

Fig. 9.19 The shape of the Kawasaki airbox (this is a ZX-6R) forms a convenient tray in which the air filter element sits

Note the two centre intake stacks are significantly longer than the outer ones, making them resonate at different engine speeds to increase the width of the power band (Kawasaki)

others must be renewed, depending on the manufacturer's recommendations (see Figs. 9.18 and 9.19). Aftermarket air filters with a low restriction to air flow offer more engine performance but because the depression they cause at the carburettor is less than the standard filter, it is often necessary to re-jet to compensate. This takes the form of richening the mixture, either by using bigger main jets, smaller air jets or different needle tapers.

As these filters then do their job of trapping airborne dirt, they become slightly blocked and lose their advantage of being less restrictive, at which point it becomes necessary to clean or renew the element, otherwise the engine has the double disadvantage of not having a free-flowing filter and of having enriched fuel mixture. The standard air cleaner element is likely to have a significantly longer service life before it shows the same drop in engine performance, but then the high performance element is offering a raised level of engine performance, at least in its as-new condition.

15 Exhaust systems

Design

Getting the burnt gas away from an engine is as important as getting air and fuel into it and the exhaust systems on nearly all bikes contribute a considerable amount to the total power output, as well as keeping the engine silenced. Aftermarket systems can offer more noise, some can offer more performance and a few can match the original silencing level.

Two-stroke systems have one pipe and silencer per cylinder, clamped by bolts or held by springs at the cylinder barrel, with one or two brackets to support the system to the bike's frame. Where servicing is possible, it is restricted to removing the endplate from the silencer can, removing the packing of mineral wool ('rock wool') which gradually gets contaminated with engine oil and loses its sound absorbing ability, and repacking with mineral wool. Where some models have engines restricted to a certain power level (eg to meet learner rider legislation), there is often a washer welded inside the header pipe, close to the engine. Removing this lets the exhaust system perform properly. Other restrictions involve disabling the power valve system (see *variable geometry exhausts*, Chapter 3).

Four-stroke exhausts usually have one header pipe per cylinder, joined into a collector, from which a single secondary pipe leads to one silencer can. There are variations on this, eg having the secondary split into two to feed two silencers, having cross

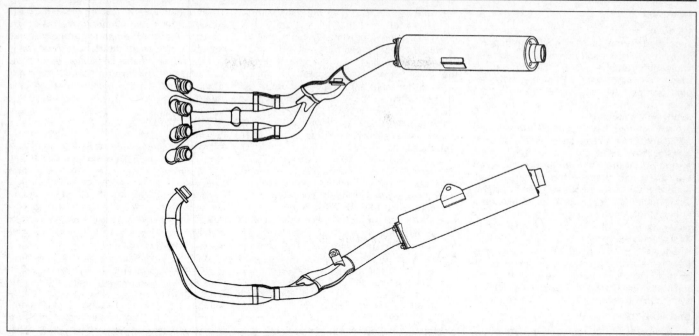

Fig. 9.20 Exhaust systems enhance engine performance by creating low or high pressure close to the exhaust valve just as it opens or closes. They also silence the engine to acceptable levels without restricting the gas flow

This is the 4-2-1 system used by Suzuki on the GSX-R750W. The header pipes have equal lengths, optimised for peak power production. The headers from #1 and #2 are joined, as are #3 and #4, into two secondary pipes, which finally join into one tailpipe and silencer can. There are stub pipes connecting #2 and #3 headers, which take out certain sound frequencies and leave less work for the main silencer to do (Suzuki)

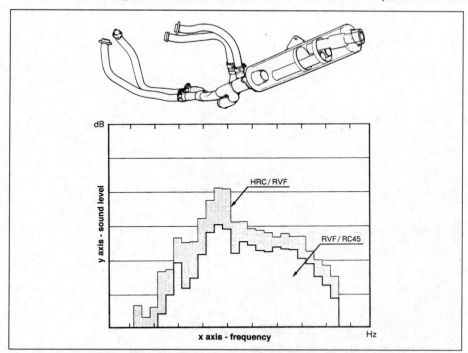

Fig. 9.21 Exhaust silencer development starts with a measurement of the sound spectrum – how much noise (in decibels) is made at each frequency (or pitch)

A simple series of baffles or a 'cheese-grater' tube reduce all frequencies more or less equally – including those where the engine hardly makes any noise, so these types of silencer are not efficient in terms of size or weight. Chambers and tubes tuned to the frequencies where the engine is noisiest are much more effective. This is a comparison of the stock silencer on the RC45, with the HRC race kit version (Honda)

connections between header pipes, etc (see Figs. 9.20 and 9.21).

Fitting

The individual components are either held together with springs or clamps and the header pipes are held to the cylinder head either by bolted flanges or by springs. Usually there is a copper ring gasket inserted between the pipe and the head. The best way to remove and refit springs is with a special tool consisting of a hook with a T-bar handle, which can be bought or made by welding a length of thick welding rod to a piece of bar and hammering the end into a hook shape (see Fig. 9.22).

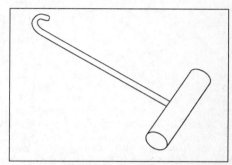

Fig. 9.22 Exhaust systems are often held together by short springs. The best tool to remove and refit this sort of spring is a simple hook with a T-bar handle

Removal

Loosen all the clamps, leave the system supported on the major mounting to support its weight. Disconnect any variable geometry cables (eg Yamaha EXUP) making a note of which way round they go. Remove the header pipe clamps – this will involve taking off the lower bodywork (at least) and possibly removing the radiator.

Some models have radiators mounted on hook and grommet arrangements, or on a bracket that can be pivoted, so they can be swung out of the way without disconnected the hoses and draining the coolant. It will usually need a slim socket, with the right-length extension or a universal joint, and a fine-toothed ratchet to get at all the header pipe nuts, especially if some have corroded or damaged threads.

Once the header pipes are free, they may have to be swung to one side or slid out of the collector to clear the engine, and then the main clamp can be undone to lower the system to the ground.

Installation

Make sure all the component parts of the system slide freely together. Assemble the system loosely and offer it up to the machine, making sure that everything will go into its final position. Slide a bolt through the main supporting bracket, just to take the weight of the system, or support it on wooden blocks, a small jack etc.

With the system approximately in place, fit the individual header pipes to the cylinder head, using a new sealing ring for each. Make sure the rings sit in the shoulder or groove provided for them and cannot slip out or get trapped while the pipe is being fitted. There are usually gaskets fitted between the collector pipes and silencer can joint – always renew these when the joint has been disturbed.

On some models it may be easier to fit the springs/nuts for the inner header pipes before the outers are positioned but don't tighten the nuts fully, you will need some room to manoeuvre the pipes to line up the collector or the mounting brackets. With the system loosely assembled, move each pipe slightly in the collector to get it firmly home and at the correct angle for the mounting brackets to line up. As each mounting comes into alignment, slide the bolt through but don't tighten it.

At this stage some judicious thumping with a rubber or leather-faced mallet is often necessary. When all the mounting bolts are aligned and the system looks to be sitting at the right attitude on the bike, check that things like centre stands, stand stops, cables for variable geometry etc have all got room to be fitted and then tighten the header pipe flanges first, followed by any other pipe clamps and finally tighten the main mountings to the bike's frame. Check for clearance for the tyre, suspension travel, brake hydraulic lines, etc and then refit cables, radiators and bodywork.

To test the gas seal on all the header pipes, run the engine at idle and hold a large bunch of rag in the tailpipe. Any leakage will easily be heard.

Catalytic converters

Catalysts speed up reactions between two other chemicals, without taking part in the reaction or changing themselves. Products of incomplete combustion – carbon monoxide, various hydrocarbons and oxides of nitrogen – would not form if the combustion process were perfect. They have a second chance in the journey through the exhaust pipe and the catalyst gives them an extra prod to complete combustion properly.

It can only do this if the correct balance of chemicals is present in the first place. The air-fuel mixture has to be stoichiometric. The catalyst cannot compensate for rich or lean mixtures. This is the reason fuel injection is used with catalytic converters: it can force stoichiometric conditions at particular engine speeds and loads.

The type of catalyst used in exhausts must also operate within the right temperature range, which means its position in the pipe is critical (see Fig. 9.23). Too close to the engine

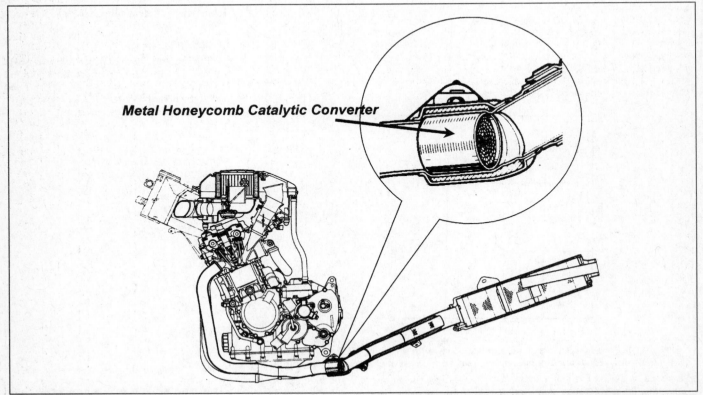

Fig. 9.23 Fitting catalytic converters can easily disrupt the power-enhancing characteristics of the exhaust. The challenge is to meet the emission laws without losing performance. Suzuki fit their catalyst in the secondary pipe, after the 4-2 joints. This drawing also shows just how much space is devoted to the intake and exhaust, compared to the engine block *(Suzuki)*

Metal Honeycomb Catalytic Converter

and it will run too hot, too far away and it will be too cool. It also needs to come into contact with all the ingredients, so it must have a huge surface area and be able to intercept the whole gas flow without obstructing it too much.

In order to make contact with the gases, the surface of the catalyst must stay clean. This is the main reason unleaded fuel is used. Leaded fuel forms deposits which would coat the surface of the catalyst and insulate it from the gas flow.

16 Two-stroke lubrication

See also Chapter 6, Testing.

Road bikes since the 1970s have had oil injection pumps but early two-strokes and most competition machines use a mixture of oil and fuel.

Pumps are driven by gear from the crankshaft or the primary drive and so turn at a speed proportional to engine speed (a few were driven from the gearbox and so would not supply oil if the engine were running in gear with the clutch disengaged). They also have a variable stroke, regulated by a cable attached to the throttle cable by means of a junction box.

The pump is supplied from a separate oil tank and its output varies with both engine speed and load. It is usually adjusted so that its linkage moves a certain amount at a certain throttle position, either WOT or when a datum mark on the throttle slide aligns with a window in the carburettor body (blanked off by a screw for normal running). Check the exact method of adjustment with the workshop manual.

Machines that use an oil-fuel mixture sometimes have a built in measure. The 1955 BSA D3 Bantam, for example, had a fuel filler cap incorporating a measuring cylinder, to add oil to the fuel. Two measures of oil per gallon of gasoline would give the recommended 20:1 mixture (if normal SAE40 engine oil was used, but if a specific two-stroke oil were used, the recommendation was for two and a half measures, or 16:1). As the tank capacity was 1¾ gallons, this probably led to a lot of mental arithmetic.

Instead of the 5% or 6.25% recommended in the 1950s, current two-stroke oils tend to run at ratios of 2 or 3% (50:1 to 33:1), although competition oils are often used in higher concentrations, typically around 20:1 in motocross engines.

Only freshly mixed fuel should be used and to mix it, first measure the amount of gasoline, say 10 litres. At 3% oil:fuel, this will need 10 × 3/100 or 0.3 litres or 300 cc but if you pour 300 cc into a measuring cylinder, it will stick to the sides and take ages to drain out. So put, say, 200 cc of the gasoline into the measuring cylinder, add oil up to 500 cc (if the cylinder isn't big enough you can do this in two halves), stir thoroughly and pour into the fuel tank. Then use the remainder of the 10 litres of fuel to swill out the measuring cylinder before adding to the tank and mix well.

There are several types of two-stroke oil and until the mid-1990s there was no standard, so apart from what the manufacturer put on the label, there was no way of knowing what you were buying. During the '90s a couple of Japanese standards (JASO) were introduced, but these are really aimed at controlling smoke from commuter engines in overcrowded cities. There still isn't a guide to the oil's performance level.

However we can put two-stroke oils into four broad groups:

1) **Forecourt oil** – The type you can buy at pretty well any filling station. Inexpensive. OK for use with injector pumps. Designed primarily for commuter-type machines, but is adequate for any standard roadster.
2) **Semi-synthetic injector oil** – Better load-bearing, rather more expensive and mostly available at bike shops. Probably gives more peace of mind than performance (a 50 cc commuter in traffic puts more stress on its engine than a bigger bike on the open road). Can also be used as oil-fuel mix.
3) **Synthetic oil** – High load-bearing and anti-seize qualities, may also contain octane-stabilising additives. May not be suitable for injector pumps – check the label. Intended for competition or highly modified machines. Expensive and only available from specialist outlets.
4) **GP racing oils** – May be vegetable-based (leaves deposits inside engine, cannot be mixed with mineral oils). Almost certainly will be too viscous for injector pumps. Even more expensive and harder to find.

There is a fifth group which is largely a scam based on the lack of standards for two-stroke oils. These are oils at the cheaper end of group 2 or even group 1, which are marketed – and priced – as if they were group 3 or 4. By careful advertising and race sponsorship many have become well-known, so it's no use recommending well-known brands. The fact that this type is successful at all shows that the vast majority of road bikes are quite happy on oils in group 1. For anything more serious, you really need to test (see Chapter 6) to find the most suitable type.

Notes

Chapter 10
Fuel injection: adjustments and settings
Refer also to Chapters 5 and 6

Contents

1 Introduction

The injection systems used on bikes are mostly the α-n type, that is, throttle position or angle (α) and engine speed (n) are used as the main parameters to calculate air flow. Early types used various ways to measure the air flow but digital processing became powerful enough to calculate the basic flow from a map based on the engine's volumetric efficiency – throttle angle and engine speed. This base quantity is then trimmed or corrected to suit information provided by various sensors, usually for air density and engine temperature.

The engine management module, referred to as ECU (electronic control unit or engine control unit) actually consists of three distinct components, although they may be contained inside the same box. There is the CPU (central processing unit, the computer that contains the program code to make the calculations and decide how much fuel is to be injected). Then there is a memory (usually an Eprom chip) in which data such as the maps are stored. Given a set of conditions, the CPU can look up the optimum fuel quantity in these tables. It may be possible for the CPU to write data to memory, such as a fault and the circumstances that surround it, which can then be read by diagnostic equipment when the machine is serviced. The third component is an I/O (input/output) module, which is responsible for receiving data from the sensors, converting it into something the CPU

can understand, receiving instructions from the CPU and converting this into signals which are sent to operate the injectors, ignition, instruments etc.

In this system the injector's open time is controlled by an electrical pulse from the ECU and it is this time that governs the fuel flow. The fuel pressure is held substantially constant by a pump capable of perhaps 5 bar delivery pressure and a pressure regulator set to lift off between 3 and 4 bar. As long as the injector dimensions remain constant, along with the fuel density and viscosity, then the quantity of fuel injected will depend simply upon the time the injector is open.

There will be small variations caused by the way the fuel flows during the time that the injector's needle valve is actually moving between the closed and open positions (and at the end of the cycle, when the valve is closed). This action depends upon the design of the needle valve and nozzle, and also upon the battery voltage applied to the injector solenoid, so there is always a correction for battery voltage. The difference between the calculated pulse time and the actual time that the injector flows fuel is called the 'dead time'. This should be added to the actual open time to calculate the pulse that is going to be sent to the injector.

All other corrections are concerned with air flow and are based upon sensors which measure air density (temperature and pressure) and engine conditions (speed, rate of change of speed, throttle position, temperature and so on).

Sometimes the injection is sequential (or timed to the intake stroke, each injector firing

once every two engine revs). This is generally at low engine speed and the end of the injection period is the most important. Injection may start anywhere during the engine's expansion or exhaust phase but it should finish before the intake stroke begins.

As the fuel requirement increases, the injector-open time has to increase, until the injector needs to be opened long before the intake valves open. At this point, timed injection starts to lose significance. In fact, because the engine is going through the intake-compression-expansion-exhaust phases so quickly, it doesn't matter when the injector adds fuel to the air stream. Some systems then switch to simultaneous injection (all injectors fire together) at this point. In simultaneous injection, each injector is fired once per engine revolution, arranged so this pulse ends in the region of 60 – 90° BTDC on cylinder #1. The pulses of fuel will be delivered just before the intake opens and just after it closes on cylinder #1 (and on #4 in an in-line four). Cylinders that are 180° out of phase (#2 and #3 on an in-line four) will have one fuel pulse during the intake stroke and another during the power stroke.

There is a half-way house between simultaneous and sequential injection, called grouped injection. On an in-line four the injectors are fired in pairs, every second engine revolution. #1 and #2 are fired together (if the firing order is 1-2-4-3, as on Japanese fours) so that #1 is timed to the intake, as in sequential injection, #2's injection occurs at the same instant, but its piston is approaching BDC, at the end of the power stroke and start of the exhaust stroke.

The same thing happens for #3 and #4, with injection on #4 happening just before its intake stroke but #3 injection occurring at BDC.

Injectors close to the valves tend to give better midrange and faster response, while those positioned much further upstream give better air-fuel mixing and more top-end power. The position of the injector in the intake tract becomes more significant than the point at which it delivers its fuel. Ultimately, as power and air flow increase, the injector spends more time open and when it is spraying fuel continuously, the system has reached its limit.

It is possible to alter the fuel injection quantity in several ways:

1) To re-program the maps in the Eprom chip at the heart of the ECU, assuming (a) this is possible and (b) the necessary software is available.
2) To replace the chip with one carrying different data.
3) To trim the output of the original chip. Sometimes an electronic control is available to give a degree of variation – typically up to ±10% – at each speed/load station.
4) To intercept the input/output of the ECU and increase/decrease the fuel delivery. This is usually done with a third party, aftermarket kit that plugs into the ECU.
5) To fool the CPU by altering the input from one of its sensors, typically the engine coolant sensor (if the CPU thinks the engine is running cold it will richen the mixture to compensate).

6) To fit an adjustable pressure regulator and raise or lower the fuel pressure. Note that raising the pressure will make the fuel pump run hotter.

Caution: when working on fuel injection systems remember that the fuel rail is kept at a pressure of around 3 bar (45 psi) and all fuel between the pump outlet, injectors and pressure regulator will be at this pressure, even when the engine is not running. If a hose or union is undone, fuel will leak from it a bit more vigorously than usual. It's not as bad as it sounds because, as a liquid, gasoline is incompressible and, if a hose is undone (engine not running) the first movement of liquid from the joint will reduce the pressure to atmospheric. To eliminate this risk, disconnect power from the fuel pump and then crank the engine on the starter for a few revolutions. The injectors opening will relieve the fuel pressure. Needless to say, the pump should never be run when anything in the high pressure line is disconnected.

2 Bosch system

Bosch systems go back a long way, to the K-Jetronic – a mechanical system with continuous injection, refined in the KE-Jetronic with open-loop electronic control of various functions (see Figs. 10.1 and 10.2).

The L-, LE-Jetronic and later Motronic had electronic control, injected at timed intervals and, in the case of Motronic, also controlled a digital ignition system.

Fuel pressure in the rail is in the 3 bar region with the pump either fitted in the tank or in the fuel line. The pump used on bikes is usually the roller cell type (see Chapters 5 and 9).

Motronic ignition control can handle a single coil with an HT distributor to each spark plug, one coil per plug or dual-spark coils that supply two plugs. The ignition is inductive discharge, with multi-stage power transistors to control the primary current. The CPU calculates the necessary dwell period (when current builds up in the primary winding: this and the inductance determine the energy stored in the coil). Obviously there must be enough energy to ignite the mixture, a requirement that will vary depending on the operating conditions and engine load, yet the energy must not rise so high that the induced voltage in the secondary winding could damage the insulation.

The secondary voltage depends on the rate of change of current in the primary winding, when this is broken by the ignition driver, and the ratio of the number of turns in the secondary and primary coils. The timing, relative to TDC, is calculated from a map based on engine speed and load, allowing for the primary circuit's rise time, which will vary with battery voltage.

When the primary circuit is switched (ignition on or off) it will induce a secondary voltage of 1 – 2 kV in the secondary, which could ignite fuel in a cylinder. On engines with distributors or twin-plug coils, the voltage isn't high enough to arc across two air gaps, but on single coil/plug layouts, this risk is avoided by using a diode in the secondary circuit. [See Haynes *Motorcycle Electrical Manual* for more details on ignition circuits.]

The system has on-board diagnosis, in which the ECU continuously tests sensors for 'plausible' output (and if one fails, it will replace the output with a default value). It also stores any errors it recognises, along with the operating conditions, and this data can be displayed when the machine is serviced and connected to a Bosch diagnostic tester.

Bosch/BMW applications

Later versions (MA2.4 on) have electronic cold running control, which matches ignition and fuelling to the conditions for both starting and idling. During warm-up it raises the idle speed by moving a 'throttle positioner' or variable throttle stop.

The main inputs to the control unit are:
● Engine speed and TDC position (Hall effect sensor on front end of crankshaft).
● Throttle position (potentiometer).
● Coolant temperature (NTC thermistor).
● Intake air temperature (NTC thermistor).
● Ambient air pressure.
● λ-sensor (heated oxygen sensor in exhaust header).

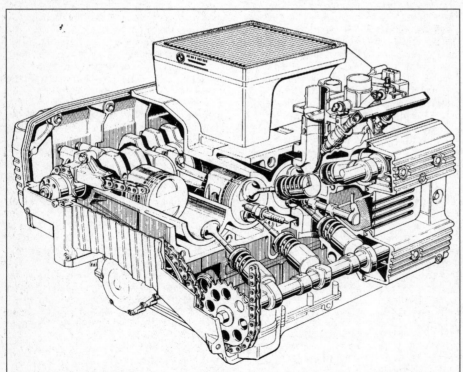

Fig. 10.1 General arrangement of BMW's two-valve K-series engine, showing the fuel rail, throttle body and injector position *(BMW)*

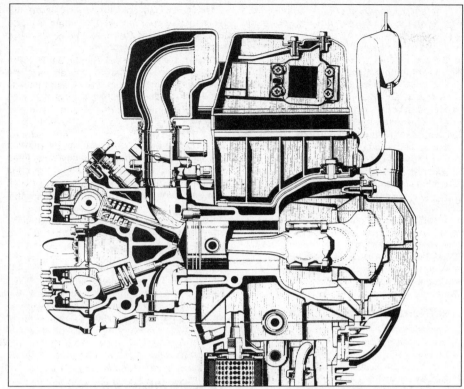

Fig. 10.2 Section through the BMW K100 engine showing the full intake tract and the injector's approximate spray pattern *(BMW)*

The outputs from the control unit are:
● Energise the ignition coil (on four-cylinder units, the secondary ignition pulses are triggered at 180° intervals, first in cylinders #1 and #4, then in #2 and #3).
● Energise the injectors (needle type, conical spray pattern, fuel at 3.0 to 3.5 bar, depending on model). They fire once per crank revolution, injecting half the required quantity each time. During starting, they fire twice per revolution.
● Throttle positioner (a servo motor with a worm drive that moves the throttle spindle to control idle speed during warm-up). Its signal is computed from engine temperature and speed, with feedback from the throttle position sensor. Closed-loop control allows this to monitor idle speed and keep it at a minimum (750 rpm on the R1200C twin) to suit the conditions (eg temperature or battery load), while adjusting the mixture to minimise exhaust emissions.
● Fuel pump.
● Instrument display and on-board computer.
● Two electric cooling fans.

On some models (eg K1200LT) the Motronic unit controls battery charging at tickover. When it detects a drain on the battery it increases the idle speed to approximately 1350 rpm, using the throttle positioner. When the reversing aid is used, it raises idle speed to approximately 1500 rpm.

When the engine is on the overrun (throttle closed, engine speed above 1800 rpm) the fuel injection is cut off. It is re-activated when the throttle is opened or the speed drops below 1600 rpm.

If any of the inputs fail (except engine speed) the control unit defaults to a substitute value stored in its memory, to allow the engine to run in a get-home mode. The error is logged in the unit's fault memory. There is a plug which is used to connect the unit to a diagnostic test computer (BMW MoDiTeC).

3 Marelli IAW system

Fitted as original equipment to Ducati, this is also the α-n type, with sequential injection (four units on 996SPS, two on 748/916). The end of the injection timing is stored in the Eprom map and as the CPU calculates the total period, this dictates the start.

Ducati use the MATHESIS tester, to check components and wiring and also to adjust injection times.

Sensors
● Absolute air pressure.
● Intake air temperature.
● Coolant temperature.
● Engine rpm and position of crankshaft relative to tdc.
● Battery voltage.
● Throttle position.

Removal and installation of Eprom

In general, do not use metallic, especially magnetised, tools inside the ECU. After switching off the ignition allow at least 15 seconds before disconnecting the ECU.

ECU 1.6M – remove the sticker in the centre of the ECU box (replace with a new one as this seals the unit). Remove the rubber plug beneath the sticker. Use plastic pull-type tweezers (Ducati tool) to remove the Eprom. To fit a new Eprom, use push-type tweezers and mount the Eprom so the reference slot in its end faces the pin board.

ECU P8 – remove the whole unit from the frame. Undo 4 screws to release the bottom cover. Remove/install the Eprom as for the 1.6M type above.

The ECUs have a trimmer – an adjusting screw on the side of the 1.6M Eprom unit or in the outside front wall of the P8, behind a rubber plug. It should be turned with a plastic screwdriver and is used to control the exhaust CO.

Its adjustment goes from 0 to 5V, in 270° (1.6M) or in 4 turns (P8). The centre of the range is 2.5V. Turning the screw further will not go beyond the range (0 or 5V) but forcing it past its end stops will cause damage.

Fuel pump and pressure regulator

Rotating lobe type, immersed in fuel. It has a non-return valve to prevent draining when switched off and a relief valve set at 5 bar to prevent the pump overheating. The regulator itself is set at 3 bar.

Throttle body

There are three adjustments which should always be made as a group, not individually, because each has an effect on the others. There are two passages that by-pass the throttle valve and air flow through them is controlled by tapered screws. These and the throttle stops will adjust the idle mixture and balance the air flow (synchronise the throttles), while the throttle position sensor (tps) must also be placed so the ECU can make accurate calculations.

Because of the overlap it is not always possible to get the best idle, CO readings and balance, and then it is necessary to choose which is the more important.

The full adjustment needs the MATHESIS tester, exhaust CO meter and mercury column vacuum gauges. This is the general procedure, using figures for the 748/916 as an illustration – check figures for other models with the workshop manual.
1 Warm up the engine
2 Lift tank from frame, remove the intake stacks and airbox.
3 Loosen or disconnect the throttle and fast idle cables.
4 Undo the throttle stop screw on the horizontal cylinder until it is well clear of its stop.

5 Turn the knob on the throttle linkage so that the master throttle (on tps side) is fully closed.

6 Connect MATHESIS power supply cable to the bike battery and to the 3-way self-diagnosis cable.

7 Connect this to the CDS self-diagnosis adapter and connect the adapter cable to the main port on the tester.

8 Connect the tps adapter cable between the tps and the COM2 port on the tester.

9 Insert the memory card in the tester: there should be a value of 150mV ± 15. If not, loosen the tps mounting screws and hold the master throttle control closed while you turn the tps until you obtain a reading within this range.

10 Clamp the tps in place. Disconnect the MATHESIS cable and re-connect the normal wiring.

11 Adjust the throttle cable.

12 Remove the vacuum take-off plugs and connect the vacuum gauge to the intakes.

13 Close the air by-pass screws.

14 Start the engine and run at a slightly high idle speed.

15 Use the knob on the linkage between the throttles to balance the vacuum gauge readings.

16 Connect the tps to the diagnostic tester, as described above.

17 Turn the master throttle adjuster to obtain a reading of 300 mV ± 15.

18 Re-connect the tps to the ECU.

19 Adjust the by-pass screws to get an idle speed of 1000 – 1100 rpm, with balanced vacuum readings.

20 Connect the CO meter and check the levels on both cylinders. If they are not within limits (1.5% to comply with street bike legislation, up to 6% for optimum race bike performance) then use the trimmer (described above). Turning clockwise richens the mixture, and has the same effect on all injectors, so if there is a difference between cylinders it will be necessary to strike an average or to re-do the by-pass adjustment on one.

21 Press the fast idle button underneath the twistgrip barrel and adjust the cables so the engine idles at 1500 – 1600 rpm.

4 Honda PGM-FI system

Honda's PGM-FI system is described as used on the VFR800, RVF/RC45 models. It is an α-n system at wide throttle angles, with intake vacuum used to monitor smaller throttle openings.

On the V4 engines, the front and rear banks of cylinders are treated separately, with their own injection-time maps, to allow for different operating conditions (mainly temperature) between the two. On some models there are maps for individual cylinders.

The base fuel quantity is calculated from engine speed and throttle opening, corrected for:

- Intake air temperature and pressure.
- Battery voltage.
- Coolant temperature.
- Acceleration (rate of change of throttle opening).
- Idle conditions.

A pulse generator on a camshaft lets the system identify individual cylinder positions enabling sequential injection, independently timed for each cylinder. Simultaneous injection is used for the first engine revolution when the starter is pressed.

Main sensors

- Throttle position (potentiometer).
- Intake manifold pressure.
- Ambient air pressure.
- Coolant temperature.
- Crank speed.
- Camshaft position.
- Battery voltage.

Additional sensors/inputs

- Engine stop relay.
- Bank angle sensor.
- Wheel speed sensor.
- Idle mixture adjuster.
- Sidestand switch.
- Starter motor switch.

Outputs

- Fuel injector-on time.
- Ignition dwell and timing.
- Idle by-pass control.
- Tacho signal.
- Wheel speed signal.
- Fuel cut relay.
- Variable intake geometry.
- Warning light.

The intake air pressure sensors are mounted in the airbox and the vacuum tube is connected to the intake downstream of the throttle valves. The sensor output is linear from 0.5V (low pressure) to 5V (high pressure). The throttle position sensor, mounted on the throttle body at the end of the throttle spindle, also has a linear output ranging from 0.5V (idle) to 4.5V (WOT).

Engine speed is taken from a rotor on the right-hand end of the crankshaft and a pick-up coil inside the right-hand crankcase cover. This serves as an ignition pulse generator, crank speed sensor and tacho signal.

There is another pulse generator on the rear intake cam with a pick-up coil in the cylinder head.

Ambient air pressure is taken from a sensor inside the seat cowling, with a linear output between 0.5V (low pressure) and 5V (high pressure).

Coolant temperature is monitored by a thermistor in the water jacket of the front block.

Air temperature is also monitored by a thermistor in the left-hand side of the airbox.

The thermistor output is not linear. Its resistance at 0°C is about 5 kΩ, at 40°C about 1 kΩ and about 0.15 kΩ at 100°C (same for coolant and air temperature).

Idle mixture adjuster: located inside the seat cowling, it regulates the AF mixture during idle and is preset at the factory. Turning the adjusting screw may cause rough idling.

Fuel pump and regulator

The pump is located inside the tank with a mesh filter at the intake (the lowest point) and a high pressure filter at its outlet. There is a banjo union to the delivery pipe with a check bolt than can be removed to measure the fuel pressure.

The regulator keeps the pressure at 2.5 bar above the intake tract.

Bank angle sensor

Mounted inside the seat cowling, this has circuitry which switches on with the ignition and powers the engine stop relay. If the machine tilts more than 60° ±5, power is disconnected to the engine stop relay and will not be switched on even if the bike is moved upright again. It only powers up when the ignition is switched off and on again, with the bike in its upright range.

Variable intake geometry

Where fitted, this has a solenoid valve controlled by the ECU which, at low engine speed, closes part of the intake area and uses a different length of tract to give best low- and medium-speed performance. At high speed, the full tract area is opened up for maximum air flow.

When the solenoid is not powered, the valve is open to atmosphere. Switching power to the solenoid closes the atmospheric vent and applies intake vacuum to the control valve, which moves a flap to alter the intake passage being used.

At low and medium speed the duct is closed, reducing intake area and selecting a tract length that gives best inertia effects for mid-range torque. At high speed the duct is opened, giving full area and a shorter length to suit peak power production.

The duct is opened by an air control valve using intake vacuum to move the operating linkage. This valve is controlled by a solenoid-valve, switched by the ECU.

In the off position the valve is open to ambient air pressure and the duct is in the wide-open (high speed) position. When the ECU energises the solenoid, it moves the valve, ducting intake vacuum to the valve controlling the linkage.

Diagnostics

The ECU lights up a warning light on the instrument panel when it detects a fault in the I/O system (ie sensors or wiring). The lamp flickers a variable number of times, depending on where the fault is, so by counting the

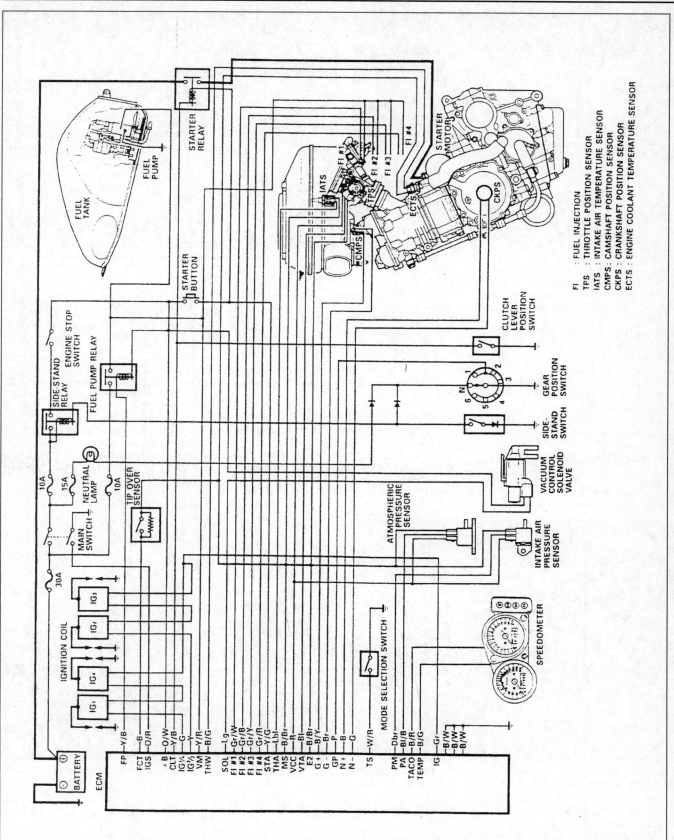

Fig. 10.3 The full wiring layout of Suzuki's GSX-R750W system (Suzuki)

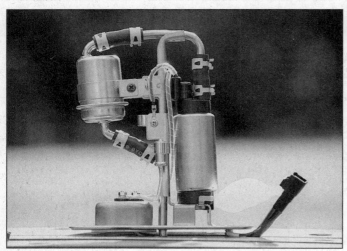

Fig. 10.4 In-tank pump and filters used on the Yamaha OW02 R7

Fig. 10.5 Pressure regulator from the Yamaha R7

number of light pulses, the general area of the fault can be seen. There is a connector under the seat cowling so that diagnostic test equipment can be plugged into the system.

Where possible, the system switches to default values in order to let the engine run in a get-home mode. These are:

Faulty circuit	Default setting
Intake pressure sensor	Simulated map
Ambient air pressure sensor	760 mm Hg
Coolant temp sensor	80°C
Air temp sensor	20°C
Throttle position sensor	Zero throttle opening

Throttle by-pass

There is an air passage that by-passes each of the throttle valves, equipped with a 'starter' valve that controls air flow during starting and idling. Air is delivered to the intake in the recess where the injector is fitted and the volume flow is controlled by the valve, from the ECU.

The valves can be manually adjusted to balance the intake vacuum of the four cylinders.

Exhaust emission control

Some models have a system to bleed filtered air into the exhausts, controlled by a solenoid valve, which is powered from the ECU when it detects suitable conditions. There are reed valves in the line to the exhaust ports, to prevent gas trying to flow the wrong way.

5 Denso system

See Figs. 10.3, 10.4, 10.5, 10.6, 10.7, 10.8, 10.9, 10.10, 10.11 and 10.12.

Fitted as original equipment to Suzuki, Aprilia and Yamaha. **Note:** *This is a general description of the Denso installation, not all aspects apply to all makes/models.*

The system has sequential injection, using α-n control at wide throttle openings or higher volume flow rates, reverting to intake air pressure to monitor smaller openings and flow rates. The base quantity is then corrected for ambient and engine conditions, with a further correction added for battery voltage.

Fig. 10.6 The Yamaha has a fuel rail mounted inside the airbox with injectors plugged into it to deliver fuel directly into the intake bellmouths

Although this looks as if it would restrict air flow, the bellmouths fitted are for the road version. The race engine uses much shorter bellmouths which are well clear of the injectors

Fig. 10.7 Yamaha's adjuster consists of a 3-button controller and uses the tacho to indicate the settings *(Yamaha)*

Sensors/inputs

● Crankshaft speed.
● Engine position (camshaft pulse).
● Throttle position.
● Airbox pressure.
● Intake air temperature.
● Coolant temperature.
● Intake air pressure.
● Starter motor signal.
● Gear position.
● Battery voltage.
● Tilt switch.

Outputs

By using a second computer in the instrument panel, signals from the ECU and the wheel speed sensor can be processed and stored, typically giving real time displays for engine speed, wheel speed, fuel level, engine temperature and distance travelled, plus stored data that can be scrolled, showing several trip distances, average fuel consumption for each trip, average road speed and peak road speed.

● Injector-on time.
● Ignition dwell and timing.
● Tacho signal.
● Coolant temperature signal.
● Fuel used signal.
● Overrev warning (adjustable).
● Error codes.

Injectors

Pintle or plate type injectors are used.

Diagnostics

A warning lamp (or the digital display normally used for oil and coolant temperatures) is used to warn the rider of a fault in the engine management system. By connecting a mode selection switch into a connector block in the harness, the instrument LCD will display an error code to locate the fault.

Fig. 10.8 The Aprilia RSV manages to fit two 51 mm throttle bodies into its 60° V-angle (Aprilia)

Reprogramming

New data can be written to the Eprom chip that stores the maps. In race kit versions such as Yamaha's R7, this is adjustable via a simple hand-held switch that selects the programming mode and then shifts the selected value up or down (ie to richen or weaken the mixture). There is a Yoshimura aftermarket adapter that is used to give a limited amount of change to the Suzuki memory: idle setting can be adjusted and off-

Fig. 10.9 The two throttle bodies are cast in one self-contained unit that houses the fuel gallery and carries the pressure regulator (Aprilia)

Fig. 10.10 A single spindle operates both throttle valves, with a throttle position sensor on one end and the cable linkage on the other (Performance Bikes)

idle the mixture can be changed by up to ±10% or the equivalent of 2 to 3 main jet sizes. In both cases the engine can be re-programmed while running on a dyno so it is fairly easy to optimise torque at a particular speed, lock in to this setting and move to the next speed.

Some machines, like the Aprilia RSV Mille and the Yamaha YZF-R7, have instrument panels with stepper motor analogue gauges for rpm and a liquid crystal digital display for things like temperature, time etc. The instruments are part of the engine management package and can be used as part of the programming/diagnostics procedure.

The R7 race kit has a different wiring loom and an ECU controller, a switch with three buttons (labelled Mode, Up and Down). Various combinations of these buttons are used to change the program's maps or to check sensors. During these operations the tacho turns into a voltmeter and its readings confirm the controller's actions.

The simplicity of having only three buttons is offset by having to use complex combinations to select modes (engine setting, diagnosis and test). This is done by pressing a sequence of buttons three or four times in succession. Two-digit code numbers then identify the area to be adjusted or an error that has been detected. The digits are indicated by the tacho reading: the tacho reads 10000 for 2 seconds when the mode switch is pressed and then, for example, code 15 is shown by the tacho indicating 1000 (meaning 1) for 1 second, 10000 for 0.5 seconds, and 5000 (meaning 5) for 1 second.

In engine setting mode there are 18 codes. The idle injection quantity can be altered on individual cylinders. Off-idle injection can be altered in four regions: low-speed/low load, low speed/high load, high speed/low load, and high speed/high load. 'Low' is defined as below 8000 rpm or 20% throttle, while 'high' is above 8000 rpm or 65% throttle. The software calculates the in-between progression but there is a code to make the transient mixture richer or weaker, to optimise the engine during acceleration.

The remaining codes adjust the ignition

timing in various speed/load conditions, reset the ECU to standard, set the rev limiter and gearshift warning, and switch the display between coolant temperature and lap timer (triggered by a switch supplied with the race kit wiring loom).

Once a code has been selected, the setting is varied by pressing the Up or Down button and acknowledged by the warning LED on the tacho flashing.

When a fault is detected the warning light flashes and, with the engine stopped but ignition power on, the tacho indicates the two-digit fault code in the same way as it shows settings codes. Where possible, the ECU reverts to a default setting to allow the engine to run in a get-home mode:

Error	Default setting
Camshaft sensor	ECU groups cylinders #1/#4, and #2/#3 in pairs
Intake air pressure	set to 760 mm Hg
Throttle position	set to wide throttle opening
Coolant temperature	set to 80°C
Intake air temperature	set to 40°C
Ambient pressure	set to 760 mm Hg
Wheel speed	set to 6th gear map
Battery voltage	set to 12V
ROM adjustment	set to standard maps

Fig. 10.11 This compact unit contains everything except the fuel pump (Performance Bikes)

Fig. 10.12 This is the fuel pump, mounted on a base plate that bolts into the bottom of the tank (Aprilia)

In test mode, the various codes select sensors which are monitored by the instruments. The tacho in voltmeter mode, reads volts x 500 (eg indicated 6000 means 12V, indicated 4000 means 8V). The sensors checked are:

● Battery voltage.
● Air pressure (760 mm Hg at indicated 8000).
● Ambient minus intake pressure (100 mm Hg at indicated 1000).
● Throttle position (closed: indicated 1300 is 0.68V, wide open: indicated 7400 is 3.72V).
● Intake air temperature (indicated 4800 at 20°C, and 5700 at 30°C).
● Coolant temperature (indicated 4900 at 20°C, 9200 at 100°C).
● Wheel speed (sensor raw data is displayed when rear wheel is turned).
● Sidestand switch (indicated 10000 means switch is on – sidestand down, ignition interrupted – indicated 0 means switch is off).
● Tilt switch status (indicated 8000 is normal, indicated 0 means switch is on (bike has fallen over and system not reset) and indicated 10000 means there is a fault in the circuit.
● The system also checks the ignition and primary and secondary injectors (individually) by switching on and off five times. If normal, the warning light flashes 5 times per second.

6 Sagem system

Fitted as OE to Triumph models.

Basically an open loop, α-n system, with a throttle position sensor covering all throttle angles, and a fuel injection quantity which is then corrected (or 'trimmed') depending on data from other sensors. Some models, fitted with exhaust catalysts, have a λ-sensor in one exhaust header pipe and this controls the fuelling by closed-loop feedback.

Most of the usual instrument/warning/safety systems (like clutch lock-out switch, low fuel warning) are routed through the ECU. The exceptions are the speedo signal and oil pressure switch.

Sensors

● Engine speed, at crankshaft. The trigger is a toothed wheel with 21 teeth on an equal pitch and one 3-teeth wide with a 3 tooth gap to calculate the crank position.
● Throttle position sensor: 0V at idle and 5V at WOT.
● Corrected throttle position – based on the output of the potentiometer at idle. The butterfly position is recorded as a percentage of the full range and need not necessarily be 0 at idle or 100% when wide open.
● Cooling fan, on or off.

● λ-sensor (not all models: only used with exhaust catalytic converters).
● Gearbox neutral switch.
● Sidestand switch, on or off.
● Clutch switch, on or off. (If the sidestand is down, power to the ECU is cut when a gear is engaged unless the clutch is also lifted.)
● Battery voltage.
● Coolant temperature.
● Intake air temperature (measured inside the airbox).
● Intake air pressure (measured inside the airbox).
● Camshaft position sensor (detects which stroke the engine is on).
● Fuel level sensor.

Outputs

● Sensor reference voltage (5V nominal).
● Cooling fan on or off.
● Idle air valve stepper motor (0 = fully closed, 180 = fully open).
● Idle fuelling and idle fuel trim (proportion above or below the base amount).
● Ignition timing and dwell.
● Injector on time (plus fuel trim).
● Fuel trim. Short term: a correction applied to the base mixture to suit current operating conditions. Long-term (closed loop control only): if the engine constantly needs the same correction, the ECU remembers it and adapts the base mixture, so reducing the amount of short-term corrections.
● Tacho signal.
● Fuel gauge signal.
● Fuel level warning lamp.
● Temperature gauge signal.
● Neutral warning lamp.
● Power to fuel pump.
● Malfunctioning indicator lamp.
● On-board diagnostics. If the system detects a fault, the details (error code, engine data at the time) are stored in memory which can be downloaded by a dealer with the appropriate test equipment (which is mandatory for all Triumph dealers).

Injectors

One, twin-jet injector is used per cylinder. They are fitted close to the intake valves and the spray pattern is aimed at the heads of the valves.

Fuel delivery is controlled solely by injector open time.

Caution: Fuel in the rail is at 3 bar (45 psi). This pressure must be released (by disconnecting power to the fuel pump and cranking the engine a few times on the starter motor) before removing any fuel lines or injector bodies.

The injectors are a push-fit with O-ring seals into the throttle bodies. They are removed by leaving them in the fuel rail and easing the injectors out of the throttle body castings. To remove the injectors from the fuel rail, unclip the circlip at the top of each injector and pull out.

Check the condition of the sealing O-rings.

Throttle position sensor

A rotary potentiometer on the end of the bank of throttle bodies, its output should be 0 – 5V between idle and WOT. If not, it may have to be replaced or removed to check for damage but if it is disturbed, the closed position must be recalibrated using the diagnostic tool. Apart from accidental damage, the most likely fault is dirty or corroded electrical connections, which can be checked without physically moving the sensor.

Idle air control

This is a valve, controlled by a stepper motor, inside the airbox, which bleeds air to a point downstream of the throttle valves. During idling and starting (usually on a closed throttle) the valve controls air flow to the engine, altering it to keep the required AF ratio based on coolant temperature and air temperature/pressure.

The ECU stores a target idle speed.

The valve is also used for altitude compensation and to bleed air into the intakes during overrun, to prevent unburnt fuel lighting in the exhaust.

It can only be tested using the diagnostic tool.

Ignition coils

Fitted directly to the tops of the spark plugs, the coils are controlled by the ECU both for dwell and optimum timing. Normally each plug is fired on its cylinder's compression stroke but if the camshaft sensor fails, the ECU triggers the coils once per revolution (ie compression stroke and end of exhaust stroke).

Power relay

Electrical power is supplied to the ECU by a relay that is switched by the ignition switch. When the ignition is switched off, the ECU holds the relay on while the ECU is powered down. During this time it writes data to memory, checks the position of the idle air control valve stepper motor, runs the cooling fan until the coolant is below the prescribed temperature, and finally turns the relay off.

The relay is located under the seat, beside the ECU.

Fuel pump

Fitted inside the tank, the pump and pressure regulator supply fuel at 3 bar ±0.5. It runs all the time the engine is running and briefly when the ignition is switched on, to make sure the fuel rail is up to pressure. The ECU controls the pump via a relay.

Cooling fan

Controlled via a relay by the ECU from coolant temperature data, the fan is switched on/off if the temperature goes above/below preset thresholds. Power to the fan is independent of the ignition switch position.

Diagnostics

The system has extensive facilities to monitor running conditions, detect faults and provide means to adjust or calibrate the set-up. This is done with a Triumph diagnostic tool, carried by all dealers, which plugs into a dedicated socket on the ECU.

When the system detects a fault, it records it and then starts to count the number of cycles that the fault remains. If this number exceeds the preset threshold, the fault is logged in the memory along with engine data (see table below) and the malfunction indicator lamp is lit up.

Where possible the ECU substitutes default values to replace data affected by the fault, to let the engine run in a get-home mode.

Once the warning lamp is lit, the system begins to count warm-up cycles (each cycle requires the coolant to reach at least 72°C, be warmed by more than 23°C from start-up, and for the system to have a controlled power-down when the engine is switched off). If the fault clears, the system switches off the warning lamp after a pre-set number of warm-up cycles (usually 3) has been achieved and erases the fault from memory when a second (higher, usually 40) number is reached.

Faults in the instruments and fuel level sensors will not activate the warning lamp.

The diagnostic tool can show real-time engine data as well as data stored at the time a fault was detected. The functions displayed, along with the range of values are:

Function Range

Function	Range
Calculated volume of air/cycle	0 to 100%
Coolant temperature	–40 to 215°C
Idle fuel trim	–100 to 99.2%
Off idle fuel trim	not used
Engine speed	0 to 16383 rpm
Intake air temperature	–40 to 215°C
Ignition advance	–64 to 63.5° BTDC
Throttle position	0 to 100%
Intake air pressure (only in stored data)	0 to 983 mm Hg
λ fuel trim*	–100 to 99%
system status*	open or closed loop
λ-sensor voltage*	0 to 1.25 V

used only when a closed-loop program is stored in the ECU

The diagnostic tool can check individual sensors, factory data stored during assembly, when the ECU was last checked and details of the dealer who made the check.

It can also be used to send signals to the fuel pump and cooling fan to run them for specific periods to test their performance, and to check the instruments.

Adjustment

Idle settings can be adjusted using the diagnostic tool:
● Throttle position sensor voltage at closed throttle.
● Idle fuelling (not with closed-loop control).
● Idle air control valve stepper motor start point.
● Long term fuel trim (only on closed-loop control).

It is possible for Triumph to supply a password (keyed in to the diagnostic tool) which allows the tool to download the data for a different engine tune (stored under model designations).

Throttle balance procedure

This can be done using vacuum gauges (analogue, mercury column or digital gauges)
1 Remove the fuel tank.
2 Remove the airbox.
3 Disconnect the idle air hoses at the throttle bodies.
4 Connect a vacuum gauge to each throttle body.
5 Refit the fuel tank, hoses and pump connector (or run from remote tank – Triumph have an extension kit for this purpose).

6 Run the engine (with exhaust extractor if indoors), use twistgrip to hold idle speed at about 1200 rpm (disconnecting the idle air hoses will disable the normal idle control, so the throttles will need to be opened slightly to keep the engine running).
7 One cylinder has no throttle adjuster – the others are matched to its vacuum reading by turning their adjusters by small amounts and leaving the engine to settle for a few seconds.
8 Get equal vacuum readings on all cylinders. As adjustment on any one cylinder will affect the other readings slightly, the adjusters should be turned in small steps, going on to each throttle in turn, rather than trying to adjust one completely before starting on the next.
9 Stop the engine.
10 Disconnect the fuel tank connections and remove the tank.
11 Remove the vacuum gauge connections.
12 Refit the idle air hoses.
13 Refit the airbox and fuel tank.
14 Check the idle speed and pick-up. If the idle is outside the normal range (usually 1150 – 1250 rpm) then the closed throttle position should be recalibrated using the diagnostic tool.

7 Aftermarket systems

See Figs. 10.13a and b, 10.14a, 10.14b and 10.14c

The OE systems described so far apply to up-to-1999 models and, although injection

Fig. 10.13a The Dynojet Power Commander II kit

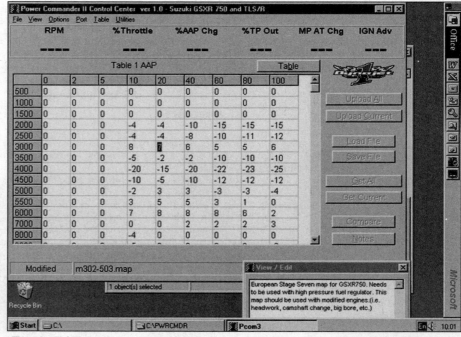

Fig. 10.13b The software for Dynojet's Power Commander has this screen editor, which displays the change being applied to the fuelling maps. The data can be altered, saved and downloaded to the module on the bike

had at this point been available for about 20 years, it is fair to say that bike applications were in their infancy. From a practical point of view, they had only been used where proven necessary – usually on big twins and V-motors, where there are special considerations like large diameter throttles, lack of space or engine heat/vapour lock problems.

By the late 1990s, only BMW and Triumph – both manufacturers with very small model ranges – had taken a decision to use fuel injection exclusively (not counting the retro-styled Triumphs). Other small manufacturers - Aprilia, Benelli, Laverda, Guzzi – were following the same route. Of the major manufacturers (with wide model ranges and relatively large production runs) Suzuki were switching to injection as newer and more powerful machines were introduced; Honda used it where it had sufficient merit; Yamaha and Kawasaki (the first to put it on a production bike) were being more cautious.

From an electronic point of view the systems will only get better (smaller, cheaper, more reliable, faster-acting, able to store more data). As the disadvantages get smaller and the needs get greater, there will be a general shift to injection. This will be accompanied by another shift to systems with more programmable features, as racers need to optimise fuelling and ignition to suit modified engines. Even owners of road bikes, who wish to fit different exhausts and air filters will need the electronic equivalent of a Dynojet kit. The original equipment manufacturers, on the other hand, are bound by emissions controls, which often include anti-tampering regulations, plus their usual reluctance to have their products modified. This implies that OEM units are likely to be non-adjustable and possibly sealed. As with other engine components, unauthorised modification will cause loss of warranty.

Consequently there will be an increasing

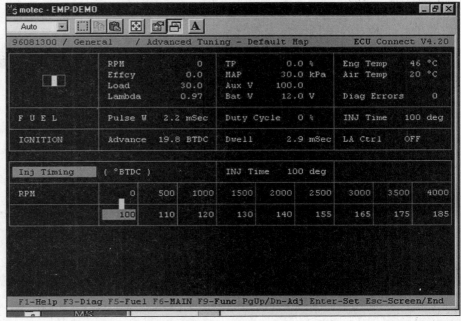

Fig. 10.14a Motec is an Australian engine management system whose software is very comprehensive and allows full editing of all the engine control features, as this and the following screen dumps show

market for replacement ECUs and other items such as sensors, injectors and throttle bodies, so that engines can be developed for competition.

This is already the case in the car world, where, at the simplest level, it is possible to buy a replacement chip, or, more drastically, to switch to another ECU, or fit a completely different motorsport set-up.

[Engine management units offer another potential, namely that they make it very easy to govern vehicle performance, either through built-in rev or speed limiters or from an outside source, not unlike the transponders used to log race bikes' lap times and positions. Worldwide, a lot of development work is going into 'smart' highways, which can communicate with vehicles – potentially making it easy to bill drivers on toll roads (without having to stop at booths), give warnings of hazards, limit speeds, detect speeding vehicles etc. The technology already exists in one form or another, it is only a matter of time before it all gets bound together in a reliable package.]

Where bikes are concerned, there are a few aftermarket car systems that can be adapted – theoretically any system could be, although there may be practical problems with the size of the ECU and of running a system designed for a maximum of 7000 rpm on an engine capable of 14000 rpm.

There are political/financial problems, too. Many of the larger manufacturers are paranoid about their software and go to extreme lengths to protect it. The result is that a license to use the software (essential for engine tuning) is very expensive and restricted to a limited period of time (so it will have no resale value). Other manufacturers who make dedicated motorsport versions, usually with built-in data acquisition and telemetry options (like Bosch and Magneti Marelli) tend to be very expensive.

Fortunately there are a few smaller firms who supply their own ECUs and software that can be adapted to other manufacturers' hardware. Ironically, as their business is small and doesn't have to order large quantities a long time in advance, they can adapt to rapid advances in electronics and may be using more sophisticated processors than the OEM suppliers. In many cases they will supply the software free, sometimes as a demonstration

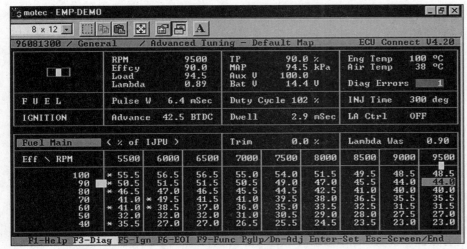

Fig. 10.14b The data can be altered while the machine is on a dyno, so fast comparisons can be made to optimise the fuelling and ignition characteristics – or to return to the original settings

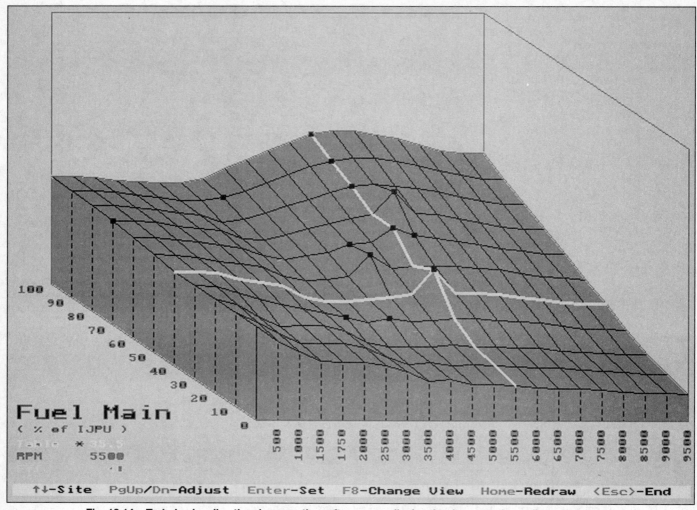

Fuel Main
(% ef IJPU)

RPM   5500

↑↓-Site   PgUp/Dn-Adjust   Enter-Set   F8-Change View   Home-Redraw   ⟨Esc⟩-End

Fig. 10.14c To help visualise the changes, the software can display the data as a three-dimensional map
This one shows fuelling against engine speed and load. The selected point (where the two white lines cross, at 5500 rpm and 40% load in this case) can also be edited from the keyboard

program which doesn't have all features available, although often it is the full working program (because the software cannot be used without the hardware which, of course, has to be paid for). In demo or working form, it gives customers a good idea of how it works, how easy it is to understand, how many features it has and so on. The software and a few sample data files can often be downloaded from the company's web site.

The questions to ask are: is it compatible with the sensors you want to use, does it have enough inputs and outputs to do what you want, and can it handle the necessary number of injectors at maximum engine speed?

When these base requirements are satisfied you need to find out how it handles cold starts and idling, and how it manages the injector's on-off characteristics (which vary with battery voltage).

Once you know how it will fit in with the

hardware, you can look at how many load/speed stations can be programmed, how much the mixture can be trimmed, and whether individual cylinders can be trimmed.

Can it handle other inputs such as a knock sensor?

Outputs are not so much of a problem – a simple signal intended for a gearshift light can be amplified and used for other purposes, eg to drive a servo motor or open a solenoid valve. It is necessary to check that the origin of the signal can be programmed (it may only be triggered by a speed threshold, whereas you may want a combination of load and speed).

The firm supplying the software can almost certainly adapt it to meet special requirements like this: it is a function of time, cost and willingness. Unless you are a large and important customer, this is more likely to be found in a small company.

As a half-way house there is the possibility

of fitting a module that sits between the original ECU and the bike's wiring harness, to intercept (and modify) input/output signals. Similar systems exist for digital ignition control, giving a degree of programmability to the ignition timing maps.

Others, such as Dynojet's Power Commander II are available for specific machines with fuel injection.

Power Commander is a module containing programmable maps that plugs in between the standard ECU and the wiring loom. It has an adapter cable that can be connected to a PC, or it can be programmed by buttons on the box. Each unit contains preset maps, other maps (suitable for modified engines, for example) can be supplied on disc or downloaded from Dynojet's website and the map currently in the unit can be edited by the PC software provided. The new version can be saved and transferred to the ECU.

Fig. 10.15 Aprilia's semi-direct injection only puts fuel into the cylinder after the exhaust port has closed *(Aprilia)*

8 Direct injection

See Fig. 10.15

There is no doubt that where power density is concerned, two-stroke engines are much better than four-strokes. Whether you measure it as power per cc displaced by the piston, or power per unit weight or space occupied by the engine, the two-stroke is superior.

The problems with two-strokes are high fuel consumption and dirty exhaust gas, which both stem from running fuel and oil through the crankcase to the cylinder, where some can 'short-circuit' – escape directly from the transfer ports to the exhaust, and not be trapped inside the cylinder. Also, when port sizes and timing are set for optimum high speed and high load performance, the engine is inefficient at low speeds and light loads. In these conditions, combustion is often irregular, the engine misfiring and creating the characteristic two-stroke stutter. This leads to unstable running on light loads and a certain amount of roughness on idle.

Aprilia addressed these problems by developing a direct injection system, called DITECH. The crankcase and cylinder are scavenged by clean air, so any losses will not affect fuel consumption or exhaust dirtiness. In other respects it is a conventional two-stroke (a 50 cc unit, as used in mopeds and small scooters) but Aprilia claim a 40% reduction in fuel consumption with exhaust emissions reduced by 80%.

Indirect injection offers no advantages to two-strokes. Whether the fuel is introduced in the intake port, the crankcase or the transfer ports, it still suffers the same problems as carburation, namely that fuel can short circuit.

Direct injection has its own problems. One is that the fuel has to be injected in the very short space between the exhaust port closing and ignition – in the region of 70° of crank travel, which doesn't leave enough time to get the fuel spray atomised and thoroughly mixed with the air in the cylinder. The second problem is the fuel pressure has to be raised above cylinder pressure, which makes pump design difficult.

Aprilia's answer to this is based on a design by the Australian Orbital company, with whom the DITECH system was developed. The injector sprays fuel into a separate chamber containing compressed air, forming a very rich mixture. This can be done over most of the engine cycle, leaving much more time for the air and fuel to be mixed.

The small, compressed packet of air and fuel is then injected into the cylinder, close to the spark plug, after the exhaust port has closed. The unburnt fuel cannot escape from the cylinder and the locally rich mixture is easy to ignite, avoiding the light load misfiring that conventional two-strokes suffer.

Once burning, combustion spreads through the remaining, much weaker air-fuel content. This process is called stratified charge combustion, where a rich mixture is used to start the burn. The stoichiometric AF ratio is 14.7:1 with something like 12:1 needed for maximum power and 16 to 18:1 used for lean cruise conditions. These overall ratios can be achieved but close to the spark plug the mixture is much richer, while the surrounding gas may be as weak as 30:1 on light load, going down to 50:1 at idle. In a conventional engine there would be a tendency to start misfiring beyond the rich and especially the lean limits. Because stratified charge combustion relies on an expanding, burning, ball of mixture, rather than a short, sharp, electric spark, it can carry a smooth burn all the way through the entire gas. Honda used a comparable injection system in their EXP-2 two-stroke (see Chapter 2) but on light loads it was engineered to auto-ignite, doing away with spark ignition altogether.

In both systems, the right amount of air and fuel can be used for either maximum power or best economy, with no risk of unburnt fuel short-circuiting, and reliable, regular combustion in light load, low speed conditions.

As they already have an engine management system to control fuel and ignition, with the usual ECU and various sensors, Aprilia make use of this to control engine lubrication as well. There is a separate oil tank and an electric, solenoid type pump delivers oil to the intake as in conventional two-strokes. The pump is controlled by the ECU and delivers oil to meet the precise engine load and speed. This gives a claimed 30% reduction in oil consumption (and as two-stroke oil is ultimately burned or blown through the exhaust, it also reduces exhaust emissions).

By keeping the oil and fuel completely separate, there are more gains. Conventional two-strokes mix the two, either in the fuel tank or in the intake where the oil is injected. This means that the oil is diluted by the fuel and is washed off bearing surfaces, so the pump has to deliver more oil than the engine actually needs to allow for these losses. Similarly the oil contaminates the fuel, altering its combustion and anti-knock qualities and adding deposits on the piston, rings and exhaust valves, plus hydrocarbon and CO content in the exhaust pipe. Aprilia's system neatly avoids these problems and is said to meet European emissions standards not only with a two-stroke cycle but without catalytic converters. It also implies a longer service life, because there is no oil dilution or washing in the crankcase bearings and lower cylinder wall.

The construction of Aprilia's DITECH is:
- Electric fuel pump. Possibly one of the biggest design challenges: the pump runs at 6 bar with low electrical drain (it is intended for lightweight machines which cannot afford the weight and cost of large generators and batteries).
- Fuel rail with automotive type of injector (Siemens).
- Air compressor. Small pump driven by a cam on one of the crankshaft's full web flywheels. It runs at 5 bar and draws its air from the crankcase (already filtered and now containing oil mist, which lubricates the compressor). The high pressure air is ducted to the injection chamber above the cylinder head.
- Injection chamber. This contains a small volume of high pressure air and has the

total amount of fuel for the engine cycle injected into it. After the exhaust port closes, a valve opens the chamber to the cylinder and this volume of rich air-fuel mixture is propelled towards the spark plug. Although the chamber-to-cylinder injection has to be completed in only 70° or so of crank travel, this arrangement means that the remaining 290° are available for fuel injection. Aprilia say that a typical car injector creates fuel particles of about 50 microns diameter, while a (high pressure) DI diesel produces particles in the 25 to 30 micron region, yet DITECH makes them only about 8 microns across. From this size the fuel can evaporate in less than 1 ms, which is within the time allowed for an engine turning at 12000 rpm.

● Pressure regulator, to maintain the pressure difference between fuel and air.

● Ignition. A powerful system, controlled by the ECU, to make sure each cycle ignites and there is no misfiring which would allow unburnt hydrocarbons into the exhaust.

● Throttle valve. As the intake flows dry air, a simple type of valve with a throttle position sensor is all that is needed.

● Oil pump. An electrical unit, controlled by the ECU (as described above).

● ECU. An α-n system, corrected for engine temperature, with maps for fuel injection, ignition and oil pump output. It also has self-diagnosis and anti-theft features.

Chapter 11
Supercharging and special fuels

Contents

1 Introduction

To get the most power from a piston engine you must persuade the maximum amount of air to enter its cylinders. Putting in the matching amount of fuel is less of a problem because there's far less of it. Gasoline, for example, needs only 1/12th the weight and, as it arrives in liquid form, it takes up negligible volume compared to the air. So piston engines are air-restricted. The first stroke – intake – is the weakest of the entire process.

There are two ways around this. One is to use a fuel (or introduce a third compound) which liberates oxygen when it gets inside the cylinder. The other is to use a compressor to force air into the engine instead of relying on atmospheric pressure to do the job (see Fig. 11.1 overleaf). This is called *supercharging* while atmospheric engines are called *naturally aspirated* (NA).

HAYNES HiNT *Superchargers are also called 'blowers', aptly because the earliest types were simply fans blowing air in the general direction of the engine.*

If the compressor is turned by the engine through a mechanical or electrical drive it is called a supercharger (possibly with a descriptive *vane, Roots-type, centrifugal* etc to distinguish the type). When the compressor is turned by an exhaust-driven turbine, the assembly is called a *turbocharger*. Turbochargers always use radial-flow (see Note 1) compressors and turbines, while there are many different types of compressor used in direct-drive superchargers.

Turbochargers appear to give something for nothing because they're driven by what would be waste energy in the exhaust – all piston engines lose at least 30% of their fuel's energy as low grade heat which disappears down the exhaust pipe. Some of this is extracted to drive the turbine but it's not something-for-nothing. It takes some energy, which means the exhaust process isn't as efficient as it could have been and, in practice, the whole engine has to be detuned (lower compression, shorter valve timing) to cope with the turbo's boost, so effectively it is starting from a lower baseline.

It simply means that turbocharged engines aren't quite as good as they would seem to be but they are still a lot more powerful than a naturally-aspirated engine of the same weight, displacement or cost (depending on what

Note 1 *At least vehicle-sized turbochargers are radial flow. Bigger engines can use axial flow turbines but these are only efficient in a narrow speed range, which doesn't suit road vehicles*

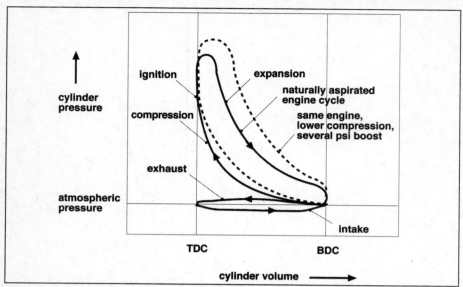

Fig. 11.1 An indicator diagram (showing cylinder pressure over cylinder volume as an engine turns through its full cycle) demonstrates how supercharged engines gain over naturally aspirated engines

During intake and exhaust the piston does less pumping work on the gas (as it is forced into the cylinder) and, at the beginning of exhaust, the gas has a higher pressure making it leave the cylinder when the valves open. To offset these gains, work has to be done to drive the compressor. More work is done on the gas during compression but then it reaches higher pressures after ignition and during the expansion stroke. The work available at the crankshaft is shown by the area enclosed in the upper, banana-shaped loops that cover compression and expansion: a larger area equals more work or torque per cycle

your criteria happen to be). They're also more efficient than supercharged engines because the supercharger has to be driven from the crankshaft and the power absorbed is directly subtracted from engine power, while the engine carries on wasting 30-odd per cent of its heat through the exhaust system.

The advantage of superchargers is they can be tailored and geared to give boost wherever you want it. Turbochargers only work when there is already a high mass flow through the engine: when you're close to maximum power they can increase it handsomely but they can't help you when you're accelerating from low rpm.

While all supercharged engines give more power in their working range they are not more fuel-efficient than NA engines, because you still have to add more fuel to go with the increased mass of air. Turbochargers gain a little because they recapture some waste energy but on the whole, all blown engines simply behave like bigger NA engines as far as fuel efficiency is concerned.

Mechanically, they tend to be more efficient. Because the base engine is still the same physical size, it has roughly the same losses caused by pumping, friction and viscous oil drag, yet in supercharged form it gives more power so the power/losses ratio is higher.

The engines tend to run more smoothly than similar NA engines because the peak cylinder pressure, although slightly higher, is

spread over a wider angle of crank travel and the rate of change of pressure is less. It also cushions the piston at top dead centre, where the inertia loadings are highest, so a blown engine, although giving more power, is less likely to suffer failure in the connecting rod or big-end bolts than a same-sized NA engine.

2   History of the Supercharger

Pre-war development

1885 – Gottlieb Daimler was given a patent for a pump alongside the engine cylinder to deliver air to, and help scavenge exhaust gas from the cylinder.

1902 – Louis Renault was given a patent for a belt-driven fan blowing air through the carburettor.

1908 – Lee Chadwick, of Pennsylvania, built a supercharged race car that did 100 mph. His first design was an 8-inch diameter fan driven at five times engine speed. Later he used three fans in series, a ploy adopted by the aircraft industry to overcome the inefficiencies involved in obtaining the desired volume flow, pressure and compressor speed in a single stage supercharger. One of Chadwick's cars won the first race (a 10-miler) held at the Indianapolis Raceway in 1909.

1909 – Buchi, employed by the Swiss firm

Brown Boveri (of which more later) drew up designs for an exhaust-driven turbocharger for diesel engines. Materials problems (to cope with the high temperatures and the high turbine speeds) meant that this would not be taken further until WW2 and wouldn't really be a practical proposition for gasoline engines until much later.

1914–18 – aircraft development in WW1 made designers quickly realise there were big advantages in cruising altitude and take-off weight offered by supercharged engines. [At high altitude the air density is less, so drag is less and aircraft can travel further on the same weight of fuel, but the same reduction in air density gives less power - a supercharger can restore this to the same as sea level power, while, for take-off, it can give a temporary increase.]

1921 – having gained experience with aero engines, Paul Daimler (son of Gottlieb) designed a Mercedes 4-cylinder (and later 6- and 8-cylinder) supercharged engine, setting a trend for sports and race engines (especially made in Germany) that would last until 1939. At the 1920s level of engine development, 6 to 7psi boost (see Note 2) gave a 50% increase in power in Mercedes' 1.5-litre sports car.

1923 – Fiat ran a supercharged GP race car. This and the Mercedes, like the other types mentioned above, blew through the carburettor (see Note 3). Instead of the centrifugal or radial flow fan, Mercedes chose a Roots-type, positive displacement compressor (see Fig. 11.11). This is named after Philander and Francis Roots, from Indiana, who developed the interlocking rotor design in 1859, to pump water.

1924 – the Duesenberg 2-litre engine featured a centrifugal blower downstream of the carburettor. By drawing air and fuel into the

>
> **Note 2**
> *Boost - manifold pressure above atmospheric, eg ambient pressure of 14.7 psi and boost of 5 psi would be absolute pressure of 14.7 + 5 = 19.7 psi. Sometimes referred to as a pressure ratio, in this case a PR of 19.7/14.7 or 1.34*

> **Note 3**
> *Bernoulli's theorem still applies to supercharged engines. Boost pressure bled into a chamber with no exit will be higher than the pressure of the gas travelling along the intake, because it is static and has no kinetic energy. Boost pressure therefore has to be applied to the float bowl of a carburettor which is downstream of the supercharger and the carburettor will then work in the usual way. It may be necessary to raise the fuel delivery pressure to prevent boost pressure forcing fuel back up the line.*

Fig. 11.2 The argument against superchargers on bikes is that they're difficult to fit, both to line up with a convenient drive and to find the necessary space. It's not entirely borne out by this sequence of pre-war race bike photographs: first the 1933 AJS 1100 cc, overhead cam V-twin record breaker at Pendine sands (Mortons Motorcycle Media Archive) . . .

Fig. 11.3 . . . AJS had a blown, air-cooled V4, which wasn't too successful and they made it liquid-cooled for 1939 . . .

The powerplant looks neat and compact but the machine was heavy – 405 lb (Mortons Motorcycle Media Archive)

blower, the fuel's latent heat could be used to cool the compressor and the air stream, resulting in higher air density and better engine performance. Previous types, blowing through the carburettor, had to have the entire fuel system pressurised. The downside to sucking through the carburettor is that compressing a combustible mixture increases the drama if the engine spits back in the intake, and it means that the blower has to be sealed against leaks (whereas a certain amount of leakage, along with high gas temperature, is acceptable if the compressor is handling dry air).

Supercharging became popular in cars and was used in quite a few bikes from the late 1920s through the 1930s (see Figs. 11.2, 11.3, 11.4, 11.5 and 11.6). With bikes there was always the problem of space and the addition of an extra drive, lubrication, cooling and weight although there were many, varied (but usually race bike) applications, such as:
1926 – DKW 173 cc, liquid-cooled two-stroke with piston compressor.
1930 – Guzzi, 500 cc 4-cylinder.
1933 – AJS 1100 cc, air-cooled V-twin.
1935 – Rondine, 500 cc, in-line, liquid cooled 4-cylinder.

1935 – Imperia, 500 cc, horizontally opposed, air-cooled two-stroke twin.
1935 – various DKW, split-single, liquid-cooled two-strokes, with third cylinder as compressor. The 250 cc racer was said to have fuel consumption of 15 mpg.
1938 – Gilera, 4-cylinder, liquid-cooled, based on Rondine.
1938 – Guzzi, 250 cc single: 0.6 – 0.8 bar boost on gasoline/benzole and 1.3 – 1.5 bar boost on methanol, 32 mm Dell'Orto carburettor, 38 bhp at 7900 rpm on gasoline, 45 bhp on methanol, 124 mph, weighed 291 lb.

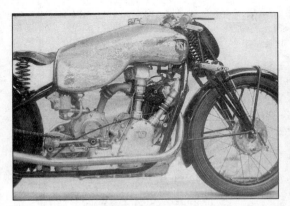

Fig. 11.4 . . . careful powertrain design creates even more room on this 350 cc DOHC NSU twin of 1938. Its blower is mounted above the gearbox, driven from the primary drive . . .

The bike was fairly heavy, at 369 lb, and thirsty – it reputedly had to carry another 50 lb of fuel (Mortons Motorcycle Media Archive)

Fig. 11.5 . . . a smaller engine leaves more room and BMW's 500 cc flat twin layout provides a drive from the nose of the crankshaft plus lots of space for the eccentric vane blower and the intake system . . .

The bike was both light (306 lb) and fast, winning the 1939 TT and 500 cc championship, taking world speed records around 170 mph in fully streamlined form (Mortons Motorcycle Media Archive)

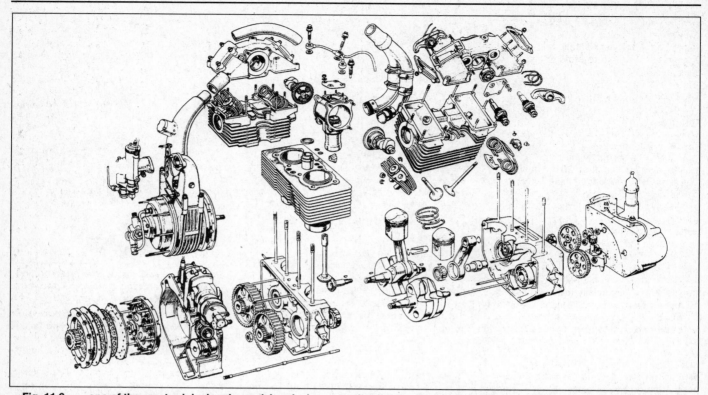

Fig. 11.6 . . . one of the most original and promising designs wasn't fully developed before WW2 put a temporary stop to GP racing

This is Velocette's twin cylinder Roarer. Two vertical cylinders with contra-rotating crankshafts give perfect balance and an ideal driveline, with the 6-blade Centric supercharger mounted on one and the clutch on the other. The transmission has all-indirect gears – the norm today but unusual then – to make the drive step out past the rear wheel to an enclosed shaft, like the BMW. With a 1 1/16 inch carburettor and 13 psi boost, the 500 cc engine was said to make 54 bhp (Mortons Motorcycle Media Archive)

1939 – AJS, liquid-cooled (previously air-cooled), V4, weighed 405 lb.
1939 – Benelli, 250 cc, 4-cylinder.
1939 – BMW, 500 cc, air cooled flat twin, weighed 306 lb.
1939 – Guzzi, 500 cc, 3-cylinder, weighed 386 lb.
1939 – NSU 350 cc twin, weighed 419 lb.
1939 – Velocette Roarer, 500 cc, air-cooled, twin cylinder, 54 bhp.

In cars of the same era these considerations weren't important because designers simply made the car bigger. The engine compartment was already the dominant part of the design, while passenger and luggage space was made to fit in whatever was left. Forty-odd years later this would change completely, as cars were designed as a whole, with the emphasis on passenger safety and comfort, and the mechanical parts squeezed into ever-smaller spaces. In these opposite conditions, turbochargers became popular as a means of getting more power from down-sized engines.
1939-45 – virtually all high-performance and high-altitude piston-engined aircraft used supercharging of one kind or another, usually multi-staged or with a variable gear drive, so that blower speed, pressure and delivery could be kept in step with the engine's demands.

Post-war development

After the war, aircraft switched to gas turbines (which can be viewed as a turbocharger which just got bigger and bigger until the base piston engine disappeared altogether...) while car manufacturers, still under no pressure to limit under-bonnet size, simply used bigger engines to get more power. This had the same overall effect as supercharging and it meant there was only one thing to manufacture and develop, instead of two.

In racing, which had permitted supercharging before the war, resulting in bikes like the NSU, Benelli, Gilera, DKW, BMW, Velocette and AJS, plus many blown cars such as Mercedes and Auto Union, there were now restrictions. Superchargers were still permitted, but the base engine had to have a smaller displacement than NA engines.

In GP car racing this was still a practical proposition and the 1.5-litre V16 BRM of 1950-51, fitted with a Rolls Royce two-stage, radial flow supercharger, was said to produce 330 bhp at 8000 rpm. F1 rules restricted supercharged engines to 1500 cc against NA engines of 4500 cc but in 1952 the rules were changed to 2000 cc NA and 500 cc supercharged, which killed off further supercharger development.

For a long time motorcycle racing rules said that supercharging was permitted if the engine displacement was half of the NA engine class. As the biggest racing class then was 500 cc, this meant a blown engine would be 250 cc at most. In addition to the difficulty of finding the space for a blower, there was now the problem of finding one small enough to match a 250 cc engine. Nobody made anything like this, while designing and manufacturing one would come close to doubling the cost of a single cylinder engine.

Supercharging all but died out. The exceptions were some two-stroke diesels, which used blowers, sometimes not strictly for supercharging but to scavenge burnt gas from the cylinders, leaving them full of air at atmospheric pressure.

There is also a spark ignition engine that uses a supercharger to permit very late intake closing and a short compression stroke. Called a Miller cycle (after Ralph Miller, the engineer who devised it during the 1940s), it is constructed like a four-stroke with poppet valves in the cylinder head and a blower with fuel injection. The disadvantage of the conventional Otto cycle is that compression and expansion strokes are equal in length and while thermal efficiency is theoretically improved by raising the compression ratio, the benefits are limited to the point at which the fuel knocks. The high temperatures cause

NOx production. This and other emissions are traditionally tackled by 3-way catalysts or lean-burn engines. Catalysts require the engine to run close to stoichiometry, which means it cannot use a mixture suitable for full power, so output is not as good as it might be. Lean burn has more long-term promise but at this stage could not beat the emissions of a catalytic converter.

The Miller cycle attempts to address all these problems by giving the intake phase late timing, and shortening the compression phase. During the first 20% or so of the compression stroke, the intake valves remain open, as they would on a very high-speed engine, yet this is only turning at 6000 rpm. The piston would normally push gas back past the valves, but a very efficient blower means that intake gas keeps flowing into the cylinder.

The compression stroke is that much shorter and there is a small loss in efficiency caused by the artificially low compression (it reduces a geometric 10:1 to about 8:1 from the point at which the valves close). This is not all bad, though, because it also reduces the risk of detonation and NOx emissions. The following power stroke is the usual length. The asymmetry between compression and expansion reduces the pumping work done on the gas (although work has to be done to drive the compressor).

From 1987 to 1991, Mazda developed a 2.2-litre V6 Miller cycle engine, using a Lysholm compressor and an intercooler. The compressor had one three-lobed rotor and one five-lobed. The gearing between rotors was 5:3 and they turned at a maximum 35,000 rpm and 21,000 rpm respectively, driven by a belt from the crankshaft. It gave a claimed 162kW at 5500 rpm, compared to their conventional, 2.5-litre V6 with 147kW at 6500 rpm, with fuel consumption as good as a 2-litre engine. The high specific output means less fuel is used for a given level of performance, so emissions are reduced in proportion and the power is obtained without high temperatures being developed. The implication then is that less has to be done to clean up the exhaust or that the engine could be run close to stoichiometry with a catalyst and could afford the loss of power that this produced.

3 Turbochargers

Supercharged diesel applications expanded in the late '50s and early '60s, particularly for larger engines – trucks, buses, earth-movers, agricultural machinery etc.

There were also a few car manufacturers who had made supercharged aero engines during WW2 and used this experience, like Buick who had a blown 335 bhp V8 in its 1951 LeSabre and XP-300. Studebaker used superchargers in three of its last production models.

Along with Oldsmobile, Buick (part of General Motors), went on to try turbochargers in the early 1960s, gaining experience that would be resurrected in 1978 to put them at the head of a fashion for turbos that extended even unto the motorcycle manufacturers. By then, advances in materials (and oils and a gradual shift to fuel injection) had made turbos a practical proposition.

They have a big advantage over superchargers in size and weight (to deliver the same quantity of air at the same pressure, a supercharger and its drive might weigh four times as much). The weight and the need for a mechanical drive restricts the position in which a blower can be fitted. To carry the weight and provide the necessary stiffness to keep the driveline straight means it also has to have fairly substantial castings and mountings.

A turbo can be mounted almost anywhere, in any attitude. The only installation problems are mounting it close enough to the exhaust valves (so heat energy isn't lost before arriving at the turbine) and finding a reasonable route for ducts from the compressor to the intake side of the engine. If a (large) carburettor has to be included in this route it makes it more complex, while fuel injectors can be neatly adapted to it.

The turbo has one other practical advantage. Although it interferes with the exhaust passage, it also acts like a silencer, so the vehicle can be silenced down to road levels fairly easily, by adding light, small, silencer cans and resonators, saving the weight, space and development time of a full silencing system.

Positive-displacement superchargers actually *make* noise, producing their own characteristic whine, plus the noise of their drive gears or belts. High speed turbines, especially if the compressor intake is open (as it often is on competition vehicles), make a high-pitched whistling sound but the volume is very low compared to that of superchargers.

4 Pressure wave supercharger

There is one other device which fits into the supercharging category. Known as a pressure wave supercharger, its function is to transfer exhaust energy to the intake air. It is called Comprex and was designed in the 1940s by Brown Boveri (the first to recognise the potential of exhaust turbochargers back in 1909), although its real development happened during the 1960s.

It consists of a drum (see Fig 11.7), with radial vanes forming lengthways cells, which

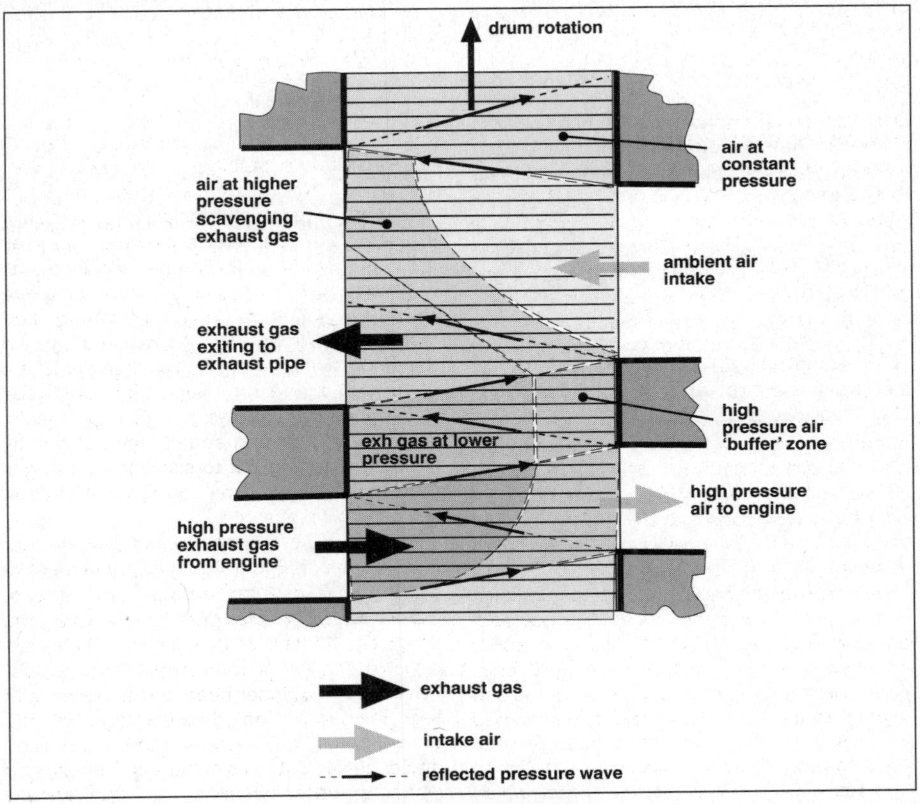

Fig. 11.7 Comprex design

The rotating cylinder unrolled, so the relationship between the moving cells and the exhaust/intake ports can be seen more clearly

run from one end of the drum to the other. The drum is able to rotate and is driven at roughly 1.5 times engine speed. There are static covers at each end, with port windows opening into the drum's cells. One end cover is connected to the exhaust header and has an exit to the exhaust silencer. The other has similar intake connections (a high pressure port leading to the engine and a low pressure port, which receives atmospheric air).

In operation, it allows the intake gas to come into brief, timed, contact with the hot exhaust gas and can, surprisingly, achieve up to 45 psi boost. As there is no physical compression of the gas, the driving losses merely amount to the inertia and windage of the drum, plus the effect of the back-pressure in the exhaust.

The physical movement of the exhaust gas along the cells is controlled by matching the exhaust flow to the size of the ports, the speed of the drum and the timing of the ports. To see how this works, follow one cell around a complete revolution, starting as it goes past the exhaust port, where hot, high pressure exhaust gas forces its way into the cell, compressing the air that is already there.

It pushes intake air out into the open port leading to the engine's intake (and fuel injectors). As the intake port closes, the exhaust gas pressurises residual intake air in a critical 'buffer zone'. The next event is that the exhaust exit opens. Exhaust gas, still at some pressure, bursts out, beginning the flow. It is encouraged further by the pressure of the air 'buffer', which then starts to follow the escaping exhaust gas.

Having got the exhaust stream started in the correct direction, the air intake port is opened and the inertia of the exiting exhaust draws fresh air into the evacuated cell. All of the exhaust gas and possibly some of the air go into the exhaust pipe. The cell, now full of air, continues to rotate until once again it is opened to the exhaust flow.

There are a couple of improbable stages in this cycle, where you can envisage things going wrong and exhaust gas flowing towards the inlet or, cycle by cycle, gradually filling the cell until fresh air cannot get in. This is prevented by pressure waves in the gas, in much the same way as a two-stroke's expansion chamber helps to scavenge exhaust gas. When the cells are first opened to the exhaust, a pressure wave travels across to the opposite end of the drum (at the speed of sound). By the time it reaches the opposite side, the cell will have travelled a short way and the crux of the design is to match the speed of rotation to the port window positions, so the pressure wave is reflected, raising air pressure again. High pressure reflections from the port window will return as low pressure waves, which dominate the cells in the region after the exhaust port closes. These reflect across and back to the exhaust exit, helping the flow. Subsequent reflections to the low pressure inlet encourage air to enter the cells and keep exhaust gas moving in the right direction.

The obvious 'problems', adding heat to the intake charge (when it is usual to cool it to raise its density) and contamination of the intake with burnt exhaust are turned into advantages.

The drum's movement and the intake porting arrangement act as a trapping valve, so instead of expanding the intake gas and reducing its density, exhaust heat raises the pressure of the gas in a triumph of Charles's Law (see Chapter 3) over intuition. At high speed there isn't time for contamination of any consequence. This may apply at low speed too, although a little exhaust gas recirculation can actually be useful in reducing emissions and controlling knock (see egr in Chapter 2).

As it depends upon very small pressure changes, it is very sensitive to back pressure in the remainder of the exhaust system, making silencing a bigger than usual problem. In conjunction with this, Comprex has one design disadvantage. Being constructed like a siren, it tends to sound like one. According to ear witnesses it has more than a passing similarity to a Stuka dive bomber (which used an air driven siren both as an air brake and to intimidate its victims).

Comprex has been used by Opel (General Motors), Steyr-Daimler-Puch, Saurer and Mazda in diesels (diesels are more amenable because their exhaust temperatures are considerably lower than gasoline engines, they flow full air, so there is no throttle requirement and the fuel is better suited to high pressure, direct injection, so the compressor can handle clean, dry air). Comprex has also been used in many experimental applications ranging from a Perkins diesel in a Land Rover through to an F1 Ferrari engine.

5 Turbo matching

Supercharging in bikes has long been restricted to sprint and drag bikes, partly because of competition regulations and partly because these long wheelbase machines were one of the few types with enough room to fit a blower. With no requirements other than the highest power to weight ratio, straight-line traction and stability, the design of these machines isn't compromised by considerations for handling, cornering clearance or braking.

There is another reason that bikes haven't had much use for superchargers: it has always been hard to find small enough units to match motorcycle engines and while riders can usually find a use for more top-end power, low- and mid-range delivery has always been more than adequate. Unlike cars and trucks, bikes never need to pull a heavy payload up steep hills and torque back-up isn't a priority. Superchargers tend to be best at improving midrange torque.

But turbochargers are another matter. They tend to leave low-speed performance alone and concentrate on delivering boost in high speed and high load conditions, which is just what high performance bikes need.

When the car-led fad for turbos took off in the late 1970s, it was no surprise to find bike manufacturers following. All four major Japanese manufacturers brought out turbo models in the sports-touring category, while aftermarket applications like Luftmeister did highly improbable things with BMWs.

The bike makers' experience with turbos showed two flaws. First that it is difficult to match a turbo to a small engine. Second that it was just a fashion fad, not a serious engineering expedition.

Not that they didn't take the engineering itself seriously. Honda did the full exercise on their CX500T, using an IHI (Ishikawajima-Harima Heavy Industries) RHB51A turbo, which was the smallest production turbine available, at 50 mm diameter (see Fig. 11.8). It span at speeds up to 180,000 rpm. With it they developed full fuel injection, new engine parts (but keeping the same layout as their popular 500 cc V-twin) and completely new rolling chassis and bodywork. A small V-twin is not the ideal candidate for a turbocharger

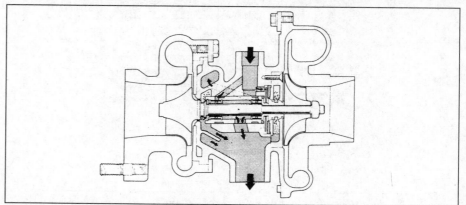

Fig. 11.8 Section through a turbocharger, showing the oil passage, which is used to cool the exhaust turbine and provide lubrication for the floating bearing (Honda)

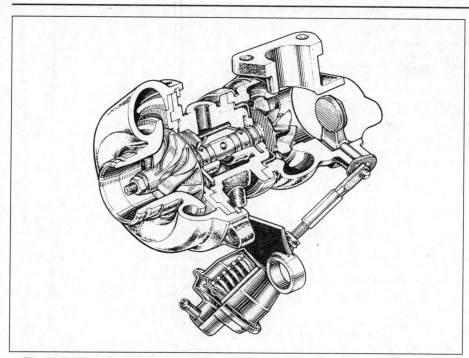

Fig. 11.9a The Hitachi turbocharger used on Kawasaki's ZX750T showing the boost pressure-operated wastegate. When open, this diverts exhaust gas from the turbine directly into the exhaust pipe (Kawasaki)

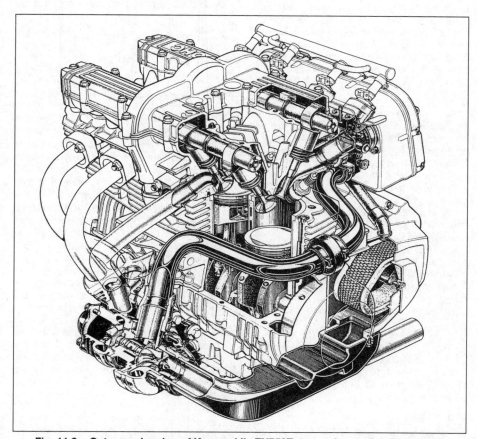

Fig. 11.9c Cutaway drawing of Kawasaki's ZX750T, two-valve engine (Kawasaki)

Fig. 11.9b The turbocharged Kawasaki ZX750T engine, showing how neat the final installation was (Kawasaki)

but the engine layout let Honda place the turbine in the V angle, conveniently close to both the exhaust valves and the engine's intakes.

They succeeded in giving the 500 roughly the same performance as their CB900 but in the process they demonstrated the something-for-nothing fallacy. The CX500T had the performance of the 900 but unlike the small, extremely agile CX500, the T was the same physical size and weight as the 900. It also had big-bike rather than middleweight price.

Even then the mismatch between turbo and small piston engine was evident and Honda soon shifted to a bigger base engine, with the CX650T.

However the turbo gave 17 psi boost and most certainly was a serious engineering exploit. So was Kawasaki's ZX750T which was designed as a 650 in 1980, but became a 750 for the 1981 prototype, with a new Hitachi turbo and digital fuel injection, similar to that of the 1983 GPz1100. Like Honda, Kawasaki went to some trouble to place the turbine close to the exhausts, making a neat 4-1 set of headers and having to use tough steel alloys to prevent the metal cracking under the thermal stress (see Figs. 11.9a, 11.9b and 11.9c).

Its wastegate was set to lift at 560 mm Hg boost (10.6 psi) giving a power output closer to the GPz1100 than to the base GPz750. And so was the weight – it was only 11 kg less than the 1100, and it was the lightest of the turbos.

Yamaha and Suzuki also produced turbo models, the XJ650T and XN85 respectively. On both the turbine performance was limited by poor design and by wastegates that opened at low levels of boost.

The 673 cc XN85 used fuel injection with an air flow meter (not unlike Kawasaki's first EFI attempt). The turbine was located above the gearbox, behind the cylinder block, creating a tortuous exhaust route which couldn't have been very efficient. The 50.4 mm turbine was designed to give 7.4 psi boost but the bike's performance was less than startling.

Yamaha's attempt was just as half-hearted. Mitsubishi's TC03-06A turbine was even smaller than the IHI unit, at 39 mm diameter. It

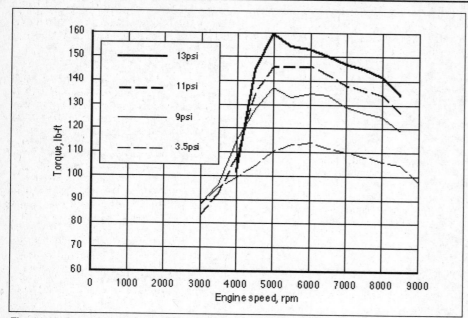

Fig. 11.10 Torque curves for a Suzuki GSX1100E bored to 1498 cc and fitted with a Rajay F40 turbo, at various levels of boost

The general effect is obvious, raising torque with no losses, although the effects below 3500 rpm are small. The curve for 13 psi boost is also a sort of measure of turbo lag. The other curves were taken on an eddy current dyno, which lets the motor stabilise at each rpm station. In doing so it had plenty of time to build up full boost (the figures quoted are the wastegate settings and don't necessarily mean the engine was receiving this boost for the full run). This dyno couldn't contain the power output above 11 psi boost, so the machine was switched to an inertia dyno, which only gives transient figures. Now, when the throttle was opened wide at 3000 rpm, the turbo wouldn't respond immediately but, of course, the engine was capable of accelerating without boost. At 4000 rpm it behaved more or less as it had with 3.5 psi boost, and it had got to something like 4500 rpm before the boost had reached its full working level

would turn at 210,000 rpm but that's where the promise ended. Yamaha placed the turbo behind and under the gearbox, a long way from both the exhaust valves and the intake. They didn't even bother to develop fuel injection, letting it blow through four BS30 Mikuni carburettors instead. It was the bare minimum to qualify for a *Turbo* logo and it behaved like it. The wastegate was set to open at 7.2 psi boost but, like the Suzuki, it's debatable whether the system ever became that energetic.

It was clear the manufacturers were responding to a styling fashion (as were most of the car makers, too). If people had bought them in droves, they'd have developed them further. If not, then they'd make something else. Perhaps if they'd been allowed to race them... Kawasaki, whose 750s then held two FIM Endurance World Championships and four AMA Superbike Championships, hinted that they wouldn't mind racing the turbo, when they said, 'For those who may want to race without the standard air cleaner, the compressor wheel is specially treated to withstand increased abrasion from unfiltered air.' But nobody did.

The general perception was that turbos had

little to offer and no-one was sorry when the fad petered out. Of course it is a false impression – I have ridden turbocharged bikes engineered for performance which make normal machines of the same weight look seriously underpowered.

One example is a 1986 Harris-framed 750 Kawasaki, which gave 97 bhp at 8,000 rpm and covered a standing-start quarter mile in 10.8 seconds at a time when no road bikes could manage anything less than 11 seconds and the base GPZ750 gave 73 bhp at 9,000 rpm and took 12.03 seconds for the quarter mile.

Another is Steve Burns' *Monster*, which had a big bore Suzuki GSX1100 motor with a Rajay turbine in a Spondon frame, was capable of more than 200 bhp and would wheelie at 150 mph (see Fig. 11.10). And as this is written in 1999, a turbocharged ZZ-R1100 in 1994 is still the fastest machine *Performance Bikes* magazine has tested, at 203 mph (the same speed that Honda's 500 GP machines reach at Hockenheim, the fastest GP circuit).

Wastegate

Turbos can be self-regulating by means of a wastegate – a valve that lets exhaust gas by-

pass the turbine and go straight to the tailpipe. It's a spring-loaded valve operated by a linkage connected to the intake, where boost pressure pushes on a piston. When the pressure reaches a predetermined level, the force on the piston overcomes the spring and opens the valve. Exhaust pressure is dumped, the turbine slows down and boost pressure is reduced. Alternatively, the ECU can monitor boost pressure and control the wastegate electrically.

Floating bearings

Because turbines turn at such high speeds they need to be light (to respond quickly to changes in load), to have carefully designed lubrication systems and bearings that can survive the speed and the high temperature.

A high flow lubrication system can help cool the rotors but it needs some sort of reservoir because the turbine will carry on spinning for some time after the engine is shut down, when the normal pressure lubrication will stop.

Floating bearings can help to handle both high speed and high oil flow. Basically the bearing consists of a bushing with a large radial clearance and a large oil supply. Once up to speed, the shaft and bush centre themselves on the cushion of oil and literally float. There is a separate thrust bearing coupled with a labyrinth type oil seal to prevent the shaft sliding along its axis and to stop oil getting into the turbine or compressor.

6 Supercharger types

Positive displacement

Reciprocating piston

Although too heavy and inefficient for vehicle supercharging, a piston reciprocating in a cylinder, with inlet and exhaust valves in the cylinder head (identical to a four-stroke cylinder) can be used as an air pump and is an easy-to-visualise way to demonstrate the actions of a compressor. Of course, pistons have been used in many designs: two-strokes use the underside of the working piston; some two-strokes have had a separate cylinder responsible for scavenging and charging the working cylinder; some (Dunelt, Wolf) have had pistons with two diameters, using the lower, larger diameter to pump gas into the combustion chamber above the upper part.

If the valving is arranged so that the inlet opens when the piston is descending from TDC to BDC, then air at atmospheric pressure will flow in as a substantially constant-pressure process, with no change in temperature or air density. The inlet then closes and the piston begins to travel up towards TDC.

There is now a choice:
1) The exhaust could open immediately and the air would be pushed out at the speed of

the piston, again a more or less constant pressure process and the cylinder volume of air would be delivered at atmospheric pressure and temperature. This would only happen in practice if the piston moved very slowly. When it moves with any speed, the air will not be able to get out of the valve as fast as the piston is travelling and it will either accelerate or compress the air. A high velocity stream of air may be what's required in some applications (eg a paint sprayer). If the piston speed becomes too high for the capacity of the valve, it will also start to compress the air, delivering it at a higher pressure and density than it started at. This may be necessary eg in pumps to inflate tyres to a certain pressure, while the volume displaced is not important.

This compression, as you've probably noticed from holding a bicycle pump, raises the air's temperature. The air passes on some heat to raise the temperature of the cylinder head or the end of the bicycle pump and this is one measure of the pumping efficiency, called the *adiabatic efficiency*. Adiabatic describes a process that occurs without heat entering or leaving the system and the fact that heat obviously does leave the air means the pump isn't very efficient in this sense.

You have had to put work into moving the air and some of this work is being wasted in raising the temperature of the pump's housing, instead of doing the original job of shifting the air to somewhere else. This leads to the second option.

2) It may be advantageous to delay the opening of the exhaust valve until the piston is somewhere in mid-stroke and has raised the

gas pressure (and temperature) significantly. This will encourage the gas to leave at a higher velocity and take more of its heat with it. Because it will not be in contact with the valve and port for such a long period, there will be less time for heat loss and the adiabatic efficiency will increase.

There are several characteristics of the air flow that the pump can alter: the mass flow, the volume flow, its velocity, its density, pressure and temperature.

The design of the pump can tailor these features (eg to get large volume flow at low pressure), by changing the bore and stroke of the piston, the pump speed, the valve size, the valve timing and the compression ratio of the piston in the cylinder. All these factors (or their equivalents) will apply in the various types of compressors that follow.

The piston will deliver the flow in a series of pulses, with a gap equal to the intake stroke between them. This could be smoothed out by having more pistons or by pumping through a large tank which would damp out the pulses.

However, a piston is a heavy and expensive way to pump gas. As well as the piston, cylinder and sealing rings, it needs a connecting rod, crankshaft, sturdy crankcases, a cylinder head with valves, some kind of cam and valve gear, a drive to the cam and a lot of components to be lubricated and cooled. It also pumps on the unused underside of the piston (although some types have double acting pistons to avoid this waste). And it vibrates.

Most automotive compressors have simple

rotating elements, using the minimum of moving parts and keeping the assembly in balance or at least in a form that is easy to balance.

Roots type

Contra-rotating rotors with interlocking (but not touching) lobe shapes (see Fig. 11.11). Early types had two lobes, later types used three to smooth out the pulsing nature of the flow at low speeds. Later still the rotors were twisted (lengthways) into a helical curve to improve delivery further and Lysholm made multi-lobed rotors which gave better adiabatic efficiency.

The two rotors are coupled by spur gears with a 1:1 ratio (when they have equal numbers of lobes) and the whole thing is driven usually by toothed or V-belt. Air is carried in the chamber formed between the housing and the rotor lobes and pushed out of the exhaust port when the lobes of the two rotors 'mesh' and the volume reduces.

This design gives high volume flow with little increase in pressure, although helical rotors and the positioning of the port windows can add boost pressure to the delivery.

Vane types

These rely on a rotor mounted eccentrically in a cylindrical housing, with four vanes dividing the rotor into quadrants (see Figs. 11.12 and 11.13). In the simplest type the vanes are free to slide in slots, centrifugal force pushing them out until they touch the housing to make a seal. The Centric or Shorrocks type is a refinement on this. The

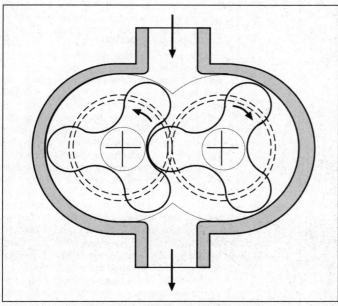

Fig. 11.11 Roots type supercharger
Originally developed with two-lobe rotors, the design was refined to three-lobe, lobes that are twisted in a helical form along the length of the rotors, and rotors with five and three lobes, and a 5:3 gear between them

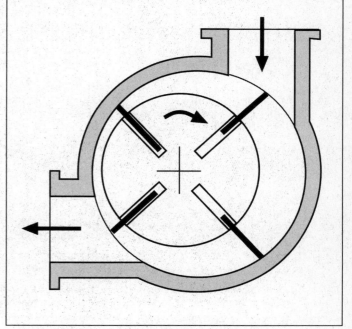

Fig. 11.12 Vane type blower
The vanes are free to slide as the rotor turns in its eccentric housing

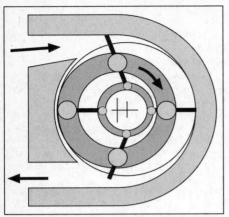

Fig. 11.13 Development of the vane type made by Centric and Shorrocks

The vanes now slide in trunnions and are anchored to prevent them making contact with the outside wall

rotor is mounted eccentrically on a shaft, physically creating a volume that expands as it passes the inlet port and contracts, pressurising the air before it passes the exhaust port. As with Roots type blowers, raising the pressure improves the adiabatic efficiency.

The air is kept in compartments by four vanes, which force it to move with the rotor. The vanes are able to slide in the eccentric rotor, but are anchored to their carrier so they never actually touch the outer housing. The clearance is kept to within a few thousandths of an inch. To allow the vanes to slide and to accommodate the eccentric travel of the rotor (which turns the vanes through a small angle) they are held in trunnions: bushes which can rotate in the rotor.

Another variation on this theme is the epitrochoid (Wankel) type, with a three lobed, eccentric rotor whose tips trace a roughly oval shape, which the housing matches. Once again the volume between rotor and housing expands and contracts over each cycle and it is possible to obtain very high compression ratios with this type. The eccentric motion produces vibration, which may be balanced by using a twin rotor machine.

NSU used this type of supercharger in their world record breaking bikes of the 1930s.

Helical screw type

A rotor with a square-form thread, inside a close fitting casing was patented in 1936 by Svenska Rotor Maskiner in Sweden, although the principle goes back into antiquity, having been used for water pumps and machines to extrude clay for pottery.

Zero displacement types

In these designs gas dynamics are used to create the flow, the air passing over the blades of a rotor, like a domestic fan or the fan on a radiator cooling system. All systems depend on the rotor moving at high speed and the blades have to be carefully designed so their angle matches the relative velocity of the air and the rotor. This is like an aircraft wing whose angle of attack must be kept within a certain range if the airflow is to maintain a high pressure on the underside and a low pressure on the topside.

The turbine blade is driven so that it should maintain a high pressure on one side and a lower pressure on the other and this depends on the geometry, the flow rate of the air and the delivery pressure. If this equilibrium is upset, for instance by the engine being too small and not being able to handle the air flow, the rotor's blades will go into an inefficient region. Where the pressure is too low or the flow rate too high, the efficiency will drop considerably. More seriously if the pressure is too high or the flow too low, the compressor will *surge*. This is analagous to the aircraft wing stalling. It loses control of the flow and the sudden, violent fluctuations that follow can be severe enough to cause mechanical damage.

Radial flow type

Also called a *centrifugal* compressor, this is the most common type used on road vehicle engines (see Fig. 11.14). The intake is at the centre and air flows along the almost-radial blades, being accelerated outwards into the expanding (*involute*) housing, with the exit running at a tangent to the rotor.

The delivery pressure is proportional to the square of the rotor speed and this has to be very high, in the region of 50,000 to 100,000 rpm, which makes mechanical drive a bit of a problem. Without a variable drive, getting the compressor in its working range at peak engine revs would mean that it would be turning too slowly to be of any use in the low-midrange. The obvious drive is something that will turn naturally at the required speeds – an exhaust-driven turbine.

This takes a similar form to the compressor, except that exhaust gas enters the outer housing, tangentially to the rotor, and exits at the rotor's centre. On large diesels the turbine will turn at 70,000 to 100,000 rpm, while the smallest type made by IHI is rated at 180,000 rpm.

Matching both the turbine and the compressor to engine requirements is critical. The compressor must be running near peak efficiency when the engine is in its power band, yet mustn't get too close to its surge line. The turbine needs to match the exhaust flow so it can spin the compressor to the right speeds to achieve this.

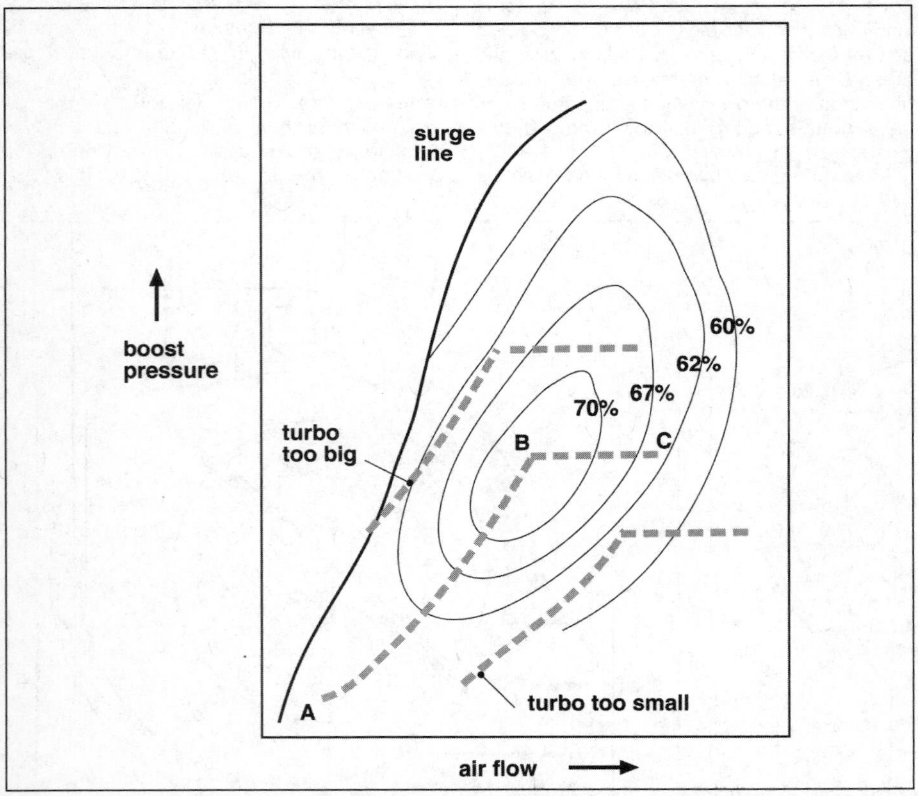

Fig. 11.14 The efficiency of radial flow turbines depends on their dimensions and speed, making them better at certain combinations of pressure and air flow

Ideally the engine's requirements for gas flow should run through the regions of maximum efficiency (A – B) and the wastegate will crop the boost pressure at peak efficiency (B – C). Choosing a wrong-sized turbo for the engine will make it run in less efficient regions and either will not develop sufficient boost or the boost will get too high, running into the surge region

While the size of the blades give more or less air flow at any one speed, the geometry of the turbine housing determines what this speed is. The ratio of the area of the nozzle which forms the entry to the turbine to the radius of the centre of this area from the rotor's axis is called the A/R ratio. A larger A/R ratio will make the turbine turn at a lower speed for a given exhaust flow. A smaller A/R ratio will make the turbine speed up.

If the A/R ratio is too big for the engine then the compressor will not turn fast enough to make useful boost in the engine's midrange and will only just be getting into its stride when the engine is making maximum power. It will simply be inefficient and not work very well.

If the A/R ratio is too small, the turbocharger will become efficient at fairly low engine revs, but as the engine speeds up the compressor will give too much boost and will get closer to its surge line.

Having a too large A/R is the most common mismatch on bikes, simply because most turbochargers are designed for larger engines, which tend to flow a lot of gas at low rpm.

Axial flow

There is another type of zero displacement compressor, which looks rather like the turbines used in jet engines. The air flow is along the axis of the rotor, which has rows of blades in several stages, with stationary blades between them, to prevent the air picking up the blades' rotary motion. This type is only efficient over a narrow speed range and is only suitable for extremely large engines.

Intercooler

All compressors heat up the air that passes through them and this is bad for several reasons. First it reduces the air density and thus reduces the number of oxygen molecules that will find their way into the cylinder. Second it takes the fuel closer to its ignition point and some types of fuel may even ignite before they get to the engine. With gasoline this is not likely, but having the mixture at a high temperature means the engine has to do less to it to bring it into the pre-ignition or detonation range. As detonation is the limiting factor in high performance engines, it is obviously worth keeping the fuel as far away from it as possible.

Many applications have an intercooler to do just this. It takes the form of a heat exchanger between the compressor and the engine, usually with a water jacket and a radiator, working in the same way as the engine cooling system.

Water injection

Using water as an internal coolant was first tried during the 1920s. Liquid water can be drawn in with the intake gas and expanded into steam, taking its heat of evaporation away from combustion and reducing the likelihood of knock or pre-ignition. It can be supplied via a jet, in the same way that fuel is drawn in, or some pre-war bikes had a wick, like a candle, along which the water would climb by capillary action.

However, it is not needed all the time, only on full load and when the engine is in danger of running into a dangerous region. This makes it well suited to supercharged engines, because it can be fed to a reservoir which is subject to boost pressure and when the pressure reaches a certain level, water will be delivered to the intake.

It needs its own reservoir and often it is mixed with methanol, which acts as an antifreeze and also adds its own considerable latent heat of evaporation to the overall cooling effect.

Water injection can be an effective way to increase an engine's thermal efficiency. It is introduced as a liquid, with negligible volume compared to the gas flow (water is usually added at roughly the same rate as fuel, in the region 25:1 to 5:1, air:water, by weight). If some stays in liquid form during compression, then no compression work will be done on it. If it then takes heat from its surroundings to turn into steam it will expand, raising the pressure on the piston and reducing the heat which would otherwise be lost into the metal of the piston and cylinder.

7 Fuels

See also Chapter 2

Alcohols

Alcohols are a branch of the hydrocarbon family distinguished by the presence of an hydroxyl radical, an OH tacked on to the end of the chemical formula, indicating an oxygen and a hydrogen atom respectively. During combustion the oxygen component becomes available to burn more fuel. Sometimes alcohols are blended into gasoline at the refinery. Sometimes they are themselves modified and then put into the fuel as additives called oxygenates, whose job is to reduce emissions and/or increase the fuel's knock resistance.

The most common alcohol fuels are methanol (CH_3OH) and ethanol (C_2H_5OH). The first, synthesised from natural gas (mostly methane) is used in grass-track, speedway and drag bikes. The second, distilled from fermented vegetation, is used in the US and many third world countries, either blended with gasoline or used in spark ignition or diesel engines for trucks and buses.

Alcohol fuels have several characteristics:

High latent heat of evaporation – which cools the intake charge, giving maximum air density and also helps to cool the engine.

Good knock resistance – so that high compression (or high boost) pressures may be used, which raise the engine's thermal efficiency.

Miscibility with water – Alcohols are often used in conjunction with water injection (as a means of providing internal engine cooling to suppress knock, especially on turbocharged machines). As methanol is hygroscopic this can be a problem, where storage is concerned, needing sealed containers and the vehicle tank to be drained after each use.

Corrosion – Because alcohols contain oxygen they can react with materials that oxidise and if an engine is converted to run on alcohol fuel it is necessary to change fuel line fittings in brass, aluminium, magnesium, copper and some plastics, to components specifically developed for alcohol. Even then it is usually necessary to drain float bowls and tanks if the engine is not going to be used for some time.

Low heat content – Methanol has about half the calorific value of gasoline and so twice as much has to be used to generate the same power. With a stoichiometric AF ratio of 6.45:1 it gives maximum power at 4:1 (compared to gasoline at 12 – 13:1). Although it has half the heat content, a given amount of air uses three times the quantity of fuel, and therefore has the potential to develop 1.5 times the power. At 30% thermal efficiency, only 30% of this gain will appear at the crankshaft (ie 15% more power than gasoline) although it is made easier to extract by the fuel's knock resistance and cooling properties. The greater volume flow of fuel also means that tank range is a problem: a vehicle running on methanol will require something approaching twice the tank capacity to achieve the same range.

Slower burning than gasoline – As the fuel takes longer to burn, more ignition advance is needed, with a more powerful ignition system to ensure combustion in difficult conditions such as starting and cold-running.

Wider misfire limits than gasoline – allows the fuel to be run at very rich mixtures (for maximum power) or lean mixtures (for maximum economy) and makes initial set-up and tuning that much easier.

Oil dilution – The increased amount of fuel and the tendency to use rich mixtures for their cooling means that cylinder bore washing and oil contamination are more of a problem than with gasoline, demanding frequent oil changes.

Volatility – Not as volatile as gasoline, which can make cold-starting difficult, especially with neat ethanol, which requires such a high ambient temperature that auxiliary starting fuels (gasoline, propane, ethers etc) are needed. Gasoline is a blend of hydrocarbons with different boiling points and can be tailored to suit the ambient conditions, eg in the UK a more volatile blend is used during winter to help cold starts.

Handling – Methanol is very toxic and can be absorbed through the skin. It attacks the central nervous system and the optic nerves (hence the expression *blind drunk*, caused by alcoholic drinks that have been contaminated with methanol). Drinking as little as 50 cc can be fatal and, while exposure to the vapour for an hour or two can cause drowsiness, longer exposure is followed by narcosis.

Methanol can be made from natural gas, often burnt off as waste at oil wells, which is ironic as it was initially used as motor fuel around 1900, until it was replaced by cheaper gasoline, which itself had been seen as a useless by-product of the oil refining process and had also been burnt off as waste. Methanol was originally made from wood, giving it the name *wood alcohol*.

Ethanol can be made from anything that can be fermented – pretty well any carbohydrate that can be converted into starch and then into sugar. The alcohol concentration is then increased by distillation, in the same way that alcoholic spirits are made.

In poorer countries or where crude oil is not easily available, alcohols (especially ethanol) are attractive alternatives. Brazil pioneered the conversion of vehicles (including locally built Honda and Yamaha motorcycles) to run on the fuel, made from sugar cane, and it can be used neat or blended with gasoline.

There has been a lot of research into vehicles that can run on a variety of fuels, or mixtures of fuels, which would be useful both for military applications and for third world countries (the supplies for both are erratic and highly variable). Now fuel injection using fast-reacting oxygen sensors as part of a closed loop control can adjust the fuel mixture sufficiently to permit this hybrid use of fuels. Other experiments included sensors to 'analyse' the fuel (usually by measuring its specific gravity) and tell the engine management which map to use.

Nitromethane (CH$_3$NO$_2$)

During combustion, nitromethane releases its not inconsiderable oxygen content, which can be used to burn more fuel, which releases more oxygen... it can even be burnt without any outside oxygen being supplied. Thus it can combust in huge quantities, liberating equally huge amounts of heat.

It is one of a family called nitroparaffins (there is also nitroethane, nitrobenzene and nitropropane). While some of the nitroparaffins were used in pre-war race cars, nitromethane was first used as a rocket fuel in the 1940s. Later it was tried as a fuel, either neat or mixed with methanol, but its only real applications are in model aircraft engines and Top Fuel dragsters.

It is corrosive to aluminium and magnesium alloys, it has a low heat content and is not very resistant to knock but the large quantities more than make up for these deficiencies. It may be run at AF ratios of 1 or 2:1., to make possibly twice the power produced on gasoline. No-one knows how much it makes in practice because its combustion is so rough that engines don't last long enough to be tested.

A Top Fuel dragster, revving to 10,000 rpm, covers a quarter mile in under 5 seconds. As it has a single gear, its average engine speed while it is on load is going to be around 6,000 rpm, or 100 revs per second. In five seconds therefore, it will turn over something like 500 times. And then it will be overhauled.

Nitrous oxide (N$_2$O)

See Figs. 11.15 and 11.6

The final option is to introduce a third component to release oxygen inside the cylinder, which is what nitrous oxide does. In atmospheric conditions it exists as a fairly stable gas, used as an anaesthetic and a propellant in some aerosols.

The high temperature and pressure conditions inside an engine's cylinder destabilise it into its component parts: the nitrogen joins the rest of the atmospheric nitrogen, which (ideally) takes no further part in the chemical reaction and is simply the working gas, to be compressed and expanded. The oxygen is liberated to react with more fuel (which has to be provided as a metered amount when the nitrous oxide supply is switched on).

The means of storing nitrous oxide endow it with one significant advantage. It is kept as a liquid, which requires immense pressure (around 800 psi) and therefore a strong (heavy) container. This residual pressure means there is no problem getting the gas into the engine cylinder. It could be injected directly at any point on the compression stroke before ignition but in fact there is more to be gained by injecting it into the intake tract.

In this way it is easier to regulate the additional fuel flow and, as the high pressure liquid immediately expands into gaseous form, its latent heat of evaporation has a considerable chilling effect on the normal air flow.

This both raises the air density, improving

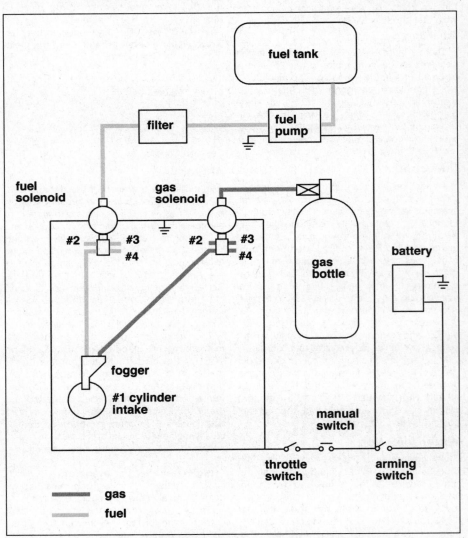

Fig. 11.15 Typical layout for nitrous oxide injection

the engine's volumetric efficiency, and lowers the temperature, taking the air/fuel mixture further away from its detonation threshold.

During combustion, more fuel can be used and therefore more heat liberated and pressures which would normally cause detonation may be reached safely.

The end result is a massive increase in torque. Changes in the order of 100% are possible, limited only by detonation (which makes changes of 20 – 30% more realistic), and the adjustment is by simply altering the jet sizes controlling the flow of nitrous oxide and additional fuel.

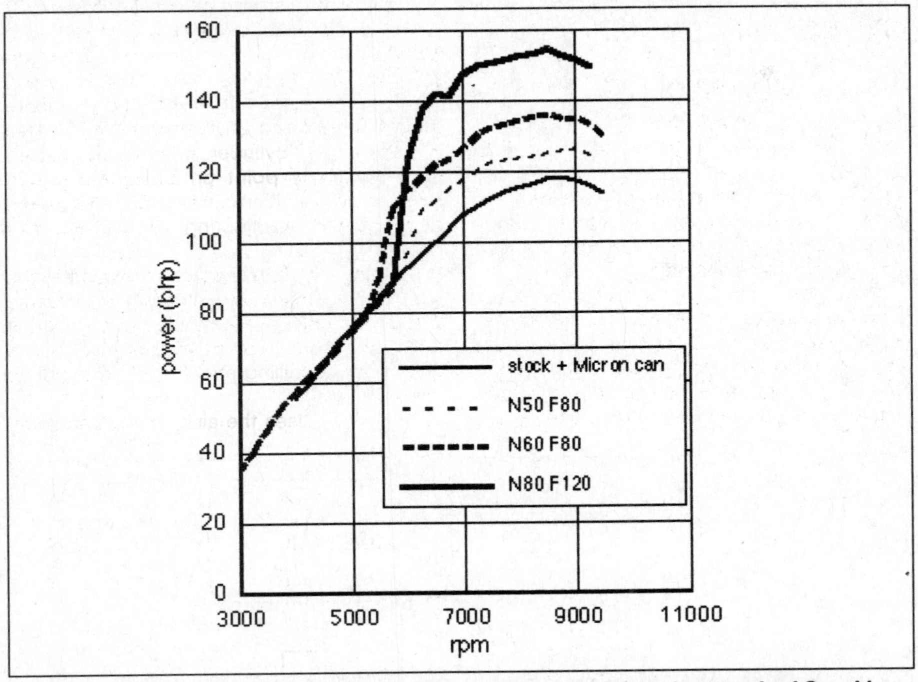

As nitrous oxide is not a fuel (it provides the oxygen to burn more fuel) it may be used legally on the road (in the UK) although it is prohibited in most kinds of racing.

Its disadvantage is the limited range available from a practical-sized container. On most bike applications this is a 2.5 lb steel bottle (that is 2.5 lb of liquefied gas, the bottle itself weighs more), which will last anywhere from a few seconds on a high-powered drag bike, where the nitrous could be contributing to an extra 50 bhp, through to many minutes on less powerful installations. As it is not used continuously but only during WOT acceleration, this translates to several quarter-mile runs or up to perhaps 20 minutes track time.

It can be used on any engine, including supercharged machines and two-strokes. There is an open race class in the US, in which bikes like TZ250s were equipped with nitrous oxide to compete with much bigger racers.

As a more extreme example, I had a Suzuki TS50 moped, which gave 2 to 3 bhp as standard, was tuned conventionally to give 5 to 6 bhp and then UK-based TMS developed what is possibly the world's smallest nitrous kit, using tiny jets to double the engine's output. At 11 bhp, on the tight circuits used for moped racing, where the engine would be on WOT for probably 50% of the time, the bike could reach more than 70 mph and the nitrous bottle's range was about 20 minutes.

Fig. 11.16 The dramatic effects of nitrous oxide on an otherwise standard Suzuki GSF1200

The amounts of N_2O and gasoline are shown by the jet sizes (N – nitrous, F – fuel) (DynoSpeed Developments)

Notes

Chapter 12
Fault finding

Contents

1 Introduction

Logical steps

The essential part of any fault-finding mission is to work out a logical sequence of steps that will home in on the culprit with the minimum of effort. These steps should alter one thing at a time and be organised to eliminate the broadest range of possibilities first – there is no point in fiddling about with pilot screws if there is no fuel in the tank. Then, in the tradition of Sherlock Holmes, once you have eliminated the impossible, 'what you are left with, however improbable, is the truth'.

It is very satisfying to sit down, work out several possibilities (on a 'if it's not this, then it must be this and then this must happen' basis), test the parts and locate the fault. Of course, you could have spent the time taking the system to pieces and testing parts at random as they appeared. Sometimes this is as quick, after all there isn't that much that can go wrong with carburettors, but it isn't as intellectually satisfying and it is very easy to create a large pile of stripped-down parts only to discover the fuel tap wasn't turned on, or something of an equally basic order. I feel sorry for race mechanics, particularly in endurance teams, because they don't have the luxury of time and even if they do stop and think about something, then, to the rest of the world it looks as if they're doing nothing, when quite obviously they should not only be doing something but doing it quickly. Being resourceful people, they've developed their own answer. Instead of trying to locate faults, they simply swap whole assemblies – a complete bank of carburettors, the entire ignition circuit etc – and they have these assemblies ready in a quickly fittable, plug-in form that takes only seconds to change.

Apart from the obvious, no-fuel-in-the-tank type problems, there is the fact that fuel systems are always prime suspects when an engine starts to misbehave, while the fault is much more likely to be electrical or mechanical. Two things follow from this. One is that carburettors in particular cannot function well if the rest of the engine isn't working properly. The second is that carburation can be used to cover other faults, such as a flat spot caused by a defective exhaust system being minimised by richening the mixture in that load/speed region.

The general procedure is to check the obvious, check the rest of the engine and only then work out a sequence to analyse the fuel system.

Checking the obvious

● Is there fuel in the tank? Can it flow freely at least as far as the carburettor? A blocked air breather (the vent in the top of the tank, sometimes in the filler cap, that allows air in to replace fuel as it is used) can prevent fuel flowing just as easily as a kinked or blocked fuel line.

- Is fuel leaking, or a carburettor flooding?
- Are the throttle and cold start controls working normally?
- Is everything switched on and set correctly?
- Is there electrical power – do the warning lights come on, is there sufficient battery voltage to, say, operate the headlamp or horn?
- Does the engine turn freely?
- Can you hear the fuel pump when you switch on?
- Is anything blocking the exhaust?
- When was the engine last run and how did it perform? Has anything happened since?
- Do you number practical jokers among your friends? Nothing should be too simple or too general to be overlooked.

2 Engine/electrical faults

From a diagnostic point of view, the engine is either electrical or mechanical and, statistically, the electrical circuits are the most likely candidates for failure. However, if this is ultimately leading to a fault in the fuel system, all we need to know for the time being is whether there is a healthy spark. This is easy enough to test in principle, although with some combinations of bodywork, tank and airbox, it's not always so easy in practice.

Remove a spark plug. If it is in poor condition, particularly with carbon fouling on the centre electrode or insulator or with varnish or dirt on the outer insulator, this may point the way to the root of the trouble. Take a look at the other plugs. If one is significantly different to the rest, it will suggest a fault on that cylinder. Similarly, old or dirty HT leads and caps may let the spark voltage track away to earth without reaching the spark plug, so all wiring and connections should be cleaned or renewed.

Signs (or smell) of fuel on the plug's electrodes prove that fuel is reaching the engine. A lot of liquid fuel suggests there may be too much or it may be arriving in neat rather than atomised form. If there is a danger of liquid fuel accumulating in the cylinders (it can 'hydraulic' and cause mechanical damage when the engine is turned over), it should be expelled by switching off the fuel and spinning the engine on the starter for a few seconds, with the spark plugs removed, connected to their HT leads and grounded (well out of the way of the potentially flammable mixture about to be expelled from the engine), and with the throttles wide open.

Using plugs in as-new condition, there should be a good spark when the starter spins the motor, whether it is a kickstart or electric

start. 'Good' means bright blue, as wide as the gap it is jumping, visible in direct sunlight and making an audible click. Less than this will still be enough to run an otherwise healthy engine but as the spark gets less energetic, smaller in width and becomes more yellow in colour, your attention should start to turn away from the fuel system towards the ignition system.

You should also check the spark occurs close to TDC on the firing stroke. Many four-strokes have a wasted spark, that is the plugs fire every TDC like a two-stroke, but the spark timing should be checked especially if you have not seen the engine running recently or if it has been overhauled since it last ran.

Testing for sparks usually means connecting the plug to its HT lead, resting it on the cam box and spinning the engine over. Take care when doing this: (a) that the plug is effectively earthed, (b) that other plugs are also connected and earthed. This is because ignition systems can be very powerful and if the high voltage isn't given its proper path it may break down the insulation in the coil or the HT lead to create not only its own path but a future fault.

A possible problem with HT or magneto coils is the so-called layer short, in which a breakdown of the internal insulation shorts out a portion of the windings (there are thousands of turns in an HT coil). If 10% are inactive, the secondary voltage will be 10% lower but will still be ample to make a spark in air and in most engine conditions. Only when full energy is needed (high load, full acceleration, starting) will the spark break down.

Also many engines run the plugs in pairs, one plug connected to each end of the HT coil, and both are needed to complete the circuit. Voltages as high as 30kV are possible. I'm not sure if there's enough energy to do you any physical damage but there's certainly enough to make you jump quite energetically and most injuries are not from the electric shock but from the recipient leaping up and banging his head or causing some other indirect damage.

Plugs actually require more energy to fire under engine load conditions, so this isn't a complete test although it's usually a good enough indicator. Another possible problem is that the starter motor may not turn the engine as fast under load as it does when the plugs are removed. The low speed or the starter's drain on the battery (sapping current needed by the ignition system) can both make the engine difficult to start.

At this point you should be able to form an opinion about the ignition system. If it seems OK then continue with the mechanical checks. If there's any doubt, check it further. Put down this book, pick up the Haynes *Motorcycle Electrical Manual*.

3 Engine/mechanical faults

Ideally, the engine should be in perfect condition throughout but, as with the ignition, it is enough to know that the major functions are good. Does it turn freely and at its usual cranking speed on the starter motor? Are there any leaks or unusual noises? Traces of oil or coolant around the top-end are symptoms of a blown head gasket (as is the appearance of coolant in the oil or the loss of coolant with no external sign of a leak). Is there good compression and is it the same on all cylinders (see Fig .12.1)?

'Good' compression means whatever pressure is listed in the workshop manual. However as this is normally given for a fully warmed engine and as the problem engine is likely to be cold and cranking at a lower speed because of the extra oil drag, the figures will probably not be achieved. Typically, compression pressures above 130 psi are good, while anything over 100 psi is acceptable in the sense that it will support combustion. Two-strokes are generally lower, by as much as 15%. The main thing is that low readings should be caused by adverse conditions, not by a mechanical fault, and all cylinders should be the same. On bikes fitted with kickstarts, the compression figure is usually the result of, say, five, consecutive swings on the kickstart – the workshop manual may specify the precise number.

Low compression can indicate a problem like piston or ring damage, bore wear, a valve not seating or a leaking head gasket. A better indication of this kind of fault is given by a

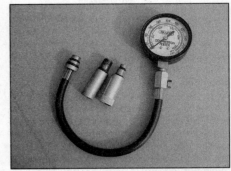

Fig. 12.1 A cylinder compression tester

Using a cylinder compression tester is a useful way to check that an engine is mechanically sound. It screws into the spark plug hole and has several adapters for different plug thread sizes. A Schraeder type valve in the stem of the gauge lets it hold the maximum pressure it receives and can release the pressure before the next test. The test should be made with the engine at normal working temperature, all spark plugs removed, wide open throttles and normal cranking speed leak-down test, in which the cylinder is pressurised to a given level and the time taken to reach a lower pressure is recorded.

You should be happy there are no mechanical faults before considering the fuel system and even then there are circumstances which conspire to make engines difficult to start. Large, single cylinder motocross machines are notoriously bad at starting. I raced a Honda CR500 in supermoto trim, using revised suspension and 17-inch magnesium alloy wheels with road race tyres, which was so bad at starting that I eventually saved the weight of the kickstart and had a set of rollers made. [A car is parked with one driven wheel on the rollers, while the bike sits with its rear wheel on the other end, so the car can take the bike engine up to speed and, at 15 – 20 mph in first, the CR would start easily.]

The reason it wouldn't start easily on its own starter had nothing to do with faults, just a series of unfortunate design features.

● The big, single cylinder two-stroke needed a big, 38 mm carburettor. Gas flow through large venturis is slow and, at low engine speeds the air speed can be so low it doesn't pick up enough fuel and certainly doesn't atomise it. For this reason, anything with borderline starting capability will usually fire up most easily on a closed, or just fractionally open, throttle. When the throttle is closed the gas velocity in the venturi is at its highest and the idle mixture is always richer than on quarter to half throttle (where the fuelling will be at its leanest, to give best economy in cruise conditions).

● Motocross riders often lay the whole bike on its side until the carburettor floods, to provide some extra richness.

● The long-travel suspension is very soft in its initial movement. Downward force aimed at the kickstart is divided between compressing the suspension springs and turning the engine.

● The kickstart itself has an arc of travel limited by the footrest and is geared so a full swing only turns the engine once.

● The magneto CDI has to turn fast enough to generate the voltage that will charge up the capacitor, or no spark. For reasons of awkward kickstart gearing and stubbed toes, this was not always possible.

Given all these conditions it was rare to persuade combustible mixture to reach the combustion chamber while the crankshaft was still turning fast enough to make a spark. Once it did, the engine fired straight away.

4 Fuel system faults – carburettors

The fuel system has two jobs, one to regulate the air flow to control the engine load and speed, and two to mix the appropriate amount of fuel with the air. Any fault will basically affect either the control system or the ability to mix fuel and air.

The control system should really come under the heading *Obvious* above, in the sense that the throttle linkage and cold-start mechanism either work or they don't. However there are subtleties that are not so obvious. Carburettor icing is one (when the chill effect of forcing fuel to evaporate makes atmospheric water vapour freeze). If ice builds up over the idle jets or around the throttle valve it can produce a range of symptoms from stalling or flat spots to the throttle sticking open. Long before you can even remove the fuel tank, heat soak from the engine will have melted the ice and removed the evidence.

Fuel starvation can be another elusive problem. A partly blocked fuel filter or tank vent will restrict fuel flow to a certain level. Below this level the engine will run normally. Above this level it will have the reservoir of fuel in the float bowls and it will only be at sustained high flow rates that the symptoms appear. By the time you've stopped to investigate, fuel will have trickled through, filled the float bowls and all will appear to be normal again.

There is another cause of fuel starvation: when bikes with vacuum-operated fuel taps have a less restrictive airbox or filter fitted. Even though the carburettors are re-jetted, the intake vacuum on WOT can be reduced enough to stop the fuel tap working. A manual type of tap is then needed. Going a stage further, tuned engines require more fuel flow and it isn't unknown for this to exceed the fuel tap's capacity. The tap effectively takes over the job of the main jets!

Heat from the engine can, in the wrong circumstances, make fuel vaporise and cause vapour locks in the fuel lines, interrupting the fuel supply. By its nature, the fault is intermittent, unpredictable and goes away as soon as you start looking for it (because the engine cools down).

Using the 'wrong' fuel can make these faults worse. If you have some fuel bought in winter and stored through to spring, for example. There are different grades sold seasonally – winter fuel will evaporate more easily, which aids cold starting but is more prone to vapour lock. Winter fuel is also likely to have more anti-icing additives – different companies use different ingredients, so if you have a long-term, intermittent problem it's worth changing brands and keeping a note of the results.

Very nearly all motorcycles since the 1970s have been designed to run on unleaded fuel. Except for those with catalytic converters in their exhausts, it should not do any mechanical harm to run them on leaded fuel. However there is one condition, called lead fouling, which can be caused by this type of fuel. In a properly set-up engine, the spark plugs run in a self-cleaning temperature range. Near the cool end of this range there is a narrow region in which the lead additives form a sort of varnish on the central insulator and as the varnish can conduct electricity it effectively shorts out the plug. If the centre insulator has a shiny, light green or yellow appearance and leaded fuel has been used, then this is probably the cause of misfiring or losing one cylinder. It's probably an outmoded fault, too, as most leaded fuels now contain scavengers – ethylene dibromide or dichloride – that are meant to react with the lead, turning it into lead bromide or chloride, which escape with the exhaust gas instead of being deposited in the engine.

As far as the fuel mixture is concerned, there are two basic dysfunctions, rich mixture or lean mixture. The engine will tolerate small amounts of either and as both cause a drop in power (see Chapters 2 and 4, mixture loops), often it's not obvious to the rider whether the mixture is rich or lean.

Rich mixtures

A very rich mixture will carbon-foul the spark plugs causing misfiring and refusal to run until the plugs have been cleaned. Moderately rich mixtures, make the engine response feel woolly, not crisp, although the engine will accelerate well. Starting will be easy but idling or steady speed, low-load running may be erratic or unstable. There may be popping and banging in the exhaust on the overrun as unburnt fuel lights on the hot baffles. The engine may make dark smoke, but note that black smoke is also caused by detonation.

When all fuel was leaded, a correct mixture would leave light grey deposits in the exhaust and the carbon produced by a rich mixture would make this darker, tending to black. Unleaded fuel has more additives, some of which leave dark deposits, so the colour inside exhaust tailpipes is no longer a reliable guide to mixture strength.

Weak mixture

Causes misfiring in the extreme condition, and tends to make the spark plugs run hot, burning off deposits and leaving the centre insulator looking white, almost bleached. Slightly weak mixtures give the engine a crisp edge and make it respond with a sharp crackle that feels attractive to the rider. Going slightly weaker still tends to make the combustion chamber run hotter, possibly causing pre-ignition, auto-ignition or detonation. Long-term, this will accelerate wear of things like plug electrodes and valve seats, while detonation at high rpm can rapidly damage pistons. Weak mixtures make for difficult starting and cold running, with poor acceleration and a tendency to spit back in the carburettors.

Wet mixture

There is a third mixture condition, which we could call a *wet* mixture. It can apply to rich,

Fig. 12.2 Air filters should be checked for blockage. If in doubt, run tests with the filter element removed

Fig. 12.3 An exhaust gas analyser can detect fuelling faults such as a rich mixture (high CO) or incomplete combustion (high HC)

lean or correct AF ratios and it happens when the fuel arrives in the cylinder in large, liquid particles instead of a fine, atomised spray. Here we have a condition where, regardless of the overall AF ratio, the region around the droplet is very rich, while other regions that don't contain any droplets are very weak. Such a mixture will be very hard to ignite and the burn will probably vary from cycle to cycle, so the engine will tend to run rough and erratically. In this condition, the fuel will probably wet the walls of the inlet tract and liquid fuel will form in puddles which then evaporate. The lighter fractions will evaporate first so, during acceleration, this is what will reach the engine and it may have different ignition characteristics and anti-knock properties to the fuel as a whole. This will produce symptoms of too much or too little ignition advance, maybe coupled with

knock and a tendency to auto-ignite (typically running on when the ignition is switched off).

Symptoms

From the above summary of the things likely to go wrong with carburation, the main conclusion is that it can get very confusing if you allow it to. It's important to collect a list of all the symptoms and compare this with the engine's recent history, ie was it running well up to a certain point, did anything change between then and now? Obviously if the symptoms coincide with something that happened, then check this first.

Carburettor components mostly control one area of load and speed. If the symptoms occur over the whole range, then the problem is likely to lie outside the carburettor, such as a blocked air filter (see Fig. 12.2), water in the fuel etc.

Symptoms that only occur in specific

conditions will automatically narrow the focus to this region, covered roughly by the chart 6.1 in Chapter 6. At this point, if the engine will run safely, it will probably be possible to try some tests to see if the results confirm your suspicions. It may be possible to make a temporary fuel supply, to rule out problems with the standard tank, tap, filter or pump; or to make the mixture richer by using the cold start (this will only make a significant difference at light loads); or to run the machine with the airbox or filter element removed, which may also make the carburettor slides visible. If it needs to be run on load, it will be easier and safer to do this on a dynamometer (see Figs. 12.3, 12.4 and 12.5).

Fuel supply

Such tests may reveal other things. If the problem is restricted to one cylinder, its header pipe will be cooler than the others (or

Fig. 12.4 When stripping the carburettors, check the float bowls carefully for signs of dirt or water in the fuel

Fig. 12.5 Check for smooth movement in the sprung throttle linkage. The throttle valves can be roughly synchronised by making sure they all line up with the idle by-pass holes (or the cold start hole as shown here) simultaneously

Symptom	Other symptoms	Likely reason	Tests
engine won't start	plugs fouled	too much fuel or neat fuel reaching engine	blocked air cleaner, cold-start defective, carb(s) flooding, try starting with fuel tap turned off
engine won't start	plugs OK	mixture too weak or no fuel reaching engine	temporarily richen by partly blocking intake (if possible), check float bowls are filling, inspect cold-start linkage, suspect blocked jet
idle erratic	—	incorrect adjustment, possible carb icing	if adjustment is ineffective, check throttle valves and carb mountings for wear/air leaks, check float bowls and jets for blockage. Check multi-carb synchronization. If fault happens intermittently, try different brand of fuel, check carb heaters if fitted.
flat spot just above idle	[can be caused by changes to exhaust system or air filter]	idle settings wrongly adjusted or blocked by-pass	test with idle screw(s) set ±1/2 turns. Test with idle speed raised 100 – 200 rpm. Reverse any recent changes to exhaust or intake systems
flat spot elsewhere	—	transient settings wrong	torque curves on high output engines have a natural midrange dip: if the mixture goes rich or lean at the same spot it affects driveability. Test with different needle positions or CV piston vent hole size
stuttering or misfire on acceleration or engine won't accelerate when throttle opened wide	—	slide carb opening too quickly CV carb piston fluttering	employ more skilful rider. CV piston flutter can be caused by too large vent holes or mismatch between engine spec and carbs (in acceleration AF goes rich, engine slows down, piston drops, airspeed increases, AF now correct, engine speeds up, and so on)
sticking throttle	—	dirt build-up on linkage, damaged cable worn air slide or dirt on air slide	
sticking throttle	only in certain weather conditions [typically 4°C and high humidity]	carburettor icing	test with different brands of fuel, check carb heating if fitted, if not ask dealer if carb heaters are available
part-load richness	high mileage, misfire on part-load	wear between needle and needle jet	
erratic running/loss of power on one cylinder	—	CV carb: torn diaphragm or leak at O-ring seal	slide doesn't lift at same rate as others when throttle opened
one cylinder cuts out during hard acceleration	happens above, say, half throttle/half max rpm	main jet unscrewed	massive richness on one cylinder
intermittent cutting on one or more cylinders	worse during acceleration	dirt or water in float bowls	drain float bowls into dish so contents may be examined (also check line filter and tank)
lean running	high mileage, auto-ignition	build up of varnish in jets	
misfire during acceleration	immediately after heavy braking	fuel swill in float bowls, CV pistons lifted during deceleration (downdraught carbs)	this is a design fault, cured in extreme circumstances by using the front brake stoplight switch to turn off the fuel pump
carburettor flooding	—	dirt in needle valve or wear on needle valve seat	older types, with brass floats: punctured float or soldered joint failed, allowing fuel into float (float rattles when shaken)
light tapping noise	slight vibration, power fade after a few seconds	detonation	light tinkling ('pinking') is not unusual on four-strokes at low rpm/high load. At high rpm, or if power fade is noticed, it is dangerous. Two-strokes will not tolerate detonation for very long
blue or white smoke	on load or on overrun	oil being burnt (ring or bore wear, big-end journal wear, valve guide wear)	two-strokes: moderate amount is normal when engine is cold and piston clearance is at a maximum. Four-strokes: check for overfilled sump, try compression/leakdown tests
grey or black smoke	on load	rich mixture	short puffs of black smoke indicate detonation
brown smoke	on load	weak mixture	
water vapour (steam) in exhaust	engine cold	normal by-product of combustion, visible until engine and exhaust system get up to temperature	exhausts usually have small drain holes at lowest point so water doesn't accumulate and corrode pipes from inside

12.6 Typical fuel system faults

occasionally hotter, although this would suggest a problem with combustion or the exhaust valve rather than the carburettor). If the fuel supply is suspect, either rig up a separate tank (with about 6 to 10 inches of fuel head above the carburettors) to by-pass the original tank, tap, filters and pump. Or test the output from the original system by disconnecting the feed to the carburettors and running it into a suitable can. Unlike fuel injection systems (see Section 5), pumps used with carburettors run at low pressure but make sure the can is large and splash-free enough for the test. Open the tap and if necessary apply a 12V source to the pump connections (by-passing any relays or protective tilt switches). Use a stopwatch to time the flow and switch it off after, say, 10 seconds. Measure the volume of fuel in a measuring cylinder, multiply this by 6 to get the flow per minute, or 360 for flow per hour. Compare this to the figure quoted in the workshop manual or, if this is not available, use the following formula to work out a safe flow rate for your engine.

Four-strokes tend to run an sfc of about 0.5 pt/hp-h on full load. If your engine is rated at P horsepower, it will need at least 0.5P pt/h (0.284P L/h). That is, for a 100bhp engine, the flow should be a minimum of 50 pt/h or 28.4 L/h. Note that this is a rock-bottom minimum, the system should be capable of flowing considerably more than the engine requires. Also note that 28.4 L/h is only 473 cc/min or 7.89 cc/s and this is for a fairly large engine: for less powerful machines you may need to run the fuel for longer than 10 seconds to get a quantity to measure with reasonable accuracy.

Two-strokes run between 0.7 and 1.0 pt/hp-h and so will need a minimum flow rate of roughly twice as much as a four-stroke: 1.0P pt/h (0.568P L/h) for an output of P bhp.

Two-stroke oil

Two-strokes also introduce engine oil at the intake, either via a pump or mixed with the fuel, which is an extra source of potential 'carburation' problems. As long as the pump and cable is in correct adjustment and the correct type of oil is used, pumps don't usually give any trouble. Check with the workshop manual for details of adjustment and oil grades but note that many competition oils, with better load-bearing properties than 'normal' oils, are not suitable for injector pumps. This is because the pumps are designed, typically, for an oil of SAE30 viscosity while the competition oils are frequently thicker, to SAE40 or SAE50.

Where fuel and oil is mixed, it's essential to keep to the recommended proportions. Too much oil will not give more lubrication, it is merely surplus and will be burnt, creating deposits in the engine and exhaust and lowering the fuel's octane rating while it's at it. Pre-mix should be used as soon as possible and not stored because the more volatile fuel will evaporate and, if the oil is not completely soluble, it will start to settle out.

5 Fuel system faults – fuel injection

Most injection systems have some kind of self-diagnostic ability, either flashing a warning light or displaying a message on one of the LCD instrument panels. Some have combinations of LEDs on the main processor box, others can be plugged into the manufacturer's diagnostic equipment to reveal their message. The workshop manual will probably be necessary to decode the warning signal.

If a non-essential sensor or part of the wiring has failed, most systems will resort to a default map, which will allow the engine to run in a get-home mode, with a suitable warning display. Apart from making a check of the wiring (and repairing any damage, or broken or corroded connections), there is not very much you can do, other than locate the failed component and renew it.

As well as the electronic control circuits, the system will have a pump, filter, pressure regulator and return to the fuel tank, plus the injectors themselves. 'Mechanical' failures include blocked filters, blocked or kinked breather pipes and varnish from the fuel building up and blocking the injector nozzles. Some fuels contain additives to prevent this and it is possible to buy additives to put in the fuel to clean the deposits off the injectors. These are among the few worthwhile additives and it's not a bad idea to run a tankful of treated gasoline after each service or when the machine has been laid up for a few weeks.

The pump will be operated by the ignition switch, probably via a relay and a tilt switch (lean angle sensor – turns off the pump if the machine falls over). Relays make an audible click, while the pump makes its own noise, sounding heavier under load and finally stopping as it builds up pressure. The sounds (or their absence) can give a good indication of a fault in the fuel's pressure circuit.

For more detailed information on testing electrical circuits, see the Haynes *Motorcycle Electrical Manual*. For diagnostic purposes, parts like the relay and tilt switch can be by-passed with a length of heavy gauge wire, while the pump is tested by running its output into a suitable can, connecting it to a 12V source and timing the output for 5 or 10 seconds with a stopwatch. Check the volume of fuel delivered in a measuring cylinder and multiply by 12 or 6 to get the output per minute and compare this with the rated value in the workshop manual. Take care, because most injection systems run at a pressure of 3 to 4 bar (45 to 60 psi). Most workshop manuals recommend using kerosene (paraffin) instead of gasoline for this test.

Injector systems often have a by-pass system to handle idle requirements, there may be an adjusting screw, a throttle stop screw and a linkage similar to that used on CV carburettors. Adjustment, synchronisation and faults like blockages in the pilot drillings are the same as for carburettors.

Chapter 13
Overhaul

Contents

1 Introduction

The main key to overhauling fuel systems is cleanliness. Tiny specks of dirt cause all sorts of trouble, because the fuel and air jets are not exactly big, filters can become clogged and needle valves need only a minute particle to prevent them closing. When fuel evaporates it tends to leave a layer of varnish, which can also build up until it blocks passages or makes moving parts stick. And this, in one paragraph, accounts for the majority of carburettor and injector problems. The remainder are caused by torn 'rubber' mounts, seals and diaphragms, either through careless handling, old age or... dirt.

On high mileage engines, or machines that don't have very good air filters, dirt also causes wear on air slides, throttle valve spindles and accelerator pump linkages. This creates air leaks, which aren't significant on full power but stop the idle circuit adjustments having proper effect.

If it's not possible to reassemble the carburettor in a clinically clean condition, then there is no point in overhauling it in the first place.

The next step is to check with the workshop manual. This chapter is not a substitute for the manufacturer's procedures, it is intended to supplement them, with points that apply to most carburettors and, insofar as they can be overhauled, injectors. And one of the first things the workshop manual will mention is... cleanliness. The manufacturers are very fond of recommending a 'high flash-point solvent' to wash out carburettors and other engine parts. Obviously they don't want to recommend anything that is going to burn you or corrode you or do anything else unpleasant but some solvents are capable of attacking carburettor parts, especially those in plastic or synthetic rubber. So what do you use? There are special carburettor cleaners and the only other solvent you know won't harm carburettors is gasoline, of which you have already got at least one float-bowl-full per carburettor.

Gasoline is harmful to you in several ways. It's inflammable and it will cause all manner of discomfort if it gets inside your body, which is possible via mouth, nose, eyes and skin. Many mechanics still use it when working on carburettors, but don't touch it or breathe it. Wear those disposable, medical type gloves you can get at chemists, work in a well-ventilated area, do not smoke and try not to set fire to yourself. The only responsible recommendation is to use a special carburettor cleaner – but who knows how safe they are? Anything that's capable of removing the gunge that builds up in fuel systems is not going to be too friendly to the carbohydrates that make up your body, so you still need the gloves and the wide-open door.

2 Taps and hoses

Even with a workshop manual, it's important to make a note of what goes where, with little sketches if appropriate, and to figure out what each part is supposed to do (see Chapter 4 and Fig. 13.1). The Japanese stamp ID numbers on carburettor bodies, which can be helpful, especially if you're renovating an old machine. A dealer or the importer can look up the model to which the carburettor was fitted and discover the original sizes of jets etc. It can also identify a unit imported from another market, where the same carburettor body may be used but with different drillings etc to match that specification.

If you need to remove the fuel tank, undo the mountings and support the tank on a block of wood, unless there is a prop already built in, so you can reach the fuel lines and electrical connections. Some tanks have a removable fuel tap handle, others have hidden fuel taps simply to cut off the supply when the hoses need to be removed. More recent types, mainly with fuel injection, have self-sealing, snap-together connectors. To undo, either pull the two halves apart or squeeze a sprung part of the clamp and then pull apart. As the line is broken, the connectors seal so no fuel is lost, but check it is this kind of connector beforehand.

You will now discover that whoever fitted the wire clips that clamp the hoses had a pair of pliers that were a different shape to any that you can find. Make a note of where the breather and vent pipes go, and of electrical connections for the fuel gauge, pump or low fuel warning light, although most manufacturers use connectors that can only be fitted the right way round.

Depending on the design you may have to remove the airbox or just the connections to it. Either way, it gives a good idea of the state of the engine as a whole (see Fig. 13.2). The build-up of dirt inside indicates the mileage (or perhaps the type of mileage), oil deposits (the crankcase breather vents to the airbox, which acts as a catch tank, draining liquid back to the sump and letting oil mist carry on through the engine to be burnt) show the state of the bores and piston rings, while the hoses themselves, which gradually harden and then split, show the machine's age.

There may also be carburettor heaters, to prevent icing. Some are electrical and will have a simple block connector to the main wiring harness. Others use engine coolant and there will be a hose connector inlet and outlet. Check with the manual to see if it's necessary to drain any coolant or if there are taps that need to be turned off. Often the hoses can be disconnected with just the loss of a few cc of coolant – have some rag or a dish ready for this, and for the coolant which will come from the carburettor bodies.

3 Carburettor overhaul

Removal

Most carburettors are spigot mounted – their bodies push into rubber mounts, with a simple metal clamp around them. Undo the screws until the metal bands are loose and simply pull the carburettors out of the rubber mounts. Flange-mounted types usually have two bolts or studs running through the flange, through an insulating spacer with gaskets, into the cylinder head. Undo the nuts or bolts and withdraw the carburettors. In both types the carburettors may have to be moved away from the engine to clear their mountings, so it will be necessary to remove any airbox connections, hoses or cables that will restrict this movement.

The carburettors will be in a bank of two, three or four, depending on the engine configuration, and should be left connected together all the time. While overhauling the carburettors is easy, separating one unit from the bank is a major exercise to be avoided with gusto. This is because it isn't merely a matter of bolting the four bodies to a plate. The throttle and cold start linkages have to be separated, with all their springs and seals and adjusters, there are fuel feed pipes connected to a common rail and possibly connections for engine coolant, and it all has to be reassembled again and bolted to the plate with the carburettors correctly spaced to match the intake stubs on the cylinder head. This isn't so bad (just tedious) if the engine is out of the frame but otherwise it can be a time-consuming operation.

Make a note of the action of the throttle and cold start controls, which cable opens and which cable closes the throttle. It seems obvious when you take it to pieces, but less so a day or two later when it all has to go back together.

A bank of carburettors is usually coupled in pairs, with a linkage that then operates each pair. There is a 'master' unit, usually #3 in a bank of four, to which all the other carburettors are aligned. Its throttle valve will not have an adjuster, because all the other carburettors are adjusted to match it.

Drain the float bowls into a container. Professional mechanics usually have a steel tray (see Fig. 13.3), deep enough to hold the fuel, large enough to take the carburettor assembly and with small compartments for the jets and other small parts. The carburettors can be stripped and washed in this, thoroughly cleaned and then inspected on a bench.

Clean the outside of the carburettors first and drain the high flash-point solvent into the waste can. Next remove the float bowls, cleaning any residue of dirt or varnish from them. If flooding or contaminated fuel has been a problem, it's as well not to drain the carburettors but to keep them as upright as possible until the float bowls are removed. This way you can see the state of the fuel in the float bowls, along with any dirt or water that would otherwise have been flushed away.

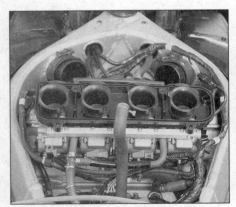

Fig. 13.1 Make a note of all hose and cable connections before dismantling

Fig. 13.2 The airbox will typically have a steel strainer, the filter element and some kind of supporting framework

Fig. 13.3 Work is easier if there is some kind of tray to drain fuel into, to support the bank of carburettors and hold any parts as they are removed

Fig. 13.4 Two type of cross-head screws are different enough to be damaged if the wrong bit is used (Phillips, right, and Pozidriv, left)

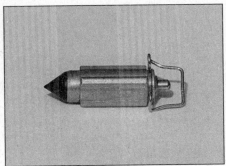

Fig. 13.5 Inspect needle valves around the tapered seat area for damage, wear or small particles that can prevent the valve closing

Stripdown

Carburettor bodies are cast in zinc alloy, which is not very strong and is easily scratched. The float bowl, and other covers are held on by small, low quality screws, usually with a cross-head slot. There are two types of cross-head screws, Phillips and Pozidriv (see Fig. 13.4), they are cut at different angles and both come in a variety of sizes. With such weak materials it is essential to use the correct size and type of screwdriver bit – if it doesn't fit the slot exactly it will easily ride up and burr the edges of the slot. When refitting, don't overtighten because it is very easy to strip the weak alloy threads.

Turn the carburettors upside down and check the action of the floats. If you connect a tube to the fuel feed, the weight of the float holding the valve closed should prevent you blowing through the tube. The needle valves should have clean, unworn seats (see Fig. 13.5). If there is any sign of damage or scoring, fit new valves. Above each valve there will be a gauze strainer – remove it and thoroughly clean the gauze and the fuelway behind it.

You should now be able to identify and inspect the main jet, pilot jet, cold start jet and their respective air bleeds but don't remove them yet (see Chapter 4 for a detailed description and location of the component parts). Now the main sources of accumulated dirt have been cleaned (the exterior and the float bowls), you can move on to the tops of the carburettors and, if necessary, any little diaphragm-controlled vents or accelerator pumps fitted to the sides of the carburettor body. These areas must be kept scrupulously clean as they depend on tiny air ways and gaskets with small seating areas where any dirt at all can cause a failure.

The tops of CV carburettors usually have a pre-formed diaphragm, with an O-ring seal around its edge that seats in a groove in the top of the carburettor body. Later types fit neatly and can simply be pressed carefully into the groove, staying politely in place while the carburettor top is fitted and clamped on to the diaphragm. Earlier types were not so well-behaved, needing a smear of grease or petroleum jelly to prevent the fitted portion popping out as you eased the opposite side into position.

This whole area needs a lot of care because if it doesn't seal, the carburettor won't work properly. Inspect the diaphragm for tears, especially where it is bonded to the top of the piston slide. Inside the piston will be some sort of guide for the spring and a clip to locate the needle. Note how the clip is fitted because it is often possible to get it the wrong way round and, although it looks OK, it does not hold the needle properly. Once fitted and with the spring on top, it should not be possible to slide the needle up through the piston.

Slide type carburettors are not so critical. There is a top cover, inside which there is the operating arm connected to the air side, or the cable, running through a spring, held to the slide by a nipple in an elongated hole. Simply disconnect the slide from the arm or the cable (holding the spring compressed so you can slide the cable along its slot until the nipple moves through the widest part of the hole). The needle either pushes out once the spring has been removed or has to have its clip pulled out of a slot in the air slide.

For both types of carburettor, when the needle has been removed, you can unscrew the main jet and emulsion tube, which sometimes holds the needle jet or nozzle in place, sometimes the whole assembly is in one piece and sometimes the nozzle is a press fit in the venturi casting and normally stays in place. To remove pressed-in nozzles requires a special tool in the form of a drift shaped to fit the nozzle and not damage it, plus ideally a small press, although a gentle thump with a mallet is often OK.

Some jets have a hexagon end, for a spanner, or a screwdriver slot. If you use a screwdriver, choose one that is a snug fit in the slot and use a bit that is hollow ground. This type (see Fig. 13.6a) is made so that the blade has parallel edges at the working end, unlike the chisel type, whose shaft is simply ground in a taper until the blade is the right thickness. Over time the screw threads of the brass jet and the zinc alloy casting fuse together and you may need to use a fair amount of force to undo the jets. The chisel type of screwdriver forms its own ramp, which lifts it out of the slot when a twisting force is applied to the blade (see Fig. 13.6b). This can easily damage the soft brass.

Main jet

Check for signs of screwdriver damage around the entry to the jet and for any deposits inside the fuel orifice. This can be difficult to clean without scratching the soft brass. If you renew the jet or wish to use a different size, make sure you use the same type – same thread, same length, same hexagon/screw thread. Different jet types, even if they fit the screw thread and have the same number stamped on the side, will not flow the same amount of fuel. Even the right type of jet but from a different manufacturer may not have exactly the same calibration.

Emulsion tube

Check for blockage in the small holes in the sides.

Air jet

Clean the passageway from the inside outwards, ie the opposite direction to the air flow. If the jet is removable, unscrew and clean it, again being careful not to scratch the

Fig. 13.6a Hollow ground screwdriver bits have a blade with parallel faces where it fits the screw slot. The correct size bit then gives maximum purchase with the least risk of damaging soft materials like brass

Fig. 13.6b Conventional screwdriver blades are tapered and the wedge shape tries to lift the blade from the screw when it is turned

brass or enlarge the hole. Usually the jet is pressed in or doesn't exist – the air passage drilling being made the right size.

Pilot jet

As for main jet except that above it there will be drillings through to the venturi, with by-pass drillings and a tapered adjusting screw. Remove this, check the taper hasn't been damaged and make sure all drillways are clear. Aerosol contact cleaner is perhaps the best way of doing this.

Needle and needle jet

Inspect for wear – scoring or polishing marks on the needle and elongation of the needle jet's bore, which should be circular. It's not easy to assess wear because only a few thousandths of an inch can make a significant difference to fuel flow. If in doubt, renew them as a pair. Note that the nozzle sometimes has a right and wrong way round. Occasionally there is a peg to locate it but not always. If there is any kind of screen or cutaway, the screen goes upstream and the cutaway goes downstream (see Fig 4.14 in Chapter 4). The exception is in some Mikuni flatslides that have a screen with an orifice in it and this goes downstream of the nozzle. Test needles for straightness by rolling them along a flat surface such as a pane of glass or a Formica worktop. Any bending will show up as wobble. Press fit jets need to be removed using a drift, with a 'pilot' to locate inside the jet bore, and a small press (or a thump from a mallet). Make sure the weak alloy body of the carburettor is well supported and that the jet is being pushed in the correct direction. Check whether it is available as a service item. If not, new components may have to be made using the old as a pattern.

Air slide or piston

Look for signs of wear or scoring between it and the guides in the venturi as an excessive clearance here can let the slide wobble and stick. The piston will have a small vent hole (or two) alongside the needle's hole. Check they aren't blocked or obscured by the needle's clip.

Air chamber

On the airbox side there will be a fairly large vent to (filtered) fresh air. On the engine side there may be other tiny vents and possibly connections to the cold start plunger. Check that these are clean and clear.

Carburettor body

There may be small chambers, each containing a spring and diaphragm, typically to bleed fresh air into the venturi or to block the pilot feed when the engine is on the overrun and intake vacuum is high. Inspect the diaphragms and gaskets, clean out the drillings.

Throttle valve

The butterfly type is mounted on a spindle and after a lot of use there may be wear in the bushes that support the spindle. If you can feel any radial movement, there is too much. It won't affect performance but a small air leak here will make tickover erratic and difficult to adjust, while dirt getting into the bush will accelerate wear and may build up to the point where it makes the throttle action sticky. These undesirables have to be weighed against the cost of a new bank of carburettor bodies or having the carbs line-bored and re-bushed.

Reassembly

To rebuild the carburettor, fit any small covers with their diaphragms, springs and plungers carefully located. Next fit the jets into the underside of the main body, making sure the threads are nipped but not overtightened. Push the needle clip into the correct groove and place the needle into the piston, making sure it is properly clamped into position.

The needle can then be carefully slid into the needle jet and the air slide/piston located in its grooves. Press the diaphragm's O-ring evenly into the groove in the top of the casting, taking care not to stretch it, or you'll have a surplus bulge in the last few millimetres. There's usually a locating tab to make sure the diaphragm isn't twisted – fit this first and then work progressively around the ring. When the diaphragm is in place, fit the spring and the top housing, pressing it as squarely as possible on to the diaphragm and holding it firmly in position while you fit the four screws. From finger-tight, tighten the screws half a turn each until the housing is fully clamped down.

The float and needle valve can now be assembled. Check the float heights (see Chapter 4, Fig. 4.4), even if you plan to do it later using the actual fuel level method. The procedure is usually to turn the carburettors upside down with the float bowl gasket face horizontal and measure from this face up to the (now) top surface of the float, with only its weight pressing on the sprung plunger of the needle valve. Gently bend the metal tang that bears on the needle valve to adjust the height. Adjust to the specified height. This is not critical, it's more important that all the carburettors should be the same.

When the float bowls have been replaced, the carburettors are ready for refitting to the machine, although now is a good time to get them roughly synchronised (or 'balanced'). This will save work later, when you do it more accurately with the engine running because there will be less adjustment to do, and you'll already have found the best tools to fit the linkage, while it's still accessible on the bench.

Rough balancing

Synchronising the carburettors simply means making sure that all the throttles are in the same position and they all open at exactly the same time. This makes idling and the initial pick-up noticeably smoother. It makes no difference to other running conditions but you should check that on WOT all the air slides are lifted clear of the venturi, or, on CV carburettors, that all the butterfly valves are completely edge-on to the air flow.

To balance the carburettors roughly, find some lengths of thin welding rod that will fit under the throttle valves and just be held by each valve when the throttle is closed. As you slowly open the throttle, all the rods should be released simultaneously. Use the main throttle stop on the master carburettor (probably #3 on a four-carburettor bank) to close them to the point where the throttle valve just grips the welding rod.

Now use the throttle adjuster on carburettor #4 to match it. Adjust carburettor #1 and #2 until they are both equal, and finally use the adjuster between #2 and #3 to bring both pairs of carburettors into synch.

For more precise settings, see *synchronisation*, opposite.

Set the idle mixture adjusters to the position specified in the workshop manual. A figure like '1½ turns' means the tapered screw is turned in (clockwise) until it lightly seats and then it is turned out 1½ revolutions.

Gaskets

Current carburettors have O-ring seals which last well and stay in position. If one is damaged and the part is not available, there are O-ring kits from motor factors with various diameters of rubber which you cut to length and use a special clamp and adhesive to join the two ends.

Older carburettors have gaskets that really need renewing at each stripdown after a long interval (with care, they'll survive several jet changes as the gasket won't have had time to stick to the metal surfaces or harden itself). If gaskets are not available you can buy sheets of the thicker gasket material and cut your own. Cut a rough shape to more than cover the area. Then either smear a thin layer of grease on the gasket face and press it firmly on to the gasket material, to leave a clear outline which you can cut using a scalpel. Or hold the material firmly against the face and use a small hammer to tap around the edges. Where the edges are sharply defined, this will cut through the material, elsewhere it will leave a clear enough outline to finish off with a scalpel. Use a small punch or a nail to pierce holes, for mounting screws and wherever there are passageways in the casting – take great care not to obscure any of these.

As a last resort, a fuel-resistant RTV compound may be used, as float bowls do not have to be clamped with great force and the dimensions are not critical. But take care that the compound cannot be squeezed out on the inside of the joint and do not use on any sealing areas which contain drillings or passageways.

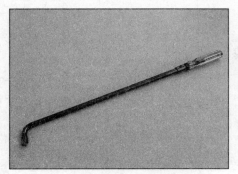

Fig. 13.7 Long thin screwdrivers are essential to get at pilot adjusters, drain screws etc. This type has a flexible drive inside the hollow shaft, with a 90° bend at its end, specifically designed for pilot screw adjustment

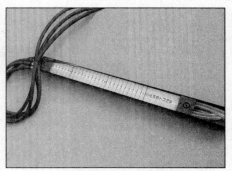

Fig. 13.8a Mercury column vacuum gauges are the classical tool for synchronising carburettors as they are more reliable and easier to read than clock-type gauges

Fig. 13.8b This version is more compact, using steel rods instead of the liquid mercury (which is easy to lose and toxic)

When the carburettors are refitted, check the condition of all the hoses and renew any that have hardened, cracked or been torn. Make sure all hoses – vents, overflows, engine breathers, carburettor heaters, fuel supply – and all electrical connections are in place and routed correctly. Test the throttle cable and cold start action, with the steering moved from lock to lock and check that the cables cannot be trapped.

Final adjustment

With the fuel supply connected and the engine ready to run (the airbox doesn't necessarily have to be fitted for this part), the carburettors are ready for final adjustment – cable adjustment, float heights, idle settings, synchronisation (in this order).

Cables

Throttle cables are normally set so there is 2 – 3 mm of free play at the twistgrip. More than this spoils the control, less runs the risk of the cable tightening when the steering is turned. The cold start cable can be set up with slightly more free play.

Fuel levels

Should be set accurately on the bench but can be checked in situ. Fit a piece of clear tube over the overflow stub and hold it up alongside the body of the carburettor. With fuel switched on and the float bowls full, undo the float bowl

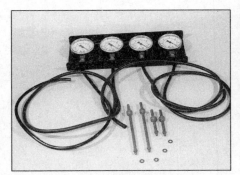

Fig. 13.8c Clock-type vacuum gauges

drain screw and the fuel level can be seen in the clear tube. Normally it should align with (or be a measured height from) some datum mark on the casting. For this you will need a long, thin screwdriver to reach the drain screws. Some models have small plastic funnels mounted over the drain screws, to guide the screwdriver. Make sure they're pointing in the most convenient direction when you fit the float bowls.

Idle settings

There are three choices
a) *Use the figure in the book*
b) *Tune by ear*
c) *Tune by instrument*

If you intend to tune the settings, the engine will need to be fully warmed up first and reasonably well synchronised (see next item). Tuning by ear aims to get the smoothest, slowest tickover. For this you will need a screwdriver to reach each pilot adjusting screw. There are suitably long, thin screwdrivers whose shafts turn through 90° an inch or so before the blade (see Fig. 13.7)

If you alter the mixture on one cylinder so that it is better, the engine will speed up. You can then use the throttle stop to slow it down and repeat on all cylinders. This is more easily said than done.

You can use an instrument, either exhaust

Fig. 13.9 An adapter like this replaces a blanking plug in each intake stub, to connect a hose to the vacuum gauge

gas analyser or a transparent spark plug, made by Gunson, which lets you see the colour of the combustion flame, yellow being too rich, turning to blue as the mixture is weakened. With many current machines this is impractical to use because of the juxtaposition of the spark plugs and frame, ignition coils and airbox.

Having optimised the idle mixture, use the main throttle stop to bring the idle speed to the specified level, usually 1000 - 1200 rpm for a road bike.

Synchronisation

See Figs. 13.8a, 13.8b and 13.8c

Undo the vacuum connectors (screws or rubber plugs just downstream of the carburettor bodies) and fit adapters to connect them to vacuum gauges (see Fig. 13.9). With the engine fully warmed and idling at the correct speed, check the vacuum levels. The difference between any two carburettors should typically be less than 2 cm Hg (2.7 kPa). If the levels of the mercury columns or the gauge needles flicker too much, fit restrictor jets in the connections (see Fig. 13.10). This will lower the reading slightly as well as damp the

Fig. 13.10 A section of narrow-bore tube is used as a damper to reduce flutter at the vacuum gauge caused by pressure fluctuations in the intake. Other types use a tapered needle or a mechanical clamp to restrict the hose connection

gauge motion, so all cylinders must have the same restrictors. If you use an adjustable tapered needle to damp the gauges (or kink the hose with a small clamp), connect each gauge to the same cylinder in turn to ensure that they all have the same level of damping and give the same reading. Its not a bad idea (especially if you're using clock-type gauges) to connect each in turn to the same cylinder anyway just to make sure they all read the same.

Use the throttle adjusters to make cylinders #1 and #2 equal. Then make #3 and #4 equal. Finally use the adjuster between #2 and #3 to equalise both pairs. At each adjustment you may need to use the throttle stop to correct the idle speed.

Road test

The airbox and filter should be fitted for this test. Check the throttle cable adjustment. With the engine idling, the speed should not change when the steering is moved from lock to lock. Blip the throttle by opening the twistgrip between finger and thumb until the engine revs reach 40 – 50% of full speed and then abruptly let it go. Do this several times. The idle speed should rapidly stabilise. If not, the idle settings are incorrect or the idle speed is too low (or there is some stickiness in the cable, twistgrip or linkage).

Check that the machine will pull away smoothly from minimal revs with minimal throttle. This obviously depends on the size and type of engine. Now check that it can be ridden along slowly in first gear, with the throttle closed or just open and can be driven away smoothly without slipping the clutch. Finally, ride along in a higher gear and at various engine speeds in the normal working range, close the throttle for a few seconds and then open it. Repeat this several times, opening the throttle a small amount at first and progressively further each time.

In all cases the engine should run smoothly and pick up progressively, responding in proportion to the throttle opening, without hesitating or stuttering. If there is a flat spot or a misfire, it will be necessary to go over the idle settings again, possibly settling for a slightly rich mixture in exchange for better driveability. If this proves difficult to achieve, raise the idle speed by 50 – 100 rpm and try again. For further test procedures see Chapter 6, Tuning.

Air filters

There are two main types, re-usable foam types and non-re-usable paper types. The life of the latter elements can be extended by tapping them to shake loose some of the dirt and by using an air line to blow through the element in the reverse direction to normal air flow.

Foam types can usually be cleaned by washing in gasoline or a specific air filter solvent, taking the usual precautions, and squeezing dry. Be careful not to tear the foam. Soak in light engine oil (SAE30) or a specific air filter oil, squeeze out the excess, wrap in cloth or kitchen paper and squeeze again to remove as much oil as possible. Then refit to the filter framework.

Glossary:
technical terms and symbols explained

A

ABDC After Bottom Dead Centre (*see* BDC)

Activated radical Radicals are relatively unstable chemical components. If the temperature and pressure of an air-fuel mixture is raised enough, it will break into these components, which will then ignite and burn automatically, without needing the impetus of a spark.

AF Air-fuel. (Also *'across flats'* – a dimension to measure hexagonal etc, shapes, as in bolt heads: the distance between two parallel flat surfaces.)

Air bleed A small jet or orifice through which a stream of air is drawn to mix with the stream of fuel.

Air cleaner Either a porous foam or paper element, through which the engine intake air is drawn, to filter out dirt that would otherwise cause engine wear.

Air filter *see Air cleaner*

Air jet A small orifice, whose dimensions precisely regulate a flow of air, see *Air bleed*.

Air slide A valve that is able to slide across the venturi of a carburettor either to control the air flow or to control the open area and thus control the air velocity.

Airbox A chamber in the engine's air intake, which acts as a still air reservoir and contains the air filter.

Analogue A signal or an output that varies continuously. Compare with *Digital*. A traditional clock with hands is an analogue instrument, as opposed to a digital watch that flicks from one number to the next.

API American Petroleum Institute

ATDC After Top Dead Centre (*see* TDC)

Atomisation Breaking a liquid up into a very fine spray.

Auto-ignition A state (of temperature and pressure) in which fuel will burn of its own accord. Also called *dieseling* and *run-on*.

Avgas Aviation gasoline

B

Balance (of throttles) Making two or more throttle valves open the same amount and move in unison. Also called *synchronisation*.

BBDC Before Bottom Dead Centre (*see* BDC)

BDC Bottom dead centre. The engine position when the centres of the piston pin, crankshaft and big-end are all in line, with the piston at its furthest from the cylinder head.

Bellmouth The shape of an air intake funnel which is radiussed outwards.

bmep brake mean effective pressure. The steady gas pressure that would produce the same amount of engine torque (units: lb/in^2 or bar).

Brake specific fuel consumption The fuel consumption at a particular engine speed, divided by the power output at that speed (units: pt/hp-h or kg/kW-h).

bsfc *see Brake specific fuel consumption*

BTDC Before Top Dead Centre (*see* TDC)

C

Catalyst A material that enables or accelerates a chemical reaction without taking part in the reaction.

CD Constant depression. Type of carburettor in which the air velocity above the fuel jet is kept constant and therefore its pressure is constant. Also called *CV* or *constant velocity* or *constant vacuum* carburettor.

Coefficient of discharge A measure of the efficiency of an orifice or jet at flowing a fluid.

Combustion (burning) A chemical reaction between fuel and air, in which the fuel is oxidised and gives off heat.

Compound A substance in which two or more chemical elements are bonded together at the molecular level.

Compression ignition Combustion of fuel caused by raising its pressure and temperature to the point at which it burns spontaneously. The principle of diesel engines.

Constant depression *see CD*

Constant vacuum *see CD*

Constant velocity *see CD*

Correction factor A number or a percentage to multiply raw data in order to allow for deviations or to bring it to standard conditions. An example is the correction factor applied to engine power to compensate for changes caused by different air densities.

CPU Central Processing Unit. The computer that stores data concerning the engine's operating conditions and calculates the optimum ignition timing and fuel needed.

Cracking Chemical decomposition of a hydrocarbon into one or more different hydrocarbons.

CV *see CD*

D

Detonation Instantaneous combustion of an air-fuel mixture. Also called *knock*, because of the sound it makes in an engine.

Digital Compare with *analogue*. A signal or an output that changes in clearly defined steps or takes the form of discrete pieces of data instead of varying continuously (the computer term *bit* is a contraction of *binary digit*.)

DIN Deutsche Industrie Norm. German industrial standard, equivalent to BS. Also Deutsches Institut für Normung – German Standards Institute, equivalent to BSI.

Direct fuel injection Method of introducing fuel by pumping a metered amount into the cylinder. Because of the high cylinder pressures reached, the injection also has to be at high pressure.

Downdraught The angle of a carburettor venturi above the horizontal.

Dwell The time (or the distance) that a system stays open (open dwell) or closed (closed dwell). Applies to things like valves that are opened and closed regularly, and to electrical circuits, particularly ignition circuits, in which the closed dwell is the time available for the current to build up in the primary winding of the coil.

E

Earth A common, return circuit for electrical loads. Also called *ground*.

Efficiency A measure of how good something is at a particular job. One way or another it is usually defined as the result you get out, divided by the effort you have to put in.

Element The simplest state of a substance, chemically, that can exist on its own.

Engine management Electronic control of air-fuel ratios and/or ignition timing.

Eprom Erasable programmable read-only memory

Excess air An air-fuel mixture which contains more air than is needed for complete combustion of the fuel. Also called a *weak mixture* or *lean mixture*.

Exhaust An engine process in which burnt fuel and air are scavenged from the cylinder.

F

Flame speed During combustion, the speed at which burning gas ignites neighbouring particles. In regular combustion it usually propagates as a flame front or kernel which can be seen travelling at a certain speed through the gas.

Flash point The temperature at which fuel or fuel vapour will ignite in normal atmospheric conditions. See also *ignition*.

Frequency The number of cyclic events that happen in a given period of time, usually measured in *Hertz* (Hz – cycles per second). For example, an engine rotating at 3000 rpm completes 3000 revolutions in 60 seconds, so its frequency is 3000/60 = 50 Hz.

Fuel mixture loop The effect on engine output of changing the AF mixture from fully rich to fully lean, at a constant engine speed and throttle position.

Fuel slope The engine's AF mixture requirements over its useful speed range.

G

g Acceleration due to gravity. At sea level it is approximately 32.2ft/s^2 or 9.81m/s^2.

Ground *see earth*

H

Hall effect An electronic phenomenon in which a transverse electric field is generated in a conductor (or semi-conductor) carrying current and moving relative to a magnetic field. Used to pick up the frequency of a moving part, like a crankshaft, and so measure its speed.

Heat A form of energy, also used for the internal energy content of substances.

I

ic Internal combustion. Type of engine in which the fuel is burnt inside the working cylinder, as in all motorcycle engines. Examples of *external* combustion are steam engines and Stirling engines.

ic Integrated circuit. Electrical circuit in which several components are formed on one layer of a semi-conductor.

Idle (no load) An engine running on closed throttle, ie so the fuel burnt and power produced are only enough to overcome friction, oil drag and pumping losses at its idle speed and there is no surplus power to be used.

Ignition The point at which an air-fuel mixture begins to burn, caused either by adding energy locally in the form of an electric spark or by adding pressure/heat energy to all of the mixture. The ignition point, or flash point, of fuel and its vapour are important safety aspects for the storage and handling of the fuel.

Indirect fuel injection Method of introducing fuel into an engine's air stream before it reaches the working cylinder. It may be pumped in metered quantities into the intake tract or into a separate chamber, which is then pressurised and opened to the cylinder. Also called low-pressure injection as the fuel does not have to be at as high a pressure as for direct injection. If the injection is timed to coincide with the intake phase, it is called *sequential injection*.

Intake An engine process in which air is drawn into the working cylinder and, at some stage, fuel is mixed with it.

Internal combustion *see ic*

ISO International Standards Organisation

Isomer A chemical compound with the same number of atoms as the normal compound, but organised in a different way, giving it different characteristics. Applies to many hydrocarbons and is used to tailor fuels' characteristics such as knock resistance and ignition quality.

J

Jet A small orifice used to meter the flow of fuel or air.

K

Kinetic energy Energy due to the speed at which an object travels. Is proportional to the object's mass and its velocity squared.

Knock *see Detonation*

L

Lambda sensor λ-sensor. Electrical unit which screws into exhaust header pipe and whose output changes abruptly when oxygen is present in the gas. This signal is sent to the engine management system, which uses it to correct the AF ratio. Also called *excess air sensor*.

Latent heat (of vaporisation) The heat required to turn a certain mass of liquid into vapour.

Lean An air-fuel mixture with more air than is necessary to completely burn the fuel.

Lean burn A design or technique enabling spark ignition engines to run on very lean AF mixtures (as weak as 28:1, air:gasoline) without misfiring. See also *stratified charge*.

Load The throttle opening at which an engine is running, or the surplus torque available for useful work. [So called because early dynamometer designs loaded the engine through a fluid, electrical or friction drive and the dyno was restrained by fixing a weight or spring balance on an arm fastened to its body, so the torque measurement would be directly proportional to this simple load.]

M

Manifold Literally 'hand-shaped' – a duct which branches into two or more ducts, usually to flow gas into or away from an engine's cylinders.

Map A graphic representation of how ignition timing or injection fuel quantity varies against things like engine speed and throttle opening.

MBT Minimum advance for Best Torque. The optimum ignition timing for a given set of engine conditions.

Mixture cf compound A compound is a chemical substance in which two or more elements are bonded together atomically, ie atoms of the various elements join to form molecules of the compound. A mixture is formed of two or more substances which do not bond chemically but keep their own identities and properties and can be separated physically (by filtering, distillation, dissolving one, using magnetic attraction, centrifugal force, freezing, etc).

Molecule The smallest part of a substance that can exist (keeping the characteristics of that substance) or take part in a chemical reaction. Formed from atoms of the element(s) that make up the substance.

MTBE Methyl Butyl Tertiary Ether. An oxygenated hydrocarbon used as an anti-knock additive in gasoline.

N

Nitrogen An element that exists naturally as an inert gas, making up roughly 4/5 of the earth's atmosphere.

No-load *see idle*

Non-volatile memory Computer memory that is not lost when electrical power is switched off.

NA Normally aspirated

O

Octane rating A measure of a fuel's knock resistance, made by comparing it to the performance of iso-octane in carefully defined tests.

OE Original equipment

OEM Original equipment manufacturer

Optimise To find the best engine settings (eg ignition timing, AF mixture) that give the most power or the lowest fuel consumption.

Overlap (of valves) The period during which the intake and exhaust valves are open together.

Overrun Engine condition in which the throttle is shut and the engine is running higher than idle speed, being driven by the inertia of the vehicle.

Oxygen An element that exists naturally as a gas, making up roughly 1/5 of the earth's atmosphere. Reacts with many substances (in which they are said to be oxidised – or burnt).

P

Part load Partial throttle opening *(see Load)*.

Potential energy The energy of an object due to its height above a datum level (and the force of gravity pulling it towards that datum). Is proportional to its height, its mass and the acceleration due to gravity.

Potentiometer A variable resistance or rheostat. Connected to a moving part, like a throttle linkage, the resistance varies with the movement and the output (usually a varying voltage) can be used to measure the movement.

Power A form of energy in which a force or a torque is moved along its line of action at a certain speed. The power is proportional to the force (or torque) and the speed.

Power density The amount of power developed by an engine, divided by its displacement (or weight).

Pre-ignition Ignition of the air-fuel mixture before the spark occurs. Possibly caused by a hot component such as a valve or the spark plug ground electrode or by conditions in the gas causing local detonation or auto-ignition.

Pressure energy The energy level in a gas which is caused by its pressure. Is proportional to its mass times its pressure divided by its density.

psi pounds per square inch. Imperial unit of pressure.

R

Ram effect Utilising gas inertia to continue filling a cylinder after the piston has reached BDC, **or** the effect of the bike's forward speed forcing air into the airbox and raising its pressure.

Relay (switch) A switch that is opened and closed by a small electrical current.

Resonance The phenomenon of two oscillating systems having the same frequency and reinforcing each others oscillations, usually with a large increase in amplitude. Can happen to any vibrating object, pulsating column of gas or electrical circuit with alternating current.

Rich mixture An air-fuel mixture which contains more fuel than can be burnt by the amount of oxygen present in the air.

S

SAE Society of Automotive Engineers.

Scavenge To remove the contents of eg an engine cylinder, usually by replacing them with something else.

Sensor A device, usually electrical, which monitors the position, speed, temperature etc of a component.

sfc specific fuel consumption (*see brake specific fuel consumption*).

si *see Spark ignition*

Spark ignition Type of internal combustion engine in which the air-fuel mixture is ignited by an electrical spark.

Specific fuel consumption see *brake specific fuel consumption*

Stack The intake to a carburettor or throttle body (also called bellmouth and trumpet).

Stoichiometric The weight of air containing the necessary amount of oxygen to completely burn one weight unit of fuel.

Stratified charge An air-fuel mixture formation which is not uniform but consists of layers or streams with varying mixture strengths. Typically, a rich mixture is delivered to the region around the spark plug, while a lean mixture is delivered elsewhere.

Supercharger A compressor driven by the engine, which supplies intake air at higher than atmospheric pressure.

Synchronisation *see Balance*

T

TDC (Top Dead Centre) Engine position in which the centres of the piston pin, big-end and crankshaft are all in line, with the piston at its closest to the cylinder head.

Torque A twisting force, defined as the force multiplied by the radius on which it acts. Also called *moment*.

Trapping efficiency The amount of air-fuel available for combustion inside an engine's cylinder, compared with the amount the piston displaces. Usually applied to two-strokes, which, having drawn air into the cylinder can let it escape ('short-circuit') through the exhaust port. Compare with *volumetric efficiency*.

Transducer A sensor. Something that converts one kind of energy (eg pressure) into another (eg electrical).

Turbocharger A compressor driven by exhaust gas that supplies intake air at higher than atmospheric pressure.

V

Valve overlap The period of engine rotation when the intake and exhaust valves are open at the same time.

Variable geometry The ability to change the length or volume of chambers, pipes etc making up part of the intake or exhaust system.

Volatility The willingness of a liquid to evaporate, to change from liquid to vapour.

Volumetric efficiency The amount of air drawn into a cylinder compared to the amount the piston displaces.

W

Weak mixture An air-fuel mixture which contains more air than is necessary to completely burn the fuel.

WOT Wide Open Throttle

Chemical symbols

Hg	Mercury	**CH_3NO_2**	Nitromethane	**H_2O**	Water
O_3	Ozone	**CO**	Carbon monoxide	**HC**	Hydrocarbon
N_2O	Nitrous oxide	**CO_2**	Carbon dioxide	α	Alpha
H_2	Hydrogen	**C_2H_6**	Ethane	λ	Lambda
O_2	Oxygen	**C_4H_{10}**	Butane	>	Greater than
CH_4	Methane	**C_8H_{18}**	Octane	<	Less than
		NO_x	Nitric oxides		

Note: *References throughout this index are in the form –* "Chapter number" • "page number"